THE COMPANY SHE KEEPS:

The Medieval Swedish Cult of
Saint Katherine of Alexandria
and its Transformations

MEDIEVAL AND RENAISSANCE
TEXTS AND STUDIES

VOLUME 362

ARIZONA STUDIES IN THE
MIDDLE AGES AND THE RENAISSANCE

VOLUME 31

THE COMPANY SHE KEEPS:
The Medieval Swedish Cult of Saint Katherine of Alexandria and its Transformations

by

TRACEY R. SANDS

ACMRS
(Arizona Center for Medieval and Renaissance Studies)
Tempe, Arizona
in collaboration with
BREPOLS
2010

ASMAR Volume 31: ISBN 978-2-503-53378-0   D/2010/0095/53

Library of Congress Cataloging-in-Publication Data

Sands, Tracey Renée.
The company she keeps : the medieval Swedish cult of Saint Katherine of Alexandria and its transformations / by Tracey R. Sands.
    p. cm. -- (Medieval and Renaissance texts and studies ; v. 362)
    Includes bibliographical references (p.   ) and index.
    ISBN 978-0-86698-410-2 (alk. paper)
    1. Catherine, of Alexandria, Saint--Cult--Sweden--History--To 1500.
    2. Sweden--Religious life and customs. I. Title.
    BX4700.C45S26 2009
    282'.4850902--dc22

2009039460

Front Cover
The photo shows the corpus of an altarpiece, presumed to be of Swedish workmanship from the fifteenth century, from the parish church of Bälinge, Uppland. The figures are St. Katherine of Alexandria and a bishop saint, possibly St. Nicholas.
Photo by Tracey R. Sands.

∞
This book is made to last.
It is set in Adobe Caslon,
smyth-sewn and printed on acid-free paper
to library specifications.
Printed in the United States of America

To Mom, Dad, and Jim, with love and gratitude.

TABLE OF CONTENTS

ABBREVIATIONS

ÄSF   *Äldre svenska frälsesläkter*

DgF   *Danmarks gamle Folkeviser*

DS   *Diplomatarium suecanum*

KHLM *Kulturhistorisk leksikon for nordisk middelalder*

NMB   *Norske mellomalder balladar*

RA   Riksarkivet (Swedish National Archive)

RPB   Riksarkivets pergamentsbrev (Parchment charters housed at the Swedish National Archive: see *Svenska riks-archivets pergamentsbref från och med år 1351.*)

SMB   *Sveriges medeltida ballader*

SRS   *Scriptores Rerum Suecicarum Medii Ævi*

TSB   *The Types of the Scandinavian Medieval Ballad*

Acknowledgments

It is a pleasure to have the opportunity of acknowledging the many people who in one way or another have contributed to the completion of this book. This project has been a long one, and has progressed through many stages.

My research on the medieval Swedish cult of St. Katherine, and on its post-Reformation echoes, began as a doctoral thesis in the Scandinavian department of the University of Washington. Two members of my doctoral committee, Patricia Conroy and Thomas DuBois have been especially important in helping me to develop and refine my thinking during and since the years that that I worked on my dissertation. A 1993 fellowship from the American Scandinavian Foundation helped to fund the research for the dissertation, and much of that work has continued to be of importance in the current book. I also wish to express my gratitude to the late Bengt Jonsson of Svenskt visarkiv, who met with me in the early 1990s to discuss my ideas concerning the Swedish and Nordic ballad tradition arising out of the medieval legend of St. Katherine.

At various stages in its genesis, this project has benefited from the comments and suggestions of wise readers including Stephen Mitchell and Elizabeth Robertson. I am extremely grateful to the anonymous readers engaged by the press, whose thoughtful comments, suggestions, and in some cases corrections were profoundly helpful to me. Their influence spurred me to strengthen my arguments, refine my analysis, and tighten the structure of the overall work.

I would also like to express my appreciation for the patient guidance I have received from the staff of ACMRS, including Robert Bjork, Roy Rukkila and Todd Halvorsen. I am profoundly grateful to Leslie MacCoull, not only for her painstaking work on editing the manuscript, but also for her pointing out possible comparisons between Swedish and Byzantine sigillographic traditions and providing me with bibliographic references, and for identifying biblical references in the medieval texts.

Closer to home, I owe an enormous debt of gratitude to dear friends and family members, only some of whom will be mentioned here. My parents, Susan and Donald Sands, have been a constant source of love and encouragement. My gratitude to my husband, James Massengale, is beyond measure. He has been my constant sounding board, by his own claim my most critical reader, and my companion on innumerable visits to churches large and small. His influence on this work cannot be overestimated. Kjell, Lena and Karin Rickegård have for years provided me a safe haven in Sweden, and have listened patiently to many aspects of my developing argument. Gunnar Danell and Dorothy Kim might be regarded as godparents to chapter 4 of this book, since their invitation to visit them on Gotland in the summer of 2005 led directly to my exploration of that island's churches and their importance to understanding the larger cult of St. Katherine. Among the friends who have helped to keep me on track, personally and intellectually, at the various stages of this project are Barbara Mason, Ellen Rees, Mary Bjork, Paul Norlén, Ari Santander, Lori Talcott, Björn Ambrosiani and Phyllis Anderson Ambrosiani Ursula Lindqvist, and Enozar, that best of equine companions.

As greatly as I value the contributions of all of these wise friends and colleagues, and as much as they have added to the final product, it must be stated that all of the faults and errors that may yet be found in this book are my responsibility alone.

INTRODUCTION

This study examines the cult of St. Katherine of Alexandria, one of the most widely venerated saints of the medieval Christian world, in what was in many ways a far-flung and remote corner of Christendom. As a number of recent studies have established, this saint appealed to a wide range of different groups across medieval Europe, and her legend and cult were capable of generating and fulfilling many different meanings, both for individuals and for organizations.[1] In spite of the saint's great popularity in other parts of Europe, the subject of her cult in Sweden nonetheless raises a number of interesting questions. How did this Mediterranean saint, a Greek-speaking 'princess' or 'queen' of Alexandria, come to be one of the most beloved saints in a cold and remote northern region? How did a figure renowned for her learning become an intercessor for people whose access to the written word was limited at best? What possible functions could this cult fulfill for the Swedes? These are among the questions this study will address.

The cult of St. Katherine was certainly well established in other parts of the Nordic region in addition to Sweden. There is strong evidence of her veneration in Denmark, where many churches, chapels and altars were dedicated to her, and where images depicting her are widespread. It is clear that St. Katherine was a great favorite of the Franciscan and Dominican friars in medieval Denmark, where as many as eight Franciscan and three Dominican houses appear to have been dedicated to her. There is also good evidence that this saint enjoyed significant popularity in Norway and Iceland, though her popularity there does not seem to have approached that in Denmark and Sweden.[2] Although aspects of the cult of St. Katherine have been discussed in works on the cult of the saints,

---

[1] See, for example, Katherine J. Lewis, *The Cult of St Katherine of Alexandria in Late Medieval England* (Woodbridge: Boydell Press, 2000) and *St Katherine of Alexandria: Texts and Contexts in Medieval Western Europe*, ed. Jacqueline Jenkins and Katherine Lewis, Medieval Women: Texts and Contexts 8 (Turnhout: Brepols, 2003).

[2] See Tue Gad, Bernt C. Lange, Erik Moltke, Magnús Már Lárusson, Oloph Odenius, and C. A Nordman, "Katarina af Alexandria," *KHLM* 8: 335–45; Ellen Jørgensen, *Helgendyrkelse i Danmark,* (København: H. Hagerups Forlag, 1909), 27–28, 138–39; Margaret Cormack, *The Saints in Iceland: Their Veneration from the Conversion to 1400*, Subsidia Hagiographica 78 (Brussels: Société des Bollandistes, 1994), 86–88.

or related topics, in the other Nordic countries, no study has been done for those areas that is comparable in scope to this investigation of the cult of St. Katherine in Sweden. Although there was certainly considerable cultural contact between medieval Sweden and, especially, the neighboring kingdoms of Denmark and Norway, the three kingdoms (not to mention Iceland) were nonetheless separate and distinct as political and cultural entities, and as ecclesiastical provinces. This study, then, focuses on the cult of St. Katherine in medieval Sweden.

The legend of St. Katherine of Alexandria, as it is known from preserved medieval Swedish textual sources, may be summarized as follows.[3] Katherine is a young, learned, and beautiful virgin, the daughter and heir of King Costus of Alexandria, said to have lived and died in the early years of the fourth century. When Katherine is eighteen years old, the Roman emperor Maxentius comes to Alexandria to hold public sacrifices to the gods of the Roman state, and he demands that all citizens must participate in these sacrifices or be executed. Katherine, who is a Christian, hears the cacophony of the sacrifices and rushes to upbraid the emperor, whom she accuses of devil-worship. As she argues against the pagan sacrificial practices, Maxentius finds himself impressed by her beauty and her eloquence. He offers her great honor if she agrees to participate in the sacrifices, but threatens her with torture if she should refuse. When she nonetheless persists in her opposition, the emperor summons the fifty wisest philosophers in his realm to debate with Katherine, and show her the error of her ways. To the emperor's astonishment and fury, it is Katherine who defeats the fifty wise men in debate, and all profess their faith in Christ before they perish in the bonfire to which Maxentius condemns them. The emperor continues his efforts to sway Katherine to his will, offering her rich gifts and honors, including a position with all the rights of the empress except that of sharing Maxentius's bed. When Katherine continues in her refusal to sacrifice, and also in her demand that the emperor abandon his gods in favor of Christ, Maxentius has her brutally beaten and thrown into prison, giving orders that she should be given neither food nor drink. While the emperor is away on an extended journey, an angel in the form of a dove brings Katherine food. The empress sees a strange light issuing from the prison, and, along with the captain of the guard, she goes to investigate. They see how Katherine has been healed of her wounds by the angel, and when Katherine preaches to them, they are immediately converted to the Christian faith, along with the hundred knights who have accompanied them. Katherine prophesies that the queen will become a martyr, and Christ himself appears in the cell with a host of angels, to offer encouragement to Katherine and the empress.

---

[3] This summary follows the earliest Old Swedish version of the life of St. Katherine (complete translation in Appendix 6). The earliest, fragmentary text is found in a manuscript dated to c. 1340–1385. Complete texts are found in manuscripts dated c. 1440–1450 and 1502.

When Maxentius returns from his journey, he is enraged to find Katherine in flourishing good health. Once again he offers her the choice of sacrifice or torture, and when she indicates her preference for the latter, he orders the construction of a cruel machine, with four spiked wheels that will crush Katherine and tear the flesh from her body. When Katherine is placed on this device, an angel appears suddenly in response to her prayers, and smashes it before Katherine can be harmed. Four thousand pagans are killed by the fragments. The empress is now moved to chastise Maxentius, and to reveal that she has become a Christian, and she is tortured and beheaded. When the captain of the guard buries her body and confesses his faith, he too is martyred, together with the hundred knights. Maxentius now offers to make Katherine his empress if she will sacrifice to his gods, but she refuses in the strongest of terms, and is condemned to death. Just before she is beheaded, she prays for mercy for those who call upon her name, and a voice from heaven replies, "Betrothed of God, come to God's happiness. Those who honor you will be saved." When her head is struck from her body, milk runs from her veins instead of blood. Angels carry her body to Mount Sinai, and bury it with great honor.

Medieval Sweden is a region for which we have overall relatively few surviving manuscripts or copies of texts, but many surviving images. This circumstance, unusual for medieval Europe, is in part a result of the Protestant Reformation, which led to the widespread destruction of the contents of ecclesiastical and monastic book collections. At the same time, the materials that have survived to the present may present a somewhat skewed impression, since the majority come from the convent library at Vadstena Abbey, the last of the monastic foundations to be dissolved.[4] However, it is uncertain whether the lay population of medieval Sweden, even at the highest levels of society, ever achieved a degree of literacy, or of book ownership, approaching that of, for example, England during the same period. Although a small number of individuals (such as Birgitta Birgersdotter [1303–1373], later known as St. Birgitta) are known to have been able to read and even write, the extent of general literacy is difficult to estimate. Birgitta Fritz has pointed out that some aristocratic laymen are known to have attended cathedral schools, and that certain political positions, notably the office of *lagman*—a provincial magistrate—would require at least the ability to read. At the same time, such officials would have had the help of a clerk or scribe to produce written documents.[5] Thus it is no surprise that there are only three surviving manuscripts containing versions of the Life of St. Katherine in Old Swedish, alongside

---

[4] See Monica Hedlund, "Medeltida kyrko- och klosterbibliotek i Sverige," in *Helgerånet: Från mässböcker till munkepärmar*, ed. Kerstin Abukhanfusa, Jan Brunius, and Solbritt Benneth (Stockholm: Carlsson Bokförlag/Riksarkivet/ Stockholms medeltidsmuseum, 1993), 25–36, here 33.

[5] Birgitta Fritz, "Privata böcker och boksamlingar under folkungatiden," in *Helgerånet: Från mässböcker till munkepärmar*, ed. Abukhanfusa et al., 37–45.

a single Latin version, and one rhymed Low German text. In spite of the paucity of textual sources, however, the saint's exceptional popularity in medieval Sweden can be understood by the fact that over three hundred images of her, in the form of murals, sculptures, paintings on glass or wood, and other objects, survive from Swedish churches. The only female saint depicted in a greater number of surviving images is the Virgin Mary.[6] In addition to these images, St. Katherine is depicted in a large number of seals belonging to monastic foundations, clerics, and noble women. Given factors such as the Protestant Reformation, set in motion during the 1520s, the ravages of time and neglect that are a natural consequence of the suppression of the cult, and even more benign factors such as the desire to replace outdated furnishings or even the medieval churches themselves, it is clear that the three hundred images that survive are only a fraction of the number that must once have existed.

Katherine of Alexandria is not, of course, the only popular saint whose cult became established in Sweden at a relatively early point. The cults of St. Mary Magdalene and St. Margaret of Antioch, both of whom were among the most widely venerated saints of medieval Christendom, are attested in the same early sources as the cult of St. Katherine. However, although these three saints appear in the same calendars, and are frequently depicted together (especially Katherine and Margaret) in the Swedish churches, the feast of St. Katherine is nearly always celebrated with a higher degree of veneration than either of the others. Clearly, this saint and her image had special significance for medieval Swedish Christians during almost the entire history of the Roman Catholic church in Sweden, and even beyond the suppression of the cult by the Protestant Reformation.

In contrast to many of the other regions where the cult of St. Katherine became established, Christianity was relatively new in Sweden when the cult arrived here.

Located on the far northern frontier of Europe, Sweden was among the last areas of medieval Europe to accept Christianity. Even in comparison to its Nordic neighbors, Denmark, Norway, and Iceland, Sweden was late in establishing ecclesiastical structures, and accounts of pagan backlash against the efforts of missionaries occur later here than in neighboring regions. Several factors may contribute to this. Jónas Gíslason has suggested that the Icelanders made the collective decision to accept Christianity as their national religion at the General Assembly in AD 1000 in part because the old pagan faith had been weakened

---

[6] These statistics are based on the unpublished Catalog of Iconography (Ikonografiska registret), a card catalog housed at the Antikvariskt-topografiska arkiv (ATA) at the National Board of Antiquities in Stockholm. The portion of the catalog pertaining to the saints has recently been published in Ingalill Pegelow, *Helgonlegender i ord och bild* (Stockholm: Carlssons förlag, 2006), 272–326.

by its transplantation to a new land, far from the graves of ancestors.[7] By contrast, many Swedes in the late Viking Age lived and farmed within view of grave mounds and other monuments that dated not only from the Iron Age (c. 500 BC to AD 1050—if the Viking Age is included in this period), but in some cases from the Bronze Age (c. 1800–500 BC). While the presence of such monuments may be a contributing factor in the relatively late Christianization of Sweden, it is certainly not the only one. The Christian church gained a foothold in Denmark, which is extraordinarily rich in ancient monuments, a century or more before it became solidly established in Sweden. In this case, it is clear that the Frankish empire exerted much greater influence on leading circles in Danish society than in Sweden, and indeed posed a significant military threat at the Danish borders from which the Swedes were completely spared. It is clear that the relatively early Christianization of Denmark was to a great extent a result of this Frankish, and later German influence.

It also appears that there is a close connection between the interests of kings in the Nordic countries and the process of Christianization of those areas. It may well be significant, then, that while kings with relatively limited, local power are mentioned in early sources (including a king at Birka mentioned in the *Vita Anscharii*), the process of centralization and consolidation of Sweden into a single kingdom was slower by several centuries than in Denmark and Norway.[8] It is known that missionaries from the Frankish empire were active in Sweden beginning in the 820s, including the well-known St. Ansgar, sent by Emperor Louis the Pious to evangelize the Danes and the Swedes. Nonetheless, it is thought that the earliest Swedish king to be baptized was Olof Skötkonung, in the early eleventh century.[9] Although almost all known kings of the Swedes after Olof were Christian, the sources suggest that acceptance of Christianity among their subjects was far from universal. There is nonetheless strong evidence of a Christian presence in many parts of Sweden from this point. Although Uppsala was considered to be one of the most important pagan religious centers of the entire Nordic region, in the surrounding province of Uppland a large number of rune stones, many decorated with crosses, and many whose inscriptions are explicitly Christian in content, were erected during the second half of the eleventh century. The diocese of Skara in western Sweden was the first permanent Swedish

---

[7] Jónas Gíslason, "Acceptance of Christianity in Iceland in the Year 1000 (999)," in *Old Norse and Finnish Religions and Cultic Place Names*, ed. Tore Ahlbäck (Åbo: The Donner Institute for Research in Religious and Cultural History, 1990), 223–55.

[8] Birgit Sawyer and Peter Sawyer, *Medieval Scandinavia* (Minneapolis: University of Minnesota Press, 1993), 58–63; see also Bertil Nilsson, *Sveriges kyrkohistoria I: Missionstid och tidig medeltid* (Stockholm: Verbum, 1998), 65–67, and Rimbert, "Vita S. Anscharii," in *Scriptores Rerum Suecicarum*, vol. 2, ed. E. M. Fant, E. G. Geijer, and J. H. Schröder (Uppsala: Palmblad, 1828), chap. 10–13, 192–99.

[9] Nilsson, *Sveriges kyrkohistoria I*, 65–66.

diocese to be established, probably by the middle of the eleventh century.[10] From that time, it would be approximately another century before the boundaries of the other mainland Swedish dioceses were settled. Finally, the diocese of Åbo, encompassing much of present-day Finland, was incorporated into the Swedish ecclesiastical province in the late twelfth or early thirteenth century.[11]

These circumstances form the background for the arrival of the cult of St. Katherine of Alexandria in medieval Sweden. Although it is not certain precisely when the cult was introduced, it is clear that this must have occurred relatively late in comparison to other parts of Europe, but nonetheless relatively early in the development of the church in Sweden.

The geographical area covered by this study does not correspond to the boundaries of present-day Sweden. As noted above, Sweden's consolidation into a single kingdom appears to have been a relatively slow process, and even when that was accomplished its boundaries remained somewhat fluid. The area examined in this study will correspond to that of the archdiocese of Uppsala, the Swedish ecclesiastical province, during the Middle Ages. This means that the provinces of Skåne, Halland, and Blekinge, which Sweden acquired from Denmark in 1658, are excluded from this study, as is the western Swedish province of Bohuslän, which belonged to the archdiocese of Nidaros. The Baltic island of Gotland was part of the Swedish diocese of Linköping for the entire medieval period, even though it was invaded by Denmark in 1361, and only returned to Swedish control in the Peace of Brömsebro in 1645. In spite of its inclusion in the diocese of Linköping, Gotland appears to have maintained a degree of autonomy in relation both to the bishops of Linköping and to the political authority of Sweden and Denmark. At the same time, it is clear that there were strong cultural ties to the Swedish mainland both during and after the Middle Ages, and these are certainly sufficient to justify the island's inclusion in this investigation. The diocese of Åbo, comprising much of what is now Finland, was an important and fully integrated province of the medieval Swedish church. Although sizeable portions of the population of this diocese were linguistically and culturally distinct from the rest of Sweden throughout the Middle Ages, Finland remained part of the kingdom of Sweden until 1809, when it came under Russian control. Even today, a minority of the population of Finland speaks Swedish as a first language, and members of this community have been of great importance as bearers of Swedish-language oral traditions well into the twentieth century. For this reason, in spite of present-day Finland's status as an independent nation, it is also included in this study.

The organization of the study is as follows. The first chapter attempts to trace the cult of St. Katherine from its earliest apparent manifestations, trying to

---

[10] Nilsson, *Sveriges kyrkohistoria I*, 79–81.
[11] Nilsson, *Sveriges kyrkohistoria I*, 84–85.

assess when and from whence the cult arrived in Sweden. There are some indications that early interest in the saint was fostered among royal circles, based both on early naming traditions and on several early images of the saint. One possible early manifestation of interest in St. Katherine is the naming of a Swedish princess in the early twelfth century. Together with her mother, Helena, and her two sisters, Margareta and Kristina, this Princess Katarina is the first known Swedish woman with a name of Christian derivation. In the generations that followed, many female members of the competing royal dynasties of medieval Sweden would come to be named Katarina. The earliest preserved images of St. Katherine in mainland Sweden occur in churches that may be connected to one of the early medieval Swedish royal dynasties. Certainly, the royal dynasties' interest in the saint is not likely to be the only source of her early arrival in Sweden, but it may well have played a role in the cult's eventual popularity.

The second chapter examines the meanings and uses that the cult of St. Katherine held for the wide range of different monastic and mendicant orders of medieval Sweden and their individual members, as well as for the secular clergy, including both higher prelates and parish priests. At least by the thirteenth century, there is a clear trend that connects the active cult of St. Katherine with the various Swedish cathedral chapters, including a prominent place for the saint in the liturgy of Uppsala Cathedral. Canons and other clergymen often chose to portray St. Katherine on their personal seals. One of the oldest and most important chapels in Uppsala Cathedral is dedicated to Sts. Katherine and Nicholas together, and these two saints frequently appear together in Swedish churches. What is it about St. Katherine that makes her so attractive to members of the clergy? There is evidence to suggest that St. Katherine gradually came to symbolize certain aspects of the activities and functions of the archdiocese. Several altarpieces and murals in churches closely connected to the chapter at Uppsala Cathedral depict St. Katherine (along with, at times, St. Mary Magdalene) together with the official patron saints of the cathedral. But the saint's image is not solely associated with the cathedral chapter and higher prelates, nor is it only associated with Uppsala. St. Katherine also appears in seals of canons, and also of parish priests, from the dioceses of Åbo, Strängnäs, Västerås, and Linköping.

Along with the secular clergy, members of all of the religious orders active in medieval Sweden appear to have venerated St. Katherine and to have contributed to the popularity of her cult. The first monastic order to become established in Sweden was the Cistercian order. Although the Cistercians regarded the Virgin Mary as the primary patron of their order and of all its churches, there is strong evidence to suggest that many of the churches dedicated to St. Katherine have some connection to the Cistercian order. St. Katherine is well known as a particular favorite of the two major mendicant orders, the Dominicans and Franciscans. Several of the Franciscan order's friaries in the Nordic region were dedicated to St. Katherine, including the one in Visby on the island of Gotland. It appears likely that both the Dominicans and the Franciscans, both of whose activities involved considerable contact with lay populations, helped to promote devotion to St. Katherine in Sweden. Many members of the Order of the Most Holy Savior (*Ordo Sanctissimi Salvatoris*), the only monastic order of Swedish origin, also venerated St. Katherine. Not only does one of the earliest sculptures in the order's convent church at Vadstena depict St. Katherine, but the saint's mystic marriage is also depicted in a mural in the nuns' quarters that dates from several decades after the Protestant Reformation of Sweden was set into motion.

The third chapter of the study explores the well-established devotion to the saint among the lay nobility, especially, but not exclusively, among noble women. Naming traditions, images in seals, donations of and to altars and other foundations all suggest that St. Katherine was a favored intercessor for members of this group, as she was for clerics. Interestingly, it appears that St. Katherine may have been a particularly appropriate patron saint for active women, even married women and widows, including many who did not share the saint's name. In many cases, it appears that devotion to St. Katherine, and the use of her image in personal seals, becomes a family tradition of sorts, and the chapter explores possible motivations and meanings for this use in several families. Nonetheless, the saint's image in aristocratic circles was not restricted to the seals of noble women, nor were its meanings always associated with family connections. During the later Middle Ages, the image of St. Katherine occasionally appears in contexts that suggest that she has been enlisted as a symbol and intercessor in a political struggle. This use of St. Katherine's image does not in any way restrict its appearance in other contexts.

The fourth chapter of the study takes a somewhat different approach from the preceding two, focusing not on a particular segment of society but on a geographic region. During and after the Middle Ages, the island of Gotland, located off the southeast coast of Sweden, had a unique position, both part of and separate from the rest of Sweden. In many ways, social structures here seem more closely to resemble those of Iceland than of mainland Sweden. For example, royal influence on the island during most of the period was minimal. There were no royal estates on the island until after the Reformation. Although there was clearly a local elite, perhaps a powerful one, it is notable that the aristocratic families of the Swedish mainland never became established here. In part because of these two factors, the written charters that provide so much information about mainland Sweden during the medieval period are largely absent here. Trade was clearly the most important source of wealth on the island from a very early point, and it appears that trade contacts here may have differed to some extent from those of other regions of medieval Sweden. For example, at least until the middle of the fourteenth century, Gotlanders maintained a strong presence in the important Russian trading center of Novgorod. Here as well, many notable images of St. Katherine are found in the medieval churches, and at least two parish churches were dedicated to her. The unique position of Gotland in medieval Sweden may suggest some specific reasons for the importance of St. Katherine here, as well as ways in which circumstances in Gotland may mirror those in other areas of medieval Sweden.

The final chapter of this study concerns the piety of commoners living in urban and rural areas. In contrast to their ecclesiastical and aristocratic counterparts, these groups have left relatively little documentation of their devotions, which means that the sources on which the discussion is based in this chapter differ markedly from those employed in the earlier chapters. One possible means of gaining an understanding of the non-noble laity is to study the relatively numerous guilds dedicated to St. Katherine, found in both urban and rural areas. One church dedication in the province of Uppland may also reflect the specific interests of commoners. If these were the only resources for the study of non-aristocratic lay spirituality in medieval Sweden, the chapter would be a thin one. However, Swedish tradition offers another possibility—in many ways an unexpected one — for understanding the roles that St. Katherine has played for this population. Along with its neighbor Denmark, Sweden has preserved one of Europe's largest and most important collections of traditional ballads, the bulk of them collected from oral performance. One very important ballad in this corpus is "Liten Karin" ("Little Karin"), a narrative clearly based on elements of the vita of St. Katherine of Alexandria. In this ballad, a young woman fends off the advances of a powerful male, a king who, it appears, is already married. Although he offers her a series of rich gifts in exchange for her favors, and indeed threatens her with severe torment, Karin, the heroine of the ballad, is steadfast in her refusal, admonishing the king to give his gifts to the queen and leave her alone. Once the king realizes that he cannot possess Karin, he places her in a barrel lined with spikes, and has her rolled to her death. At this point, miracles occur. In some variants of the ballad the dead girl speaks, while in others doves fly down from heaven to carry her soul to its reward. Although this ballad was first collected at the beginning of the nineteenth century, from the time it was first recorded it became one of the most widely collected ballads in Sweden and Swedish-speaking Finland, collected well over a hundred times from oral performance. Because of the nature of ballad collecting in Sweden in the centuries following the Reformation, the ballad's absence in written sources from this period in no way undermines the possibility of its having existed in oral tradition for centuries before the time of its earliest recording. The relationship of oral narratives collected long after the Protestant Reformation to the medieval saint's cult is complex and dynamic, and has little to do with the old national-romantic notion that "the folk" preserve archaic elements of culture that their social and economic superiors have abandoned. In this chapter I argue that the "Liten Karin" ballad is in many ways rooted in lay—and possibly peasant—devotions to St. Katherine during the Middle Ages. As such, aspects of this post-Reformation narrative tradition may provide important insights into the piety of an otherwise almost undocumented population. At the same time, the prominence of this ballad in later tradition may suggest that the boundaries between pre- and post-Reformation spirituality are more fluid than has often been asserted. Thus the ballad tradition may also reflect the attitudes of later, rural Swedes toward the innovations of the Reformation, and the lingering echoes of the old cult long past the centuries in which the highest authorities in the land sanctioned its existence. This chapter does not restrict its examination of the "Liten Karin" ballad to aspects directly traceable to the medieval cult, but rather attempts to analyze it as a part of a productive living tradition in the period during which it was widely collected. For this reason, I examine the use of formulaic language in this and several other related ballads, including an examination of the use of formulaic sequences typical of the "Liten Karin" tradition in the repertoires of several different singers. In addition to examining the ways in which the ballad plot may arise directly from medieval traditions, and the ways in which its singers and audiences may have understood it to do so, I also discuss an apparent shift in the way the ballad was understood in the later nineteenth century, when it came to be widely associated with an historical figure from the Swedish renaissance. Sven-Bertil Jansson has suggested that certain aspects of post-Reformation oral ballad tradition seem to support the aptness of Jacques Le Goff's term "the long Middle Ages" as a designation of the period up to the "final breakthrough of the modern period."[12] This statement also seems productive as a way of analyzing the later history of the ballad based on the legend of St. Katherine in relation to the saint's medieval cult. The shift away from what I argue is a specifically spiritual understanding of the ballad toward an explicitly historical, if not entirely historically accurate, interpretation may signal a shift in Swedish society as a whole away from a world view with its roots in the Middle Ages toward a more strictly secular one. Thus, in spite of the complete absence of medieval recordings of the "Liten Karin," I contend that an understanding of the ballad tradition as it is known from the nineteenth and twentieth centuries is critical to an exploration of the cult of St. Katherine among the non-noble laity of medieval Sweden, whose piety is otherwise almost entirely undocumented.

---

[12] Jansson does not, however, discuss "Liten Karin" in his article: Sven-Bertil Jansson, "'Och jungfrun skulle sig till ottesången gå': om kyrkan i den medeltida balladen," in *Kyrka och socken i medeltidens Sverige*, ed. Olle Ferm, Studier till Det medeltida Sverige 5 (Stockholm: Riksantikvarieämbetet, 1991), 512–43, esp. 538.

I

EARLY MANIFESTATIONS

The arrival of the cult of St. Katherine in medieval Sweden, like the earliest manifestations of the cult, has thus far been impossible to trace, and will almost certainly remain so. Nonetheless, there is evidence that this cult was among the earlier arrivals following the Christianization of Sweden, and that its popularity was considerable from a relatively early point. Although it may not be possible to pinpoint the cult's arrival in Sweden, it may nonetheless be possible to piece together at least part of its earliest history by examining liturgical calendars, naming practices, and images of the saint in churches, frescoes, or sculptures.

It is sometimes asserted that the cult of St. Katherine of Alexandria, like so many other popular medieval saints' cults, was brought to Western Europe, and possibly even to Sweden, by returning crusaders.[1] Although a number of Danes and Norwegians are known to have fought in the Crusades, there is little evidence of Swedish participation in the campaigns in the Middle East,[2] which suggests that the introduction of the cult of St. Katherine to Sweden occurred by other means. Nonetheless, the assertion of a connection between the saint's cult and the Crusades contains a hard kernel of psychological truth. Like many of the other virgin martyrs who were popular individually and collectively throughout the medieval Catholic world (other examples include St. Margaret of Antioch, St. Barbara, often associated with Nicomedia, St. Dorothy of Cappadocia, and St. Agatha of Catania, Sicily), Katherine of Alexandria is associated with a major Christian center that fell—and remained—under Islamic control. The narratives of young virgins who resist the temptations of apostasy, while in many cases achieving the conversion of many heathens (and the death of many others), must have been read, at least by some audiences, as a kind of symbolic victory over Islam, or even as a presage of a hoped-for reconquest.

The ultimate origins of the cult and legend of St. Katherine of Alexandria as a whole lie outside the scope of this study. Whatever its beginnings, the veneration of this saint was well established in western Europe by the time that

---

[1] Sigurd Pira, *Om helgonkulten i Linköpings stift* (Lund: Svenska kyrkans diakonstyrelses bokförlag, 1952), 24–25.
[2] Jarl Gallén, "Korståg," *KHLM* 9, 210–15.

Christianity can be said to have achieved a solid foothold in Sweden. Nonetheless, a few remarks on the early development of the international cult may be in order. The most reliable information about the spread of the Katherine cult in medieval Europe suggests that the veneration of the saint, as well as, possibly, her relics, came from Sinai to Rouen, possibly as early as 1030.[3] There may also be evidence of a very early cult in Rome, in the form of a mural dated to 731–741.[4] From the eleventh century onward, evidence of the cult begins to appear not only in Normandy but also in England, where St. Katherine's name appears in a calendar produced by the scriptorium of the old Minster of Winchester in about 1050.[5] It should not be forgotten, however, that the origins of the legend of St. Katherine, and possibly of her cult are to be found in the Greek and other eastern churches, not the Roman one.[6] While Norman influence was certainly the decisive factor in the spread of the Katherine cult in most of the medieval West, the picture is not equally clear for the Nordic countries.

Liber ecclesiae Vallentunensis and its background

The earliest reliable evidence for the veneration of St. Katherine of Alexandria in Sweden is a liturgical calendar from the *Liber ecclesiae Vallentunensis*, dating from 1198. This is the earliest known Nordic calendar in which Katherine's feast, 25 November, occurs.[7] In this calendar her feast is noted in black ink, rather than the red which would indicate heightened importance. However, it is also among the feasts to which a cross was added in a later hand. This is taken to indicate a higher degree of veneration, though the exact degree has not been determined.

---

[3] R. Fawtier, "Les reliques Rouennaises de Sainte Catherine d'Alexandrie," *Analecta Bollandiana* 41(1923): 357–68; Charles W. Jones, "The Norman Cult of Sts. Catherine and Nicholas Saec. XI," in *Hommages à André Boutemy*, ed. Guy Cambier (Brussels: Latomus, 1976), 216–30.

[4] Lewis, *Cult of St Katherine*, 47.

[5] Lewis, *Cult of St Katherine*, 53

[6] Jones appears to contest this assertion, suggesting that the cult was new and obscure in the East at the time it was introduced to Rouen: "Norman Cult," esp. 221–22.

[7] The feast of St. Katherine does not appear in two twelfth-century Nordic calendars associated with the archdiocese of Lund, those of the *Necrologium Lundense* and the Annal of Colbaz (see Odenius, "Katarina av Alexandria," *KHLM* 9, 340–42; *Necrologium Lundense: Lunds domkyrkas nekrologium*, ed. Lauritz Weibull, Monumenta scaniæ historica [Lund: Berlingaska boktrykeriet, 1923]; Rosenstock, "Kalendarium," *KHLM* 2, 577–78). Likewise, the feast is absent from the runic calendar stave discovered in Lödöse, an early medieval trading center in western Sweden, near present-day Göteborg. Svärdström has dated the stave to the middle of the twelfth century. She suggests that it is of Danish origin, probably from western Jutland: see Elisabeth Svärdström, *Kalenderstickan från Lödöse*, Antikvariskt arkiv 21 (Stockholm: Almqvist & Wiksell, 1963), 65.

Schmid has suggested that the simplest crosses may indicate the degree of what is termed duplex (or double feast), and that these may have been added during the 1290s.[8] Jarl Gallén has argued convincingly that the Vallentuna calendar was greatly influenced by an early cathedral chapter at Gamla Uppsala, which, he suggests, predated the foundation of the archbishopric in 1164. He argues that the founders and most of the members of this chapter must have been Benedictine monks of English, or more exactly, Anglo-Norman origin.[9] If this assumption is correct, it may be possible to speculate that these Benedictines played a role in the early spread of St. Katherine's cult in Sweden. Sven Helander has argued that the original cathedral chapter at Uppsala must instead have followed the Cistercian rule, and that its founder was the Cistercian monk Stephen, Sweden's first archbishop, rather than King Erik Jedvardsson (St. Erik, d. 1160), as suggested by Gallén. He does not, however, dispute the connection Gallén suggests between the Vallentuna calendar and the chapter.[10] Whether the earliest canons in Uppsala followed the Benedictine or Cistercian rule, the appearance of the feast of St. Katherine in the Vallentuna calendar may suggest that the saint was known to them, and that she was a recipient of their devotions. If this was indeed the case, it might suggest that these canons played a role in introducing the cult to Sweden.

Royal connections: the evidence of names

Benedictine foundations are otherwise almost unknown in Sweden. Only one other can be traced: the earliest known monastic foundation of any kind in Sweden is thought to be Vreta Abbey, apparently founded as a Benedictine convent by King Inge the Elder and his queen, Helena, around 1100.[11] The mother house of this convent, which was located in Östergötland very near Linköping, is unknown. It is thus difficult to trace any kind of national tradition. Vreta Abbey was apparently reconstituted under the Cistercian rule in 1162, at the behest of King Karl Sverkersson and his sister Ingegierd, who would become its first abbess.[12] There is no direct evidence from any period linking the cult of St. Katherine with Vreta Abbey. Nonetheless, there is evidence to suggest that the cult of St. Katherine became established in Östergötland, and not least in the

---

[8] *Liber ecclesiae Vallentunensis*, ed. Toni Schmid (Stockholm: KVHAA, 1945), 93.

[9] Jarl Gallén, "De engelska munkarna i Uppsala—ett katedralkloster på 1100-talet," *Historisk tidskrift för Finland* 61 (1976): 1–21.

[10] See Sven Helander, *Den medeltida Uppsalaliturgin. Studier i helgonlängd, tidegärd och mässa* (Lund: Arcus förlag, 2001), 60–68.

[11] Nils Ahnlund, "Vreta klosters tidigaste donatorer," *Historisk tidskrift* 89 (1945): 301–51.

[12] Ahnlund, "Vreta," 302.

area nearest to Linköping and Vreta, at an early point by Swedish standards (see Chapter Two). There may be a further link between Vreta and early devotion to St. Katherine. According to *Knytlinga saga*, a thirteenth-century Icelandic work about the Danish royal dynasty, the youngest daughter of King Inge the Elder and his consort Helena was named Katherine. This Katherine is said to have married a son of the Danish king Harald Kejsa, and their daughter Kristina would become the consort of the Swedish king Erik Jedvardsson, later venerated as St. Erik.[13] Katherine is the least well documented of the daughters of King Inge and Queen Helena, not mentioned in any surviving contemporary document. However, her historicity, like that of her better-documented sisters Margareta and Kristina, is widely accepted by historians, who regularly include her in royal genealogies without comment.[14] Among the children and grandchildren of Erik Jedvardsson and his Kristina, several have names that would seem to connect them with the family of Inge the Elder and with Katarina Ingesdotter specifically (Margareta, Christina, Katarina, Fillip).[15] Although the reliability of *Knytlinga saga* has been called into question on many points, given the well-established medieval Swedish tradition of naming children for their grandparents, it appears that on this particular point *Knytlinga saga* may be reliable. Together with her mother and her sisters, Katarina Ingesdotter is the earliest known woman in Swedish history with a name of Christian derivation.[16]

Inge the Elder, the father of these three daughters named for well-known saints, is an important and interesting figure in early Swedish history, not least through his special role in the establishment of the church. Although the kings of Sweden are generally thought to have been Christian from the early eleventh century onward, the few written sources that discuss eleventh-century Sweden suggest that the new religion had not found universal acceptance there. Inge was in fact the first king of Sweden to receive—and respond to—a communication from the pope. In 1080, Pope Gregory VII sent two letters to "I" (one of them was addressed to "I" and "A"), congratulating him on the conversion of his kingdom, and expressing gratification over the presence in Sweden of French missionaries.[17] The letters from the pope intimate—as later medieval Icelandic

---

[13] "Knytlinga saga, "*Danakonunga sögur*, ed. Bjarni Gudnason, Íslensk fornrit 35 (Reykjavík: Hid Íslenzka fornrítafélag, 1982), 91–321.

[14] See, for example, Knut B. Westman, "Erik den helige och hans tid," *Erik den helige: Historia, kult, reliker*, ed. Bengt Thordeman (Stockholm: Nordisk rotogravyr, 1954), 18–23; Curt Wallin, *Knutsgillena i det medeltida Sverige* (Stockholm: KVHAA, 1975), 182–85; Carl M. Kjellberg, "Erik den heliges ättlingar och tronpretendenterna bland dem," *Historisk tidskrift* 43 (1923), 351–74.

[15] Kjellberg, "Erik den heliges ättlingar," 353.

[16] Anders Grape, "Studier över de i fornsvenskan inlånade personnamnen" (Ph. D. diss., Uppsala University, 1911), 81.

[17] In *DS* nos. 24, 25

sources also suggest—that Inge had, shortly before, succeeded in putting down a heathen rebellion. According to the Icelandic sources, Inge had been driven from power by a rival with the suspiciously attributive name of "Blót-Sveinn," which might be translated as "Sven the Sacrificer" (or even "man who sacrifices").[18] The religious center for early Sweden—some would say for an even wider area—was undoubtedly Uppsala, with its enormous Iron Age barrows. According to *Hervarar saga*, Blot-Sven drove Inge into exile in the more solidly Christian province of Västergötland, where his predecessor Olof Skötkonung had also taken refuge for similar reasons decades before. Eventually, though, Inge was able to overthrow his heathen rival and regain the throne.[19] Along with putting down the heathen rebellion, receiving French missionaries, and corresponding with Pope Gregory VII, Inge has been credited with appointing perhaps the earliest provincial bishops in Sweden, and also with working together with the other Scandinavian kings to establish the archbishopric of Lund.[20]

Although our information about his reign is sparse, Inge the Elder is a fascinating and important transitional figure in the Christian history of Sweden. Given what we know of his history, the fact that his three daughters are named for three popular virgin saints—all of them martyrs for their Christian faith—takes on particular significance. Without a doubt, the names of Inge's daughters must reflect his (and his queen, Helena's) relationship to the world around him. It is a well-attested fact that Viking Age and medieval Swedes (and other Scandinavians) generally named their children according to one of two systems. Runic inscriptions and other sources suggest that it was a common practice during the Viking Age that all names in a particular family contained the same root or prefix. During the Middle Ages, children were commonly named after deceased family members. By the thirteenth century, if not earlier, there was an established order according to which children were named after maternal and paternal grandparents, and then after other family members.[21] As noted above, there is no record of any Swedish woman with a name of Christian derivation earlier than that of Queen Helena and her three daughters with King Inge. It is therefore unlikely—though of course not impossible—that Inge's own family history is reflected in the choice of names. What other relationships might then be reflected? Should we look to Queen Helena's background, or are there other factors at work?

There seem to be two schools of thought regarding the origins of Inge the Elder's consort. The Icelandic *Hervarar saga* refers to Inge's queen as

---

[18] *Hervarar saga ok Heidreks*, ed. Gudni Jónasson, Íslendingasagnaútgáfnan, Fornaldar sögur Nordurlanda 2, (Reykjavík: Prentverk Odds Björnarssonar H. F., 1959), 70–71.

[19] Hervarar saga ok Heidreks, 70–71.

[20] Westman, "Erik den helige," 13–14.

[21] Roland Otterbjörk, "Namngjeving," *KHLM* 12, 210–11.

"Mær"—"Maiden"—and calls her a sister of Inge's heathen rival, Blót-Sveinn.[22] For this reason, some scholars, among them Ander Grape, have assumed that Helena (a name which does not appear in the Icelandic sources) was of Swedish origin.[23] Another school of thought asserts, though without offering any evidence, that Inge the Elder was married to a Russian princess.[24] The name of Inge's queen is generally not questioned, in spite of the rather mythic-sounding appellation assigned her in *Hervarar saga*, for, as Niels Ahnlund has remarked, "no fact in our royal geneaology from the incompletely known time around 1100 is attested with greater certainty than that Inge the Elder's consort was named Helena." She is mentioned in a number of Danish sources, including Saxo's *Gesta Danorum* and Abbot Wilhelm's geneaology of the kings of Denmark, and the anniversary of her death is included in the *Necrologium Lundense*, which records the deaths of the canons of the cathedral chapter at Lund, of members of related communities, and of individuals who become members of the community by other means, such as donations.[25] There is no doubt that the name Helena was well established in early medieval Russia by the time Inge came to power in Sweden. According to the *Russian Primary Chronicle*, Helena was the baptismal name adopted by the Russian regent Olga upon her baptism in the year 955.[26] Jarl Gallén does not attempt to trace the origins of the Swedish Queen Helena, though he does assert that her name comes from Byzantium or Kiev.[27] What significance does Helena's background have in a discussion of the cult of St. Katherine in Sweden? If none of Inge's ancestors can be shown to have had names of Christian origin, should we not look for these names among Helena's family? There is no doubt that communications and relations between the various royal dynasties of Scandinavia on the one hand, and the rulers of Novgorod and Kiev, themselves of at least partially Scandinavian ancestry, on the other, were strong

---

[22] We may be justified in expressing scepticism over the given names "Young Man" and "Maiden." *Knytlinga saga* does not mention the name or origins of Inge's consort, though it does mention Inge, and refers to his daughters and their descendants in several passages.

[23] Ahnlund ("Vreta kloster," 338) also offers a possibility for reconciling the account in *Hervarar saga* with the other accounts of Queen Helena. He suggests that the Icelandic word "mær" means not only "maiden," but also "nun." Thus, he says, "it is possible, even probable, this idea about a Queen Mær goes back to a story about a Swedish queen who ended her days in a convent."

[24] Roland Otterbjörk, "Helgner (Sverige)," *KHLM* 6, 338; Jarl Gallén, "Knut den helige och Adela av Flandern. Europeiska kontakter och genealogiska konsekvenser," in *Studier i äldre historia tillägnade Herman Schück 5/4 1985*, ed. Robert Sandberg (Stockholm: Minab/Gotab, 1985), 49–66.

[25] Ahnlund, "Vreta kloster," 323.

[26] *Nestorskrönikan*, trans. A. Norrback (Stockholm: P. A. Norstedt & söners förlag, 1919), 41.

[27] Gallén, "Knut den helige," 49.

in the late Viking Age and early Middle Ages. Not only was Olof Skötkonung's daughter Ingegierd married to Jaroslav the Wise, ruler of Novgorod and Kiev, by about 1019, but a daughter of this couple married Harald Sigurdson Hardradi in about 1044.[28] Kristina Ingesdotter, the second daughter of Inge and Helena, was married to Mstislav, Grand Prince of Kiev, in 1095 and their two daughters in turn married into the Danish and Norwegian royal families.[29] If Helena herself was of Russian origin, then the names of her three daughters may well reflect the fact that the names and cults of Sts. Margaret, Christina, and Katherine were well established in Russia by the later eleventh century. There is, in fact, every indication that these three saints were venerated in the Byzantine church by the period in question. Although it is difficult to find solid, concrete evidence of the influence of the Byzantine church in late Viking Age and early medieval Sweden, it is clear that there was some contact. It is well known, for example, that Swedes and other Scandinavians formed the core of the Byzantine emperor's famous Varangian Guard, and that many of these men also made their way back to their own countries. It is more than likely that some of these men became Christian converts and brought their new faith home with them. It is also clear that there was extensive trade between Sweden (perhaps especially Gotland) and points east, with much of the main activity located in what is now Russia.[30] For many of the traders active in this region, the most natural form of Christianity would be that of the Byzantine church. One school of thought has asserted that the earliest Christians, and possibly even the earliest churches, in Sweden were Orthodox, rather than Roman Catholic.[31] If the names of Inge and Helena's three daughters reflect Helena's own Orthodox Christian background, there is the possibility that the names, and perhaps the cults, of Sts. Margaret, Christina, and Katherine were introduced to Sweden from the east rather than from the west, and that the early and enduring popularity of (especially) Sts. Margaret and Katherine might then be connected to their Byzantine origin.

Given that there are records in both Scandinavian and Russian sources of marriages between Scandinavian princesses and Russian rulers on the one hand, and Scandinavian kings and Russian princesses on the other, records that both pre- and postdate the reign of Inge the Elder, should we not expect to find some record of Helena's origins as well? In fact, no such record has been found. None of the early sources that mention Queen Helena by name gives any information

---

[28] Simon Franklin and John Shepard, *The Emergence of Rus 750–1200* (London and New York: Longman, 1996), 202.

[29] N. de Baumgarten, "Généalogies et mariages occidentaux des Riurikides russes du Xe aux XIIIe siècle," *Orientalia Christiana*, 9 (1927): 1–94, here 68.

[30] See Michael McCormick, *Origins of the European Economy* (Cambridge: Cambridge University Press, 2001), 562–64, 608–10.

[31] Leon Rhodin, Leif Gren, and Werner Lindblom, "Liljestenarna och Sveriges kristnande från Bysans," *Fornvännen* 95 (2000): 165–81.

about her nationality or origins. It is tempting, nonetheless, to speculate about her background. To the extent that sources of information exist about the marriages of Swedish kings to non-Swedes during the late Viking Age and early medieval period, it appears that the kings married women from Norway (Ulvhild, consort first to Inge the Younger and later to Sverker the Elder), from nearby Slavic regions (Olof Skötkonung's mother as well as his consort, the mother of Inge-gierd), or Denmark (Sofia, married to King Valdemar Birgersson). Given the degree to which the Icelandic sources focus on Norway, it might be expected that Snorri or the author of *Hervarar saga* would remark on the Norwegian origins of Inge's queen, if such had been known. The same might be said of the Danish historians, in particular Saxo, especially since Helena's daughter Margareta became queen of Denmark and was the object of considerable attention from Saxo. As far as the names of Helena and her three daughters are concerned, either Norway or Denmark could have provided a source of Christian names. Norway may have had a Benedictine monastery, Nidarholm, as early as 1028,[32] which could both reflect and support an increasingly Christian culture. Although there is no indication of equally early monastic foundations in Denmark, there is strong evidence of Christian faith and Christian naming practices. As an example, Adam of Bremen noted that Estrid, who was the sister of King Knut the Great (king of Denmark 1018–1035, king of England 1016–1035) and the mother of King Sven Estridsen (king of Denmark c. 1047–1074), was also known as Margareta.[33] Another interesting example is a large ivory crucifix, possibly intended for processional use, the inscriptions on which, both in Latin and in Danish runes, refer to "Helena who is also called Gunhild." Ahnlund and a number of other scholars have asserted that this Helena is an otherwise unknown daughter of Sven Estridsen, which would make her a near contemporary of our Helena.[34] Given this correspondence in time, it is tempting to connect Gunhild/Helena with Helena of Sweden. One circumstance, though, makes this connection nearly impossible. Helena's daughter Margareta, in her second marriage, was married to Niels, a son of Sven Estridsen. Even if, as Wallin asserts, "the ecclesiastical

---

[32] Helander, *Den medeltida Uppsalaliturgin*, 59. According to Tore Nyberg, this dating was favored by nineteenth-century historians, while twentieth-century scholars generally date the foundation of Nidarholm to c. 1100 or slightly earlier. See Tore Nyberg, *Monasticism in North-Western Europe, 800–1200* (Aldershot: Ashgate, 2000), 74–76.

[33] Adam of Bremen, *Adam av Bremen. Historien om Hamburgstiftet och dess biskopar,* trans. Emanuel Svenberg, commentaries by Carl Fredrik Hallencreutz, Kurt Johanneson, Tore Nyberg, and Anders Piltz (Stockholm: Proprius förlag, 1984), 100.

[34] Ahnlund, "Vreta kloster," 310. It must be noted, however, that least one scholar has argued on stylistic grounds that the crucifix must instead have belonged to a daughter of Sven Grathe (king of Denmark 1146–1157), who was actually a great-grandson of the Swedish Queen Helena: see Harald Langberg, *Gunhildskorset* (Copenhagen: Selskabet til udgivelse av danske Mindesmærker, 1982).

determinations regarding forbidden degree were accorded little respect during this period," a marriage between such near relations as uncle and niece seems very unlikely indeed.[35] Thus, if Helena of Sweden came from Denmark, she was probably not a direct member of the royal line.

While there is no evidence that Helena, consort of King Inge, was of Danish royal lineage, it is possible, at least judging by naming traditions, that she might have come from Denmark. With our present state of knowledge, it is unlikely that we will come any closer to solving the mystery of Queen Helena's origins, and of her personal influence on the names of her daughters or the cults of their patron saints. On the other hand, there may be good reason to suspect that the names of the three daughters of Inge and Helena represent a break with older naming traditions, and an emphasis on relationships other than familial ones. In this context, it might also be possible to speculate that Inge's queen could have borne her Christian name alongside a name of Nordic derivation (as did Estrid-Margareta and Gunhild-Helena), possibly as a mark of (adult) baptism or newly deepened faith. The two letters from Pope Gregory VII to King Inge may also be an important clue to the source of the names. Several scholars have noted that Pope Gregory's emphasis on the French nationality of the clerics preaching in Inge's Sweden reflects the pope's bitter fight with the Holy Roman (German) Emperor Henry IV over the right of investiture.[36] Clearly, the French church has taken its stand on the side of the pope, and is therefore to be regarded as pure and correct. Still, Ahnlund and others have also suggested that the statement about nationality might reflect the origins of the individual missionaries, as well as their affiliation, and that it might perhaps refer specifically to clerics from Normandy. Since the cult of St. Katherine is well attested in Normandy by the middle of the eleventh century, it is possible that the earliest arrival of the cult of St. Katherine (and perhaps of Sts. Margaret and Christina as well) occurred with the arrival of these missionaries in Sweden.

Whatever the ultimate source of the names of Inge's daughters, it is clear that they derive from contact with other Christian cultures, and that they are a break with earlier nomenclature. There is no evidence that the introduction of the the name Katherine (or for that matter Margaret or Christina) arises out of an already-extant cult.[37] On the other hand, it appears likely that the introduction

---

[35] Wallin, *Knutsgillena*, 182.

[36] See Ahnlund, "Vreta kloster," 317; Henrik Janson, *Templum nobilissimum: Adam av Bremen, Uppsalatemplet och konfliktlinjerna i Europa kring år 1075*, Avhandlingar från Historiska institutionen i Göteborg 21 (Göteborg: Historiska institutionen, 1998); Westman, "Erik den helige," 13.

[37] In fact, the earliest Nordic calendar to include the feast of St. Margaret of Antioch is the Vallentuna calendar of 1198. Like Katherine, Margaret is omitted from the Danish calendars of the twelfth century, even though her name is found among the Danish royal family, and even though several Danish churches are known to have been dedicated to her

of these names—given that they were clearly adopted for a reason—would generate some level of interest in the saints from whom they derive. Whatever the path by which the names Margaret, Christina, and especially Katherine reached Sweden, they must have been introduced by practicing Christians, and their adoption must reflect at least partially Christian concerns. Given the popularity of these three saints, especially Margaret and Katherine, in medieval Christianity as a whole, it seems plausible that the nuns at Vreta might have venerated the patron saints of the daughters of their founders. While the connection cannot be proven, it is possible that Vreta Abbey might have been one of the means by which the cult of St. Katherine was introduced to the region of Östergötland (Diocese of Linköping), where many of the earliest surviving images of the saint are also found.[38]

Early images of St. Katherine

No piece of artwork depicting St. Katherine in Sweden has been assigned a date earlier than 1200. As may be expected, the number of works in general surviving from the earliest Christian period (i.e., the twelfth century) in Sweden is limited indeed, and most of the earliest works depict either Christ, the Madonna, or an occasional apostle. Katherine is, however, among the saints portrayed in sculptures dating from the thirteenth century. In addition to the early sculptures, a small number of murals in the Romanesque style has survived in Swedish churches, especially in the diocese of Linköping, which included the province of Östergötland and the islands of Gotland and Öland. Although the group of saints appearing in these early paintings is quite limited, Katherine is among those represented. It seems reasonable to conclude that the churches in which early representations of St. Katherine survive participated actively in her veneration from an early date.

Two of the most fascinating early depictions of St. Katherine are murals from Östergötland. In the Romanesque parish church of Asby, on the east wall of the chancel above the apse, and above the late medieval vaults, is a very unusual scene from the martyrdom of St. Katherine. As described by Aron Borelius, who photographed and published the frescoes in the 1950s, the scene depicts St. Katherine in prison, where she has been placed by the emperor Maxentius after her steadfast refusal to sacrifice to the pagan gods. Although it was the emperor's

---

before 1200: See Ellen Jørgensen, *Helgendyrkelse i Danmark* (Copenhagen: H. Hagerups Forlag, 1909), 16; Tue Gad, "Margareta (af Antiochia)," *KHLM* 11, 346–47.

[38] No images of St. Katherine have been connected to the church at Vreta. However, the surviving medieval inventory from this church is minimal: a twelfth-century Madonna, a thirteenth-century rood, and a font from the same period: See Birger Börjesson, *Om Vreta klosters kyrka* (Vreta kloster: Vreta klosters hembygsförening, 1986), 6–12.

intention that Katherine should starve to death (or perish from her severe beatings), she was fed and healed by a white dove. The dove was surrounded by a light so intense that it attracted the attention of the empress and the captain of the guard, who visited Katherine in prison, along with two hundred knights. Convinced by Katherine's preaching and by her miraculous recovery, the empress, the captain, and all the knights were converted to the Christian faith, which, in a later section of the legend, would lead to their martyrdom. The painting in Asby church depicts a crowned and haloed female figure, looking to the right and reaching in that direction with her hands. Immediately to her right—clearly the object of her attention—is a large white dove, descending from above, and bearing in its beak a round object that closely resembles the host. Interestingly, the dove seems to be placing the object into a chalice-like dish, so that the arrangement resembles the chalice and host often depicted in later images of St. John the Evangelist or St. Barbara. To the right of the dove are two objects that might be described as candles, or perhaps torches, while to the right of these is a haloed figure whose hand is raised in benediction. Borelius asserts that the mural in Asby without a doubt depicts Katherine's imprisonment, her miraculous healing, and the angel's visit to her cell. Although the murals in their present condition do not include depictions of the empress or Porphyrius, the captain of the guard, the legend makes them witnesses to the event. Borelius dates the mural to the middle of the thirteenth century, in part because a compass was clearly used to draw the haloes, but he also notes the presence of archaic details.[39]

Another interesting, if problematic, mural is a depiction of a woman with a halo, wearing a massive crown, holding a book, and sitting enthroned between two angels, on the east wall of the nave of Kaga church in Östergötland. This painting, which is quite damaged, has been identified as a depiction of St. Katherine in the Catalog of Iconography at ATA, and also by Mereth Lindgren in a 1995 article, even though the image does not include Katherine's most usual attributes, a wheel or sword, nor is the figure standing on the body of her tormentor.[40] Borelius, who discusses this painting at length in his study of Romanesque murals, prefers to interpret the image as that of a worldly queen, and does not suggest Katherine or any other saint as a possible identification. His analysis is not completely convincing on this point, however. On the same wall as the painting of

---

[39] Aron Borelius, *Romanesque Mural Paintings in Östergötland* (Norrköping: Norrköpings museum, 1956), 145–58; plates CXCIX and CCI, color plate V. It should be noted that Åke Nisbeth has a different interpretation of this mural: he prefers to interpret it as a depiction of "Ecclesia", and thus identifies another female figure on the south wall as "Synagoga" (see Åke Nisbeth, *Bildernas predikan: Medeltida kalkmålningar i Sverige* (Stockholm: KVHAA/RAÄ, 1986), 54–55.

[40] Mereth Lindgren,"Kalkmålningarna," in *Den romanska konsten (Signums svenska konsthistoria vol. III)* (Lund: Bokförlaget Signum, 1995), 299–335, here 335.

"the queen" is a corresponding image of an enthroned, bearded, crowned male, also with a halo, and also flanked by two angels. This figure holds an axe in one of his hands, which clearly identifies him as St. Olav, the Norwegian king who fell in battle in 1030, and quickly became one of the most popular saints of the Nordic region, not least in Sweden. In his other hand he holds a book. Borelius does identify this figure as St. Olav.[41] Given the almost identical composition of the two images, the fact that both wear haloes, and the unequivocal identification of St. Olav, it seems more likely than not that the figure Borelius calls "the queen" is intended to represent a saint, rather than an earthly queen.[42]

Even more interestingly, Kaga church is closely associated with one of the royal dynasties that ruled Sweden on and off during the twelfth and thirteenth centuries. This church, or perhaps an earlier wooden church on the same site, is said to have been built in the early twelfth century by the father of King Sverker the Elder, who ruled Sweden from around 1130 to 1156. The church was built as a private "magnate's church," in other words, not initially as a parish church, but for the personal use of the nobleman on whose estates it was located. The church then formed part of the inheritance of members of this family until 1275, when the deposed and disgraced King Valdemar Birgersson voluntarily gave up his share of the right of patronage.[43] According to canon law, including the ecclesiastical codes of the Swedish provincial laws of Uppland and Södermanland, the right of patronage is defined as the right to appoint or at least suggest a candidate for the office of parish priest. In some cases, the patron would have the right to reject the bishop's candidate for the post.[44] In practice, however, the right of patronage could include other privileges or duties. Certainly the church patron would be the most likely donor of murals or other works of art for the decoration

---

[41] Borelius, *Romanesque Mural Paintings,* 60–62; plates LXXXV, LXXXVII, LCIX. Anne Lidén has identified this painting as the earliest Nordic image of St. Olav: *Olav den helige i medeltida bildkonst: Legendmotiv och attribut* (Stockholm: KVHAA, 1999), 38.

[42] A similar pair of images in the chancel arch of Dädesjö church, Småland, has been tentatively interpreted as a depiction of St. Knut (or one of the three Danish royal saints to bear that name) and St. Katherine of Alexandria. Although the paintings, dated to 1275 or later, are in good condition, the identification is far from certain. See Mereth Lindgren, "Kalkmålningarna," in *Den gotiska konsten (Signums svenska konsthistoria vol. IV)* (Lund: Bokförlaget Signum, 1996), 308–411, here 341; also Wallin, *Knutsgillena,* 152.

[43] Gunnar Redelius, *Kyrkobygge och kungamakt i Östergötland* (Stockholm: KVHAA/ Almqvist & Wiksell, 1972), 4; Herman Schück, *Ecclesia Lincopensis: Studier om Linköpingskyrkan under medeltiden och Gustav Vasa,* Acta Universitatis Stockholmensis 4 (Stockholm: Almqvist & Wiksell, 1959), 198 ff. Interestingly, the other partial holders of the right of patronage for Kaga church at this time were Svantepolk Knutsson, a powerful aristocrat married to the sister of Queen Katarina, and Svantepolk's son-in-law Johan Fillipsson (see Ahnlund, "Vreta kloster," 351, n. 4). This suggests that the right of patronage could also be inherited through the female line.

[44] Ivar Nylander, "Patronatsrätt" *KHLM* 13, 136–38.

of the church, and this probably means that the patron exerted a degree of influence on the choice of motifs. There are several reason why it makes sense to interpret the painting in Kaga church as a depiction of St. Katherine. Other images of this saint are known from Sweden, and even from the diocese of Linköping, by the time this image was painted, which Borelius suggests was around 1230.[45] Members of the Sverker family are known to have been named Katherine, most notably Katarina Sunesdotter, a granddaughter of King Sverker the Younger (c. 1196–1208), who was the consort of King Erik Eriksson, the last direct heir of the Erik dynasty, which had been the main rival of the Sverkers. Although it is not known how long Katarina reigned as queen, she is known to have died in 1252, two years after her husband. Even if the images of the two saints on the east wall of the church are also to be understood as a reference to worldly monarchs, St. Katherine would be an appropriate choice for a church patron with royal ambitions. It is often noted that St. Katherine is the only one of the virgin martyrs who was also a reigning monarch, according to some versions of her legend. As such she makes a particularly appropriate female counterpart for St. Olav, whose sainthood seems to be closely linked to his royal status. Her legend and image have often been associated with kingship, not only with queenly status.[46] Further, descendents of Katarina Sunesdotter's sister Benedicta depicted St. Katherine in their seals for generations, as a reference to their own royal lineage.[47] Finally, St Katherine and St. Olav are frequently depicted together in medieval Swedish murals and retables. All of these factors suggest that it is reasonable to identify the "queen" in Kaga with St. Katherine, even if the identification is not certain.

Many of the earliest Swedish images of St. Katherine are found on the island of Gotland. Among these is a mural in the chancel (formerly the nave) of the parish church of Kräklingbo. An inscription in this suite of paintings dates them to 1211. If this inscription is reliable, this is the earliest known image of St. Katherine from Sweden. The Katherine images from Gotland will be discussed in detail in Chapter Four of this study, which focusses on the the island's special position in medieval Sweden, both part of and distinct from the country as a whole. One point relevant to the present discussion, however, is that the images of St. Katherine from Gotland are unlikely to reflect ideas of kingship or aristocracy. As I will discuss in Chapter Four, there were no royal estates in Gotland during the entire Middle Ages, and the aristocratic families of the Swedish mainland never

---

[45] Borelius, *Romanesque Mural Paintings*, 86.

[46] Lewis, Cult of St Katherine, 65–79; Karen Winstead, "St Katherine's Hair," in *St Katherine of Alexandria: Texts and Contexts in Medieval Western Europe*, ed. Jenkins and Lewis, 171–200.

[47] Tracey R. Sands, "The Saint as Symbol: The Cult of St Katherine of Alexandria Among Medieval Sweden's High Aristocracy," in *St Katherine of Alexandria. Texts and Contexts in Medieval Western Europe*, ed. Jenkins and Lewis, 87–108.

became established here. Thus the meanings that St. Katherine and her image held for medieval Gotlanders must have been distinct, at least in some aspects, from those evident in the early murals of Östergötland.

While the diocese of Linköping is by far the richest source of early depictions of St. Katherine, one early piece of wooden sculpture has also survived from Uppland. The church of Östra Ryd owned a hardwood sculpture of impressive size (115 cm), dated to around 1300. Although the sculpture is damaged, it is clearly recognizable as a depiction of St. Katherine. The sculpture's right hand is gone, and although the left hand has a hole indicating that it once held an attribute, that attribute has disappeared. Sven Brandel, in his description of the church for *Sveriges kyrkor*, incorrectly – though tentatively – identified it as an image of St. Margaret, but because the sculpture depicts a young woman standing on the prone form of a man, not a dragon, it can only be Katherine.[48] This figure, now headless, is the emperor Maxentius, St. Katherine's great antagonist. It should be noted that the sculpture is correctly identified as St. Katherine by Peter Tångenberg.[49] This depiction is among the oldest surviving sculptures from Östra Ryd, and its size would suggest that it must have occupied a prominent place in the church, perhaps indicating that one of the altars was dedicated to St. Katherine. However, although Östra Ryd had an impressive collection of wooden sculptures from the fifteenth century, and a suite of murals painted in 1449, it has no other depictions of St. Katherine. The church's reredos from 1488 features Sts. Erik and Barbara in its corpus, but again, Katherine is not represented, nor is she mentioned in the now-lost inscription listing the patron saints of the church.[50] As I argue in Chapter Three, the earliest church at Östra Ryd (which was replaced in the fifteenth century) appears to have been a magnate's church, and the large sculpture of St. Katherine may suggest that the aristocratic patron of the church had some connection to the cathedral chapter at Uppsala.

It was not unusual for sculptures to be replaced or modernized during the Middle Ages. Indeed, if they were not, it may be concluded that the church in which the sculptures stood suffered from difficult economic circumstances.[51] For this reason, it cannot be stated with certainty that St. Katherine did not occur more widely among early medieval Swedish sculpture than the small number of

---

[48]   Sven Brandel, "Östra Ryds kyrka," in *Uppland I: Danderyds, Värmdö och Åkers skeppslag*, ed. O. Johansson and Johnny Roosval, Sveriges kyrkor, (Stockholm: Riksantikvarieämbetet och Statens historiska museum, 1931–1942), 273–399.

[49]   Peter Tångenberg, *Mittelalterliche Holzskulptur und Altarschreine in Schweden* (Stockholm: KVHAA, 1986), 29.

[50]   See Brandel, "Östra Ryds kyrka," 307–8; also Anna Nilsén, *Program och funktion i senmedeltida kalkmåleri: Kyrkmålningarna i Mälarlandskapen och Finland 1400–1534* (Stockholm: KVHAA, 1986), 184–85.

[51]   Carina Jacobsson, *Höggotisk träskulptur i gamla Linköpings stift* (Visby: Ödins förlag, 1995), 226.

survivals would appear to indicate. In some of the churches with early depictions of St. Katherine it is possible to find evidence of continued devotion through the medieval period, while in others no further depictions of the saint survive.

Whatever the means by which the cult of St. Katherine of Alexandria arrived in Sweden, it is evident, based on liturgical calendars, naming traditions, and images in churches, that devotion to the saint was well established by the middle of the thirteenth century, if not well before. Although it may not be possible to locate the earliest centers from which the saint and her cult were introduced, even the earliest representations of the saint suggest that her image could convey and reflect different concerns and meanings in different contexts. The following chapters of this book will explore these different contexts, and attempt to tease out the rich and varying significance that St. Katherine of Alexandria appears to have had for each of them.

II

St. Katherine and the Clergy

This chapter discusses the many meanings and uses that the cult of Saint Katherine, and more specifically her legend and image, held for a range of different monastic and mendicant orders and their members, for cathedral chapters and rural parishes, and for individual secular clerics. Although the main focus of the chapter is medieval Sweden, it nonetheless begins with a discussion of the relation of the saint's cult to these groups in a broader medieval Christian context, as a necessary framework for understanding specifically Swedish meanings. One of the major issues addressed, then, is how aspects of the international cult of St. Katherine motivate and influence the specifically Swedish interpretations—and uses—of her cult and image.

As might be expected, one major group with an interest in the cult of any saint is comprised of the church as a body, as well as members of the clergy and the religious orders as individuals. Not surprisingly, given her popularity throughout the medieval Christian world, St. Katherine has a prominent place in the liturgies of all medieval Swedish dioceses. While her cult is so widespread in medieval Sweden that it might be regarded as a kind of common property for all medieval Swedish Christians, it appears clear that this saint was regarded with particular affection by the mendicant orders, especially the Dominican and Franciscan friars. In addition, there is considerable evidence that certain individual clerics, ranging in rank from parish priest to archbishop, regarded St. Katherine as a personal patron. In all of these cases there are specific reasons for choosing this saint over others.

There is no doubt whatsoever that St. Katherine of Alexandria's importance in medieval Swedish ecclesiastical circles is directly related to her prominence in the medieval church as a whole. Nor is there any doubt that St. Katherine was one of the most popular saints of medieval Europe, one whose legend was translated repeatedly into the vernacular languages of Europe.[1] The *Legenda Aurea*, written c. 1262–1266 by the Dominican friar, later Bishop of Genoa, Jacobus of Voragine, was undoubtedly the most widely translated and disseminated of

---

[1] Jacqueline Jenkins and Katherine Lewis, "Introduction," in *St Katherine of Alexandria*, ed. eadem, 1.

all medieval legendaries. In addition to its remarkable influence on the textual traditions of a wide range of saints in most of the vernacular languages of the Roman Catholic world, the *Legenda Aurea* also helped to influence the way that saints were depicted in visual images.[2] According to her legend in the *Legenda Aurea*, "it is worthy of note that blessed Katherine is admirable in five respects: first in wisdom, second in eloquence, third in constancy, fourth in cleanliness of chastity, fifth in her privileged dignity."[3] In elaborating on the last point, the author notes:

> Some saints have received special privileges at the time of death—for instance, a visitation by Christ (Saint John the Evangelist), an outflow of oil (Saint Nicholas), an effusion of milk (Saint Paul), the preparation of a sepulcher (Saint Clement), and the hearing of petitions (Saint Margaret of Antioch when she prayed for those who would honor her memory). Saint Katherine's legend shows that all these privileges were hers.[4]

Given the range and degree of qualities attributed to her, it is not surprising that St. Katherine would appeal to a broad array of individuals and groups across medieval Europe, including both clergy and laity. Few saints and few cults seem to achieve a degree of multifunctionality approaching that of St. Katherine, a fact that has been widely noted.[5] It would appear that the versatility of this saint derives both from her status as a virgin martyr—not least, a virgin martyr originating in the eastern Mediterranean—and from specific traits in her legend. Many scholars have remarked on the extraordinary popularity of virgin martyrs in medieval Europe, noting their appeal both to laity and clergy.[6] Not least, as Winstead remarks, these legends of steadfast and chaste virgins could serve an important purpose for the clergy in their relations with the laity:

> Of course, the clergy retained a professional interest in propagating the legends of holy virgins, for those legends reinforced the barrier between the laity and a celibate elite of saints and clerics. Though a fifteenth-century

---

[2] Tue Gad, "Legenda aurea," *KHLM* 10, 410–11.

[3] Jacobus de Voragine, *The Golden Legend: Readings on the Saints*, trans. William Grainger Ryan (Princeton: Princeton University Press, 1993), 2: 339.

[4] Jacobus, *Golden Legend*, 2: 341.

[5] See, for example, Lewis, *Cult of St Katherine*; also Jenkins and Lewis, "Introduction."

[6] Eamon Duffy, "Holy Maydens, Holy Wyfes: The Cult of Women Saints in Fifteenth- and Sixteenth-Century England," in *Women in the Church*, ed. W. J. Sheils and D. Wood, Studies in Church History 27 (Oxford: Blackwell, 1990), 172–96, 172–78; Thomas Heffernan, *Sacred Biography: Saints and their Biographers in the Middle Ages* (Oxford: Oxford University Press, 1988), 255–99; Winstead, *Virgin Martyrs*, 10–18; Sherry L. Reames, "St Katherine and the Late Medieval Clergy: Evidence from English Breviaries," in *St Katherine of Alexandria*, 201–20, here 206.

mother might see herself in the image of a well-dressed St. Barbara reading in her parlor, Barbara's virginity would subtly remind her of the distance that separated her from God's aristocracy. Maintaining some barrier—no matter how fragile—between clergy and laity must seemed all the more important during the later Middle Ages, when an enthusiastic and informed lay public threatened the clergy's hegemony over the dispensation of religious and moral truths.[7]

In a similar way, the legends of virgin martyrs as a group, together with those of a handful of male saints (such as St. Nicholas of Myra or St. George), could provide a symbolic means of dealing with the successful expansion of Islam that functioned alongside and after the military campaigns of the crusades. As Anke Bernau notes,

> The crusades themselves had frequently reinforced and promoted the popularity of particular saints, as is seen in the example of St Margaret, whose cult grew even stronger after the capture of the place of her martyrdom, Antioch, during the First Crusade. In addition, references to the saints' shrines (and their desecration) were also used to motivate crusaders and garner support among the wider populace . . . The images and language of martyrdom and *imitatio Christi* serve to connect crusaders, saints, Christ, and the Christian community in an intricate web of shared and mutually reinforcing associations.[8]

The legends of the saints whose shrines or places of origin were located in territories that fell to Islam could in many cases be read as a narrative reconquest of those territories. The powerful male judges who persecuted St. Margaret, St. Barbara, or St. Dorothy could as easily be understood as representatives of Islam as of the pre-Christian Roman cult. By rebuffing the threats and blandishments of their tormentors and remaining steadfast in their faith, the virgin martyrs are able to effect a form of textual resistance that contrasts with the more dismal facts of real life.

Certainly St. Katherine has all the traits of the typical virgin martyr, and as such is a powerful intercessor, symbol, and example both of pious behavior and of the inherent nobility of the celibate life. But there are aspects of her legend that make her "first among equals" both in the company of virgins and among the general community of saints. Among the community of virgin martyrs, St. Katherine is the only one who is not only of noble blood, but is, according to many versions of her legend, herself a reigning monarch. Many images depicting a group of virgin martyrs including St. Katherine reflect this idea, and show

---

[7] Winstead, *Virgin Martyrs*, 11.

[8] Anke Bernau, "A Christian Corpus: Virginity, Violence, and Knowledge in the Life of St Katherine of Alexandria," in *St Katherine of Alexandria*, 109–30.

Katherine alone wearing a crown. The legend and figure of St. Katherine might also be seen as rising above those of other virgin martyrs as texts of resistance to the spread of Islam. Among the important Christian centers that fell under Muslim control during the seventh century were Antioch (in 638) and Alexandria (in 641), each the seat of a powerful Christian patriarch.[9] It is surely not a coincidence that St. Margaret of Antioch was the virgin martyr whose popularity came closest to rivaling that of St. Katherine in many parts of the medieval Christian world. As important as Antioch was, however, its symbolic importance must have been surpassed by that of Alexandria. This city's central role in late antiquity and the early medieval period derived both from the strategic importance of its location and from its ancient reputation as an intellectual center, not least because of its famous library. The various versions of the legend of St. Katherine, in Sweden as elsewhere, stress the saint's remarkable learning, exemplified by her miraculous success in overcoming the fifty wisest philosophers of the Roman Empire in debate. Many versions of the legend, including the two Old Swedish versions, reproduce the content of the debates at length, which suggests that the saint's association with scholarship was a central part of her appeal for many of her devotees. Surely it is no coincidence that the virgin martyr most renowned for her learning was the one associated with the city that housed the most famous library of the ancient world.

It appears clear that the theme of scholarship in the legend of St. Katherine is a central part of her importance for the church in general, for certain specific religious orders, and for a number of individual clerics as well. Although the cult of St. Katherine of Alexandria was well established in the Roman Catholic church before the foundation of the Dominican and Franciscan orders in the early thirteenth century, both of these orders played a role in perpetuating and increasing the saint's popularity. For the Dominican order in particular, and perhaps later for the Franciscans as well, St. Katherine's close association with scholarship seems to be one of the primary motivations for this preference.

St. Katherine and the rise of universities

By the end of the twelfth century, universities had been founded in Bologna and Paris, heralding the beginning of a trend that would spread throughout the medieval world. The University of Paris was to become perhaps the most important intellectual center in Europe, and it was especially known for its focus on Greek philosophy, most notably the work of Aristotle. By the middle of the following century, much of this work was being carried out by members of the Dominican

---

[9] Henry Chadwick, *The Early Church*, The Pelican History of the Church 1 (1967; repr. Harmondsworth: Penguin Books, 1987), 211–12.

order, most notably by Albertus Magnus and his famous pupil, Thomas Aquinas.[10] St. Katherine, connected as she is to the famous tradition of Alexandrian learning, is a fitting patron for such activities, and indeed, together with St. Nicholas, she came to be recognized as the official patron saint of the University of Paris.[11] The various versions of the legend of St. Katherine explicitly connect the saint with Greek philosophical tradition. In the text of the widely translated eleventh-century Vulgate life,[12] St. Katherine refers directly to Plato during her debate with the fifty philosophers. The only surviving Swedish translation of this life, dating from the early sixteenth century,[13] retains this emphasis on St. Katherine's knowledge of Plato, suggesting that this remained an important aspect of her legend throughout the Middle Ages (see Appendix 5). The most widespread version of the legend of St. Katherine (including both the Vulgate and the *Legenda aurea* traditions) focuses on the events leading up to her martyrdom, with particular emphasis on her debates with the fifty philosophers and with her primary antagonist, the emperor Maxentius. In this textual tradition, Katherine demonstrates her knowledge of Greek philosophy as a scholar among scholars. The somewhat younger, but also widely diffused narrative of St. Katherine's conversion and her betrothal to the Christ Child might allow a slightly different reading of her relationship to classical philosophy. By the middle of the thirteenth century, a narrative tradition began to emerge in which St. Katherine was depicted as a Bride of Christ not just through her martyrdom—like all virgin martyrs—but through an actual betrothal (in some versions taking place in a dream or vision), leaving her with a physical sign in the form of a ring.[14] Bruce Beatie suggests that there may be evidence to support a much earlier origin for this tradition, perhaps as far back as before 1100.[15] While no extant textual versions of this narrative are preserved in Sweden, a number of visual images depict episodes from St. Katherine's conversion and mystic marriage, while still other representations of the saint include a ring as one of her attributes, which would

---

[10] Sten Lindroth, *Svensk lärdomshistoria: Medeltiden, Reformationstiden*, 2nd ed. (Stockholm: Norstedts, 1989), 38–39; Bengt Ingmar Kilström, *Dominikanska perspektiv* (Lund: Verbum/studiebokförlaget, 1976), 63–74.

[11] Jones, "Norman Cult," 217.

[12] For a discussion of the date and provenance of this version, see, S. R. T. O. d'Ardenne and E. J. Dobson, *Seinte Katerine, Re-Edited from MS Bodley 34 and the Other Manuscripts*, Early English Text Society s. s. 7, (Oxford: Oxford University Press, 1981), xv-xxvi.

[13] Jonas Carlquist, *De fornsvenska helgonlegenderna: Källor, stil och skriftmiljö* (Stockholm: Svenska fornskriftsällskapet, 1996), 36.

[14] See Lewis, *Cult of St Katherine*, 107.

[15] Bruce A. Beatie, "Saint Katharine of Alexandria: Traditional Themes and the Development of a Medieval German Hagiographic Narrative," *Speculum* 52 (1977): 785–800, here 797.

constitute a reference to the mystic marriage.[16] Oloph Odenius has suggested that this legend may be of Dominican origin.[17] Whether or not this is the case, it could be argued that the conversion of the heathen Alexandrian queen Katherine into a *sponsa Christi* could be read as an allegory for the largely Dominican project of the conversion of Aristotelian philosophy. Like St. Katherine, the learning of the ancient world is to be brought into the service of the church, and made a handmaiden of Christ, incorporated into the greater scheme of Christian theology.

Although her association with an ancient center of Christian leadership and Greek learning certainly contributes to an understanding of St. Katherine's popularity among the clergy of medieval Europe, there are further factors at work that might appeal even to less scholarly orders and individuals. While St. Katherine's debates with the fifty philosophers and with the emperor Maxentius are certainly central to the legend, an equally important point is the saint's deep and unassailable bond with her heavenly bridegroom. While this motif is in no way unique to the legend of St. Katherine, it is particularly strongly asserted as the main point of Katherine's many speeches, and the legend of the mystical marriage underscores Katherine's special status in this right. Although the emperor Maxentius repeatedly offers Katherine honor, power, and status that exceed even that of her already exalted position, she rejects his offers of earthly glory as false and transient goods, in contrast to the eternal glory of union with Christ. Here, then, might be a key to the saint's appeal to the Franciscan order, which, at least in the first decades after its foundation, did not share the scholarly inclinations of

---

[16] Murals dating from the fifteenth century in Lojo parish church and possibly in Hattula (both in Finland) depict scenes from St. Katherine's conversion and mystic marriage (see Olga Alice Nygren, "Helgonen i Finlands medeltidskonst," *Finska fornminnes-förenings tidskrift* 46 (1945):1–230, 80–94; Nilsén, *Program och funktion*, 207. St. Katherine's conversion is one of the scenes in the murals depicting her legend in the parish church of Gökhem, Västergötland. The mystic marriage is depicted on the outer doors of a fifteenth-century altarpiece from the parish church of Djursdala, Småland, and in the post-Reformation murals donated to the nuns' chapel at Vadstena Abbey by King Johan III (see below). In addition, St. Katherine is occasionally depicted with a ring as one of her attributes when she is depicted together with one or more of her fellow virgin martyrs. This ring can only refer to her mystic marriage, and it can be seen on the outer door of the altarpiece from Kräklingbo, Gotland (see chapter 4) and in a mural in the tower arch of Gamla Uppsala church, Uppland. In her survey of late medieval murals in central Sweden, Nilsén identified this last figure as "a female saint with a golden object in her hand" (*Program och funktion*, 83). She does identify two of the other three female saints in the grouping as Barbara and Dorothy, Katherine's frequent companions. Since the "golden object" is readily identifiable as a ring, the identification of St. Katherine is well warranted.

[17] See Odenius' discussion in Gad et al., "Katarina," 341.

the Dominican order.[18] In spite of her own royal status, St. Katherine recognizes that there is no true glory that does not come from the individual's relationship to God. Thus even an earthly queen may be a fitting saint for barefoot friars who have taken a vow of poverty.

Still another aspect of the legend of St. Katherine makes her a suitable patron saint for men, especially religious or clerics, to a much greater extent than other female saints, and especially other virgin martyrs. As Katherine Lewis notes, this legend presents a much more nuanced view of masculinity than other legends of female saints, mainly through the inclusion of characters such as the fifty philosophers and Porphyrius:

> In most other virgin martyr narratives all of the male protagonists who play a role in the actual passion are irredeemably evil, or at the very least inherently unsympathetic. The more complex narrative of the life of St. Katherine uses gendered distinctions to explore the difference between the sexes. It ultimately demonstrates that, despite the fixed nature of biological sex, both men and women can be similarly gendered by properties and qualities identified, through the figure of St. Katherine, as feminine. Man is not presented as an automatic paradigm in these texts; the feminine, embodied in both man and woman, is. By embracing Christianity and accepting its concomitant suffering, Porphyrius and the philosophers are feminised, spurred on by the example of St. Katherine, and ultimately of Christ. They are also seen to be good men by their ability to recognise the truth of Katherine's doctrine and her ability to expound upon it.[19]

Thus, while Katherine herself functions as a possible role model for male clerics, in addition to being an intercessor, her legend also provides these same male clerics with examples of scholarly and virtuous male devotion to the saint. At the same time, the legend may also provide a means of distinguishing between a cleric's purely spiritual relationship to the feminine (possibly including actual women) and the sinful ways of lay males. As Lewis continues,

> On the other hand, Maxentius cannot see beyond her beauty, or be directed by anything other than his animal lust. He is impressed by Katherine's eloquence, but he is really more interested in her great beauty, and it is this which prompts him to invite her back to the palace on the pretext of a further debate on Christianity. . . . He is even worse than the usual virgin-martyr villain, because, as we subsequently discover, he already has a wife . . . Nevertheless, it is telling that there is no indication that the philosophers or Porphyrius react to Katherine's appearance at all. It can be seen,

---

[18] See also Henrik Roelvink, *Franciscans in Sweden: Medieval Remnants of Franciscan Activities* (Assen: Van Gorcum, 1998).

[19] Lewis, *Cult of St Katherine*, 218–19.

therefore, that the good men recognise that Katherine's sex has nothing to do with her mind or her capacity to teach. Whereas Maxentius cannot consider her mind without reference to the body which houses it.[20]

Without doubt, the widespread evidence of devotion to and interest in St. Katherine of Alexandria among the clergy and religious of medieval Sweden is directly related to the importance of her cult for the Roman Church as a whole. St. Katherine came to be represented prominently in the liturgy of every medieval Swedish diocese. Although the degree of veneration accorded to her feast varied from one see to another, the feast was invariably accorded high honors in comparison to those of most other saints (see Appendix 3). The Uppsala tradition is an interesting example. According to the Uppsala Breviary, published at the end of the fifteenth century, the degree of *totum duplex*, the cathedral's highest degree of veneration, was accorded only to the feast of the cathedral's two patrons, St. Lawrence and St. Erik, to the feast of All Saints, and to feasts associated with Christ and the Virgin. Of the eleven feasts celebrated with the degree of *duplex*, the next highest degree, three were feasts of the Virgin and one the Translation of St. Erik. The remaining feasts are those of St. Henrik (who, according to Helander, was a third patron of Uppsala Cathedral), St. John the Baptist, Sts. Peter and Paul, St. Michael, and St. Katherine.[21] Thus, although the feast of St. Katherine was not celebrated with the highest possible degree in the archdiocese of Uppsala, no individual saint, with the exception of the cathedral's own patrons, was accorded higher honors. Similar circumstances can be noted in the calendars of the breviaries of several other dioceses, published in the late fifteenth and early sixteenth centuries. In the dioceses of Skara and Strängnäs, St. Katherine's feast, along with a handful of other important saints' days, was celebrated with the degree of *duplex*, while the highest degree was reserved for the feasts of Christ and the Virgin Mary, for homegrown saint of the diocese (Bishop Brynolph in Skara, St. Eskil in Strängnäs), and for the feast of All Saints. In other Swedish dioceses, St. Katherine's feast was celebrated with the highest degree. This is true in Västerås, where the saints honored with this degree in addition to Katherine were the archangel St. Michael, St. John the Baptist, St. Birgitta, St. Erik, and the local St. David of Munktorp. Linköping accorded the highest degree of veneration to the various feasts associated with the Apostles Peter and Paul, the patron saints of the cathedral, along with St. Henrik, known as the Apostle of Finland, St. Erik, St. Olav, and St. Birgitta. St. John the Baptist and the early local missionary, St. Sigfrid, were also thus distinguished. In both extant copies of the published Linköping Breviary, the leaves of the calendar for the months of November and December are missing. As Grotefend reconstructs them, St. Katherine is accorded the degree of *duplex*. However, in a table of feast days

---

[20] Lewis, *Cult of St Katherine*, 219–20.
[21] Helander, *Uppsalaliturgin*, 243–45.

included in the edition of the *Breviarium Lincopense* published in the 1950s, St. Katherine's feast, along with that of St. Nicholas, is celebrated with the highest degree.[22] Finally, Åbo was the medieval Swedish diocese that was most generous in celebrating saints' feasts with high degree. Here the feast of St. Katherine was accorded the degree of *totum duplex* along with the feasts of St. Henrik, St. Thomas the Confessor, St. Erik, the translation of St. Henrik, St. John the Baptist, the Apostles Peter and Paul, St. Lawrence, St. Michael, St. Birgitta, the Eleven Thousand Virgins (with or without St. Ursula), St. Nicholas, St. Anne, St. Stephen, St. John the Apostle/Evangelist, and the Holy Innocents.[23]

Among the possible means of determining levels of clerical devotion to a given saint might be a survey of churches, chapels, altars, prebends, and other related foundations dedicated to that saint. Like so many other aspects of religious life in medieval Sweden, such dedications are only partially documented in extant sources. It is unlikely that the extant records of dedications to St. Katherine reflect the full extent of her popularity as a patron saint. However, it is notable that chapels, altars, or prebends in her honor are documented in cathedrals and other important churches throughout the Swedish ecclesiastical province. It is to be presumed that these foundations both reflected the saint's importance in the cult and liturgy of their respective cathedrals and helped to reinforce devotion to the saint among the clerics who served there.

It is also important to note that although there is a degree of separation between the hierarchy of the secular church and the organization of the various monastic and mendicant orders active in medieval Sweden, in practice, there was considerable overlap between these two groups. Not only were members of the secular clergy, including bishops and even archbishops, recruited from the membership of the various orders, but it also appears that monasteries and friaries could influence parish churches in various ways, either because of their proximity, or, in a few cases, because they actually held the right of patronage to a particular church.

Church Dedications

The parish churches of Sweden are of varying ages, and apparently of varying origins. There seems to be good evidence that some of the earliest churches in some parts of Sweden, perhaps especially Östergötland, Västergötland, and Uppland, were so-called "magnates' churches," built by a powerful landowner

---

[22] See *Breviarium Lincopense*, ed. Knut Peters, 4 vols. (Lund: Laurentius Petri sällskapet, 1950–1958), 4: 68–69.

[23] See the late medieval calendars reprinted in Hermann Grotefend, *Zeitrechnung des deutschen Mittelalters und der Neuzeit* (Hannover and Leipzig: Hahn, 1891–1898),2: 215–49.

primarily for his own use.²⁴ In such cases, it seems likely that the choice of the saint in whose name the church is dedicated would fall to its builder or patron. However, it must be noted that while quite a few churches have been suggested as possible magnates' churches, few have in fact been specifically identified with a known builder. In the cases where no private builder of a church is known or suspected, parish churches are generally considered to have been built and funded by the laity of the parish. In these cases, it is not certain how the dedication of the church is determined, or who makes the decision, but it seems clear that the decision must fall under the authority of the secular clergy. Leaving aside for a moment the question of who chooses the dedication saint for any given church, there is the question of the basis on which such saints may be chosen. In an article on the dedications of churches in early medieval Lund, Per Beskow suggests that some church dedications, not least in important cities with royal ties, may reflect political relationships such as the Danish King Sven Estridsen's ties to the Holy Roman Emperor Henry III. Another possible influence, he suggests, is the range of church dedications in Rome, a popular destination for Nordic pilgrims during the early Middle Ages.²⁵ Anders Fröjmark, writing about church dedications in the Swedish province of Östergötland, comments that

> beginning in the twelfth century there are indications that more 'subjective' criteria dominate the choice of church patron, and by the late Middle Ages, these dominate completely. In general, then, it is not possible to assert that patron saints of churches must be chosen from among the saints with general popular support; on the other hand, it may be surmised that the popular cult of the saints played an increasing role in the selection of dedication saints during the later Middle Ages. During the period when most of the churches were founded in our land, we must instead count on the fact that whether patron saints were chosen on "objective" or "subjective" grounds, they have ultimately been dependent on the identity of the patron of the church in its temporal sense (that is, the identity of the person possessing the right of patronage over the church, perhaps in the person of its builder) and what ability that person has to exert his will.²⁶

---

²⁴ See, for example, Gunnar Smedberg, *Nordens första kyrkor: En kyrkorättslig studie* (Lund: CWK Gleerups förlag, 1973); Redelius, *Kyrkobygge*; Olle Ferm and Sigurd Rahmqvist, "Stormannakyrkor i Uppland," in *Studier i äldre historia tillägnade Herman Schück 5/4 1985*, ed. Robert Sandberg (Stockholm: Minab/Gotab, 1985), 167–84.

²⁵ Per Beskow, "Kyrkodedikationer i Lund," in *Nordens kristnande i ett europeiskt perspektiv: Tre uppsatser av Per Beskow och Reinhard Staats*, Occasional papers on medieval topics 7 (Skara: Viktoria bokförlag, 1994), 37–62, here 51.

²⁶ Anders Fröjmark, "Kyrkornas skyddshelgon i Östergötland 'västanstång' under tidig medeltid," in *I heliga Birgittas trakter: Nitton uppsatser om medeltida samhälle och kultur i Östergötland "västanstång,"* ed. Göran Dahlbäck (Uppsala: Humanistisk-samhällsvetenskapliga forskningsrådet [HSFR], 1990), 133–49, here 134.

For the purposes of this chapter, it will be assumed that the dedication saints of churches not specifically connected to monastic orders or identified as possible "magnates' churches" in some way reflect the preferences of the church as a body, or of the secular ecclesiastical hierarchy of the diocese in question.

Along with several Franciscan friary churches, a number of parish and other churches within the borders of medieval Sweden are known or thought to have been dedicated to St. Katherine of Alexandria. Because none of these has been suggested as a possible magnate's church, it will be assumed that the dedications of these churches reflect the interests of the ecclesiastical hierarchy.

The diocese of Linköping, which during the Middle Ages encompassed the province of Östergötland, part of Småland, and the islands of Gotland and Öland, included five known churches dedicated to St. Katherine within its boundaries. Of these, the parish churches of Alskog and Björke will be discussed in Chapter Four, which concerns the special circumstances of medieval Gotland.

In the parish of Skeda, located just south of the city of Linköping, a medieval stone church considered to date from the early thirteenth century is said to have been dedicated to St. Katherine of Alexandria.[27] The evidence for this identification is derived primarily from an eighteenth-century description of monuments in the local landscape, Carl Fredric Broocman's *Beskrivning över the i Öster-Götland befintliga städer, slott, soknekyrkor, m. m.* (Description of the cities, castles, parish churches, etc., of Östergötland). According to Broocman, an old document, earlier housed in the church but lost by the time of his visit, named St. Katherine as the patron of the church.[28] Skeda appears to have been a normal parish church, serving the needs of the local population. It may be significant, however, that Skeda is among the parish churches in the immediate vicinity of Linköping which were often assigned as benefices to canons from the cathedral chapter of Linköping, or whose parish priests were often also promoted to canons.[29] Interestingly, there are no known or surviving depictions of St. Katherine from the church. However, because there has been significant loss of such material since the Reformation, the present lack of images allows no conclusions to be drawn regarding the possible existence of depictions of this or any saint in the past. Perhaps the dedication of the church reflects a close tie to the liturgy of Linköping Cathedral, and/or the more personal devotions of canons from the chapter.

Another church dedicated to St. Katherine within a short distance of Linköping was the hospital chapel at Skänninge. Although Skänninge was also the site of a convent for nuns of the Dominican order, there is no indication that the hospital was associated with the convent, which it predates by some sixty

---

[27] Pira, *Helgonkulten*, 134; Fröjmark, "Kyrkornas skyddshelgon," 141.

[28] See Fröjmark, "Kyrkornas skyddshelgon," 141.

[29] Schück, *Ecclesia Lincopense*, 427.

years. While the convent was founded in 1281, it is known that the hospital was designated to receive the lepers' portion of the tithes for the region west of the river Stång, sometime before the year 1220.[30] It is not certain when St. Katherine was chosen as patron of the chapel, but it is mentioned under the name *hospitalis beate katerine skæningie* in a document from 1324.[31] Fröjmark suggests that this chapel had earlier been dedicated to St. George, who was a more typical dedication saint for lepers' hospitals. However, this is only speculation, and he offers no concrete evidence with regard to this specific chapel.[32] In his survey of the dedication saints of eighteen early (pre-1300) churches in the area around Linköping, Fröjmark notes that almost all of the dedication saints belong to a group whose cults are more or less universal in the Western church. If the range of dedications is influenced from any particular direction, it would appear to be from Lund, whose liturgy was apparently the primary influence in the formation of the early calendar for the diocese of Linköping.[33] In fact, St. Katherine is the only one of the saints discussed by Fröjmark whose feast is not found in the *Necrologium Lundense* from around 1120, and who did not have a Romanesque church named for her in Lund.[34] Even if St. Katherine was not represented in the earliest records of liturgical practice in Lund, she nonetheless soon came to play a prominent role both in the Danish archdiocese and in Linköping, where she was well represented in later medieval dedications of altars, prebends, and guilds.

The city of Linköping was the seat of the ecclesiastical hierarchy of the diocese, and it is to be expected that the dedications of churches in and near the city reflect considerable influence from the circles nearest to the bishop. Whether this is also the case for dedications of churches on the islands of Gotland and Öland is not certain, though it must be assumed that some members of the clergy, either parish priests or rural deans, exerted their influence.

One other church in the diocese of Linköping has been identified as dedicated to St. Katherine. This is the parish church in Ås (spelled "Othanby" or "Ottanby" in medieval documents) on the island of Öland. The small stone church apparently dates from the twelfth century, and it has a tower over the chancel. At least during the tenth century, church towers, especially when placed at the east end of the church, were widely associated with royal privilege.[35] Some hundred years later, at least in Sweden, parish churches with towers over their

---

[30] Sven Ljung, "Hospital," *KHLM* 6, 684.

[31] *DS* no. 2489.

[32] Fröjmark, "Kyrkornas skyddshelgon," 143–44.

[33] Fröjmark,"Kyrkornas skyddshelgon," 134–35; Sven Helander, *Ordinarius Lincopensis c:a 1400 och dess liturgiska förebilder,* Bibliotheca theologiae practicae 4 (Lund: Gleerup, 1957).

[34] Fröjmark, "Kyrkornas skyddshelgon," 146.

[35] Heinrich Fichtenau, *Living in the Tenth Century: Mentalities and Social Order,* trans. Patrick J. Geary (Chicago and London: University of Chicago Press, 1993), 71.

chancels often appear to be associated with royal estates.[36] Tuulse argues that many church towers in the Kalmar region, and especially in Öland, were more important for their defensive functions than for their royal connections or liturgical meanings. As he notes, Ås church is the island's only preserved church with an east tower. If, as Tuulse suggests for other nearby churches, the tower at Ås is secondary, it may well be that its function is more closely linked to the need to defend the island against Estonian pirates than to other concerns.[37] No images of St. Katherine survive from this church, or indeed from any church on Öland. However, it is known that there was a guild dedicated to the saint in the parish of Bredsätra, attested in 1413.[38] This guild was connected to the Franciscan friary in Visby, whose friars were obligated to perform annual masses for the souls of guild members in exchange for a payment of 4 silver marks per year.[39] Certainly a connection between Öland and the Franciscans of Visby, who dedicated their friary church to St. Katherine, could help to explain the dedication of one of the island's churches to this saint. It should be noted, however, that Ås is the southernmost parish on this long, narrow island, while the parish of Bredsätra lies on the northern part of the island.

The chancel in Ås has a vaulted wooden ceiling, which suggests considerable age, and is a feature seldom preserved in Swedish churches.[40] Further, the age of the church in Ås suggests that if the dedication is original, it, like that in Björke (see discussion below in Chapter Four), might be more likely to reflect the influence of the Cistercian order. Although there was no Cistercian monastery on Öland, there are records indicating that land in the parish was donated to the Cistercian monastery of Nydala during the 1280s.[41] In fact, in a charter dated 1279, Bishop Henrik of Linköping conferred the rights of patronage of Ås church on Nydala monastery, to be used in any way allowed by the rules of the order.[42] It is not known whether the connection between the monks of Nydala and the parish of Ås during the later thirteenth century is also indicative of circumstances a century earlier. However, it is interesting to note that there are two churches in the diocese of Linköping, both located on the major offshore islands, that are dedicated to St. Katherine of Alexandria and connected to the Cistercian Order.

[36] Armin Tuulse, *Romansk konst i Norden* (Stockholm: Albert Bonniers förlag, 1968), 41–42.

[37] Tuulse, *Romansk konst*, 63–66.

[38] Roger Axelsson, Kaj Janszon and Sigurd Rahmqvist, *Det medeltida Sverige 4:3: Öland* (Stockholm: Riksantikvarieämbetet, 1996), 140–50; Sven-Erik Pernler, "S:ta Katarina-gillet i Björke," *Gotländskt arkiv* 58 (1986):67–92, 67; see also Chapter Five of the present study).

[39] Wallin, *Knutsgillena*, 180–81.

[40] Axelsson et al., *Det medeltida Sverige 4:3*, 314.

[41] *DS* no. 805

[42] *DS* no. 661; Axelsson et al., *Det medeltida Sverige 4:3*, 320.

Aside from the Franciscan friary church in the city of Skara, there are no certain instances of St. Katherine as patron saint in Skara diocese, in western Sweden. There is however, one somewhat uncertain instance. According to local tradition (and a recent Swedish road atlas), during the Middle Ages there was a chapel of St. Katherine on the island of Kållandsö near the entrance to Ullersund. It fell into ruin at some point, perhaps as a result of the Black Death, until Magnus Gabriel de la Gardie (1622–1686) came into possession of the estate of Läckö. He is said to have transformed the chapel into a hospital. It was badly damaged in 1694, and in 1707 the pulpit and altarpiece were taken to Skara hospital. In 1709, stones from the chapel were used for construction work at Sunnersby church. According to an account from the 1920s, only fragments of the foundation remained. However, the church is said to have been sixteen ells long and twelve ells wide. The church was apparently built of sandstone, like other early medieval churches in the district. There is evidence in the form of a very early cross-shaped grave marker that there was a church on the site as early as the twelfth century.[43] Although the evidence of the existence of the church is solid, and the local tradition of the name apparently well established, there is no information about how or when this chapel came to be dedicated to St. Katherine. The chapel's proximity to the royal estate of Läckö might suggest a connection to royal power. As I suggested in the previous chapter, there are indications that the cult of St. Katherine may have been favored in royal circles in early medieval Sweden, possibly as early as the beginning of the twelfth century. The apparent fact that the chapel was built of sandstone might support this notion, since, at least in Uppland, sandstone was a very exclusive building material used only in very early churches associated with royal patronage.[44] Interestingly, even in this case there maybe a connection between the chapel of St. Katherine and the Cistercian order. In the middle of the 1140s, a Cistercian monastery was founded on the island of Lurö, no more than fifteen kilometers by boat from the site of the chapel. This monastery was a daughter house to Alvastra, which had been founded only a couple of years earlier, in 1143. By 1150, the site at Lurö must have proved unsuitable, for the monastery was relocated to Varnhem, some fifty kilometers to the southeast.[45] The monastery at Varnhem, like the one at Alvastra, was known for its close ties to the Swedish monarchy. It is not unlikely that the short-lived Cistercian house at Lurön also enjoyed royal patronage. Though there is no way of knowing whether the chapel might have dated from the brief

[43] Ernst Fischer, "Sankta Katarinas kapell," in *Västergötland, Bd. I: Kållands härad*, Sveriges kyrkor (Stockholm: Gunnar Tisells tekniska förlag, 1913–1922), 48–51, 48–50.

[44] Ann Catherine Bonnier, *Kyrkorna berättar: Upplands kyrkor 1250–1350*, Upplands fornminnesförenings tidskrift 51 (Uppsala: Upplands fornminnesförening och hembygdsförbund/Almqvist & Wiksell, 1987), 25–26.

[45] Jan O. M. Karlsson and Ragnar Sigsjö, *Varnhems kloster: kyrkan, ruinerna, museet*, 2nd ed. (Varnhem: Varnhems församling, 1987), 3.

period of Cistercian presence in the area, or, if it did, whether the Cistercian monks had any influence on the piety of local church builders, the fact that several Katherine churches appear in areas of known Cistercian presence or influence suggests that Cistercian influences on the cult of St. Katherine, at least in Sweden, merit further study.

In the portion of the archdiocese under the direct control of the archbishop of Uppsala, two churches appear to have been dedicated to St. Katherine. The parish church of Ununge in the eastern section of Uppland does not seem to have been one of the province's most important churches. It is a rubble church dating from the late fourteenth century or about 1400,[46] which would seem to indicate that it was probably built by the farmers of the parish, and not as a magnate's church.[47] Most of the land in the parish appears to have been taxed in the normal way, though the estate of Berga functioned as the seat of members of a noble family during the fifteenth and sixteenth centuries.[48] No medieval paintings and relatively little medieval inventory from the church survive, but the great bell, cast in 1521, has an inscription that identifies St. Katherine and St. Christopher as the church patrons.[49] The paucity of evidence makes it difficult to speculate about how the church patrons came to be chosen. St. Christopher is also an unusual choice. He is, however, a saint sometimes called on to prevent his devotees from dying unshriven,[50] and both he and St. Katherine were venerated among the Fourteen Holy Helpers, a popular group of saints in late medieval Europe. Perhaps the choice of these two Holy Helpers, and the relatively late date of this church, would indicate that in this case the church patrons were chosen based primarily on the interests of the laity. St. Katherine's membership in the group of Holy Helpers is derived from a passage in her legend. Just before her head is struck off, St. Katherine prays that those who call on her will find mercy, and the reply comes: "Those who call upon you will be saved." This passage establishes the saint as an especially powerful intercessor, who, together with St. Christopher, could be trusted to keep the needs of rural parishioners close to her heart.

As noted below, Litslena is a parish church located just outside of Enköping, in southwest Uppland at one of the region's most important crossroads. There is no written record of the patron saint of this church, nor any local oral tradition. Instead, the identity of the church patrons has been established on the basis of

---

[46] Rune Janson, Sigurd Rahmqvist, and Lars-Olof Skoglund, *Det medeltida Sverige: Uppland: 4, Tiundaland,* (Stockholm: Almqvist & Wiksell, 1974), 310.

[47] See Ferm and Rahmqvist, "Stormannakyrkor"; Bonnier, *Kyrkorna berättar.*

[48] Janson, Rahmqvist and Skoglund, *Det medeltida Sverige: Uppland: 4* , 312–13.

[49] Mats Åmark, "Kyrkopatroner i Ärkestiftet," *Julhälsning till församlingen i ärkestiftet* (1951): Uppsala.

[50] Anna Nilsén, "Kult och rum i svensk bondbygd. Om gudtjänstens inverkan på kyrkorummet," in *Tidernas kyrka i Uppland,* ed. Karin Blent, (Uppland: 1997), 57–78, here 62.

their prominence in a set of fifteenth-century murals. Although the church was originally Romanesque (which in Sweden refers to churches built in the twelfth and very early thirteenth centuries), it underwent several phases of remodeling, including the enlargement of the chancel between 1250 and 1350,[51] and was adorned with murals by a painter of the so-called "Mälardal" school some time between 1430 and 1470.[52] No medieval documents record the identity of Litslena's dedication saints. There seems to be general acceptance that John the Baptist was a church patron, though as Anna Nilsén points out, the basis for drawing this conclusion—that the mass celebrating the consecration of the church was held on St. John's day—is not relevant. Of greater relevance would seem to be the fact that St. John the Baptist is portrayed in large format on the east wall of the chancel.[53] Saint Katherine is portrayed on the same wall, in similar format, and in a position that places her in relation to St. John. This has led a number of scholars, including Bengt Ingmar Kilström, to assert that St. Katherine was one of the patrons of Litslena church.[54] This opinion is not universal, however. Nilsén is inclined to ignore St. Katherine's prominent position among the murals, and instead suggests St. Anne as the second patron, based on the fact that she is portrayed prominently in the church's altarpiece and on an early sixteenth-century paten.[55] While St. Anne is featured among the suite of murals, her position, in one of the ceiling vaults of the nave, is far less prominent than St. Katherine's. Further, examination of the retable on which Nilsén bases much of her conclusion reveals that there is little difference between the position and size of St. Anne's statue and St. Katherine's. The corpus of the altarpiece depicts the Madonna and Child. While the figure of St. Anne is nearest to the Virgin of the figures in the lower register of the left wing of the triptych, it is no larger than that of John the Baptist, directly beside it, or of St. Katherine, two positions to the left. There are three other figures placed as near to the figure of the Virgin as that of St. Anne: St. Erik, St. Andrew, and St. Peter. Interestingly, no one has suggested any of these as a potential co-patron of the church. If Kilström is correct, this might indeed, as I suggest below, be a case of Franciscan influence in the parish's choice of patron. Although the oldest parts of this church are older than the Franciscan friary in Enköping (and the Franciscan order as a whole), the major expansion of the church may well have required its rededication. It is possible, though far from certain, that St. Katherine's role as church patron dates to this period.

---

[51] Bonnier, *Kyrkorna berättar*, 275.

[52] Nilsén, *Program och funktion*, 11–12.

[53] Nilsén, *Program och funktion*, 13.

[54] Bengt Ingmar Kilström, "Litslena kyrka," in *Upplands kyrkor* 14, 5th edition. (Strängnäs, Strängnäs tryckeri, 1981), 11; idem, "Patronus," *KHLM* 13: 147.

[55] Nilsén, *Program och funktion*, 113.

The medieval Swedish diocese of Åbo encompassed the archipelago of Åland and Finland proper, including most of the territory of present-day Finland. In this diocese, three churches are known to have been dedicated to St. Katherine. In fact there is considerable evidence that the cult of St. Katherine was especially strong in this region, and it is possible that explanations of her popularity here lie nearer at hand than they do in certain other areas.

The parish of Hammarland, on the main island of Åland, has an early thirteenth-century stone church dedicated to St. Katherine, and still known in the present day as "Sta Catharina kyrka." Among the medieval inventory of the church is an altarpiece containing a wooden sculpture of St. Katherine, who wears a crown and holds a sword in her left and a wheel in her right. This piece is thought to have been imported from Gotland in the fifteenth century.[56]

The parish of Karis (Finnish Karjaa) in southern Finland, between Åbo and Helsingfors (Helsinki), is believed to derive its name from "Katarina," and thus the church is believed to have been dedicated to St. Katherine of Alexandria.[57] A well-preserved late fourteenth-century sculpture from this church depicts St. Katherine holding the remains of a small wheel in her right hand, and standing on top of her antagonist, the emperor Maxentius.[58] The presence of this sculpture suggests that the association of the church with St. Katherine, and the supposition that she was the parish's patron saint, is likely to be correct.

A third church in Åbo diocese has also been identified as a church dedicated to St. Katherine. This church, S. Karins (Kaarina) is located a short distance from Åbo cathedral. The name of this church is unambiguous, and as Nygren notes, it is confirmed by a very early sculpture that almost certainly depicts the saint:

> Among the wooden sculptures still preserved in Finland, St. Katherine is often represented. The oldest is an admittedly uncertain image from S. Karin's church. Because no other attributes remain than a book in her left hand, the saint's identity cannot be positively confirmed. The saint has worn a crown, which has by now disappeared, and the right hand has been struck off. With regard to the fact that St. Katherine was the patron saint of the church, however, it is highly likely that the identification is correct. Especially when one considers that the image is dated to the first half of the fourteenth century, the assumption seems well motivated. At that time, the saints represented in our art were not many. St. Katherine belongs, as we see in conjunction with the murals in Sund church, to their number.[59]

---

[56] Ann Catherine Bonnier, "Hammarlands kyrka," in *Ålands medeltida kyrkor* ed. Armin Tuulse, Acta Universitatis Stockholmiensis, Stockholm Studies in Art 25 (Stockholm: Almqvist & Wiksell, 1973), 84–102; Henrik Helander, *Hammarland Sta Catharina kyrka*, (Mariehamn: Mariehamns tryckeri, 1991); Nygren, "Helgonen," 81.

[57] Nilsén, *Program och funktion*, 199.

[58] Nygren, "Helgonen," 81–82.

[59] Nygren, "Helgonen," 81.

Nilsén comments that a note in a Finnish work on the churches of Finland asserts that while St. Katherine of Alexandria was the original patron saint of the church, that role was taken over by St. Catherine of Siena during the fifteenth century.[60]

The single strongest influence on the religious life of medieval Finland, at least until the very end of the period, seems to have been the Dominican order. The order's influence in the diocese of Åbo dates from that region's earliest Christian period, and was of great significance during the missionary period. The extent of its importance may be seen in the fact that the diocese of Åbo adopted the Dominican liturgy intact in the year 1330.[61] In fact, however, it appears that the Dominican influence on the religious life of Åbo diocese begins at a much earlier date. The Dominican friary of St. Olav was founded in the town of Åbo at some point before 1250, and the Dominicans were the earliest mendicant or monastic order to become established in Finland, which had only recently become part of the Christian world. The Dominican influence on the liturgy of Åbo diocese has been shown to be particularly important.[62] It is very likely that the relative popularity of Katherine of Alexandria as a church patron in this diocese reflects the preferences of that order, and this is assumption is especially motivated in the case of the church of S. Karins. The saint is well represented in Åbo cathedral as well, both in the artwork and as the patron of a very well endowed altar. It is also worth noting that St. Katherine is regularly among the saints accorded the highest degree of veneration in the liturgical calendars of Finland. In the earlier calendars known from this diocese, she tends to be accorded the degree of *duplex*, which was a relatively high degree in comparison to other cults. By the end of the fifteenth century, however, the feast of St. Katherine, along with the feasts of such saints as St. Sigfrid, St. Erik, Sts. Peter and Paul, St. Lawrence, St. Birgitta, and St. Anne, is celebrated in the diocese of Åbo with the degree of *totum duplex*.[63] If it is true that Catherine of Siena later took over the role of patron saint of S. Karin's, this may be seen as a confirmation of continued Dominican influence, as this saint, who died in 1380 and was canonized in 1461, was herself a Dominican tertiary. Interestingly, Jarl Gallén, a Finnish expert on the Dominican order and its history in Scandinavia, while mentioning that Catherine of Siena is depicted in a mural in the church of

---

[60] Nilsén, *Program och funktion*, 217, n. 317.

[61] Jarl Gallén, "Dominikanorden," *KHLM* 9: 181.

[62] Aarno Maliniemi, "Grundandet av dominikankonventet i Åbo och dess förhållande till Sigtuna," in *Sigtuna Mariakyrka 1247–1947*, ed. Holger Arbman, Wilhelm Holmqvist, and Rolf Hillman (Sigtuna: Sigtuna fornhems förlag, 1947), 83–94, 84–86.

[63] Aarno Malin(iemi), *Der Heiligenkalender Finnlands: Seine Zusammensetzung und Entwicklung*, Finska kyrkohistoriska samfundets handlingar 20 (Helsingfors, Finska kyrkohistoriska samfundet, 1925), 154–73, 251.

S. Karins, refers to Katherine of Alexandria as the patron saint.[64] Either Gallén was unaware of the note cited by Nilsén, or he did not consider it to be reliable or significant.

Mendicant Devotion to St. Katherine

In addition to their influence on the official cults of Åbo and Uppsala, the traditions of various monastic and mendicant orders also influenced the religious life of medieval Sweden in other ways. Their traditions are not always easy to reconstruct, however, since one of the consequences of the Protestant Reformation in Sweden was the dissolution of monastic foundations. The resultant dismantling of most of the physical fabric (buildings) of monasteries and friaries, not to mention the gradual destruction of their libraries, means that the surviving evidence of the interests and activities of medieval Swedish monks, nuns, and friars is often quite sparse. Nonetheless, in some cases it is possible to find indications of the saints particularly venerated by various religious communities.

Although the Dominican friary in Sigtuna was not the first such foundation in Sweden (that was in Visby), it is perhaps the best documented of medieval Swedish Dominican houses, and its church, dedicated to the Virgin Mary, is the only Swedish Dominican church to survive more or less intact to the present day. There are many indications that St. Katherine of Alexandria was one of the more prominently venerated saints for this community. It is to be expected that a Dominican church would include an altar dedicated to St. Katherine, and this is confirmed by the testament of a local noblewoman, Katarina of Steninge, dated 5 November 1311. Among the considerable property she donates to the church is the bequest of a canopy "pro altari beate Katerine in domo fratrum sictunensium. . . ."[65] Another important source of information on the devotional preferences of the Dominican house in Sigtuna is a series of letters of indulgence issued on behalf of the friary by a range of Swedish prelates during the late thirteenth century.[66] Several of these documents grant indulgence for visits to the Dominican church in Sigtuna on various feast days connected with the life of Christ, or on the feast days of various saints. Not surprisingly, all of them emphasize the feast days of the Virgin Mary, to whom the church is dedicated. The other saints who appear in most of the letters include St. Mary Magdalene, the Eleven Thousand Virgins, St. Nicholas, and St. Katherine of Alexandria, as well as St. Damian, St. Augustine, whose rule the Dominican order followed, and the specifically Dominican saints St. Peter the Martyr and St. Dominic. It is not surprising that

---

[64] Jarl Gallén, "Dominikanerorden," *KHLM* 3: 174–85.

[65] *DS* no. 1821.

[66] *DS* nos. 1715, 1027, 1229, 1365, 732, 733, 954.

Saints Peter and Dominic, both of them specifically Dominican, are mentioned in all of these documents. However, it may be of significance that St. Katherine is the only one of the other saints mentioned, in addition, of course, to the Virgin Mary, whose name appears in every one of these letters of indulgence. It seems reasonable to consider this as evidence that the Dominican friars in Sigtuna held St. Katherine in especially high regard, even in comparison to other saints also favored by the order. The church in Sigtuna also preserves a relatively large number of portrayals of St. Katherine. These include a unique fifteenth-century wooden reliquary in the shape of a bust of a crowned maiden. Although the image includes no other attributes, it has generally been regarded as a depiction of St. Katherine. A wooden sculpture in one of the wings of the late fifteenth-century triptych from the lay altar depicts St. Katherine, placed between St. Peter (the apostle, not the Dominican Peter Martyr) and St. James the Greater. Like the reliquary, this image depicts a crowned virgin. The right hand and its attribute are missing, while the position of the remaining hand suggests that it held either a sword or the rim of a wheel, two common attributes of St. Katherine. Of particular interest is a mural dating from the fourteenth century in the west end of the church. St. Katherine is depicted wearing a crown and halo, holding a book in her right hand, while her left hand appears to rest on the hilt of a sword. This image is paired with an image of St. Dominic, the founder of the order. Surely this placement reveals something about St. Katherine's importance to the Dominicans. Finally, a silver communion chalice dated to 1532 includes an image of St. Katherine on its foot, which also includes the other virgin martyrs Sts. Barbara, Margaret, and Dorothy, as well as the Madonna and Child.[67]

Like the Dominicans, the friars of the Franciscan Order also demonstrated particular devotion to St. Katherine. As Henrik Roelvink notes,

> Franciscan saints in a broad sense are the saints who were venerated by the Friars Minor and the Poor Clares. In this case, we cannot restrict ourselves to those who formally belonged to the First, Second or Third branch of the order, but must also look at the saints who were honored specifically by the friars and sisters, as patron saints of their churches and friaries or convents, as well as the saints that are represented on their various seals.

> Strictly speaking, the saints who had an altar in the friary churches or who were depicted there also belonged to them. But since there is no survey of the medieval altars in the convent churches, and only Arboga of the remaining friary churches has saved many of its mural paintings, it is impossible to identify any specific Franciscan saints in this manner.[68]

---

[67] ATA, Wilhelm Holmqvist, "Mariakyrkan och klostret," in *Sigtuna Mariakyrkan 1247–1947*, ed. Arbman et al., 7–44.

[68] Roelvink, *Franciscans in Sweden*, 64.

In fact, although Roelvink is correct that there is no survey of the altars in Franciscan friaries in Sweden, there is evidence of an altar dedicated to St. Katherine in the friary church in Stockholm. This altar was apparently located along the eastern wall of the north aisle of the church, and was mentioned in two testaments from the later fifteenth century. On 14 July 1468, Hela Bærensdotter, widow of the late mayor of Stockholm, Olaus Norumberg, donated to the Franciscan friary

> . . . ett sælaboda rwm liggiande a sudramalm . . . for mins husbonda herra Olauus norumberg fornemda oc hans kæra husfrua Taala oc telseka siæla skyld. Swa oc for mik oc min förra bonda peter van brinken. gud allas thera siæla nade oc allas waara waardnade til æwerdeliga ægo med swadana fordom oc wilkor. At fornemde grabrodra j stockolm sculu pligtoge wara ena æwerdelica messo at læsa hwan fredag aff them helga fæm undom wider sancte katerine altare j thera kirkio for forscripna siæla oc allom cristnom siælum til Roo oc nade [69]

> [. . . a hut for the rendering of seal blubber on Södermalm. . .for the sake of the souls of my aforementioned husband Olaus Norumberg and his dear wives Taala and Telseke(?), and also for me and my late husband Peter van Brinken, God have mercy on all their souls and ours as well. To the Franciscan friars for perpetuity with the following conditions. That the forenamed Franciscan friars in Stockholm shall have the obligation of performing a perpetual mass of the Five Holy Wounds each Friday, at the altar of St. Katherine in their church, for the mercy and peace of the souls mentioned above, and of all Christian souls.]

At least one other testament mentions this altar, this time emanating from one of the most influential families of fifteenth-century Sweden. Gustav Karlsson, belonging to the family later referred to as Gumsehuvud on the basis of their coat of arms, was himself a knight and the magistrate ("lagman") of Uppland. His sister Katarina, who had died in 1451, was the wife and consort of the Swedish king Karl Knutsson (Bonde). On 28 September 1475 Gustav donated two properties to the Franciscan friary in Stockholm, stipulating that a mass should be sung each week as long as the friary might exist. The masses were to benefit the souls of his parents and his late wives, and were to be performed at the altar of St. Katherine in the northeast section of the church. [70]

Following Roelvink's line of reasoning, it is of interest that an image of St. Katherine is to be found among the preserved murals in the Franciscan friary church in Arboga. This painting is located on the south wall of the nave, in the

---

[69] Sigurd Curman and Johnny Roosval, *Riddarholmskyrkan*, Sveriges kyrkor 28 (Stockholm: KVHAA, 1937), 267.

[70] Curman and Roosval, *Riddarholmskyrkan*, 267.

immediate vicinity of a suite of scenes from the Passion of Christ. St. Katherine
is clearly identifiable on the basis of her sword and wheel, as well as a crown and
halo. Bengt Ingmar Kilström has noted a degree of kinship between the murals
in Arboga and those in a pair of parish churches in Uppland, Ärentuna and
Litslena, whose paintings he describes as having "Franciscan influence."[71] Both
of these churches have significant depictions of St. Francis and patron saints of
the Franciscan order, and both include depictions of St. Katherine. As Kilström
notes, the church at Ärentuna is located 14 kilometers north of Uppsala, where
there was a Franciscan friary. Litslena is located just outside of Enköping, site of
another Franciscan friary.[72] In this church, St. Katherine is depicted prominently
on the east wall of the chancel, which prompts Kilström to identify her as the
church's second patron saint together with St. John the Baptist, who is portrayed
on the same wall.[73] Although this parish church was not itself a friary church, it
is possible that the choice of St. Katherine as one of its patron saints (if Kilström
is correct in his reasoning) might reflect the influence of the nearby friars.

   Although this study focuses on medieval Sweden, it is interesting to note
that within the borders of present-day Sweden (including the provinces of Skåne,
Halland, and Blekinge, which were Danish until the 1650s) more Franciscan
friaries, convents and friary churches were dedicated to St. Katherine than to any
other saint. According to Jørgen Nybo Rasmussen, five friaries and their churches
within this area were dedicated to St. Katherine, three to the Virgin Mary, two
to St. Anne, and one each to St. Michael, St. Clare, St. Nicholas of Myra, and
Sts. Peter and Paul.[74] For St. Katherine's part, this number included friaries in
Skara, Ystad (Skåne), Lund (Skåne), Malmö (Skåne), and Visby. Since frequent
contact between the orders' various houses was typical for both the Dominican
and Franciscan orders, it is likely that there is some connection between dedications to St. Katherine in these two areas.

   With regard to the popularity of devotion to St. Katherine among Franciscans in general, and especially in Sweden, Roelvink remarks:

> St. Katherine of Alexandria also takes quite naturally a prominent place,
> since she was honoured highly in the whole of the Western world at that
> time. The legend of Katherine expresses an ideal of steadfast witness in
> a non-Christian world and the Franciscans felt a kinship with this. Her
> example could have helped ordinary Swedish Christians, and especially
> women, in their vocation to live as consistent believers in their still half-

[71] Bengt Ingmar Kilström, *Heliga trefaldighets kyrka i Arboga* (Västerås: Västerås Stifts kyrkobeskrivningskommitté, 1998), 9.
[72] Bengt Ingmar Kilström, *Franciskanska perspektiv* (Stockholm: Verbum/studiebokför-laget, 1974), 102.
[73] Kilström,"Litslena kyrka," 11; see also discussion of this church above).
[74] Cited by Roelvink, *Franciscans in Sweden*, 64.

heathen surroundings. Perhaps the friars promoted the cult of St. Katherine more than others, since they had special relations with the Holy Land, where the saint's grave was maintained on Mt. Sinai.[75]

Individual Piety: The Evidence of Seals

Although there is a good deal of evidence of devotion to St. Katherine as part of the official cult in the various medieval Swedish dioceses, and for the mendicant orders, there is also considerable evidence of individual devotion to the saint on the part of members of the medieval Swedish clergy. Evidence of individual piety includes personal seals with iconography that includes images of saints or other religious imagery, as well as donations or bequests to altars or other foundations dedicated to a saint. In some cases, individuals fund the foundations of altars, prebends, or the like in honor of their patron saints. On occasion it is documented, or can be surmised, that a particular mural, sculpture, or other image in a parish church was commissioned by an individual cleric. This is especially notable in the case of parish churches that were connected to the cathedral chapters in the various Swedish dioceses.

An examination of published and unpublished sources has yielded twenty-three seals belonging to medieval Swedish clerics that depict St. Katherine, either alone or in the company of another saint. Of these, thirteen belong to parish priests (including one former parish priest who had become a monk in the Birgittine abbey at Vadstena), five to canons or prelates at Uppsala and Linköping, two to Dominican friars, two to clearly ordained priests whose further affiliations are unknown, and one to a holder of a prebend at the City Church (S:t Nikolai) of Stockholm. It must be emphasized that this number is unlikely to reflect the full extent of clerics' seals depicting St. Katherine. The surviving seals of medieval Sweden have neither been fully published nor fully documented.

Among the canons and prelates whose seals depicted St. Katherine are two of the most prominent figures in the hierarchy of later thirteenth-century Uppsala. Andreas Andreasson (And) was a member of a prominent aristocratic family. His brother Israel Andreasson was for a time the magistrate of Tiundaland (one of the three subprovinces that make up the province of Uppland), and the family was closely related to the powerful Finsta family, whose most prominent member was Birger Petersson, himself the magistrate of Uppland for many years. Andreas was for many years the dean of the cathedral chapter at Uppsala, and he was a member of the committee that compiled the Uppland Law, ratified in 1296. He is especially known for his efforts on behalf of the intellectual

---

[75] Roelvink, *Franciscans in Sweden*, 65.

culture of the archdiocese, both in France and in Uppsala.[76] On documents as early as 1280, Andreas used a seal depicting St. Katherine as his main seal. The same seal appears as a counterseal on a document from 1315. The seal is not the only evidence that Andreas venerated St. Katherine. He is also known to have founded a "Helgeandshus," a foundation for the care of the indigent poor and sick, in Uppsala. In his document of foundation, he made a point of granting special privileges to the Dominican friars from Sigtuna, allotting them rooms and kitchen space during their visits to Uppsala, which were to take place on the fourth day after Whitsun, and on the feasts of St. Katherine and St. Nicholas. In the chapel of this foundation, an altar was consecrated in honor of the Virgin Mary, St. Nicholas and St. Katherine. Interestingly, the archbishop who consecrated the altar, Nils Alleson, had contributed some of the land on which the house was constructed. He had also used a seal depicting St. Katherine at an earlier point in his career, and it is possible that he also influenced the choice of patron saints in this chapel.[77]

It is likely to be significant that St. Katherine is depicted in the seals of these two prominent members of the cathedral chapter of Uppsala. During the first half of the thirteenth century, a secular cathedral chapter was established in Uppsala, most likely between 1235 and 1250.[78] The establishment of this chapter, with its need for an increasing number of canons, meant that a considerable number of Swedes began to study abroad, since holders of higher clerical offices were expected to have completed a number of years of university education in theology and canon law. The University of Paris was, as noted above, an important center for these disciplines, and although Swedish students are also known to have studied at other European universities, Paris became the one most famously and most prestigiously associated with the Swedish cathedral chapters, not least with Uppsala.[79] Andreas Andreasson is known to have studied in Paris, and he is known for having donated a house there for the use of students from Uppsala studying at the university.[80] Nils Alleson, too, studied in Paris, where he is known to have been during the year 1278.[81] Indeed, the cathedrals in Linköping and Skara also owned properties in Paris that were used to house their students.[82]

---

[76] Jarl Gallén, *La province de Dacie de l'ordre des frères prêcheurs, I: Histoire générale jusqu'au grande schisme* (Helsingfors: Söderström & C:o Förlagsaktiebolag, 1946), 111.

[77] See *DS* nos. 1467, 1652; Helander, *Den medeltida Uppsalaliturgin*, 132.

[78] Carina Jacobsson, *Beställare och finansiärer: Träskulptur från 1300-talet i gamla ärkestiftet* (Visby: Ödins förlag, 2002), 57.

[79] Jacobsson, *Beställare*, 63.

[80] *DS* no. 1045.

[81] Eric Öhlin,"Nils Alleson (Nikolaus Allonis)," in *Svenska män och kvinnor: Biografisk uppslagsbok*, ed. Torsten Dahl, vol. 5 (Stockholm: Albert Bonniers förlag), 430.

[82] Schück, *Ecclesia Lincopensis*, 492; Jacobsson, *Beställare*, 64.

Medieval Swedish clerics, like aristocratic women, had a wide range of possible motifs among which to choose for their personal seals. Although bishops and archbishops seem always to have the patron saints of their respective dioceses in their counterseals (the seals of their office almost always depicting an enthroned bishop), the choices for even high-ranking members of cathedral chapters do not seem to be restricted. Thus Nils Alleson's counterseal from his reign as archbishop depicts St. Lawrence and St. Erik, the patron saints of Uppsala Cathedral, who clearly symbolize his office. [83] On the other hand, there is good reason to believe that Andreas' seal depicting St. Katherine, which he used during his long service as dean of Uppsala Cathedral, is a reflection of his personal devotional preferences, since St. Katherine, while well represented in the Uppsala liturgy, is not one of the cathedral's named patrons. Much the same thing might be said of the counterseal depicting St. Katherine used by Nils Alleson himself during the year before he was elected archbishop. It appears that Nils used this as his primary seal during his years as a canon of the Uppsala chapter. [84]

St. Katherine would appear to be an attractive patron saint for well-educated clerics for several reasons. First, her widespread popularity in the church was certainly connected to her reputation as a powerful intercessor. Her legend also offers many examples of behavior worthy of emulation, including the steadfastness of her devotion to her heavenly bridegroom. Not least, however, St. Katherine's extraordinary learning, and her ability to use it in the service of Christ, would surely contribute to her attractiveness. At the same time, there is no doubt that it was a mark of high prestige for a Swedish cleric to have studied at the University of Paris. As St. Katherine was one of the patron saints of this university, devotion to her, and the placement of her image in a personal seal, might be seen as symbolic of the seal-bearer's own studies. The connection with the University of Paris would appear to be a likely explanation for the appearance of St. Katherine in the seals of Andreas And and Nils Alleson. This possibility is only confirmed by the fact that the altar of the "Helgeandshus" founded by Andreas was dedicated not only to St. Katherine and the Virgin Mary, but also to St. Nicholas, himself a patron of the University of Paris. It is possible that the seals of three clerics associated with the cathedral chapter at Linköping, and one from Strängnäs, depict St. Katherine for similar reasons. Vemund, a canon in Linköping and Växjö, affixed his seal to a document in 1331. The seal depicts St. Katherine, identified by her wheel, crown, and sword, together with a male saint, possibly St. Andrew. [85] Lekr Salmonsson, the *officialis* of the Bishop of Linköping, used a seal depicting St. Katherine with crown, wheel, and

---

[83] Bror Emil Hildebrand, *Svenska sigiller från medeltiden*, vol. 2 (Stockholm: KVHAA, 1862, 1864), ser. 2, 154, 155.

[84] Hildebrand, *Sigiller*, vol. 2, ser. 2, 109.

[85] *DS* no. 2839.

sword, and Lekr kneeling below in veneration. This seal appears on a document from 1347.[86] Finally, Hook Ofradsson, a canon in Linköping, also used a seal depicting St. Katherine with a crown and wheel. This was affixed to a document from 1353.[87] While none of these clerics is documented among the Linköping students who studied in Paris, it appears clear that many more students studied there than appear in contemporary sources. In any case, large numbers of students from the diocese of Linköping are known to have been in Paris during the first half of the fourteenth century, and the diocese had purchased buildings in which to house them before 1329.[88] Johan Petersson, a canon of the cathedral chapter of Strängnäs and parish priest in Vadsbro, affixed his seal to his brother's letter of mortgage in 1369.[89] His seal, a partly fragmented pointed oval, depicts St. Katherine with crown, wheel, and sword. Here too, the saint's image may reflect the bearer's studies.

St. Katherine appears in the seals of at least two friars of the Dominican order. Interestingly, one of these men, Lars Agmundsson, had also been the confessor to Archbishop Nils Ketilsson. His seal, a cleric's typical pointed oval, depicts the bearer kneeling in veneration of St. Lawrence and St. Katherine, the latter crowned and holding a wheel and a martyr's palm frond. Over these two saints, the seal depicts the Madonna and Child. This seal is affixed to the testament of Archbishop Nils, dated 1314. It is interesting for several reasons. The presence of St. Lawrence in the seal, and Lars' obvious veneration of him, certainly reflects their common name, but perhaps it also signifies the friar's connection to an archbishop of Uppsala. St. Lawrence was the earliest patron saint of Uppsala Cathedral, and although St. Erik came to be his co-patron, St. Lawrence's importance and central role in the Uppsala cult were never eclipsed. The Virgin Mary is certainly a frequent motif in the seals of medieval Swedish clerics (as well as aristocratic women), and the object of universal devotion. In addition, she was the patron saint of the Dominican friary in Sigtuna, which had explicit ties to Uppsala. Finally, it may be significant that Archbishop Nils stated in his testament that he wished to be buried in the chapel of the Virgin Mary in Uppsala Cathedral. The presence of St. Katherine is especially interesting. Does her image and the devotion it suggests reflect the fact that she was a favorite saint of the Dominican order? Does it perhaps indicate that Lars, like many of his Dominican brothers, studied in Paris? Perhaps it, too, may signify the seal-bearer's association with the archbishop. Given the general requirement that prelates and canons must have studied theology and canon law at university

---

[86] *DS* no. 4211.

[87] *DS* no. 1353.

[88] Schück, *Ecclesia Lincopensis*, 489–99.

[89] *DS* no. 7944.

level for a period of years, it is likely that Nils Kettilsson had conducted at least part of his studies at the University of Paris.

Like Lars Agmundsson's seal, the seal of Nils, a Dominican friar, and also prior, at St. Martin's friary in Skänninge, depicts St. Katherine together with the bearer's name saint. This seal, affixed to a document from 1298, also suggests multiple interpretations. As in the case of Lars, it is likely that Nils chooses to place St. Nicholas in his seal primarily because of the correspondence of names. Here, too, St. Katherine may have been chosen largely because of her importance to the Dominican order as a whole. At the same time, St. Katherine shares her status as patron saint of the University of Paris with one other saint, St. Nicholas.[90] Here too, then, there is the possibility that both St. Katherine and St. Nicholas reflect that the bearer of this seal had studied abroad. Given his high position within the Dominican hierarchy, it is likely that Prior Nils had indeed studied in Paris.[91]

In addition to appearing in the seals of prelates and canons, St. Katherine also appears in the seals of a large number of medieval Swedish parish priests. In some of these cases, we know that the bearer of the seal served in a church dedicated to St. Katherine. For example, the seal of Jakob, the parish priest of St. Katherine's church in Nummis, Finland, is affixed to a document from 1309.[92] This pointed oval seal shows a crowned female saint holding a book. By her side, the head of the priest in prayer can be seen. Here, the fact that St. Katherine is the dedication saint of the church seems to confirm that she is also the saint depicted in Jakob's seal. While the book is not the exclusive attribute of St. Katherine, it is not infrequently associated with her. Indeed, it might well reflect the strong Dominican influence in Åbo diocese that this seal depicts the saint with a book in preference to other attributes. At the same time, St. Katherine's status as patron saint of the church may also explain why this parish priest would choose to place her image in his seal. While this identification in no way excludes other factors that might influence this priest's personal devotion to St. Katherine, it would appear that this is a cleric whose identity is closely linked to his office.

Although Jakob's seal demonstrates that an image of a saint in the seal of a parish priest may indicate the identity of his church's dedication saint, other

---

[90] Jones, "Norman Cult," 217.

[91] See *DS* no. 1254; Gallén, *Province de Dacie*, 130, 223; According to John Cotsonis, St. Nicholas is second only to the Virgin Mary in the number of Byzantine lead seals on which he is depicted, and the bearers of these seals belong to a wide range of occupations. In spite of St. Nicholas' popularity in Sweden, his representation in Swedish seals does not approach Byzantine levels, nor does it appear that the specific understandings of his image in Sweden are directly comparable to those in the Byzantine context. See John Cotsonis, "The Contribution of Byzantine Lead Seals to the Study of the Cult of the Saints (Sixth-Twelfth Century)," in *Byzantion* 75 (2005), 383–497, 431–37.

[92] *DS* no. 1626; Hildebrand, *Svenska sigiller*, vol. 2, ser. 2, 226.

examples make it clear that this need not be so. Nils, parish priest in Estuna, Uppland, affixed his seal to a deed of sale in 1331.[93] The seal is a pointed oval depicting St. Katherine with her customary attributes of crown, sword, and wheel. Estuna church was not dedicated to St. Katherine. According to a strip of parchment dated 14 December 1298, found when the high altar was rebuilt in 1733, the church and its high altar were consecrated on that date by Archbishop Nils Alleson in honor of St. Lawrence, St. Olav, and St. Erik. The relics deposited in the altar were of St. Mauritius and the Eleven Thousand Virgins.[94] A considerable number of other parish priests, whose churches have no known images of the saint and are not known to be dedicated to her, nonetheless depict St. Katherine in their seals. Björn, priest of Vassunda church in Uppland, sealed documents in 1337 and 1339.[95] His pointed oval seal shows him kneeling in veneration of St. Katherine, a crowned female saint holding a wheel and sword. Gödkin, parish priest in Skärkind, Östergötland, affixed his seal to a letter of mortgage in 1345.[96] His round seal depicts a crowned St. Katherine with a wheel. Arvid, parish priest of Värnamo, Östergötland, and possibly a rural dean, affixed his seal to a series of documents in the 1450s (including RPB no. 1456). The seal is round, and depicts St. Katherine with crown, wheel and sword. While still other apparent priests also depict St. Katherine in their seals, it has not been possible to connect them with a specific parish, which makes it difficult to ascertain the degree to which their veneration of the saint might have been influenced by the dedication of their churches. Nonetheless, the cases listed above make it clear that factors other than the liturgical traditions of the churches in which they served influenced some parish priests in their choice of personal patron saint and sigillographic imagery. One possibility is that the seals of these parish priests, like those of canons and prelates, refer in some way to their educational background. Educational standards for parish priests in the diocese of Uppsala, for example, at least following the foundation of the secular cathedral chapters in the thirteenth century, required that priests in training study Latin, dialectics, and the basics of rhetoric at the cathedral. In 1261, following the standards used in the Danish sees of Lund and Roskilde, Archbishop Lars of Uppsala established that all candidates for the priesthood should be required to serve at the cathedral for the first year (later two years) after their ordination. By 1291, a cathedral school is known to have existed in Uppsala, and the post of *doctor studencium* had been established for its supervision.[97] Clearly, then, some degree of standardized education was a necessary component of the personal training and

---

[93] *DS* no. 2862.

[94] Ingrid Wilcke-Lindqvist, "Estuna kyrka," (Upplands kyrkor 92) *Upplands kyrkor*, vol. 7 (Uppsala: Stiftsrådet i ärkestiftet, 1960), 105–6.

[95] *DS* no. 3306.

[96] *DS* no. 3914.

[97] Jacobsson, *Beställare*, 62–63.

identity of any given parish priest. It is less clear to what extent the educational background of individual parish priests went beyond the minimum standards established by the archbishop. As Jacobsson notes, however, it was not only men of aristocratic birth and aspirants to cathedral chapters who undertook courses of study at universities, including the University of Paris. There are indications that men of more humble background also studied there, perhaps in the hope that a more prestigious educational background might lead them to a better parish.[98] What, then, is indicated by the image of St. Katherine in the seals of parish priests? Two possibilities present themselves, in addition, as always, to the saint's general prestige as an intercessor and as a patron saint of scholars. Perhaps some or all of the parish priests who placed St. Katherine's image in their seals had studied at the University of Paris, and chose her as their personal patron for much the same reasons as canons or higher prelates like Nils Alleson or Andreas Andreasson And. Another possibility, though, is that the saint's image might serve as a symbol of the years of study that parish priests spent at the cathedral chapters of their own home dioceses, under the guidance of masters who had themselves studied at Paris.

St. Katherine and her saintly companions

St. Katherine's apparent association with the University of Paris in the minds of many clerics appears to some extent to have been shared with St. Nicholas, co-patron of the University. The fact that these two saints are closely linked in Uppsala may be related both to the strong Dominican influence on the Uppsala liturgy and to the cathedral's strong connections with France in the thirteenth and fourteenth centuries.[99] While their primary interest for the clergy of Uppsala and other Swedish sees may indeed lie in their association with the University of Paris and other seats of learning, it is worth noting that these two saints, often as a pair, were particularly strongly associated with the archdiocese of Rouen.[100] One of the earliest and most important chapels in Uppsala Cathedral was dedicated to St. Nicholas and St. Katherine, and this chapel was the chosen burial place of a number of prominent clerics, including Archbishop Jakob Israelsson (d. 1281) and Andreas And, as well as high-ranking members of the Swedish aristocracy,

---

[98] Jacobsson, *Beställare*, 65.

[99] For example, the master builder employed for the construction of the new cathedral at Östra Aros (or "new Uppsala") in conjunction with the move of the archdiocese from its earlier site at (Gamla) Uppsala was a Frenchman, Estienne de Bonneuil, who arrived in Uppsala in 1287, with a corps of "workmen and apprentices": See Maria Ullén, "Kyrkobyggnaden," in Sven-Erik Pernler, *Sveriges kyrkohistoria: hög och senmedeltid* (Stockholm: Verbum, 1999), 254–67, 254–55.

[100] Jones, "Norman Cult."

such as Birger Petersson and his second wife, Ingeborg Bengtsdotter. As noted above, the altar in the chapel of the "Helgeandshus" founded by Andreas And and Nils Alleson was consecrated to the Virgin Mary together with St. Katherine and St. Nicholas. I would argue that this pairing of saints is directly related to the importance of the University of Paris for the cathedral chapter of Uppsala and its individual canons and prelates. It can sometimes be difficult to identify images of St. Nicholas in murals or sculptures. This is because he is one of several saints regularly depicted in the regalia of a bishop, and if his specific attributes are missing or unclear, it may be impossible to tell which bishop is represented. St. Katherine is occasionally depicted in the company of such a holy bishop, and in these cases it is more than likely that he should be identified as St. Nicholas.

One especially interesting example of this pairing is a reredos from the parish church of Bälinge, just outside of Uppsala. The corpus of this very unusual altarpiece consists of two large figures, one of St. Katherine wearing a crown, holding a fragment of a wheel and a sword and standing on the emperor Maxentius, the other a bishop without specific attributes. Surrounding the two central figures are panels, originally twenty-four in number, depicting scenes from the martyrdoms of a variety of different saints, including the apostles Peter, Paul, Bartholomew, and Andrew, the virgin martyrs Agatha and Barbara, St. Stephen Protomartyr, and St. Lawrence, the patron of Uppsala Cathedral.[101] One of the panels also depicts a scene from the legend of St. Katherine. The precise origin of this late fifteenth-century piece, which is thought to be of Swedish workmanship, is unknown. It is worth noting, however, that Bälinge church was closely connected to the cathedral chapter at Uppsala. It was, in fact, the benefice for the archdeacon, and an annex church for the cathedral.[102] Perhaps the presence in the church of such an altarpiece, depicting these particular saints, suggests the involvement, even the donation, of the archdeacon himself. It is known, for example, that the other altarpiece from Bälinge church, completed in 1471 by the Lübeck artist Johannes Stenrat, was commissioned by Kort Rogge, who at that time held the post of archdeacon, and was therefore also (at least) the nominal parish priest of Bälinge.[103] In fact, Ingalill Pegelow goes a step further, and suggests that the Katherine reredos from Bälinge may actually have come from the

---

[101] Bengt Stolt, "Bälinge kyrka," *Upplands kyrkor* , vol. 2 (Uppsala: Stiftsrådet i Uppsala ärkestift, 1948), 137–52, 142–46.

[102] Göran Dahlbäck, *Uppsala domkyrkas godsinnehav med särskild hänsyn till perioden 1344–1527,* Studier till det medeltida Sverige 2 (Stockholm: KVHAA/Almqvist & Wiksell International, 1977), 81; Ingalill Pegelow, "En sky av vittnen: om ett märkligt altarskåp i Bälinge," in *Den ljusa medeltiden. Studier tillägnade Aron Andersson,* The Museum of National Antiquities, Stockholm Studies, 4. (Stockholm: Statens historiska museum), 219–38, here 236.

[103] Jacobsson, *Beställare,* 74–75; also suggested as a possibility by Pegelow, "Sky av vittnen," 236.

altar of St. Nicholas and St. Katherine, in their chapel at Uppsala Cathedral. Certainly, that altar should have had an altarpiece much like this one, though none is known from the inventory of the cathedral. It is quite possible, Pegelow reasons, that, following the Protestant Reformation, such vestiges of "papist" worship would have been deemed inappropriate in the foremost church in Sweden, even though many parish churches retained, and even continued to display their medieval artworks. She quotes the reformer Lawrence Petri's statement on this topic, demanding that all superfluous ornamentation be removed from the churches, especially "the images that foolish people often pray to." [104]

Although St. Nicholas appears in murals, altarpieces, and other images in Sweden throughout the Middle Ages, and although he continues to be featured prominently in the liturgical calendars of Swedish dioceses, it appears that St. Katherine gradually surpasses him in importance, and that she becomes one of the saints most prominently associated with Uppsala Cathedral.

By the fifteenth century, St. Katherine is regularly depicted in the company of St. Lawrence and St. Erik, the titular saints of Uppsala Cathedral. St. Olav, who was closely associated with the cathedral, though Helander contends that he was never among its patron saints, [105] is also frequently included in the grouping, as is St. Mary Magdalene, another patron saint of the Dominican order. Churches that have depictions of St. Katherine in such groupings are often closely associated with Uppsala Cathedral and its chapter. A good example is Börje church, located a few kilometers from Uppsala. There is no image of St. Katherine among the well-preserved murals, dated to approximately 1500, that cover the vaulted ceiling of this church, nor among the much more fragmentary murals covering the west wall of the chancel arch and the north side of the stairway. It is uncertain whether she was represented among the images on the walls of the nave, which were destroyed in conjunction with the post-medieval enlargement of the windows. [106] Perhaps of greater importance, however, is the church's late fifteenth-century altarpiece. The corpus of this piece depicts Christ in Judgement, surrounded, as usual, by the Virgin Mary and St. John. Surrounding this central motif, but still part of the corpus, are four smaller figures depicting St. Lawrence, St. Katherine, St. Erik, and St. Mary Magdalene. During most of the Middle Ages, Börje church was the benefice of the treasurer of Uppsala Cathedral. One holder of this office, Lars, who made his testament in 1343, donated a new image of the Madonna to the church. [107] Although there is no record of how, when, or by whom the altarpiece featuring St. Katherine was commissioned, there is good reason to believe that the holder of the benefice at the time was

---

[104] Pegelow, "Sky av vittnen," 236.

[105] Helander, *Uppsalaliturgin*, 237.

[106] Gustaf Unestam, "Börje kyrka," in *Upplands kyrkor*, vol. 8 (Uppsala: Stiftsrådet i ärkestiftet, 1964), 153–76, here 164–67; Nilsén, *Program och funktion*, 59–60.

[107] Jacobsson, *Beställare*, 74; *DS* no. 3691.

involved. The wings of the reredos contain images of the twelve apostles, which is quite common in medieval Swedish altarpieces. As noted above, St. Katherine's feast, celebrated with the degree of *duplex* in the late fifteenth-century Uppsala Breviary, was among the most honored in the calendar of Uppsala Cathedral. Perhaps because of her connection to the University of Paris, and the general idea of scholarship in service of the Christian faith, St. Katherine seems to have become closely associated with the cathedral chapter as a body.

St. Katherine is also seen in the company of the patron saints of Uppsala Cathedral in other churches in the archdiocese. The parish church of Tegelsmora, for example, has an altarpiece that is extremely similar to the one in Börje, in terms of motif, composition, and age. The resemblance is so great, in fact, that it is suggested that both altarpieces were produced by the same workshop.[108] A third altarpiece, from the parish church of Älvkarlaby, like Tegelsmora located in the northern part of Uppland, also shows strong similarities to the other two. In this triptych, of similar date and workmanship, the corpus depicts the Apocalyptic Madonna (the Woman standing on the Moon) from Revelation 12:1. She is surrounded by the somewhat smaller figures of St. Erik, St. Olav, St. Mary Magdalene, and a crowned female saint whose attributes have been lost, but who is assumed to be St. Katherine. As in the other two altarpieces, the wings contain statues of apostles, most of whom have lost their attributes, with the addition of John the Baptist.[109] Interestingly, neither Älvkarlaby church, nor Tegelsmora was as closely connected to the cathedral chapter as Börje church. Ties did exist, however. Although the cathedral owned relatively little land in Tegelsmora, it did acquire holdings in the parish in the will of a vicar ("vikarien Knut") in 1309.[110] The parish also paid the so-called "canon's tithe" to the Second Canonry at Uppsala Cathedral.[111] Although this was strictly a parish church, it is worth noting that, like several other such churches in the same part of Uppland, Tegelsmora also owned a fourteenth-century wooden sculpture (in this case of St. Olav) of very high quality, or as Jacobsson says, "cathedral quality."[112] Jacobsson notes further that while sculptures of "cathedral character" are most often found in churches with close ties to the cathedral, often through its canons, there are examples of such high-quality sculptures in a small number of churches, including Tegelsmora, without such near ties. It is quite possible that such connections once existed however, perhaps through certain parish priests who are no

---

[108] Unestam, "Börje kyrka," 16; Nils Sundquist, "Tegelsmora kyrka," in *Upplands kyrkor*, vol. 10 (Uppsala: Stiftsrådet i ärkestiftet, 1969), 33–68, here 56.

[109] Bengt Ingmar Kilström, "Älvkarlaby kyrka," in *Upplands kyrkor*, vol. 10 (Uppsala: Stiftsrådet i Uppsala ärkestift, 1969), 17–32, here 24.

[110] Janson et al. , *Det medeltida Sverige: Uppland: 4*, 179 ff.; *DS* no. 1605.

[111] Dahlbäck, *Uppsala domkyrkas godsinnehav*, 82.

[112] Jacobsson, *Beställare*, 318.

longer documented.[113] The altarpieces in Tegelsmora and Älvkarlaby parishes, in the composition of their central motifs, are likewise suggestive of close ties to the cathedral chapter at Uppsala, even if the documentation is relatively scant.

Like Tegelsmora, Älvkarlaby parish was also connected to Uppsala Cathedral. As early as 1185, fishing rights in the parish were among the cathedral holdings specifically covered by Pope Lucius III's letter of protection.[114] During the thirteenth and fourteenth centuries, salmon from this parish made up the king's tithe to the tenth canonry at Uppsala, and these rights came to be tied to the benefice. In a charter dated 25 July 1280, King Magnus Ladulås refers to a chaplain in Älvkarlaby.[115] Although the present rubble church is known to have been begun in 1478 and consecrated in 1490, it would appear that it was preceded by an earlier chapel, perhaps made of wood.[116] Interestingly, the consecration of the new stone church does not appear to have changed the status of Älvkarlaby as a congregation. During the Middle Ages, Älvkarlaby was a chapel connected to the parish of Tierp. Tierp, in its turn, was the main benefice of the tenth canonry of Uppsala Cathedral.[117] Älvkarlaby did not become an independent parish until 1641.[118] The altarpiece from Älvkarlaby is dated to about 1490, which coincides with the consecration of the new church building. It seems possible, and perhaps even likely, that the holder of the benefice might have contributed in some way to the furnishing of the new chapel in his parish. Although this altarpiece has St. Olav in its corpus instead of St. Lawrence, the grouping of figures around the central motif is comprised entirely of saints closely associated with Uppsala.

Munsö church, another early stone church in the archdiocese with strong ties to the archbishop, may also have had similar sculptural expression of these bonds. It has been suggested that this church was built at the initiative of a late twelfth-century archbishop of Uppsala on his personal lands, as a private church for the estate.[119] Relatively little remains of the medieval inventory this church must have possessed. Of the four medieval sculptures remaining, two depict the Madonna and Child, while the remaining two depict St. Katherine and St. Mary Magdalene. One of the Madonnas, along with the statues of St. Katherine and Mary Magdalene, appears to have come from a late fifteenth-century altarpiece of very high quality. It is not known whether this piece contained more than these three statuettes, which are all roughly the same size, ranging from 40 to 42 centimeters in height. Munsö remained one of the central estates

---

[113] Jacobsson, *Beställare*, 365.

[114] *DS* no. 96.

[115] *DS* no. 704.

[116] Kilström, "Älvkarlaby kyrka," 19.

[117] Dahlbäck, *Uppsala domkyrkas godsinnehav*, 89–90.

[118] Kilström, "Älvkarlaby kyrka," 19.

[119] Armin Tuulse, "Munsö kyrka," in *Upplands kyrkor*, vol. 6 (Uppsala: Stiftsrådet i ärkestiftet, 1957), 161–75, here 164–65.

of the archbishopric for much of the Middle Ages, though by 1470 it seems to have come under the control of the crown. According to a proclamation of Archbishop Nils Alleson in 1298, it was to be one of the points of collection for the archbishop's portion of the tithe.[120] The parish of Munsö, along with the other parishes under the authority of the rural deanery of Bro, also paid a canon's tithe to the tenth canonry of the cathedral chapter of Uppsala.[121] There is not enough evidence remaining to draw any firm conclusions about the saints depicted in Munsö church during the Middle Ages, and how these might have expressed the relationship between the parish church and the archdiocese. At the very least, however, it is interesting to note the presence of two saints who were particularly prominent on the Uppsala liturgy. Perhaps these figures once stood in an altarpiece the composition of which resembled those in Börje, Tegelsmora, and Älvkarlaby?

In addition to these striking altarpieces, there are other depictions of St. Katherine in the company of the patrons of Uppsala in other churches in the archdiocese. In the ceiling vaults at the east end of the nave of Färentuna church, paintings dated to the 1440s depict the grouping of St. Lawrence, St. Olav, St. Erik, and St. Katherine. Like Älvkarlaby, this church also contributed its canon's tithe to the tenth canonry at Uppsala.[122] Uppsala Cathedral had considerable land holdings here, distributed among most of the villages in the parish, through most of the Middle Ages.[123] Interestingly, this church was originally built on a royal estate during the late 1100s, possibly at the king's initiative, and it seems to have been closely connected with royal power, at least during its early history.[124] Although the crown maintained its strong profile in the parish, the cathedral also seems to have been influential. It is difficult to see the particular combination of saints in the east vault of the nave as anything other than a reference to Uppsala Cathedral and its liturgical traditions.

Murals in the parish churches of Nora, Vallby, and Ärentuna also depict St. Katherine in the company of some or all of the patron saints of Uppsala Cathedral. In Nora church, for example, the very fragmentary murals on the east wall of the chancel show St. Katherine standing together with St. Lawrence. Directly over them is a depiction of St. Olav. Fragments on the south wall of the chancel appear to depict scenes from the martyrdom of St. Katherine.[125] In Vallby, St. Katherine, together with St. Birgitta, is depicted in the sides of the window

---

[120] Dahlbäck, *Uppsala domkyrkas godsinnehav*, 35–41, 51.

[121] Dahlbäck, *Uppsala domkyrkas godsinnehav*, 89.

[122] Dahlbäck, *Uppsala domkyrkas godsinnehav*, 89.

[123] Olle Ferm, Mats Johansson, and Sigurd Rahmqvist, *Det Medeltida Sverige 1:7 Attundaland* (Stockholm: Riksantikvarieämbetet, 1992), 115–39.

[124] Armin Tuulse, "Färentuna kyrka," in *Upplands kyrkor*, vol. 5 (Uppsala: Stiftsrådet i Uppsala ärkestift, 1955), 97–112, 99.

[125] Nilsén, *Program och funktion*, 117.

opening on the east wall of the chancel. Flanking this window are depictions of St. Lawrence and St. Erik.[126] In Ärentuna church, which paid its canon's tithe to Uppsala's second canonry,[127] the westernmost vault of the nave includes a depiction of Sts. Lawrence, Erik, and Olav in close proximity to a depiction of St. Katherine and St. Dorothy. St. Mary Magdalene is also depicted close by.[128] In addition, according to Peringskiöld's late seventeenth-century drawings of the parish church of Västeråker, the paintings on the north wall of the chancel included the grouping of St. Erik, St. Olav, and St. Katherine, and St. Barbara together with the arms of the builder of the church, Lady Ramborg of Vik. Because these paintings are no longer in existence, it is difficult to determine their date. Other medieval paintings in the church date from the 1470s, and still others were painted in 1870, when the church was "restored."[129] Assuming that Peringskiöld is reliable in this case, a connection to Uppsala is plausible here as well. Lady Ramborg had close family connections to the cathedral chapter, where her paternal uncle, the same Andreas And whose seal depicted St. Katherine, was dean for many years. Her parents were buried in the chapel of St. Katherine and St. Nicholas, and they had made sizeable donations of property to the cathedral. The addition of St. Barbara to the grouping is interesting, but since this saint had a freestanding chapel, apparently in the exterior of the cathedral's south wall, she too may be a link to Uppsala.[130] In general it may be assumed that murals in a magnate's church, of which Västeråker is an example, may in some way reflect the personal interests of the holder of the right of patronage, and not just the choices of the parish priest or other members of the ecclesiastical hierarchy. In this case, however, whether the paintings date from Lady Ramborg's own time or from a later period, they seem to emphasize her close personal ties to the church hierarchy.

While especially strong ties to Uppsala Cathedral cannot be proved in all cases it appears clear that depictions of St. Katherine are often found in the company of the patrons of the cathedral. In many of these cases, it appears that she has become a representative of the cathedral's liturgical traditions, much like the saints she accompanies. Perhaps, then, it is not unreasonable to suppose that such depictions had similar meaning in the churches whose direct connection to the cathedral was less obvious.

---

[126] Nilsén, *Program och funktion*, 157–58.

[127] Dahlbäck, *Uppsala domkyrkas godsinnehav*, 82.

[128] Nilsén, *Program och funktion*, 178.

[129] Nilsén, *Program och funktion*, 171.

[130] See Dahlbäck, *Uppsala domkyrkas godsinnehav*, 137.

Skara Diocese

It is not only in the archdiocese that St. Katherine appears in works of art spon-
sored by members of cathedral chapters or in churches with such connections.
Another important example is the parish church of Gökhem, located in the
province of Västergötland in the diocese of Skara. According to the eighteenth-
century antiquarian Rhyzelius, who visited the church during the 1720s, an
inscription among the murals that covered almost the entire church contained
the information that they had been donated by Erik Bengtsson, a canon at Skara
Cathedral and parish priest in Gökhem, in the year 1487.[131] The images of St.
Katherine are found in the ceiling vaults of the present-day church porch. During
the Middle Ages, however, this structure was a chapel dedicated to the Virgin
Mary, and had no exterior door. Motifs from the martyrdom of St. Katherine,
including her debate with the fifty philosophers and her confrontations with
the emperor Maxentius, are depicted in a series of vignettes. The fact that St.
Katherine's debate with the wise men is depicted may suggest that the canon who
funded the murals, Erik Bengtsson, had a particular interest in the intellectual
and scholarly aspects of St. Katherine's legend and cult. Like all high-ranking
clergy, he must have studied at a European university. It is also interesting, however, that St. Katherine's martyrdom has been given so much attention — it covers the entire ceiling — in a chapel dedicated to the Virgin. The Virgin Mary
was the patron saint of Skara Cathedral, which may explain the rather unusual
circumstance that a parish church has an entire chapel, not just an altar, in her
honor. In a church that is in itself the benefice for a canonry connected to the
cathedral chapter, such a chapel might reflect the emphasis of the parish's liturgical tradition. It is not at all unusual for St. Katherine to be depicted in connection with the Virgin Mary. Many retables made for altars of St. Mary depict
the Virgin Mary accompanied or surrounded by images of two or more of the
"Four Capital Virgins" (St. Katherine, St. Margaret of Antioch, St. Barbara, and
St. Dorothy), occasionally with the addition or substitution of another virgin
martyr, such as St. Agnes or St. Agatha. As Sven-Erik Pernler notes in his discussion of a retable of St. Mary from Sorunda church in Södermanland, the Four
Capital Virgins, together with the Virgin Mary, represent the consequences of
faith. Like the Virgin Mary, each of these women responded in the affirmative
to God's call. "Just as a sword would pierce Mary's heart (Luke 2:34)," so it would
go for these others.[132] The martyrdoms of these and other virgin saints echo the
sacrifice of the Virgin Mary and her participation in the Passion of Christ. Thus
the relatively great amount of space accorded to the legend of St. Katherine in

---

[131] *Medeltida bilder: Medeltidens konst, kultur, och historia sedd genom västsvensk kyrkokonst*,
CD-ROM, SINOPIA digitalproduktioner, 1999; Jacobsson, *Beställare*, 76–77.

[132] Pernler, *Sveriges kyrkohistoria II: Hög- och senmedeltid*, 148.

the parish church of Gökhem may be reflective both of her role as a patron of scholars and of universities, including that of Paris, and of her close connection to the patron saint of Skara Cathedral.

Birgittine Connections

The last major monastic order to arrive in Sweden, and the only one to be founded there, also shows evidence of a specific interest in St. Katherine. The Order of the Most Holy Savior (*Ordo Sanctissimi Salvatoris*), the foundation of which was approved by Pope Urban V in 1370, was founded at Vadstena, Östergötland, at the behest of Birgitta Birgersdotter (1303–1373), herself a member of one of medieval Sweden's most influential families.[133] Although the nuns of Vadstena are perhaps better known, Vadstena Abbey, like its daughter houses, was founded as a double monastery, in which a sizeable population of monks, under the authority of the abbess, saw to the spiritual needs of the sisters. While St. Katherine of Alexandria does not play a role in Birgitta's famous *Revelationes*, she is represented in the convent church at Vadstena, and it is clear that she was the focus of considerable devotion from the nuns of the order. It may be of interest in this context that Birgitta's family seems to have had a history of devotion to St. Katherine, and that the name "Katarina" is well represented among both her paternal and maternal antecedents. Given this background, it is not surprising that one of Birgitta's own daughters, the first abbess of Vadstena, was named Katarina (see Chapter Three).

The convent church at Vadstena has two surviving images of St. Katherine of Alexandria.[134] The most prominent is a wooden sculpture, still in its shrine, that once stood on an altar of St. Katherine. It has been suggested that the piece may date from the 1390s. If that is the case, it is actually older than the convent's current stone church, which would indicate that it was made for the original wooden church, and that this saint was venerated at the convent from its earliest days. The sizeable sculpture depicts St. Katherine wearing a crown, and standing on the prone form of her old enemy, the emperor Maxentius.[135] An

---

[133] Catharina Broomé and Kajsa Rootzén, *Katolska ordnar och kloster* (Stockholm: Petrus de Daciaföreningen, 1963), 125–26.

[134] A distinction is made in this section between St. Katherine of Alexandria, the subject of this study, and St. Katherine of Vadstena, daughter of St. Birgitta and first abbess of Vadstena. Although she was beatified in 1489, Katherine of Vadstena was never canonized by the pope, possibly because the process was interrupted by the Protestant Reformation in Sweden, and the Swedish support for the case thereby undermined.

[135] Andreas Lindblom (*Vadstena klosters öden* [Vadstena: Vadstena affärstryck, 1973], 48, notes that in 1388 a fire destroyed the convent's wooden chapel, the adjacent stone buildings, and a large part of the nuns' dormitory. A date of around 1390 might thus suggest that this

embroidered altar cloth made by the nuns of Vadstena during the middle of the fifteenth century also depicts St. Katherine, wearing a crown and holding a small spiked wheel. Although there were many important and influential monastic and mendicant foundations in medieval Sweden, Vadstena was in many ways unique. It was supported by the Swedish crown to such an extent that it was the only religious house whose existence was allowed to continue, albeit much curtailed, after the Reformation. It was not until 1595, after the death of King Johan III, that Karl IX (still titled Prince, as he had not yet managed to topple Johan's son and heir, King Sigismund, from the Swedish throne) drove the last remaining nuns from their convent.[136] It is also notable that the nuns at Vadstena had a scriptorium, in which they produced a number of prayer books and other manuscripts. Some of these manuscripts include illuminations, and are known to have been produced by nuns. Interestingly, St. Katherine is represented in the only fully preserved manuscript from Vadstena Abbey containing texts to be read aloud during the nuns' meals. This manuscript, dated to the year 1502 and said to have been "written by a convent sister," contains, in addition to the legend of St. Katherine and an additional miracle narrative concerning her, the legends of Sts. Anne, Barnabas, Briccius, Cecilia, Clement, Crysogonus, Elizabeth of Hungary, Joachim, Lucia, Martin, Nicholas, Silvester, Simon, Theodore, and Thomas Becket, as well as two texts concerning the Virgin Mary.[137] The vita of St. Katherine in this manuscript (see Appendix 6), copied from an earlier manuscript which is in its turn is a reworking of an older source, is certainly closely related to the *Legenda aurea*'s version of her vita, while the miracle narrative (see Appendix 8) is found nowhere else.[138] Of the surviving prayer books from Vadstena, written in Latin, Low German, and especially in Swedish, a goodly number contain prayers to St. Katherine of Alexandria (sometimes designated "of Greece" or "of Egypt"). There seems to be greater variety in the prayers dedicated to St. Katherine than in the prayers to other virgin martyrs, though these other saints are certainly well represented in the material. One manuscript (Uppsala C 68), dated to the beginning of the sixteenth century, contains a number of illustrations, including one sketch of Christ surrounded by instruments of torture, one portrait each of St. Barbara and St. Dorothy, and two of St. Katherine. The prayer addressed to St. Katherine in this manuscript, also found in two other

---

sculpture was produced before the new church was finished in around 1405. Lindblom also connects the sculpture with a prebend of "sancte Katterine de gretia," whose precise age and donor are not known. This still suggests the importance of St. Katherine's cult to the convent (see A. Lindblom, *Kult och konst i Vadstena nunnekloster*, KVHAAs handlingar, Antikvariska serien 14 [Stockholm: Almqvist & Wiksell, 1965], 72, 113).

[136] Lindblom, *Vadstena klosters öden*, 138–43.

[137] Cod. Holm A3. See Carlquist, *Fornsvenska helgonlegender*, 25.

[138] See Carlquist, *Fornsvenska helgonlegender*, 26–27; Jansson, *Fornsvenska legendariet*, 3, 34.

manuscripts from the same period, makes a point of St. Katherine's special status as the bride of Christ:

O Min älskelika Oc aldra kärista jomfrw sancte katherina J thina wärio och gömo befaller jak mik, och antwardhar mädh liff och siäl Oc flyr jak enk-annelika til thin, mädh stadogh hop och gudhelikom kärlek Oc bidher jak tik för the stora nadh oc järntekn gudh giordhe mädh tik, at han wändhe tik ffran hedhindom Oc wtualledhe tik til sinna brwdh oc stadfäste tik swa i sinne troo oc kärlek, at thu förwan fämtighe mästara, mädh gudhelikom wisdom, hwilken som brände wordho, oc äro hälghe j hymmerike Oc nar thit hwffuod | war aff hwggit fför gudz troo oc kärlek skuld, tha flöth ren mölk fför blodh aff thinom likama, oc fördho han oppa synai bärgh, oc jordhado han thär mädh hedher Oc äwärdherlika flyther olio aff thinom hälga benom, thär allan siwkdom helar, tik loffuadhe Gud j thinom yther-sta tima, at alla the som a tik kalla, skulu wardha hördho af hanom . . . .[139]

[O my beloved and dearest maiden St. Katherine, into thy care and protec-tion I commend myself with life and soul. And I take flight to thee with steady hope and godly love. And I pray to thee for the great mercy and mir-acle God granted thee, that He turned thee from heathendom and elected thee His bride, and steadied thee in His faith and love, so that thou with divine wisdom didst overcome fifty masters, who were burned and are now holy in Heaven. And when thy head was struck off for the sake of God's love and faith, pure milk poured from thy body instead of blood. And God's angels took thy holy body and carried it Mount Sinai, and buried it there with honor. And an oil flows eternally from thy holy bones, which heals all sickness. God promised thee in thy last moments that all those who call upon thee would be heard by Him . . .]

Although this prayer gives a relatively detailed summary of the main points of St. Katherine's legend, it emphasizes the saint's special status as the chosen bride of Christ. Although Katherine's rejection of the Roman emperor's advances and the temptations he puts before her are implied in this summary of her passion, they are not mentioned explicitly. This is interesting, given the emphasis placed on the personal conflict between Katherine and Maxentius in many other narrative sources. Perhaps this summary, which also touches upon St. Katherine's conver-sion of the fifty wise men, provides some clues about the aspects of the saint's legend that most touched the nuns of Vadstena, and most closely reflected their interests. The crucial ideas here seem to be that Katherine was especially chosen by God to receive his gifts and favor, first in the form of conversion, and then as his specially chosen bride. While this pattern might be said to reflect the voca-tion of all nuns, it can be seen as an especially specific parallel to St. Birgitta's

---

[139] R. Geete, ed., *Svenska böner från medeltiden*, Samlingar utgifna af Svenska fornskrift-sällskapet, 131, 133, 135 (Stockholm: Svenska fornskriftsällskapet, 1907–1909), 419.

own biography, including her early determination that she would devote herself to her faith, and her conviction that she too enjoyed a specific and individual relationship to Christ. St. Katherine's legend also contains elements that might make her a particularly attractive intercessor and patron for an aspiring bride of Christ who had nonetheless been married. Katherine's relationship to the empress, whom she converts to Christianity, grooms as a fellow bride of Christ, and supports through her resulting martyrdom, could also be a source of inspiration for women like St. Birgitta, and perhaps other nuns of her order.[140]

Perhaps St. Katherine's special gift of scholarship, which allows her so utterly to convince the fifty philosophers of her position that they are willing to be martyred, is also seen as a precursor of St. Birgitta's revelations. Further, although the Order of St. Birgitta certainly did not send its nuns to Paris to study theology, the fact that its nuns actively copied and even composed and illustrated texts in Old Swedish, Low German, and even Latin shows that the order supported intellectual activity for women. Thus even the scholarly aspects of St. Katherine's legend make her a fitting intercessor for the nuns of this order. It might be argued that St. Katherine's prominence in the prayer books of the Vadstena nuns reflects her general popularity in medieval Swedish society, and this line of thought is certainly corroborated in part by the fact that many of the nuns bore her name.[141] At the same time, it is clear that St. Katherine and her image and legend hold specific meanings for the Order of St. Birgitta that go beyond the saint's popularity in the society as a whole.

Perhaps the most interesting example of St. Katherine's importance to the nuns of Vadstena is a painting dating from the reign of King Johan III (1537–1592; king of Sweden 1569–1592).[142] The convent of Vadstena was to some extent excepted from the general order that all monastic foundations be

---

[140] *Virgin Lives and Holy Deaths: Two Exemplary Biographies for Anglo-Norman Women,* ed. and trans. Jocelyn Wogan-Browne and Glyn S. Burgess (London: Everyman, 1996), xxxiv; Lewis, *Cult of St Katherine,* 247.

[141] According to Geete (*Svenska böner,* 61), forty-nine nuns at Vadstena, including seventeen who entered the convent after 1480, were called Katarina. For the sake of comparison, forty-four nuns were named Margareta, including fourteen after 1480. There is no indication that these nuns had assumed their names upon entering the religious order; on the contrary, it appears that, like St. Birgitta and her daughter St. Katherine of Vadstena, the nuns of the order retained their baptismal names.

[142] Johan III, along with his older brother, Erik XIV, and his younger brother Karl IX, were the sons of Gustav (Eriksson) Vasa (Gustav I), a member of one of Sweden's leading aristocratic families, who gained control of the Swedish throne in the 1520s. Gustav is generally given credit for once and for all establishing Sweden's status as a separate kingdom independent of the Kalmar Union. He is also the king who set the Protestant Reformation in motion in Sweden, a project that each of the three sons who followed him on the throne would continue in his own way.

dispersed and their lands and property "returned" to their original donors (or to the king himself) in the decades following the inception of the Protestant Reformation in Sweden. Although even Vadstena was severely treated, having many of its books and records confiscated and losing much of its land to the crown, King Gustav I (ca. 1496–1560; king of Sweden 1523–1560) did issue an edict in 1555 that allowed the remaining nuns of Vadstena an annual sum of money along with supplies in kind. By this time, the monks who had been so important to the spiritual life of Vadstena Abbey ever since its foundation had been driven out, and Protestant ritual had been imposed on the convent church, which had been largely taken over for use by the townsfolk.[143] In spite of these obvious difficulties, the nuns of Vadstena were relatively lucky in comparison with nuns of other orders. After having been largely ignored by Gustav's son and successor, Erik XIV (1533–1577; king of Sweden 1560–1569), the convent began to enjoy improved circumstances during the reign of Erik's brother Johan.[144]

Unlike his father and brothers, Johan III worked, though with only short-lived progress, to reconcile the Roman Catholic faith with the newer Lutheran ideals. In contrast to his predecessors, Johan not only tolerated the existence of the convent, he favored the nuns, and together with his Polish queen, Katarina Jagellonica, he treated the nuns and their abbess with warmth and respect. In addition to restoring a significant portion of the property confiscated by Gustav, and allowing the convent to admit new sisters, Johan also contributed to the reconstruction of the convent buildings after a fire in 1567.[145] After the Protestant takeover of the convent church in 1550, the nuns had moved their most precious relics to a room connected to their dormitory in the former palace of the Bjälbo dynasty,[146] in what apparently had been the sacristy of the palace chapel. Perhaps the most pivotal occurrence during this period was the visit of the papal legate Possevino to Vadstena in February 1580. During this visit, the legate professed the ten new nuns (for whom no other Catholic bishop had been available), and consecrated an altar within the cloister itself for the spiritual activities of the nuns. Even more significantly, perhaps, he encouraged them to remain stead-

---

[143] Lindblom, *Vadstena klosters öden*, 123–25.

[144] Lindblom, *Vadstena klosters öden*, 126–27.

[145] Lindblom, *Vadstena klosters öden*, 128.

[146] The Bjälbo dynasty (headed by Birger Jarl), also known as the Folkung dynasty, ruled Sweden from the middle of the thirteenth to the middle of the fourteenth century. Birgitta Birgersdotter's mother was distantly related to this dynasty, which gained power after the extinction of the Sverker and Erik dynasties that competed for the Swedish crown for most of the preceding century. The so-called Bjälbo palace had been donated to the order by the dynasty's last king, Magnus Eriksson (1316–1374; king of Norway 1319–1344; king of Sweden 1319–1356, co-regent with his son Erik 1357–1359, sole king of Sweden again 1359–1364), who was driven from the throne in 1364.

fast in their faith, following the example of the saints and martyrs.[147] Shortly after Possevino's visit, King Johan donated a suite of murals for the room in the dormitory, which had come to be known as the Sanctum Sanctorum. Along with a number of scenes from the passion of Christ, the murals depict the five female saints Possevino had suggested to the nuns as models in their faith: St. Apollonia, St. Katherine of Alexandria, St. Agnes, St. Agatha, and St. Mary Magdalene. The painting of St. Katherine is especially remarkable. It is located on the east wall of the chamber, which is also decorated with a painting of St. Birgitta and her daughter St. Katherine of Vadstena. Both in terms of its direction and in terms of its proximity to the images of the founder of the order, the placement of this image suggests high status. The choice of motif is also crucial: the scene depicts St. Katherine of Alexandria's mystic marriage with the Christ Child, who is portrayed sitting in his mother's lap and offering a ring to Katherine. To quote Andreas Lindblom:

> Why has this scene, in particular, been given such a prominent place in Vadstena's *Sanctum Sanctorum*? Certainly because of the special significance that bridal mysticism had come to have for the order, already during Birgitta's own time. Likewise, it had become increasingly popular in art by the end of the Middle Ages.

> In the *Legenda Aurea*, which was translated for the [Dominican] nuns at Skänninge already during the thirteenth century, Katherine of Alexandria is praised for her steadfast refusal to marry, even when she is offered the opportunity to become Empress of Rome. She bursts out: "Jesus is my betrothed, he is my honor, he is my love. Neither fair words nor death will ever separate me from him." A statement that could just as well have been made by Birgitta!

> St. Bernard of Clairvaux's famous sermons on the Song of Songs are generally thought to be the classic source for the bridal imagery that appears in the nunneries and in the works of Birgitta's great predecessors in the faith, such as Mechtild of Magdeburg. It is clear that Birgitta was taken with this divine mysticism through her contact with the Cistercians, primarily Prior Petrus, but also during the spouses' [Birgitta and her husband, Ulf Gudmarsson] pilgrimage to Compostela in the company of another monk, and then especially during her stay at the Cistercian monastery at Alvastra. It is characteristic that it was during her stay at Alvastra, after the death of her husband, that she removed his ring from her finger.[148]

---

[147] Lindblom, *Vadstena klosters öden*, 133–34.
[148] Lindblom, *Vadstena klosters öden*, 135–36.

Clearly, then, the image of St. Katherine's mystic marriage had a special resonance for the nuns of the Order of St. Birgitta. The prominence accorded to this particular scene from St. Katherine's marriage in the murals painted during the last flowering of Vadstena Abbey after the Reformation may also help to explain why St. Katherine appears to have been important in the cult of Vadstena from the beginning. While St. Katherine's intellectual activities were certainly not foreign to Birgitta herself and to the nuns of Vadstena, it would appear that it was the saint's special relationship to Christ, as the only saint (up to the end of Birgitta's lifetime) whose marriage to the Christ Child is explicitly depicted in her legend, that guaranteed her status.[149]

Interestingly, there is evidence of devotion to St. Katherine not only among the nuns of Vadstena, but also among the monks. A cleric by the name of Hemming had been quite prominent in Östergötland during the later fourteenth century. He is known to have served as the rural dean of Söderköping, and as the treasurer ("yconomicus") of the Cistercian convent of Askeby, as well as having been the parish priest of Östra Eneby church. In 1398 he became one of the first *fratres ab extra* for Vadstena Abbey, where he again served as treasurer, a role in which he continued for over twenty years.[150] Quite fascinatingly, Hemming's seal, preserved on a document from the year 1400,[151] after he entered the monastery, depicts St. Katherine. Does this choice of image, and the devotion it suggests, indicate that Hemming's educational background resembles the background of the other medieval clerics whose seals depicted St. Katherine? Given Hemming's prominent position as a rural dean before he entered the monastery, this is a strong likelihood. At the same time, however, it is clear that Hemming had been closely associated with Vadstena Abbey even before he became a monk there himself. At the time of his death in 1411, thirteen years after his entrance, it was noted that he had served as treasurer for over twenty years. It is quite possible, then, that Hemming's devotion to St. Katherine was influenced not only by her associations with the intellectual activities of the universities and cathedral chapters, but also by Birgittine, and perhaps Cistercian bridal mysticism. At some point after Hemming's entrance into the monastery at Vadstena, but before 1404, his former parish church, Östra Eneby, was decorated with a series of murals in which the legend of St. Katherine is depicted in a grouping of six roundels. Hemming was not the donor of these murals, which also feature a wide variety of other saints, and closely resemble murals painted is a group of parish

---

[149] The later legend of St. Catherine of Siena (c. 1337–1380; canonized 1461), would portray her mystic marriage to Christ in ways that at least in part parallel the earlier mystic marriage of St. Katherine of Alexandria.

[150] Åke Nisbeth, *Ordet som bild: Östgötsk kalkmåleri vid slutet av 1300-talet och början av 1400-talet*, Scripta maiora 1 (Stockholm: Sällskapet runica et mediævalia, 1995), 207.

[151] RPB no. 3105

churches in Östergötland during the late fourteenth and early fifteenth centuries. At the same time, however, there are indications that he had had contact with a possible donor of the paintings, so it is possible that he was not entirely without influence on the content of the paintings.[152]

Even if the influence of the Birgittine Order does not seem to dominate in the church paintings of late fourteenth- and early fifteenth-century Östergötland, it may be possible to trace its influence elsewhere. By the end of the Middle Ages, Vadstena Abbey was the largest ecclesiastical landowner in all of Sweden, with over one thousand properties spread throughout the kingdom.[153] This fact, in addition to the general interest in the cult of St. Birgitta and to some extent of other native-born Swedish saints, may have given the order a certain degree of influence of the decoration of some parish churches, and may even be responsible for certain representations of saints that are not exclusively associated with the Order of St. Birgitta. A particularly interesting example is a retable from the parish church of Kråksmåla, Småland. This piece was undoubtedly made for a side altar, probably dedicated to St. Birgitta, and was produced in Lübeck by the workshop of Johannes Stenrat shortly after the middle of the fifteenth century.[154] The central motif of this altarpiece is a sculpted image of St. Birgitta. The images on the doors are paintings of St. Katherine of Alexandria on the right, and St. Nicholas of Myra on the left. This combination of saints is especially interesting. As noted above, these two saints were the co-patrons of the University of Paris, and this fact seems to have led to their co-patronage of a chapel at Uppsala cathedral, and to their general popularity in association with the cathedral chapters of medieval Sweden. Even though the sculpture of St. Birgitta in this retable depicts her reading a book, undoubtedly a reference to her revelations, it seems unlikely that an emphasis on intellectual pursuits accounts for the presence of the two saints portrayed on the doors. Certainly the image of St. Katherine leads to thoughts of the mystic marriage and the general bridal mysticism of the Birgittines. However, this depiction (which is slightly damaged) does not appear to include a ring among the saint's attributes. It is a typical, if lovely, portrayal of St. Katherine wearing a crown, with a broken wheel at her feet and a sword at her side. There may, however, be another explanation for this particular combination of saints.

By the middle of the fifteenth century, when this piece was produced, Birgitta was not the only saint associated with Vadstena. Nicholas Hermansson (d. 1391) had been bishop of Linköping for many years by the time of his death, and

---

[152] See Nisbeth, *Ordet som bild*, 208 and passim. Although he examines the murals painted in Östergötland during this period for signs of influence from Vadstena, Nisbeth finally concludes that their depictions of the Virgin Mary more probably indicate that the artist was advised by someone connected to Dominican order, which had a priory and a convent in Skänninge (see esp. 254).

[153] Pernler, *Sveriges kyrkohistoria II*, 146.

[154] Pernler, *Sveriges kyrkohistoria II*, 146.

he had come to be widely regarded as a saint even by that time. A canonization process was begun on his behalf in 1416, though his relics were not enshrined at Linköping Cathedral until nearly a century later. His close association with St. Birgitta personally (he had tutored her children at the family estate of Ulvåsa) and with Vadstena Abbey as a whole meant that the promotion of his cult was a matter of interest to the abbey well before his official recognition by the pope. Similarly, Katarina Ulfsdotter (d. 1391), daughter of St. Birgitta and first abbess of the order, had also been venerated as a saint within the Order of St. Birgitta, long before her beatification in 1489. While a specific connection between the parish of Kråksmåla and Vadstena Abbey is not recorded, it is known that pilgrims from Småland visited the relics of Nicholas Hermansson in Linköping and those of Katherine of Vadstena at Vadstena Abbey. In addition, miracles attributed to both of these saints were collected from residents of Småland.[155]

Certainly both St. Katherine of Alexandria and St. Nicholas of Myra were of sufficient standing in medieval Sweden that their appearance in a parish church in the middle of the fifteenth century should raise no eyebrows. However, their appearance together with the central figure of St. Birgitta raises a question: can a representation of one saint refer to another saint of the same name? Certainly the evidence of personal seals makes it clear that an individual may be represented by the image of his or her name saint. If the retable in Kråksmåla is a product of Birgittine influence, perhaps the choice of the two saints flanking Birgitta reflects the veneration of these other saints, who were recognized locally and within the Birgittine order but not yet officially recognized by the church as a body. In this case, then, the images of St. Katherine of Alexandria and St. Nicholas of Myra may also be intended to represent, in some way, Katherine of Vadstena and Nicholas Hermansson. The possibility also exists that the efforts to launch the cults of the newer Saints Katherine and Nicholas might also contribute to the veneration of the already established saints who share their names. Whatever the circumstances that led to its commission, the particular composition of this retable suggests that these portrayals may reflect an even greater degree of flexibility and multifunctionality than is usually noted.

Conclusions

In spite of the inevitable losses in the centuries following the Protestant Reformation, a surprisingly large amount of evidence survives to document the importance of St. Katherine of Alexandria to the various representatives of the clergy

---

[155] Anders Fröjmark, *Mirakler och helgonkult: Linköpings biskopsdöme under senmedeltiden*, Acta Universitatis Upsaliensis, Studia Historica Upsaliensia 171 (Uppsala/Stockholm: Almqvist & Wiksell, 1992), 88–91.

and the religious orders of medieval Sweden. Although it is clear that much of this saint's importance derives from her prominence in the medieval church as a whole, it is also apparent that she was closely associated with certain sets of meanings that were of specific importance to the Swedish clergy. The saint's almost universal association with scholarship and learning made her a logical patron saint for the University of Paris, one of the most important seats of learning in high medieval Europe, and indeed also for other seats of learning. In turn, this association with the scholarly tradition of Paris meant that high-ranking Swedish clerics and friars could direct their devotions toward a patron and intercessor who was a fellow scholar, whose interests might be understood as resembling their own. At the same time, they could indicate their own educational background, and its attendant prestige, by placing the image of St. Katherine in their personal seals. As the Middle Ages progressed, the links between St. Katherine and the University of Paris, and perhaps with the idea of scholarship in general, clearly contributed to her particular centrality in the cult and liturgy of Uppsala Cathedral. During the later fifteenth century, a significant number of parish churches in the Archdiocese of Uppsala depicted St. Katherine together with the official patron saints of Uppsala, St. Lawrence and St. Erik, as well as with other saints, such as St. Olav and St. Mary Magdalene, who were closely connected with the cathedral cult. In these representations, most of which occur in churches with specific documented ties to the cathedral chapter, it appears that St. Katherine and her saintly companions comprise a specific reference to the relationship between the parish and the archdiocese. While the appearance of the official cathedral patrons in these contexts is entirely logical, the fact that St. Katherine is depicted in their company demonstrates the central importance that scholarship came to have for the cathedral chapter. There are some indications that St. Katherine was regarded in similar ways by other medieval Swedish cathedral chapters. Perhaps this is better documented for Linköping than for the other dioceses, but there is also evidence that St. Katherine was venerated by members of the cathedral chapters of Skara, Strängnäs, and Västerås, and we may assume that the motivations for this devotion were similar to those in the better-documented chapters.

For the various religious orders, St. Katherine, her legend, and her image held a wide range of meanings, some of them more or less similar to those suggested for the secular clergy. Certainly the saint's scholarly associations made her an attractive patron saint for the Dominican order, as for the Franciscans after the order's first few decades. Another important aspect of her legend is its emphasis that all true glory comes from God, and that even the most exalted earthly status is temporary and worthless in comparison with a union with Christ. Certainly this aspect of her cult would be compatible with the ideals of all religious orders and secular clergy. The apparent connection between the Cistercian order and parish churches dedicated to St. Katherine presents a fascinating problem in this connection. Although it is difficult to establish a certain connection between the

activities of the Cistercian order and the popularization of St. Katherine's cult
and image, there are some very suggestive pieces of evidence for a strong interest
in St. Katherine in areas where the Cistercians were well established and influential. If these coincidences actually reflect historical realities, they certainly
remind us of one of the most striking aspects of the cult of St. Katherine: its flexibility and multifunctionality. In contrast to the Dominican order, the Cistercian
order was, at its inception and for its first decades, directly anti-intellectual in
its ideals and activities. Although this had begun to change by the middle of
the thirteenth century, it still could not be said that intellectual pursuits were a
defining aspect of Cistercian activity.[156] Furthermore, the Cistercian order was
known for dedicating all of its monasteries and churches to the Virgin Mary and
for renouncing the rich decoration of churches that had come to characterize
other monastic foundations. What, then, accounts for the appearance of images
of and dedications to St. Katherine in areas of apparent Cistercian influence?
Perhaps, like the Franciscans, the Cistercians were attracted to St. Katherine as
an example of steadfast faith in confrontation with worldly power and authority.
Perhaps, too, she was understood as a heavenly companion to the Virgin Mary
herself, the patron of the order. Lindblom's comments about the connection
between St. Katherine and the bridal mysticism of St. Birgitta and her order are
undoubtedly relevant here. Of course the Cistercian order would have regarded
the Virgin Mary as the central figure in this context. Of all other saints, however, St. Katherine is the one whose legend most strongly emphasizes her unique
position as the spouse of Christ. In this sense, the legend of St. Katherine might
be seen as echoing aspects of the life of the Virgin Mary. Both the special connection to the Virgin, then, and the legend of her own mystic marriage might
provide an explanation for Cistercian veneration of St. Katherine.

The proliferation of images of St. Katherine of Alexandria, in comparison
with those of many other saints, cannot be explained solely by her membership
in popular groupings of saints such as the Fourteen Holy Helpers and the Four
Capital Virgins. It is clear that for many members of the clergy St. Katherine's
particular qualities made her a patron and intercessor of special power, even
alongside such central figures as the Virgin Mary and the ubiquitous St. Olav.
The specifically scholarly aspects of the cult no doubt contributed to her importance to the highly influential Dominican and Franciscan orders. Further, the
saint's close links to the center of ecclesiastical learning in Uppsala meant that
her image was likely to appear wherever the cathedral's influence reached.

At the same time, the second outstanding aspect of the legend and cult of
St. Katherine is her explicit status as the chosen bride of Christ. The general idea
of bridal mysticism, ultimately derived from the Songs of Solomon, was a central

---

[156] C. H. Lawrence, *Medieval Monasticism: Forms of Religious Life in Western Europe in
the Middle Ages* (London and New York: Longman, 1984) 146–66.

aspect of Cistercian thought, and also of the piety of St. Birgitta, Sweden's only home-grown canonized saint, and the founder of the country's only native religious order. Clearly this aspect of the cult of St. Katherine contributed to her attractiveness to both of these orders, and it continued to resonate for Birgittine nuns well into the Reformation period. The association of St. Katherine's name with that of St. Katherine of Vadstena, the first abbess of the Birgittine Order and daughter of its patron and founder, may also contribute to her lasting importance for the Birgittines.

There can be no doubt that St. Katherine of Alexandria was one of the saints most widely venerated by the clergy and religious orders of medieval Sweden. Certainly, part of the explanation for her prominence in Sweden lies in the status her cult enjoyed in the church as a whole. At the same time, however, it is clear that there were also specific circumstances within Sweden that gave a special resonance to devotions to this saint, and particular symbolic meanings to her image. Even within a group that might be assumed to have many interests in common, the range of meanings associated with the cult of this saint is remarkable. Clearly this cult had sufficient flexibility that it could adapt to suit the needs of devotees of many backgrounds.

FIGURE 2.1
Counterseal of Andreas Andreasson (And).

B.E. Hildebrand, *Svenska sigiller från medeltiden.*

FIGURE 2.2
Reredos from Bälinge parish church (Uppland).
Tracey R. Sands.

FIGURE 2.3
Reredos from Börje parish church (Uppland).
Detail: St. Katherine.
Tracey R. Sands.

FIGURE 2.4
Reredos from Börje parish church, corpus.
Tracey R. Sands.

III
Saint Katherine and the Nobility

Along with the clergy, the nobility are among the best documented groups of medieval Sweden. Perhaps the most important source of documentation for this group consists of charters such as property deeds and testaments. Charters documenting the transfer of land and other property were valuable in themselves, and were often preserved by the landowners and even transferred to the new owners when the property changed hands As a result, a considerable corpus of material documenting the names, property, and personal, social, or familial ties of medieval Swedish aristocrats has survived to the present day, and these documents, even when written on parchment, tended to escape the kinds of mutilation and reuse that often affected manuscripts of more strictly ecclesiastical character. Although the charters, and not least the seals affixed to them, are a rich and important source of information about the medieval Swedish nobility and their relationship to the various saints, including their donations, their naming customs, choice of grave location, and so on, they are not the only source. In some cases, parish churches bear witness to the interests of their local aristocratic patrons through the murals that decorate their walls and vaults or the sculptures that decorate their altars. Although the leading circles of the church, including the papacy, were at times less than enthusiastic about the idea that members of the laity might be entitled to accept or reject a candidate for the position of parish priest, or even to claim a portion of the income (tithe or otherwise) of a particular church, the phenomenon did exist in medieval Sweden.[1]

It has been suggested that many of the earliest parish churches in Sweden were originally built by powerful and wealthy landowners on their own estates and initially, at least, for their own use. Often the portion of the estate on which the church is built becomes a separate entity, no longer part of the original estate. In most cases, the "church village" is allotted sufficient farmland to provide a living for the parish priest. For the province of Uppland alone, Ferm and Rahmqvist found that five central Uppland churches show strong indications of being

---

[1] See Gunnar Smedberg, *Nordens första kyrkor: En kyrkorättslig studie* (Lund: CWK Gleerups förlag, 1973), 88–102; Ferm and Rahmqvist, "Stormannakyrkor," 67–69; Bonnier, *Kyrkorna berättar*, 167–69; Ivar Nylander, "Patronatsrätt," *KHLM* 13, 136–38.

so-called "magnates' churches," while another twenty-one churches elsewhere in the province also merited further examination. Furthermore, as Bonnier notes, several of the provincial laws make specific reference to the existence of the right of patronage. A passage in the Uppland law, ratified in 1296, notes that it is primarily the right of the parish to choose their priest. If the congregation cannot agree on a candidate, the matter goes to the bishop, whose responsibility it is to grant the choice to the holder of the right of patronage (*ius patronatus*).[2] Although the aspect of the right of patronage emphasized in the law codes is the right to select the parish priest (or at least to reject a candidate), there appear to be other expressions of the relationship between landowners and the churches once built on their estates. It was not unusual in medieval Sweden for landowners to contribute to the decoration of churches in parishes where they owned significant holdings. In some cases, when the donation seems especially significant, for example, if a donor funds the painting of a suite of murals in the entire church, it is assumed that this donor had inherited the right of patronage for the parish in question. It is worth noting in this context that the right of patronage appears to follow the original estate, not necessarily the descendants of the builder of the church.

This chapter will examine the many different meanings that St. Katherine of Alexandria had for members of the medieval Swedish aristocracy. Members of the Royal Council were to a great extent recruited from within this group. The title of "riddare" (knight) was not inherited in medieval Sweden. Nonetheless, holders of the title usually came from this segment of society. In many cases, the interests of the Swedish nobility were closely entwined with those of the ecclesiastical hierarchy. Members of aristocratic families often entered the service of the church; many of them became prominent members of the cathedral chapters, and eventually bishops or even archbishop. Another important group for the present study consists of aristocratic women. Here again, this category covers a wide range of interests. While many noblewomen in medieval Sweden entered a convent, either as young women or after having been widowed, other women married, had children, and remained active in the secular world to the ends of their lives. Some of these women took a strong interest in managing their own considerable financial holdings, and many of them had strong ties to the cathedral chapters and their prelates. Finally, several of the leading aristocratic families of medieval Sweden had members, sometimes continuously over several generations, who aspired to royal power.

As I argued in the previous chapter, an examination of personal devotions to saints and the ways that these are expressed may reveal important information about the interests and affiliations of the individual devotees. In this chapter, I will argue that this is no less true for the secular aristocracy than for members of the clergy and the various monastic and mendicant orders. While many saints'

---

[2] Bonnier, *Kyrkorna berättar*, 168.

cults show a great degree of flexibility and are able to accommodate a broad range of meanings and interests, the cult of St. Katherine seems to stand out even among these. In all cases, it must be assumed that part of St. Katherine's appeal was her reputation as a powerful intercessor, with a uniquely close relationship to Christ. In some cases, though, it is possible that the use of the saint's image has as much to do with symbolic meanings, perhaps only loosely related to her intercessory function, as with more specifically spiritual functions. Typically, veneration of St. Katherine may be surmised on the basis of donations or testaments to foundations (altars, chapels, prebends, and the like) in the saint's name, naming traditions within the family, and, not least, the use of St. Katherine's image in the seals belonging to the women of the family.

The use of St. Katherine's image in women's seals is certainly a reflection of her general popularity and her status as an especially powerful intercessor. Other female saints, including St. Margaret of Antioch and St. Barbara, occasionally appear in women's seals. However, to the extent that it has been possible to study the corpus of medieval Swedish seals, which has been published only in part and for which no catalog exists, it appears that these saints occur only in the seals of women whose names they share. Again, based on the limited material available for examination, male saints appear only occasionally in the seals of medieval women.[3] In the material published by Hildebrand, two women depict male saints in their seals. The seal of Ingeborg Bengtsdotter, affixed to several documents in the year 1302, depicts the bearer on her knees in veneration of St. Erik. The seal of her mother, Ingeborg Niklisdotter, affixed to two of the same documents, depicts its bearer on her knees in veneration of St. Lawrence.[4] Ingeborg Niklisdotter was the sister-in-law of Folke Johansson (d. 1277), archbishop of Uppsala.[5] It is quite clear that both of these women chose to represent the patron saints of Uppsala Cathedral in their seals at least in part because of their familial tie to the highest ecclesiastical authority in the land. In comparison to other female saints as well as the few male saints represented in the seals of noble women, St. Katherine appears to have a different status. Like the Virgin Mary, who appears in a large number of women's seals, St. Katherine is frequently depicted in the seals of women who are not named for her. Some of these women have names of Nordic origin, such as "Ingeborg" or "Ragnfrid," and thus had no possibility of conveying their own names through the image of a saint. However, St. Katherine's image also appears in seals belonging to women named "Christina" and

---

[3] In addition, several women in this limited group depict aspects of the Passion of Christ in their seals.

[4] See *DS* nos. 1362, 1428, 1456; *Svenska sigiller från medeltiden*, ed. Hildebrand, ser. 3, nos. 145, 146.

[5] See Bengt Thordeman, "Erik den helige i medeltidens konst," in *Erik den helige: Historia, kult, reliker*, ed. idem (Stockholm: Nordisk rotogravyr, 1954), 173–232, here 180.

"Cecilia." Both of these are saints' names with a long history in Sweden.[6] While neither St. Christina nor St. Cecilia was among the most widely venerated saints in medieval Sweden, both their feasts are included in Sweden's earliest known liturgical calendar, the Vallentuna Calendar from 1198.[7] Both also occur, if sparingly, among the murals that were painted in many Swedish churches during the later fifteenth and early sixteenth centuries.[8] It would appear, then, that women with these names could have chosen to be represented in their sigillographic imagery by their patron saints. The fact that they instead chose St. Katherine suggests a more interesting and more complex relationship between individual identity and the imagery of personal seals.[9]

Ragnfrid and her Family

Let us examine the mechanism of this aspect of the cult of St. Katherine by following a few examples. The earliest known Swedish woman with a seal depicting St. Katherine is Ragnfrid (or Ramfrid) Gustavsdotter, whose seal is first preserved on a seal from 1296.[10] This relatively large and detailed round seal depicts Ragnfrid kneeling in devotion to the crowned saint, who is clearly identified by the wheel and sword in her right hand. By the time that Ragnfrid's seal first appeared in the preserved record, she was the widow of her second husband, the nobleman, knight, and magistrate ("lagman") of Tiundaland, Israel Andreasson And. Through this marriage, Ragnfrid was the sister-in-law of the dean of Uppsala Cathedral, Andreas Andreasson And (see Chap. 2 above), with whom she clearly had regular contact. Bonnier has suggested that Ragnfrid's choice of St. Katherine for her seal may be related to the fact that Andreas also had a seal depicting this saint.[11] This may well be so, but there is also strong evidence that veneration of St. Katherine was a tradition in Ragnfrid's natal family. The first

---

[6] According to one tradition (see Westman, "Erik den helige," 22, note 80; also *Scriptores Rerum Suecicarum*, 1: 83) the mother of St. Erik, the martyred king Erik Jedvardsson (d. 1160) was named Cecilia. Christina is considered one of the earliest women's names of Christian origin in medieval Sweden. This was the name of King Inge the Elder's second daughter, who married the Grand Duke Mstislav of Kiev and Novgorod before 1100 (see Chapter 2, above).

[7] Schmid, *Liber ecclesiae*, 89, 93.

[8] See, for example, Nilsén, *Program och funktion*, 37–38.

[9] Sands, "The Saint as Symbol: The Cult of St Katherine of Alexandria Among Medieval Sweden's High Aristocracy," 95–96.

[10] *DS* no. 1156; *Svenska sigiller från medeltiden*, ed. Hildebrand, ser. 3, no. 147; contemporary documents use both forms of this woman's name (Ragnfrid and Ramfrid), as well as both forms of her father's name, Göstaf and Gustav.

[11] Bonnier, *Kyrkorna berättar*, 166.

document in which Ragnfrid is named is her mother's testament from 1286.[12] Ragnfrid's mother, Hafrid Sigtryggsdotter, was a member of one of the leading families of early medieval Sweden, one of the few that can be traced as far back as the twelfth century.[13] In her testament, Hafrid makes an especially interesting bequest to the Cistercian convent at Gudhem, where her daughter Kristina is one of the sisters. In addition to an estate in Esperyd (which has not been identified) with all its possessions, Hafrid also bequeaths to the convent "her chapel at the altar of St. Katherine, at the same place, where she also chooses her grave." It would appear that the location referred to in this statement is the convent, since convent churches were typical burial places for medieval Swedish aristocrats, while burial in a private chapel on an estate seems much less likely. Bonnier has suggested that many of the so-called "chapels" mentioned in aristocratic testaments from the thirteenth and fourteenth centuries actually referred to the movable equipment required for celebration of the mass, such as a chalice and paten.[14] Hafrid's terminology, however, suggests that her chapel has a permanent location. Perhaps her statement should be interpreted to mean that she had earlier funded the construction of a chapel in the convent church, or on its grounds. In any case, the dedication of Hafrid's chapel is highly interesting. The question of how the chapel came to be dedicated to St. Katherine is worth posing. Is this an expression of Hafrid's personal devotion? If this is so, it is interesting to note that Hafrid's seal depicts the Virgin Mary, not St. Katherine.[15] Certainly, devotion to the Virgin Mary in no way excludes devotion to other saints, and as I noted above in Chapter 2, many images of St. Katherine are so closely linked to images of the Virgin Mary that it is clear that there is a symbolic and devotional connection between them. If the dedication of the chapel is to be understood as an expression of Hafrid's own devotional preference, it is possible that it reflects an established family tradition dating from before Hafrid's own generation. However, her mother's name and identity are not known, nor is the name of her paternal grandmother. None of Hafrid's known siblings was named Katarina, though she did have one sister whose name has not been recorded.[16] However, the name Katarina does appear among Hafrid's grandchildren. Both her son Bengt and her daughter Ragnfrid have daughters by this name, and the name continues to

---

[12] *DS* no. 925; this document is remarkable for a number of reasons, including the fact that it manumits a slave woman named Tove and her two young children.

[13] *ÄSF*, 22–25; it may be an indication of her status that her son, Bengt Hafridsson, chose to use a matronymic rather than the patronymic used by Ragnfrid. There is no evidence that Bengt was illegitimate, and the fact that he became magistrate (*lagman*) of Västergötland, a position earlier held by Ragnfrid's father Gustav, suggests that he was also Gustav's son (see *ÄSF*, 115).

[14] Bonnier, *Kyrkorna berättar*, 165.

[15] *Svenska sigiller från medeltiden*, ed. Hildebrand, ser. 3, no. 137.

[16] *ÄSF*, 24.

reappear among Bengt's descendants for several generations.[17] Even if Hafrid regarded the Virgin Mary as her personal patron, the choice of St. Katherine as the dedication saint for her chapel may still reflect a degree of personal devotion. It may also be significant that Gudhem Abbey had been in existence for well over a century by the time of Hafrid's testament.[18] Since these nuns lived under the Cistercian rule, it is clear that the dedication to the Virgin Mary was already established for the entire convent well before Hafrid founded her chapel. Under these circumstances, St. Katherine seems an appropriate choice as a secondary patron saint for a devotee of the Virgin Mary. It is also possible that the choice of St. Katherine as chapel patron was not Hafrid's alone. If the nuns or the abbess of Gudhem were involved in the choice of patron saint for the chapel, there are several factors that would make St. Katherine especially appropriate. First of all, St. Katherine's general popularity makes her a nearly universal saint, in medieval Sweden as well as the rest of Europe. Further, as I have shown in the previous chapter, it appears that Katherine was at least as popular in Cistercian and Cistercian-related circles as she was among other clerical and monastic groups in medieval Sweden. In her capacity as the most explicitly chosen bride of Christ, and one who also actively helps others to achieve that status, Katherine makes an appealing example and intercessor for the Cistercian order as a whole, and for its nuns in particular. However, Gudhem Abbey had an additional reason to dedicate a chapel to St. Katherine. Although the convent's earliest buildings appear to have been largely made of wood, an important donation during the middle of the thirteenth century made it possible to rebuild in stone, and at the same time to expand the compound. The donor who made this expansion possible was Queen Katarina Sunesdotter (d. 1252), who entered the abbey after the death of her husband, King Erik Eriksson (known to later generations by the unfortunate epithet "the lame and lisping").[19] By honoring Queen Katarina's patron saint, the abbey and its subsequent donors could also honor the memory of their important donor and most prominent member. Whether the choice of patron saint for the chapel was made by the abbey, by the donor, Hafrid Sigtryggsdotter, or by both together, it is likely that it was motivated both by devotional and by personal interests.

Whether or not the dedication of Hafrid's chapel at Gudhem reflects her own personal devotion to St. Katherine, it seems likely that it inspired her daughter's choice of sigillographic image and, presumably, favored intercessor. While St. Katherine was generally known for her intercessory powers, it seems likely that a woman whose mother had built a chapel in the saint's honor would expect her to be especially attentive. In addition, of course, specific elements of

---

[17] *ÄSF* 116–19; Hans Gillingstam, *Ätterna Oxenstierna och Vasa under medeltiden: Släkthistoriska studier* (Stockholm, Almqvist & Wiksell, 1952–1953), 108.

[18] Nilsson, *Sveriges kyrkohistoria I*, 130.

[19] Nilsson, *Sveriges kyrkohistoria I*, 130.

St. Katherine's legend might be especially attractive to a woman of Ragnfrid's status and situation. Not least of these is the fact that Katherine's legend suggests that the saint has an unusually inclusive attitude toward other women, and not just virgins like herself, but even married women. This is most apparent in one passage in particular. As Katherine Lewis notes:

> St Katherine's words to the Empress [suggesting that she too will be a bride of Christ] seem to offer a strategy by which married women could reconstruct themselves as virgins and negotiate a relationship between themselves and Christ which allowed them to think of themselves as his bride.[20]

Both of the surviving medieval versions of the legend of St. Katherine in Swedish depict the conversation in which the saint comforts and encourages the empress who is confronting her own impending martyrdom. Ragnfrid's many donations to Uppsala Cathedral, and the relatively close relationship she seems to have had to her brother-in-law, Andreas Andreasson And, who was dean of the cathedral chapter at Uppsala, suggest strong personal piety and religious interests. At the same time, Ragnfrid was married twice, and had children with both of her husbands. She clearly took a strong interest in managing her considerable wealth and property, and was thus very much a woman of the world. Unlike many other pious widows, she did not end her days as a nun. The fact that St. Katherine explicitly states that a married woman is worthy to be a bride of Christ must have been deeply appealing to a woman like Ragnfrid. St. Katherine is also depicted as a reigning monarch, with great personal wealth and property. This too may have made her an attractive example and intercessor for a woman who continued to live in the secular world to the end of her lifetime. Interestingly, there is not the same degree of evidence that Ragnfrid's best-known daughter, Ramborg Israelsdotter, shared her mother's devotion to St. Katherine. However, she must have been aware of the various symbolic meanings that could reside in the saint's image, and there is at least the possibility that she made use of that image on at least one occasion.

Ramborg has a unique distinction, at least for Uppland. She is the only woman, indeed the only individual, known by name as the builder of a parish church in the province. According to an inscription in the chancel, Ramborg had the stone church at Västeråker built in 1331. An earlier wooden church had preceded Ramborg's stone church, the architecture of which shows a number of traits in common with that of Uppsala Cathedral. Given Ramborg's close relationship to Andreas And, it is not surprising that she should have had access to craftsmen connected to the building site of the cathedral, and certain features of Ramborg's church are indeed reflective of this higher level of craftsmanship.[21] Although the

---

[20] Lewis, *Cult of St Katherine*, 247.
[21] Bonnier, *Kyrkorna berättar*, 206–11.

church's medieval murals, most likely painted during the fifteenth century, were destroyed by a "restoration" in the 1870s, a drawing dating from Peringskiöld's late seventeenth-century visit to the church indicates that a painting in the chancel, perhaps dating from Ramborg's own time showed St. Katherine together with other saints connected to Uppsala Cathedral, along with Ramborg's coat of arms.[22] Whether the painting dates from Ramborg's own time, or was commissioned by one of her descendants, her mother's favorite saint remains in the grouping. The entire grouping is clearly intended to connect Ramborg with the cathedral. On the other hand, the painting does show clearly that St. Katherine is one of the saints whose image symbolizes the cathedral and its chapter.

Katarina of Steninge

A contemporary of Ragnfrid Gustavsdotter's, with many of the same connections, was Katarina of Steninge, who also depicted St. Katherine in her two known seals, dating from the end of the thirteenth century and the first years of the fourteenth. Although a relatively large number of charters issued by or concerning Katarina has been preserved, very little concrete information is known about her lineage. What is known is that by the time of her earliest preserved charter, dated 1299, she was the widow of a man named Anund.[23] Her primary estate, at least during this period, was Steninge in Husby-Ärlinghundra parish, Uppland. Katarina's only known son, Olof, was apparently a friar in the Dominican friary at Sigtuna, where Katarina chose to be buried. Katarina had dealings with Birger Petersson regarding the sale and trade of a number of properties, and it is to a great extent because of this correspondence that she appears in the record. She donated property to Uppsala Cathedral, possibly in exchange for the right to the tithe of the parish of Låssa, which she received from the archbishop. She also designated Bishop Israel of Västerås, formerly prior of the Dominican friary at Sigtuna, as the executor of her testament. All of this information suggests a woman of aristocratic origins and exalted social status, but little is known of Katarina's ancestry, or of how she came to be named as she was. On the other hand, it would appear that Katarina was a strong devotee of her patron saint, St. Katherine of Alexandria. In her testament, dated 5 November 1311, Katarina donates considerable property to the Dominican friary church in Sigtuna, including the specific bequest of a canopy ("baldachin") "pro altare beate Katerine in domo fratrum sigtunensium."[24] Both of Katarina's seals depict her kneeling in devotion to the saint. The question of how this woman came to have

---

[22] Bonnier, *Kyrkorna berättar*, 211; Nilsén, *Program och funktion*, 171.

[23] *DS* no. 1299.

[24] *DS* no. 1821.

two separate seals depicting St. Katherine is not resolved. It should be noted, however, that the later seal is considerably more elaborate and detailed than the earlier seal, and that St. Katherine is actually enthroned in the later seal, a relatively unusual depiction. With so little concrete information about Katarina's origins, it is difficult to draw conclusions about her veneration of the saint, and the degree to which her devotion was influenced by family tradition or other circumstances. In general, it seems likely that the aspects of St. Katherine's legend that appealed to Ragnfrid Gustavsdotter must also have appealed to Katarina of Steninge. Like Ragnfrid, Katarina continued to live in the secular world and to control her own property to the end of her life, which in no way hindered her piety. Perhaps Katarina, too, found St. Katherine to be a helpful intercessor under such circumstances. In addition, it is quite possible that Katarina's affection for her patron saint was strengthened by her Dominican connections, since it is known that St. Katherine was held in high regard by that order.

Cecilia Glysingsdotter

Another interesting Katherine tradition occurs in a family that may be related to Hafrid Sigtryggsdotter. Several documents, beginning in 1332 and continuing to 1358, preserve the seal of Cecilia Glysingsdotter, the widow of the knight Karl Nilsson (of the Natt och Dag lineage).[25] Cecilia's seal has the almond shape often associated with clergy. In Sweden, however, female aristocrats could and did bear such seals. The central motif of this seal is St. Katherine, who is depicted wearing a crown on her rather short, puffy hair, holding a martyr's palm frond and a wheel.[26] Cecilia is depicted kneeling in veneration of the saint, and below them is the coat of arms of Cecilia's husband. There is one further, very unusual detail in this seal. At the very top of the seal, an angel is depicted, reaching down toward the wheel in St. Katherine's hand. It is tempting to view this image as an especially strong reference to the saint's intercessory power, since the angel's destruction of the wheelworks on which St. Katherine was to be tormented is one of the high points of her legend. Cecilia was named for a saint whose cult can be traced as far back in Swedish liturgical calendars as St. Katherine's.[27] The fact that she nonetheless chose to depict St. Katherine in her seal suggests that this saint must have been of particular significance to her. Indeed, the composition of the seal image also suggests a close relationship between the bearer and the saint. Cecilia was the daughter of Henrik Glysing, the founding member of the lineage later known as Glysing. According to Hans Gillingstam and A. Fillip

---

[25] *DS* no. 2941, RPB 353.

[26] For a discussion of the meanings associated with the length of St. Katherine's hair, see Karen Winstead, "St. Katherine's Hair."

[27] Schmid, *Liber ecclesiae*, 129.

Liljeholm, Henrik must have been married twice. Cecilia, her sisters Katarina and Kristina, her brother Nils, and possibly one additional sister are assumed to have been born in this presumed first marriage, though there is no record of such a marriage, nor of the name or lineage of Henrik's presumed first wife. Henrik's only known marriage, assumed by these authors to be his second, was to a daughter of Ragvald Puke and Katarina Karlsdotter, whose mother, Ulvhild, was the sister of Hafrid Sigtryggsdotter. Two more children are suggested as offspring of this marriage, namely Hafrid Glysingsdotter and Kettil Glysing, also known as Kettil Puke.[28] If Gillingstam and Liljeholm are correct, it is difficult to account for Cecilia's choice of sigillographic imagery, as well as for the name of her sister, Katarina. We might assume that their unknown mother came from a family that venerated St. Katherine, but this is an argument *ex silentio*. Gillingstam and Liljeholm base their assumption that Henrik Glysing was married twice on a charter, *DS* no. 4553, that they take as evidence that Kettil and Nils Glysing were only half-brothers. Because Hafrid is a name otherwise borne only by an aunt of Katarina Karlsdotter (Hafrid Sigtryggsdotter), it is assumed that she must be the daughter of Katarina's daughter. On the other hand, it is to be expected that one of the first daughters born to a woman whose mother was named Katarina would also receive that name. In addition, the names Katarina and Kristina are clearly connected to the family of Katarina Karlsdotter. Hafrid Sigtryggsdotter had a daughter named Kristina, a nun at Gudhem Abbey (see above), and Hafrid's daughter Ragnfrid Gustavsdotter and her son Bengt Hafridsson each had daughters named Katarina and Kristina.[29] Judging by the names of his children, it would appear just as likely that Henrik Glysing was married only once, to the daughter of Ragvald Puke and Katarina Karlsdotter.

Based on this assumption, Cecilia's seal would seem to convey both dynastic and devotional concerns. Interestingly, although Cecilia remarried after the death of her first husband, Karl Nilsson, she continued to use the seal depicting his arms, and never added the arms of her second husband, Gustav Nilsson (Bielke). Cecilia appears to have had one known child, a daughter named Ingegärd, with her second husband.[30] What meanings might the image of St. Katherine have conveyed for Cecilia? It is interesting to note that the naming conventions for Cecilia's generation suggest that the family was strongly aware of its ties to Hafrid Sigtryggsdotter. For example, one of Cecilia's sisters is named Hafrid, but none is known to have been named Ulvhild, even though it was Ulvhild Sigtryggsdotter, not Hafrid, who was the family's direct ancestor. Perhaps, then, Cecilia's choice of patron saint reflects a sense that a connection to Hafrid is a connection to St. Katherine. Perhaps, like Hafrid's own daughter Ragnfrid, Cecilia expects St.

---

[28] *ÄSF*, 53–54; see also 164.
[29] *ÄSF* 116–117, 139, Gillingstam, *Ätterna Oxenstierna och Vasa*, 108.
[30] See *ÄSF* 53–54.

Katherine to be an especially attentive intercessor because her great-grand-aunt Hafrid built a chapel for St. Katherine. It is also possible that Cecilia, like Birgitta Bryniofsdotter (see below), regarded the image of St. Katherine as a symbol of her own lineage, with particular reference to her maternal grandmother's prestigious ancestry. If this is so, then the image of the saint can be seen as a parallel to the shield depicting the arms of Cecilia's first husband.

Birger Petersson's Family

An especially interesting example of the Katherine tradition in Sweden was the lineage that later came to be called the "Finsta family," though they are never so designated in medieval sources. Among the most prominent members of this family were Birger Petersson, magistrate of Uppland and the head of the committee that compiled the Law of Uppland (ratified in 1296), and his daughter, Birgitta Birgersdotter, who came to be known throughout Christendom as St. Birgitta of Sweden. Other members of the family included an archbishop (Jakob Israelsson, d. 1281),[31] and a dean of the cathedral chapter at Uppsala (Israel Petersson, d. 1302).[32] Several members of the Finsta lineage came to be buried in the chapel of St. Katherine and St. Nicholas at Uppsala Cathedral, as were their close relations, Andreas Andreasson And and his brother, Israel Andreasson. It has been suggested that the dedication of this chapel, like those of the other four original chapels surrounding the chancel of the cathedral, reflects the desire of the leading families of Uppland to stress their own presence, and that of their patron saints, in the most prominent church in the land.[33] Given the family's close ties to the cathedral chapter at Uppsala, it is not surprising that the name "Katarina" is given to its daughters for several generations. Andreas Andreasson (see preceding chapter), the dean of the cathedral chapter and devotee of St. Katherine, was the nephew of Archbishop Jakob Israelsson, and a cousin of Birger Petersson.[34] Birger Petersson himself is known to have founded and endowed a prebend dedicated to St. Katherine, first named in his testament of 1326.[35] If the Finsta family and their close relations, the And (Andreasson) family are as closely connected to the foundation of the chapel of St. Katherine and St. Nicholas as Lindahl seems to suggest, it seems likely that their choice of patron saints nevertheless reflects the interests of the clerical members of the families. At the same time, however, both Birger Petersson and his children may well

---

[31] *ÄSF*, 35

[32] See *DS* no. 1372.

[33] Göran Lindahl, "Uppsala domkyrka," in *Kyrkorna i Uppsala*, Upplands kyrkor, new series 1:1 (Uppsala: Almqvist & Wiksell tryckeri, 1997), 39–40.

[34] See *ÄSF*, 34–35.

[35] See Dahlbäck, *Uppsala domkyrkas godsinnehav*, 149.

have inherited an interest in St. Katherine from both their maternal and their paternal forebears. As I noted in an article published in 2003, Birger Petersson's maternal grandfather, Birger Skänkare, was known to have had two daughters, one named Ingeborg, the other named Katarina.[36] Several preserved charters specifically identify Ingeborg as Birger's aunt, which led me in my earlier discussion to conclude that Katarina must be Birger's mother.[37] Interestingly, Ingeborg is the bearer of a seal that depicts St. Katherine, along with another female saint whose only attribute, a martyr's palm frond, is too general to allow identification. The fact that Ingeborg, not named for a saint herself, has the saint for whom her sister is named in her own seal suggests that the naming customs in this family are connected to active devotion to the saint. This is a pattern that also occurs in several other families whose female members depict St. Katherine in their seals. If the relationship between Birger and Ingeborg is clear from the charters, however, the relationship between Birger and Katarina is not. One document from 6 November 1314 records Ingeborg's sale of a farm, explicitly in order to pay the debts of her sister, Katarina, and Katarina's son, Peter.[38] In another charter dated four days earlier, Birger granted Ingeborg the right to sell her property. Since Ingeborg's title ("domicella") indicates that she was unmarried, Birger was clearly one of her legal heirs, and therefore had the right to approve (or disapprove) any transfer of her property. Another document, not published in the *Diplomatarium Suecanum*, makes the relationship between the various parties somewhat clearer. In this charter, dated 5 February 1313, Katarina, daughter of Birger Skänkare, announces that she is selling several properties, with the approval of her sister Ingeborg, who is clearly one of her heirs.[39] Since no son is mentioned at all, it may be that he was no longer living at the time the charter was written, though Ingeborg's charters make it clear that his debts are still a problem for Katarina. Birger Petersson is not mentioned at all in this document. Although an unmarried woman like Ingeborg could expect to be to some degree under the guardianship of a male family member, a widow like Katarina could often control her own property. Though Katarina must also have been related to Birger, the fact that he is not named as her heir, with the right to approve the disposal of her property, shows that she cannot be his mother. Clearly, then, Birger Skänkare had a third daughter, whose name was not recorded, and it was she, not Katarina, who gave birth to Birger Petersson. What can this information tell us about Birger's prebend, and the prevalence of the name Katarina among his descendants? Several factors may have contributed to the foundation and dedication of the prebend. Given the close connection that Birger's family clearly had to

---

[36] Sands, "Saint as Symbol," 89.

[37] See *DS* nos. 1983, 1984.

[38] *DS* no. 1984, see also nos. 1983, 2007, 2026.

[39] *De svenska medeltidsbreven i Svenskt Diplomatariums huvudkartotek*, CD ROM, Version 2, Macintosh (Stockholm: Riksarkivet, 2001), 2542.

this chapel, it makes sense that he would locate his prebend here. Birger and his second wife also chose to be buried in the chapel of St. Katherine and St. Nicholas, which would also contribute to their desire to support a priest connected to this location in the cathedral. There is, interestingly, no tradition of naming sons for St. Nicholas in any of the families connected to this chapel,[40] and even if St. Nicholas had been the preferred patron, a prebend in his name had already been founded in 1291.[41] As I noted in the previous chapter, the chapel's dedication to St. Katherine and St. Nicholas may be connected to the fact that these two saints were the patrons of the University of Paris, an institution of central importance to the cathedral chapter. During the later part of the thirteenth century, the two families most closely connected with this chapel had three high-ranking members of the chapter, including an archbishop and two deans. There is thus no inherent conflict between aristocratic family interests and the interests of the clergy, at least when it comes to the choice of dedication saints. On the contrary, lay members of families that included high-ranking clergy had every reason to emphasize this connection.

Given these circumstances, Birger's decision to dedicate his prebend to St. Katherine would appear to arise out of a family tradition, but not necessarily out of a wish to honor his mother's memory. Nonetheless, it is entirely possible that his interest in St. Katherine was strengthened by the tradition of devotion to her that very clearly existed in his mother's family, even though she herself was not named for the saint. Although relatively little is now known about the family of Birger Petersson's mother, they must have been a family of considerable status, since Birger chose to use their coat of arms, rather than that of his father's family.[42] It is impossible to determine the extent to which Birger's own choices were influenced by the various Katherine traditions in his own background, but it must be assumed that all of them played some part.

Although Birger had both a daughter and a granddaughter named Katarina, it is not certain that his own family traditions played a role in their naming. All of Birger's known children were born in his marriage to his second wife, Ingeborg Bengtsdotter.[43] Ingeborg had a sister named Katarina, which, given that medieval Swedish naming traditions called for naming children after their grandparents and other close relations, suggests that the name must have been current in previous generations of either their maternal or paternal family.[44] A similar pattern arises in the following generation of Birger's descendants. Birger Petersson's two surviving daughters, Katarina and Birgitta, married two brothers named Magnus and Ulf Gudmarsson. These brothers, who also came from a

[40] See *ÄSF*, 7–8, 34–38.

[41] Dahlbäck, *Uppsala domkyrkas godsinnehav*, 128–29.

[42] *ÄSF* 34.

[43] *ÄSF*, 35–36.

[44] See Otterbjörk, "Namngjeving," 210–11.

powerful aristocratic family, had a sister named Katarina, who died without issue by 1350.[45] Katarina Birgersdotter and her husband Magnus Gudmarsson had one known child, a daughter named Ingeborg after her maternal grandmother. Among Birgitta Birgersdotter's eight children with her husband Ulf Gudmarsson was a daughter named Katarina. It is worth noting that Birgitta had children named after all four of their grandparents, as well as a son named after her maternal grandfather, and another named after her husband's.[46] Even if Birgitta (and her children) did not have a direct ancestress named Katarina, the name was so well represented in all branches of the family that it is no surprise that it turns up among Birgitta's daughters. At the same time, it is interesting to note that while Birger Petersson's third surviving child, his son Israel, had three known children, none of them is named after their paternal grandparents. However, one daughter, Helena, was named for her maternal grandmother.[47] Although there were clearly well-established traditions regarding the naming of children after their grandparents or other ancestors or family members, these rules were clearly not binding. It may thus be assumed that for at least some of the parents of children named Katarina, the association with the saint was conscious and intentional. It appears that St. Katherine has a number of different meanings even for the extended family of Birger Petersson. For Birger's maternal aunt, whose seal depicts the bearer kneeling in devotion to the saint, it would appear that Katherine is a personal patron. The fact that Ingeborg also had a sister who shared the saint's name suggests that this devotion may have been an established tradition within the family. For Birger himself, the name and image of St. Katherine are also linked to a family tradition, though perhaps largely from a different direction. Birger's founding of a prebend dedicated to the saint appears to arise out of his paternal family's close ties to the Uppsala Cathedral chapter, a group that clearly venerated St. Katherine in part because of her association with the University of Paris. Finally, the fact that the name Katarina appears in several generations of Birger's family is clearly connected to the fact that both Birger and his descendants married into families with strong Katherine traditions of their own.

Svantepolk Knutsson's lineage

In another family of prominent medieval Swedish aristocrats, the name and image of St. Katherine also appear for several generations, and, as for Birger, they are clearly reflective of the family's sense of its own rank and prestige. For

---

[45] *ÄSF*, 91–95.

[46] *ÄSF*, 92–93.

[47] See *ÄSF* 145–46.

them, however, the status symbolized or embodied by St. Katherine comes from a completely different source. For the family of Svantepolk Knutsson, St. Katherine seems to have functioned as a symbol of royal ancestry.[48]

The descendants of Svantepolk Knutsson and his wife Benedicta Sunesdotter could claim royal ancestry through both of their parents. Svantepolk, who was clearly one of the most prominent men of his time, was the son of Knut, duke of Reval, himself the illegitimate son of the Danish king Valdemar Sejr (1170–1241) and Helena, the widowed daughter of the Swedish Jarl Guttorm.[49] Svantepolk held the title of knight and was a member of the powerful Royal Council ("riksråd"), much like his contemporary Birger Petersson. At some point between 1293 and 1305, he became magistrate of the province of Östergötland. He was married to Benedicta Sunesdotter, whose ancestry was nearly as prestigious as his own. Benedicta's father, Sune Folkeson, was the son of Jarl Folke who died in battle in 1210. Sune married Helena, daughter of the Swedish King Sverker Karlsson, after abducting her from the Cistercian convent at Vreta, apparently against her will, sometime during the 1220s.[50] As if this royal ancestry were not enough, Benedicta had yet another royal connection. Her sister, Katarina Sunesdotter, was married to the Swedish king, Erik Eriksson, and thus queen of Sweden in her own right.[51] The family expressed their status in a number of different ways. For example, at least two of the daughters of Svantepolk and Benedicta were placed as small children in the Cistercian convent at Vreta, which has the distinction of being Sweden's oldest known convent. Reputedly founded as a Benedictine convent by King Inge the Elder and Queen Helena some time around 1100, Vreta was reorganized as a Cistercian abbey by King Karl Sverkersson (Benedicta's ancestor) and his sister Ingegierd during the 1160s.[52] By placing their daughters in this abbey, Svantepolk and Benedicta were following a practice well established among Benedicta's royal antecedents. It was from Vreta that Benedicta's mother Helena was abducted by Sune Folkeson.[53]

---

[48] See Sands, "Saint as Symbol."

[49] In early medieval Sweden, the title "jarl" (translated into Latin as *dux*) designates a position second in power only to the king. After the death of Birger Jarl (d. 1266), who had managed to place his own son on the throne and had effectively ruled though him, the title disappeared from Swedish usage: see *Medeltidens ABC*, ed. Karin Orrling (Stockholm: Statens Historiska Museum/Prisma, 2001), 189.

[50] See Sands, "Saint as Symbol," 96–98; *ÄSF*, 258–59.

[51] This is the same Queen Katarina whose donations enabled the expansion of Gudhem Abbey, including the stone church where Hafrid Sigtryggsdotter apparently funded a chapel of St. Katherine (see above, 73–74).

[52] See Ahnlund, "Vreta klosters äldsta donatorer"; Sands, "Saint as Symbol," 97–98.

[53] As I noted in 2003, Benedicta's family had another tradition of sorts connected with Vreta Abbey. Not only was Helena kidnapped by the man who became her husband, but Benedicta herself, and her daughter Ingrid as well. Benedicta was abducted in 1244 by Lars

Interestingly, it has been shown that Vreta's links to royal power continued long after the Abbey's foundation, and even its reorganization under the Cistercian rule. According to Kristin Parikh, between the 1160s and the 1220s it was the only religious foundation to which royalty sought entry. After this period, immediate members of the ruling dynasty no longer entered Vreta. However, members of the high nobility with close connections to the throne continued to place their daughters there.[54]

Two of Benedicta's and Svantepolk's daughters also held the position of abbess at Vreta. The first, Katarina, held this post until 1322, when she was succeeded by her sister, Ingrid. Perhaps family connections played a role here. The first abbess of Vreta Abbey after its Cistercian reorganization was Ingegierd Sverkersdotter, who was Benedicta's great-great-aunt.[55] Certainly this family's strong interest in and close connection to Vreta Abbey was one means of maintaining an awareness of its royal origins. At the same time, it appears that the name and image of St. Katherine were another important means of marking royal ties. For several generations, the descendants of Benedicta and Svantepolk have a daughter named Katarina in each generation. In addition, women in the family who are not named Katarina depict St. Katherine in their seals.

In contrast to her sisters Katarina and Ingrid, Ingegierd Svantepolksdotter does not appear to have had a particular connection to Vreta Abbey. Perhaps it is significant in light of this fact that she is the first member of the family to depict St. Katherine in her seal.[56] It is quite clear that this seal should be understood as an expression of Ingegierd's personal devotion, since, like Ramfrid Gustavsdotter and Ingeborg Birgersdotter, Ingegierd is depicted kneeling in veneration of St. Katherine.[57] As in many depictions of the saint, St. Katherine's crown is clearly marked in this seal, as is her wheel. Interestingly, the attribute in Katherine's right hand in this seal is not her usual sword, the instrument of her martyrdom. Instead, it is a spire, the tip of which is shaped like a fleur-de-lis. Many images of St. Erik, the martyred king of Sweden, depict him holding a similar

---

Petersson, at the time magistrate of Östergötland. Apparently she did not marry him, and her abduction was no hinder to her marriage to Svantepolk. Ingrid, who was at the time betrothed to a high-ranking Danish nobleman, was in her turn abducted from Vreta in 1288 by Folke Algotsson. This act turned out to have devastating consequences for Folke's family, including his brother Karl, who was beheaded a year later, and another brother Bengt, at the time bishop of Skara, who was forced to humble himself in order to prove his loyalty to the king (*ÄSF*, 1, 259; Sands, "Saint as Symbol, 98).

[54] See K. Parikh, *Kvinnoklostren på Östgötaslätten under medeltiden: asketiskt ideal—politisk realitet* (Lund: Lund University Press, 1991), 46–59.

[55] Sands, "Saint as Symbol," 98.

[56] Affixed to *DS* no. 2333, 30 May 1322; not published, housed at Riksarkivet.

[57] Sands, "Saint as Symbol," 98.

spire.[58] Many versions of the legend of St. Katherine make clear that she was not just the daughter of a king, but a reigning queen in her own right. However, it is relatively unusual for a medieval Swedish image to make this point. There are a few depictions of St. Katherine together with other virgin martyrs in which Katherine is shown wearing a crown while the other virgins are not.[59] Although these images may simply be illustrating the point made by Jacobus of Voragine in the *Legenda aurea*, that Katherine is in every way to be distinguished from other saints, it is also possible that they are pointing to Katherine's specifically royal status. Given Ingegierd's own family connections, however, there can be little doubt about the meaning of the spire in St. Katherine's hand. While St. Katherine was certainly recognized as a powerful intercessor in general, her royal status is clearly an important part of her appeal for Ingegierd Svantepolksdotter.

At some point well before 1310, Ingegierd married Bryniolf Bengtsson, who was the son of Ramfrid Gustavsdotter's brother, Bengt Hafridsson.[60] Their known children include daughters named Katarina and Birgitta, as well as sons named Knut and Algot.[61] Interestingly, none of these children is named for a grandparent. It is entirely possible that the couple had other children, named in the usual way, who died before they were old enough to enter the written record. It is, however, interesting to note that at least two of the children, Knut and Katarina, have names that refer back to some of the more illustrious members of Ingegierd's family, her aunt, Queen Katarina Sunesdotter, and her grandfather, Duke Knut of Reval. At the same time, we should not forget the prominence of the Katherine tradition in Bryniolf Bengtsson's family. Hafrid Sigtryggsdotter, who founded the chapel of St. Katherine at Gudhem, was Bryniolf's grandmother. Ramfrid Gustavsdotter, who depicted St. Katherine in her seal, was his aunt, and he had both a sister and a cousin named Katarina. Katarina Bryniolfsdotter's seal, which has been preserved, depicts a heraldic lion similar to the one in the seal of her paternal grandfather. As I noted in 2003, this seal clearly expresses dynastic rather than devotional interest.[62] Birgitta's seal, however, is far more complex and far more interesting, managing to express a broad spectrum of interests at once. Like the seal of her mother Ingegierd, Birgitta Bryniolfsdotter's seal depicts St. Katherine. The saint's crown is clearly marked, as is the wheel she holds in her left hand. The object in her right hand appears to be a martyr's palm frond, rather than the lily-tipped spire of Ingegierd's seal. Like her mother, Birgitta also includes a depiction of her own devotion to the saint, although she is placed in a separate space below St. Katherine's feet, rather than kneeling in

---

[58] For examples see Thordeman, "Erik den helige," pl. XXII.

[59] One example is the St. Olav retable from Värmdö parish church, Uppland.

[60] See *DS* 1703, *ÄSF*, 117.

[61] *ÄSF*, 117.

[62] Sands, "Saint as Symbol," 99; seal published in *Svenska sigiller*, ed. Hildebrand, ser. 3, no. 714.

front of the saint, as in Ingegierd's seal. At the same time, unlike her mother's, Birgitta's seal also includes specific references to her paternal ancestry and her marriage. By St. Katherine's right foot is a shield bearing the arms of Bryniolf Bengtsson's family (identical to the arms in Katarina Bryniolfsdotter's seal), while the shield by St. Katherine's left foot depicts the arms of Birgitta's husband, the knight, royal councilor, and magistrate of Västmanland and Dalarna, Gregers Magnusson.[63] The composition of Birgitta's seal certainly demands that we see her relationship to St. Katherine as one of devotion. Without doubt, Birgitta regards the saint as her patron and intercessor. At the same time, it is tempting to interpret the saint's image as a symbol of Birgitta's royal ancestry through her mother. In this sense, the image of St. Katherine has a function equivalent to the shields that depict the family arms of Birgitta's husband and father. The symbolic importance of St. Katherine seems also to be reflected in the naming of Birgitta's daughter. In her marriage to Gregers Magnusson, Birgitta gave birth to two known children. Her son, Magnus, was named in the traditional way for his paternal grandfather. However, Birgitta and Gregers' only known daughter was named Katarina. It is particularly interesting that the couple did not have a daughter named Ingegierd, since that was the name of Gregers' mother as well as Birgitta's.[64] The name Katarina does not figure prominently among Gregers' ancestors, and must thus be assumed to refer to Birgitta's family. Again, it is possible that there were other daughters who died at a young age, but there is no evidence of their existence. This opens the possibility that the symbolic importance of St. Katherine, most likely as a symbol of royal ancestry, was so strong for the descendants of Svantepolk Knutsson and his wife Benedicta, and especially their daughter Ingegierd, that it overrode all other considerations in the naming of their daughters.[65]

Patronage

Although sigillographic images and chapel dedications may be among the most personal demonstrations of devotion to a particular saint, they are far from being the only ones. Another important source of information about the personal relationship of members of the nobility to specific saints is the artwork in parish

---

[63] *ÄSF*, 44; Sands, "Saint as Symbol," 99.

[64] See *ÄSF*, 43–45.

[65] The only known son of Svantepolk and Benedicta, Knut, apparently died unmarried and without issue. Katarina Svantepolksdotter appears to have remained in Vreta Abbey, and did not marry. Neither Ingrid, who was abducted from Vreta, nor the other daughter of Svantepolk and Benedicta, Ingeborg, is known to have had a daughter, though each had a son named Knut. Though these sons had children in their turn, they do not appear to continue the Katherine tradition, as neither has a daughter by that name (see *ÄSF*, 4–5, 10–12, 259).

churches. As surviving medieval charters show, Swedish aristocrats tended to take an interest in the churches in whose parishes they owned land. It is quite typical that their wills include bequests to every such church. In general, however, they tended to favor the church most closely linked to their primary manors. In some cases, there is a clear link between an aristocratic donor's decoration of a church and an inherited right of patronage. In other cases, there is no documentation of such a right, but the proximity of the manor to the church seems to be sufficient motivation for the donation. Like the dedications of chapels, prebends, and other foundations, and also like the images on seals, wall paintings, altarpieces, and freestanding sculptures in the parish churches can express a wide range of meanings, some of them strictly devotional, others with personal and political overtones. The placement of the images, both within the interior space of the church, and in relation to other images, can play a crucial role in understanding their symbolic and devotional meanings.

The great majority of the medieval Swedish wall paintings, altarpieces and freestanding sculptures that have survived to the present day date from the later Middle Ages, especially from the middle of the fifteenth century and onwards. As Carina Jacobsson has noted, earlier works tended to survive most often in churches that lacked the economic resources to update or replace their aging artworks.[66] Those congregations that could afford to modernize tended to do so. Furthermore, certain familiar forms, such as the winged retable, did not come into existence until the 1450s.[67] As a result, most of the images discussed in this section of the chapter date from the middle of the fifteenth century or later.

There are exceptions to this trend, however. The church of Östra Ryd, in the coastal region of southeast Uppland, has a large freestanding sculpture of St. Katherine that has been dated to circa 1300.[68] This piece is by far the earliest image of St. Katherine to survive in Uppland, and as such, it is not surprising that its origins are mysterious. It is of exceptionally high quality, and has stylistic traits that resemble those of sculptures from churches with a close connection to the Uppsala Cathedral chapter. It is very interesting, then, that there is no known connection between Östra Ryd and Uppsala other than the fact that the parish is located in the Uppsala archdiocese. It has been noted, however, that there was a high concentration of land in the hands of the nobility in this parish during the later Middle Ages, and that the owners of the manor Rydboholm were active in donating murals and a retable during the late fifteenth century.[69] The

---

[66] Jacobsson, *Höggotisk träskulptur*, 226.

[67] Paul Crossley, "The Man from Inner Space: Architecture and Meditation in the Choir of St. Laurence, Nuremburg," in *Medieval Art: Recent perspectives: A Memorial Tribute to C. R. Dodwell*, ed. Gale R. Owen-Crocker and Timothy Graham (Manchester and New York: Manchester University Press, 1998),165–82, here 169.

[68] Jacobsson, *Beställare*, 231.

[69] Jacobsson, *Beställare*, 282.

present church, itself built during the fifteenth century (and thus considerably later in date than the sculpture of St. Katherine), is located on land that formerly belonged to the estate of Rydboholm, which is a typical indicator of a "magnate's church." However, the record of the archbishop's visitation in 1303, along with the presence of inventory older than the present church building, suggests that this church was preceded by an earlier building.[70] Interestingly, the early fourteenth-century statue of St. Katherine is the only image of this saint to be found in the present-day church of Östra Ryd. She was clearly not among the saints of interest to the donors who painted the church and donated its altarpiece in the later fifteenth century. It has not been possible to identify the presumed fourteenth-century donor of the St. Katherine statue. However, it is clear there were landowners in the parish during the early fourteenth century who had ties to the Uppsala Cathedral chapter. Birger Petersson, for example, owned land in the parish during this period, as did Archbishop Peter Fillipsson, who traded a parcel here for land in another parish in 1335.[71] While it seems clear that the statue of St. Katherine was not donated by a member of the cathedral chapter in that capacity, it is quite possible that its donor was a member of the nobility with ties to the chapter.

Although it has not been possible to link the statue of St. Katherine from Östra Ryd with a specific aristocratic donor, there are other images of the saint the donors of which are known. For these images, it is possible to reconstruct a historical and social context that allows much more specific interpretation of their meanings for their donors and other viewers.

The parish church in Tensta, north of Uppsala, is a classic example of a magnate's church. It is built entirely of brick, which was a very exclusive building material in medieval Sweden.[72] Access to large amounts of brick more or less required that the builder of a church be exceptionally wealthy and well connected.[73] In addition to its building material, the parish church in Tensta has a number of architectural traits in common with Uppsala Cathedral, and it appears to date from the late thirteenth century, during which time the new cathedral was under construction. Noting that a large proportion of the land within the parish, including the property allotted to the church, was once in the hands of the nobility, Rahmqvist not only determines that Tensta is a magnate's church, but also

---

[70] Hjörvard Norén, Inga Norrby, Curt Sandin, and Carola Selbing, "Östra Ryds kyrka," *Upplands kyrkor*, vol. 13 (Uppsala: Stiftsrådet i ärkestiftet, 1978), 233–55, here 235.

[71] See *DS* nos. 1584, 3164.

[72] This material first appears in Sweden in the abbey churches of the Cistercian and Dominican orders during the thirteenth century. In those parish churches built by local farmers, the use of brick is usually confined to small ornamental details and window surrounds, while the rest of the church is generally constructed of rubble (Sw. *gråsten*).

[73] See Bonnier, *Kyrkorna berättar*, 63–64, 182–93; Ferm and Rahmqvist, "Stormannakyrkor," 67–84.

identifies the likely builder as Jakob Israelsson (d. 1281), archbishop of Uppsala and the uncle of Birger Petersson.[74] In spite of its aristocratic origins, Rahmqvist does not consider Tensta church to have been associated with any single estate complex during the later Middle Ages. If the builder of the church in fact was Archbishop Jakob Israelsson, it makes sense that the right to appoint the parish priest in Tensta would have been awarded to the future archbishops, rather than to aristocratic landowners belonging to the laity. Still, whether or not they held a hereditary right of patronage, the owners of the nearby estate complex of Salsta donated an extensive set of murals to the church in 1437. These murals are unusual for a number of reasons. They are, for example, one of only two sets of murals known to have been painted in Sweden by Johannes Rosenrod, a painter thought to be of German origin who perhaps worked in Sweden for only a short time.[75] They are also unusual because of the extensive suite of paintings depicting scenes from the life of St. Birgitta in the west end of the church. Not least, these murals are unusual in that they include not only the donor's coat of arms, a typical element in murals financed by Swedish nobles, but also his portrait. The donor of these paintings was Bengt Jönsson of the family known as Oxenstierna. By the time these murals were painted, the Oxenstierna family had come to be one of the most powerful lineages in Sweden. Little more than a decade after the date of the murals, Bengt Jönsson and his brother Nils would be named regents of Sweden after the death of King Kristoffer, who had ruled over the Kalmar Union, comprised of the three kingdoms of Denmark, Norway and Sweden. In the same year, 1448, Bengt's son, Jöns Bengtsson, would be elected archbishop of Uppsala.[76] Although these events occurred well after Bengt's donation of the murals to Tensta, the power base and relationships out of which they developed were already in place in the 1430s. Thus it is worth examining the images in the church for their political symbolism as well as for their devotional content.

On the north wall of the chancel of Tensta church, the murals depict the donor, Bengt Jönsson, together with a considerable group of saints. Bengt is depicted on his knees, holding up his coat of arms to St. Peter, who is depicted slightly above him and to his right.[77] The saint closest to Bengt, standing on the same patch of grass on which he is kneeling, is St. Katherine of Alexandria. To Katherine's right (further from Bengt) is St. Dorothy, and to Dorothy's right, St.

[74] Sigurd Rahmqvist, *Sätesgård och gods* (Uppsala: Upplands Fornminnesförening och Hembygdsförbund, 1996), 239–41.

[75] Nilsén, *Program och funktion*, 9.

[76] See Pernler, *Sveriges kyrkohistoria II*, 153–54.

[77] At the time these murals were painted, Bengt's son Jöns, who would later become archbishop of Uppsala, was completing his studies at the University of Leipzig: see Pernler, *Sveriges kyrkohistoria II*, 153. While it is tempting to see this image in relation to Bengt's ecclesiastical ambitions on behalf of his son, it probably more appropriate to regard St. Peter, the first pope, as a symbol of the Church and its authority in more general terms.

Lawrence. This grouping, including St. Peter, is placed slightly to the west of the door into the sacristy. On St. Peter's other side, directly above the sacristy door, the corresponding group of saints, likewise standing on a grassy patch, consists of St. Barbara (closest to St. Peter), followed by St. Margaret and St. Olav. This grouping is as fascinating for its omissions as for its inclusions. The Four Capital Virgins, Barbara, Dorothy, Katherine, and Margaret, were certainly popular intercessors, and widely depicted as a group in Swedish churches. Three of the saints in the grouping, St. Lawrence, St. Olav, and St. Katherine, are closely associated with Uppsala Cathedral. As I have noted in this chapter, it is not at all unusual for the nobility of Uppland to associate themselves with the cathedral and its chapter, often by means of images of or dedications to saints important prominent in the Uppsala liturgy. If this is Bengt's intent, it is striking that the saint omitted from the grouping is St. Erik, who was the patron saint of Uppsala Cathedral together with St. Lawrence and (according to some sources) St. Olav. It may be significant that Bengt was generally a supporter of the Kalmar Union, while St. Erik had come to be seen as a symbol for Sweden as a discrete kingdom separate from the Union, and had been so used by the rebels led by Engelbrekt Engelbrektsson, who had been murdered in 1436.[78] Perhaps the image of St. Erik was too closely associated with a movement he opposed to be placed close to Bengt's own image. Instead, St. Erik is depicted on the west wall of the chancel, closest to a saintly bishop who may be St. Henrik, though the identification is uncertain.[79] Interestingly, the other two patron saints of Uppsala, St. Lawrence and St. Olav, are not only associated with the Swedish archdiocese. St. Lawrence is also the patron saint of Lund, the Danish archdiocese, while St. Olav is the patron of Nidaros Cathedral, the highest church of Norway. St. Margaret's inclusion in the grouping may reflect the fact that she was the patron saint of Queen Margareta, the first monarch of the Kalmar Union.[80]

---

[78] See Sawyer and Sawyer, *Medieval Scandinavia*, 76; also Allan Etzler, "S. Örjens gille," *Med hammare och fackla* 3 (1931), 1–55, here 46–48.

[79] see Nilsén, *Program och funktion*, 144.

[80] It should be noted that Nilsén has a very different interpretation of the murals in Tensta, based in part on images described by Peringskiöld that are no longer in existence. According to Peringskiöld's description, a painting somewhere in the church -- no one has been able to determine the location more exactly -- depicts a donor, almost certainly Bengt Jönsson, kneeling at the feet of St. Erik (Nilsén, *Program och funktion*, 232). Nilsén accepts Peringskiöld's assertion, and builds upon it without commenting on the paintings in the chancel. Instead, she suggests that Bengt Jönsson was an enthusiastic devotee of St. Erik's, and that this devotion was an aspect of Bengt's political ambition. She notes:

> At some point before 1435 he had become a member of the Royal Council, and like the rest of the Council at this time, he found himself in opposition at the time the murals were painted to the Union King, the despised Erik of Pomerania, who was deposed in 1439. In this situation, Bengt Jönsson may have had an interest in connecting his

St. Katherine's placement in the composition is not entirely easy to understand. There is no evidence that St. Katherine was a particular favorite of the Oxenstierna family. While members of the family occasionally married women named Katarina, the name does not tend to recur among the family's daughters.[81] I am not aware of any seals that depict the saint belonging to women of the Oxenstierna family, nor of their having donated to foundations in the name of St. Katherine. Although Bengt's son Jöns was engaged in university studies at the time the murals were painted, and later became a member of the Uppsala Cathedral chapter, he studied at Leipzig, not Paris. Thus there is no reason to assume that Katherine's placement in the murals indicates that Jöns Bengtsson was especially devoted to her. However, there is a possibility that the image of St. Katherine in the chancel of Tensta church serves to mediate between the depiction of Bengt Jönsson and the extensive suite of murals depicting the life of St. Birgitta in the west end. Sigurd Rahmqvist has pointed out that Bengt Jönsson was a distant relation of St. Birgitta's through his mother, who was descended from Birgitta's aunt, Katarina Bengtsdotter.[82] He suggests that Bengt's maternal relations were themselves devotees of St. Birgitta, who passed on this interest to Bengt. Birgitta, who had been canonized in 1391, was by the 1430s already a figure of high prestige in Sweden, and Bengt had good reason to regard her both as an intercessor and as a symbol of his own status. As I have argued previously, the placement of St. Katherine directly behind Bengt's image in the chancel may be a reference to the fact that his grandmother, Katarina Magnusdotter, was the granddaughter of Katarina Bengtsdotter, Birgitta's maternal aunt.[83] By linking Bengt's own image in the chancel to the depiction of St. Birgitta in the west end, the image of St. Katherine serves an important symbolic and devotional function. At the same time, it is not certain that St. Katherine herself is to be regarded as a special intercessor for Bengt. Although he is shown kneeling at her feet, his back is turned to her, as he reaches up toward St. Peter. This seems to

own person with that of St. Erik, the protector of the kingdom. It would also appear that he had major plans for his son Jöns, later archbishop and guardian of St. Erik's own church. This too may have been a stimulus to his depiction of St. Erik. Jöns entered the University of Leipzig in 1434 and was a baccalaureate already by 1436. He took his master's degree in 1438. The next time he is named, the following year, he is already Dean of Uppsala. Perhaps by this time Bengt was already aspiring to the position of Magistrate (*lagman*) of Uppland, which he achieved in 1439. If this was the case, he had yet another reason to associate himself with the figure of St. Erik, whose "own" law he would be administering. Clearly, a number of factors lie behind this depiction (Nilsén, *Program och funktion*, 441; translation mine).

[81] See Gillingstam, *Ätterna Oxenstierna och Vasa*.

[82] Rahmqvist, *Sätesgård*, 242–43.

[83] Sands, "Saint as Symbol," 104–5.

strengthen the argument that St. Katherine in this context should be regarded primarily as a symbolic mediator, and not as a central figure in her own right.

Although this interpretation of the image of St. Katherine in the chancel of Tensta church is an example of the extreme flexibility of St. Katherine's image and legend, it is by no means typical of the depictions of the saint in later medieval Sweden. A later set of murals in the porch of Tensta church, possibly commissioned by a later owner of Salsta, includes an image of St. Katherine that can be interpreted in a much more conventional way. Pernilla Nilsdotter was the widowed second wife of Bengt Jönsson's grandson Sten Kristiernsson. It appears likely that she was the donor of the murals, dated to the 1520s.[84] In the north ceiling vault of the porch, St. Katherine is depicted together with images of St. Barbara, the Virgin and Child (the Woman of the Apocalypse), and Christ in Majesty. This placement suggests a more typically devotional interpretation of the image, even though most of the images in this suite of murals are cautionary rather than devotional in nature. The motifs on the walls of the porch include the wheel of fortune, images depicting the consequences of failing to attend church, others warning of the immanence of death. Only a few other saints are depicted in these paintings, including St. James the Greater and Sts. Erik and Olav. The small number of saints depicted suggests that each of these images has a specific motivation. Pernilla Nilsdotter was one of at least sixteen siblings, of whom only three, all daughters, are known to have survived to adulthood. One of the sisters, Elsa Nilsdotter, disappears from the record in 1505, and her husband later remarried. The other sister, Katarina, died in 1520. Perhaps the image of St. Katherine in this suite was at least in part a memorial to Pernilla's sister. In this case, St. Katherine's intercession might be of particular interest to the donor.[85] None of the other saints depicted in this suite are name saints for any member of Pernilla's family, but it may be that her sister's death was of particular concern to her at the time the murals were commissioned.

Another magnate's church in Uppland has a depiction of St. Katherine that appears to arise not just out of devotional concerns, but out of specific circumstances within the family that held the right of patronage. The parish church of Vendel, a few kilometers northwest of Tensta, is also a large brick church with elaborate architecture and decoration.[86] The church had an unusually large number of secondary altars during the Middle Ages, which suggests liturgical practices much more advanced than those in the usual parish church. On at least two occasions during the thirteenth and fourteenth centuries, archbishops of Uppsala explicitly claimed the right of patronage over the church, and awarded

---

[84] Rahmqvist, *Sätesgård*, 227, n. 91.

[85] *ÄSF* 82–84; see also Sands, "Saint as Symbol," 106.

[86] See Bonnier, *Kyrkorna berättar*, 197–206.

it to members of the cathedral chapter.[87] This circumstance may help to explain some of the church's unusual features. In spite of the claims of the archdiocese, however, the right of patronage was also claimed and implemented by various owners of Örby, a large estate complex located within the parish. Rahmqvist speculates that the estate's claim to this right may have arisen out of a fourteenth-century conflict between on the one hand Dukes Erik and Valdemar Magnusson, who rebelled against their brother, King Birger Magnusson, and on the other, the archdiocese of Uppsala. During the years 1314–1315, Valdemar illegally imposed a tax on church property in the archdiocese, especially properties belonging to the cathedral. If the owner of Örby at this time was a follower of the dukes, it might help to explain how both the archdiocese and the later owners of Örby considered themselves legitimate holders of the right of patronage.[88]

No matter how the owners of Örby came to claim the right of patronage over Vendel church, we know that they made use of it on more than one occasion during the middle of the fifteenth century. In 1445, the owners of Örby, Agneta Eriksdotter and her stepson Knut Stensson (Bielke), appointed a new parish priest for the church.[89] Sometime thereafter, a suite of murals was painted in the church by Johannes Iwan. According to an inscription, the paintings were completed in 1451. Among the paintings are two scenes from the martyrdom of St. Katherine, located on the south wall of the nave. The first scene depicts an angel smashing the wheelworks on which Katherine was about to be tortured. A Latin inscription reads: 'Virgo d(u)m clamat de celis angelus astat' [While the virgin cries out, the angel from heaven is near]. In the next scene, we see Katherine's beheading. Her soul is shown flying up from her headless body toward an angel, while another angel catches her head. The emperor Maxentius may be identified among the onlookers. The inscription for this scene reads: 'Percussa gladio dat lac pro Sanguine collo' [Struck by the sword, her neck gives milk instead of blood].[90]

The owners of Örby during this period were closely connected to Karl Knutsson (Bonde), who ruled as king of Sweden in defiance of the Kalmar Union for three separate periods, from 1448 to 1457, 1464–1465, and 1467–1470. Knut Stensson, mentioned above, was Karl Knutsson's half brother, while Agneta Eriksson was the second wife of Knut's father, Karl Knutsson's stepfather, Sten Turesson (Bielke).[91] As I have discussed previously, the images from the martyrdom of St. Katherine seem to have a specific connection to circumstances in Karl Knutsson's life.[92] In 1438, Karl had married Katarina Karlsdotter (Gumsehu-

---

[87] Bonnier, *Kyrkorna berättar*, 197–206; Rahmqvist, *Sätesgård*, 154–58, 193–95.

[88] Rahmqvist, *Sätesgård*, 194–95.

[89] Rahmqvist, *Sätesgård*, 193.

[90] See Nilsén, *Program och funktion*, 164 for description of the murals.

[91] See Rahmqvist, *Sätesgård*, 139, 160.

[92] See Sands, "Saint as Symbol," 101–3.

vud), a member of another powerful aristocratic family. She was crowned Queen of Sweden in 1448, and died on 7 September 1450.[93] The particular composition of the scenes from St. Katherine's legend, together with the dating of the murals, suggests that these images should be read as a memorial to the recently deceased queen. The queen and the saint had both their name and their royal status in common, and it is likely that the murals would have included an image of St. Katherine even without the additional motivation of the death of a queen closely connected to the owners of the estate. However, the fact that the murals show the saint's death, and in particular the ascension of her soul to heaven, seems to confirm the assumption. Surely these paintings are not only a memorial, but also a plea for the saint's intercession on behalf of Queen Katarina's soul.[94]

As I have noted in the past, it is not entirely certain who owned Örby at the time the murals were painted. Late in 1451, Agneta Eriksdotter had sold part of the estate to her nephew, Johan Kristiernsson (Vasa), who was also one of her heirs, and who was married to a niece of Karl Knutsson's. Agneta died some time before 1453, the year in which her estate, along with those of her late husband Sten Turesson and his first wife, Margareta Karlsdotter, was settled. The heirs to Sten and Margareta's portion of the estate were their daughters, Birgitta and Katarina, and Margareta's son, Karl Knutsson.[95] While it is not known who commissioned the murals in the parish church of Vendel, it is clear that it must have been one (or perhaps several) of the members of this extended family.

Interestingly, another image painted just above the scenes depicting St. Katherine's martyrdom confirms the suspicion that the scenes are to be linked with the death of Queen Katarina. At the top of the south wall of the nave is a detailed depiction of St. George's battle with the dragon. In addition to the horrible dragon, the brave knight and his white horse, the scene also includes the rescued princess and her lamb (both of whom had expected to be eaten by the dragon), and in the distance, the "city" of Cappadocia. As Jan Svanberg has pointed out, the cult of St. George the Knight (as opposed to a cult focusing on the saint as a martyr) was introduced to Sweden by Karl Knutsson, and images of this saint became enormously popular during and after his reign.[96] It appears that Karl Knutsson regarded St. George as his personal patron saint. This makes it almost certain that the combination of Sts. Katherine and George, in a suite of paintings commissioned by someone close to Karl Knutsson, must be a direct reference to Karl and his recently deceased queen.

---

[93] *ÄSF*, 63.

[94] Sands, "Saint as Symbol," 103.

[95] Rahmqvist, *Sätesgård*, 160; Sands, "Saint as Symbol," 103.

[96] Jan Svanberg and Anders Qwarnström, *Sankt Göran och draken* (Stockholm: Bokförlaget Rabén-Prisma, 1993, repr. 1998), 30–31.

St. Katherine and St. George

As I will argue below, there is reason to believe that the images on this wall in Vendel church gave rise to another symbolic usage of the image of St. Katherine. In a small number of images from the end of the fifteenth and the beginning of the sixteenth century, depictions of St. Katherine together with St. George appear to enlist her as a helper in the anti-Kalmar Union, nationalist movement in Sweden. In spite of their influence on other images, however, it does not appear likely that the images of St. Katherine and St. George in Vendel church should be read as a statement of political affiliation. Indeed, it is not certain that they are even, primarily, devotional images. Vendel church was dedicated to the Virgin Mary, who is naturally featured prominently in the murals decorating the chancel. The chancel also includes a depiction of two scenes from the martyrdom of St. Barbara. Both the Virgin and Child and St. Barbara reappear among the paintings in the vaulted ceiling of the church porch, where both are depicted with donors or supplicants at their feet. The south wall of the porch also features a depiction of the three Nordic saintly kings, St. Olav, St. Erik, and St. Knut.[97] The medieval church in Vendel is not entirely intact. Portions of the wall of the nave were destroyed in conjunction with the construction of an addition in the 1730s, and one of the two original porches has been pulled down.[98] However, while some images have certainly been lost, the images in the porch convey some information about the commissioners and their interests. Clearly, someone among the commissioners of the paintings was a devotee of the Virgin Mary (which is hardly surprising) and more interestingly, of St. Barbara. St. Katherine and St. Barbara do appear together in a set of murals in the chancel arch, but Rahmqvist has suggested that these paintings may date from around the time the church was built, possibly as early as the 1290s.[99] Otherwise, however, Katherine does not appear in proximity either to St. Barbara or to the Virgin Mary, though both are her frequent companions in medieval Swedish churches. It would seem, then, that St. Katherine is not an object of the devotions of the commissioner to the same degree as these other two saints. While the paintings should clearly be seen as a plea for intercession, it would appear that that intercession is sought primarily on behalf of Queen Katarina Karlsdotter. The political opinions of the person or persons who funded and (apparently) planned these murals are also uncertain. The three saintly kings, Olav, Erik, and Knut, are martyred kings of Norway, Sweden, and Denmark, respectively. When they appear together, they may be understood as representing the Kalmar Union, which combined the three

---

[97] Nilsén, *Program och funktion*, 161–64.

[98] Nilsén, *Program och funktion*, 161.

[99] Rahmqvist, *Sätesgård*, 155–57.

kingdoms under one ruler (in practice, typically the monarch of Denmark).[100] Given the political circumstances in Sweden during the middle of the fourteenth century, it is unlikely that anyone would be unaware of the connotations of a combined depiction of the three Nordic kings, each of whom is regarded as his country's patron saint. The fact that such an image appears in the porch of Vendel church suggests that while the commissioners of the murals acknowledged their familial relationship to Karl Knutsson and his queen, they may not have been entirely sympathetic to his political views.

While I do not believe that the depiction of St. Katherine and St. George in Vendel church should be taken as a statement of the donors' political opinions, there is reason to believe that these paintings came to influence later artworks, in which the combined images of St. Katherine and St. George could indeed be understood as a political statement. After Karl Knutsson's death in 1470, his position as regent was assumed by his nephew, Sten Gustavsson Sture. Except for brief periods of effective Danish rule, Sten Sture the Elder, as Sten Gustavsson Sture is generally known, maintained control of Sweden until his death in 1503.[101] In addition to his politics, Sten Sture also shared his predecessor's devotion to St. George. The most famous and spectacular example of this devotion is the more-than-life-sized group of sculptures depicting St. George's battle with the dragon that Sten Sture commissioned for the City Church of Stockholm (St. Nikolai, also known as "Storkyrkan," "The Great Church") following his victory over Danish forces in the Battle of Brunkeberg in 1471.[102] As a knight himself, St. George was certainly perceived as the most effective of intercessors for those doing battle for a just cause. In the popular imagination, of course, the dragon could easily be equated with the enemies of the country (in this case the Danes), and the saint with the regent. Many images of St. George in Swedish churches, dating from the reign of Sten Sture, would appear at least in part to be expressions of support for Sten Sture's efforts in resisting the Kalmar Union. Although there is no evidence that Sten Sture himself was a particular devotee of St. Katherine, it is notable that there are several sets of images dating from his reign, in which St. Katherine and St. George are paired in contexts that suggest that Katherine's image, too, could be interepreted to support the anti-Union cause.

In an article published in 1991, Jan Svanberg demonstrated that a set of sculptures decorating the pulpit in the parish church of Tillinge, to the west of Uppsala, were actually the components of a winged retable originally com-

---

[100] Louise Berglund, *Guds stat och maktens villkor: Politiska ideal i Vadstena kloster, ca 1370–1470,* Acta Universitatis Upsaliensis, Studie Historica Upsaliensia 208 (Uppsala: Historiska institutionen vid Uppsala universitet, 2003), 17.

[101] See Sawyer and Sawyer, *Medieval Scandinavia,* 78.

[102] Swanberg and Qwarnström, *Sankt Göran.*

missioned for the church on the estate of Ängsö.[103] As Svanberg reconstructs it, the corpus of the altarpiece consisted of a group with the Virgin Mary in the center, flanked by St. Katherine and St. George on either side. The wings of the triptych contained reliefs depicting scenes from the martyrdoms of St. Katherine and St. George. This interesting combination of saints would appear to have a connection to the anti-Unionist politics of Sten Sture and his followers. The triptych has been dated to the end of the fifteenth century.[104] Ängsö was unusual, if not unique, in Sweden in that it functioned almost as a kind of independent state within a state. In contrast to other magnates on whose estates churches had once been built, the owners of Ängsö retained direct control of their church, without having to submit to the authority of the bishops of Västerås until shortly before the beginning of the eighteenth century. The owner of the estate retained economic and judicial control over the inhabitants of his island, and he also had the economic responsibility for making, and the right to make, decisions regarding the church and its priest.[105] The various owners of the estate have been among the leading families of Sweden, and this was no less true during the late fifteenth century than in the preceding or the following centuries. The owner at the time the altarpiece must have been commissioned was Bengt Fadersson (d. 1494), whose family is referred to on the basis of their arms as "Sparre of Ängsö and Hjulsta" (Hjulsta being their other major estate). Bengt was the son of Fader Ulfsson (d. 1488), a royal councillor and knight who had supported Sten Sture. Bengt's maternal grandfather was another of Sten Sture's supporters, Nils Bosson (Sture).[106] Both Fader Ulfsson and Nils Bosson were among the contributors to the great St. George group in Stockholm, commissioned by Sten Sture to commemorate his military victory in 1471. Their arms appear among those of other donors on the monument. As Svanberg notes, there was good reason for Fader Ulfsson, his wife Elin Nilsdotter (d. 1470s), and their son Bengt Fadersson to wish to commission an altarpiece dedicated to St. George, who by now had come to be viewed as a kind of national patron saint, for their own private church. He further suggests that the altarpiece may well have been a testamentary gift to Ängsö church, donated by Fader Ulfsson for the sake of his wife's soul and his own. Another possibility is that it was commissioned by their son, though also for the sake of his parents's souls, whether or not there was such

---

[103] Jan Svanberg, "Ett helgonskåps historia: Från altare i Ängsö till predikstol i Tillinge," in *Kyrka och socken i medeltidens Sverige*, Studier till det medeltida Sverige 5 (Stockholm: Riksantikvarieämbetet, 1991), 321–51.

[104] Svanberg, "Helgonskåps historia," 324.

[105] See Svanberg, "Helgonskåps historia," 346; Åke Nisbeth, *Ängsö kyrka och dess målningar* (Stockholm: KVVAA/Almqvist & Wiksell International, 1982), 16–17.

[106] It is important to note that these names refer to the heraldry in each family's coat of arms. They were not, for the most part, used during the Middle Ages, and do not necessarily imply a familial relationship.

a provision in their testaments.[107] Some of the reliefs depicting the martyrdom of St. George are closely related to those on the base of the Stockholm group, which strengthens the argument that the donors of the Ängsö altarpiece wanted to express their relationship to its commissioner.[108]

Given the degree of devotion accorded to the Virgin Mary in all of medieval Christendom, the presence of her image in the triptych is hardly surprising. However, the reasons for including St. Katherine are not as immediately obvious. Svanberg speculates that the reliefs depicting her martyrdom are based on an otherwise unknown triptych that must have stood on the altar of St. Katherine in the City Church of Stockholm.[109] Whatever the antecedents of the reliefs from Ängsö, however, I would contend that specific elements in the legend of St. Katherine, perhaps in combination with the knowledge of the murals in Vendel and their association with Karl Knutsson, make St. Katherine an appropriate intercessor and example for the anti-Union cause. According to one version of her legend, St. Katherine of Alexandria was a reigning monarch, who inherited her kingdom from her father. The Christian Katherine came into conflict with the heathen Roman emperor, who alternately wooed and threatened her, finally having her beheaded in frustration at her stubborn refusal to sacrifice to his gods. In her refusal to yield to either the blandishments or the threats of the more powerful emperor, Katherine might be seen as an example to be emulated by the nationalist factions of Sweden. Her status as a sovereign ruler in her own right would add to the symbolic force of her image. Although St. Katherine, like St. George, is eventually martyred, this is, of course, the ultimate source of her power as a saint. In no way does it detract from her efficacy as example and intercessor.

One other factor may have played some role in the choice of saints for the Ängsö retable. As its unusual status suggests, Ängsö was very much a magnate's church. All evidence suggests that it was built by the powerful knight Nils Abjörnsson, who owned the estate during the middle of the fourteenth century. The church, which is, like Tensta and Vendel, architecturally complex and built entirely of brick, appears to have been completed before 1346.[110] Unlike most other churches from this period, however, Ängsö has a suite of murals, damaged from having been whitewashed (perhaps as early as the seventeenth century), but relatively intact and dating from the 1340s.[111] The section devoted to saints in this suite of murals is not complete, since portions of the chancel and nave were broken up when the south transept was added in the seventeenth century, and other paintings were damaged or hidden by the construction of the organ in the

---

[107] Svanberg, "Helgonskåps historia, 346–47.
[108] See Svanberg, "Helgonskåps historia," 347–48.
[109] Svanberg, "Helgonskåps historia," 347.
[110] Nisbeth, *Ängsö kyrka*, 60–61.
[111] See Nisbeth, *Ängsö kyrka*, 197–205.

west of the nave.[112] However, a number of depictions of saints are preserved. On the south wall of the nave there are depictions of two saints whose knightly aspects are emphasized, namely St. Martin, shown on horseback with the beggar who is really Christ in disguise, and St. George, shown fighting the dragon in defense of the princess. Both of these depictions are highly unusual for the four-teenth century, and Nisbeth suggests that their presence in the church is directly related to Nils Abjörnsson's own exalted status. Above St. Martin is a depiction of the popular virgin martyr St. Margaret, shown with long, loose hair, but not wearing a crown. Near St. Margaret, on the other side of a window, is a depic-tion of St. Katherine with her wheel, and unlike Margaret, Katherine is wearing a crown. The image on the other side of St. Katherine seems to be an allegorical scene the content of which is difficult to determine. Most of the other paintings on this wall have been destroyed, though it is possible to make out scenes from the martyrdom of St. Lawrence. Over the sacristy door are several monastic or mendicant saints including St. Francis, and perhaps St. Clare and St. Bernard or Anthony of Padua.[113]

It is not my intention to claim that the images of St. George and St. Kather-ine are connected to each other in these early murals from Ängsö. At the death of Nils Abjörnsson, Sweden was still several decades away from its entrance into the Kalmar Union, and there appears to be no reason to interpret the images of St. George and St. Martin as anything but appropriate examples and interces-sors for a pious man of high social status. If anything, perhaps they are there to serve as a reminder that power also entails a responsibility toward those who need help and protection. What the image of St. Katherine does show, however, is that the donor seemed to regard her status as considerably higher than St. Margaret's. Whether this is a reflection of the fact that St. Katherine is the only reigning monarch among the virgin martyrs, or a reference to her importance in the liturgy of Västerås or, even more likely, Uppsala Cathedral is not certain. It is known, however, that Nils Abjörnsson, like his father, chose to be buried in Upp-sala Cathedral.[114] The depiction of the martyrdom of St. Lawrence, the earliest patron saint of Uppsala, may arise out of this connection. Still, whatever factors lie behind the depiction of St. Katherine in this suite of murals, it is quite pos-sible that the late fifteenth-century owners of Ängsö noted her importance in the murals that still decorated the church in their time, and considered themselves to be following an established tradition in honoring her. Ängsö church has one further depiction of St. Katherine, whose meaning would appear to be strictly devotional. She appears, together with her fellow female saints St. Barbara, St. Dorothy, and St. Mary Magdalene, in the doors to a shrine depicting St. Anne

---

[112] Nisbeth, *Ängsö kyrka*, 110.

[113] Nisbeth, *Ängsö kyrka*, 112–15.

[114] Nisbeth, *Ängsö kyrka*, 15.

with the Virgin and Child. This piece has been dated to the second half of the fifteenth century. The fact that St. Katherine is prominently featured in three different contexts in Ängsö church suggests that she was highly regarded by the owners of the estate throughout the medieval period. It may thus be reasonable to sense a degree of continuity in the depiction of St. Katherine as a crowned figure (in contrast to the uncrowned St. Margaret) in the fourteenth-century murals and her appearance together with St. George, perhaps in the specific role as intercessor for the anti-Unionist party, in the fifteenth-century winged retable.

At least two other churches have paired depictions of Sts. Katherine and George from around the year 1500, a time during which Sten Sture was embattled, but not without support.[115] Häverö parish church, in the coastal area of the archdiocese known as Roslagen, has a depiction of the martyrdom of St. Katherine on the north wall of the nave, paired with a depiction of St. George and the dragon in the corresponding position on the south wall. It is worth noting that the scene from St. Katherine's legend in Häverö depicts the angel smashing the wheels on which Katherine was to be tormented. This corresponds to the first of the two scenes from her martyrdom in Vendel church. St. Katherine is not the only virgin martyr depicted in this church, but the depictions of her fellow martyrs are quite different, which supports the hypothesis that Katherine's image is to be interpreted differently from theirs. As in a number of other Uppland churches, the murals in Häverö include a large number of scenes from the Old and New Testaments, with relatively fewer depictions of non-biblical saints. Among the images in the chancel vaults are a large number of scenes from the Old Testament. Several of these are paired with images of virgin martyrs. St. Apollonia is paired with Samson and the lion, St. Ursula with an image of Abraham and Isaac on their way to the sacrifice, and St. Margaret with Abraham's sacrifice.[116] The implication of these images clearly links the martyrs' sacrifice of their own lives with Abraham's sacrifice of his son, and with Samson's valiant fight. The images of St. Katherine and St. George are much larger and more prominently placed. Their positions on opposite walls of the nave means that anyone who enters the church will see them. The placement of the images is also, without doubt, explicitly intended to link them together. Each of the paintings is placed at the top of a deep arch, the interior of which is covered in ornamental patterns.[117] Further, both of the images are separated from the fields below them by stenciled bands. The depictions of virgin martyrs in the chancel are simple portraits of the saints with their attributes, not scenes from their martyrdoms. This too suggests that the image of St. Katherine should be accorded a different,

---

[115] See Nilsén, *Program och funktion*, 19–20, 98.

[116] Described in Nilsén, *Program och funktion*, 98–99.

[117] It is worth pointing out that the depictions of St. George and St. Katherine in Vendel church are also placed in such a niche, though in that church St. George is placed over the two scenes from St. Katherine's martyrdom.

or further, meaning. Although both St. George and St. Katherine are martyrs, it may be significant that these images depict them not at the moment of their death, but in their spectacular triumph over powerful opponents. While I do not know the precise circumstances of land ownership in Häverö parish at the time these murals were painted, their content suggests that a connection to Sten Sture is likely. Sten Sture is known to have been more restrained in his taxation of the peasantry than most late medieval rulers of Sweden, and as a result he tended to have broad support among this group. It is possible that the initiative for these particular images could have come from an aristocratic donor, from the farmers of the parish, from a local parish priest with anti-Union sympathies, or from a combination of two or all of these sources.[118]

The parish church of Söderby (now Söderby-Karl, since the neighboring parish of Karlskyrka was combined with it in the 1790s) is located some kilometers to the south of Häverö, and has murals from the same period, around 1500. Four motifs appear on the south wall of the chancel. On the east side of the window is a fragmentary depiction of Elias's ascension to heaven. Over the window are two dragons with their necks intertwined. West of the window, a depiction of St. George and the dragon is placed directly over an image of St. Katherine, who is shown wearing a crown, grasping a large sword and a large wheel.[119] The paintings on the east wall of the chancel depict the arms of Sten Sture and of Archbishop Jakob Ulfsson. This indicates that the murals were painted during their respective reigns, but does not necessarily indicate that they had any personal interest in the content of the murals.[120] It is of interest that a cousin of Karl Knutsson was among the major landowners of this and the neighboring parish beginning in the 1470s.[121] These lands were inherited in the 1520s by a son of Sten Sture the Younger, who, while not related by blood to Sten Sture the Elder, followed him in his position as anti-Union regent of Sweden. It is not unlikely that the owners of these lands had anti-Union sympathies. Since it was a frequent practice for landowners to contribute to the churches in parishes where they owned significant holdings, it is quite possible that there is a connection between the murals and the political sympathies of local landowners.[122]

---

[118] For a discussion of Sten Sture's relationship to the peasantry, see Janken Myrdal, *Jordbruket under feodalism 1000–1700*, Det svenska jordbrukets historia 2 (Stockholm: Natur och kultur/LTs förlag, 1999), 154, 194–98.

[119] Nilsén, *Program och funktion*, 140–41.

[120] Nilsén, *Program och funktion*, 223.

[121] Sigurd Rahmqvist and Lars-Olof Skoglund, *Det medeltida Sverige: Uppland: 5. Attundaland Lyhundra, Sjuhundra* (Stockholm: Riksantikvarieämbetet, 1986), 96–105, 62–71.

[122] Another set of murals that may fit into this category can be found in Vallby church in southwest Uppland (Trögd). St Katherine is shown on the east wall of the chancel together with a number of other saints, including St. Lawrence and St. Birgitta. However, on the south

Although the depictions of St. Katherine together with St. George discussed in this section represent only a tiny fraction of the images of the saint from medieval Sweden, the particular circumstances of their origin, placement, and date suggest that they can be understood to have a specific set of political as well as devotional meanings. As always, these meanings in no way exclude the possibility that other meanings were implicit in the images at the same time. Nor does the use of the image of a saint by one group necessarily exclude the possibility that other groups or individuals might depict the same saint in other contexts, and for entirely different, even opposing, reasons.

As I have tried to demonstrate in this chapter, St. Katherine of Alexandria had many devotees among the medieval Swedish nobility, just as she had among the clergy. In some cases, it is clear that the saint's status in clerical circles, especially among members of the Uppsala Cathedral chapter, is an important aspect of her popularity among the noble laity. St. Katherine is one of the saints most frequently depicted in the seals of aristocratic women in Sweden, and one of a very few to appear in seals of women not named for her. Even for these women, the saint seems to embody a wide range of meanings having to do with family connections, but perhaps also with other aspects of personal identity. While donations, seals, and naming traditions within families can convey important information about individual devotion to St. Katherine, there is also much of significance to be found in the murals and sculptures decorating many of Sweden's parish churches. In some cases, there is specific information that links a particular church, its murals, or a particular sculpture or altarpiece to a known donor. In other cases, it may be surmised that a particular image or set of images was donated by a local landowner, even if the identity of the donor is not known. Clearly, St. Katherine's ability to appeal to a large group of people with varied interests has to do in part with her general popularity, and with a widespread appreciation of her power as an intercessor. At the same time, Katherine's legend seems to have had a flexibility not shared by the legends of her fellow virgin martyrs. She seems to have been able to function as a symbol of royal origins, as a patron saint for married women as well as for virgins, and even as a symbol of political resistance.

---

wall of the nave, below a depiction of St. George and the dragon, is a damaged painting that may depict the beheading of St. Katherine (Nilsén, *Program och funktion*, 157–58).

FIGURE 3.1
Vendel parish Church (Uppland).
St. George and the dragon, St. Katherine's martyrdom
Tracey R. Sands.

FIGURE 3.2
Häverö parish church (Uppland).
St. George.

Photo: James Massengale.

FIGURE 3.3
Häverö parish church.
St. Katherine's martyrdom.

Photo: James Massengale.

IV
GOTLAND, A LAW UNTO ITSELF?

The Baltic island of Gotland, located roughly sixty miles off Sweden's east coast, presents a special set of problems for the understanding of the cult of St. Katherine of Alexandria in medieval Sweden. For much of the medieval period, Gotland fell within the area in question. For this study, the most decisive factor in determining which provinces can be termed Swedish and which cannot is their relationship to the Swedish church. Even after Gotland was invaded by the Danish king in 1361, and afterward, when it was occupied first by pirates and later by the deposed Union king, Erik of Pomerania, it remained part of the diocese of Linköping, and as such could be considered officially, if not practically, a part of Sweden's ecclesiastical structure. The unique circumstances of Gotland's relationship to the rest of medieval Sweden may also be reflected in the way that the cult of St. Katherine develops here.

Gotland's Historical Background

In order to understand the particular circumstances of the cult of St. Katherine in Gotland, and how the cult here relates to the cult in mainland Sweden, it is necessary to examine the history of Gotland's relationship to Sweden proper. Culturally, linguistically, and politically, Gotland had close ties to the Swedish mainland for centuries before the beginning of the Middle Ages, but it was not a fully integrated part of what would become the core of the Swedish kingdom. Although the nature of the Gotlanders' relationship to the rulers of the Swedish mainland is not entirely clear, it has been suggested that it may have involved reciprocal trade agreements, as well as, possibly, payment of tribute to the King of the Svear in exchange for some degree of protection. It has also been suggested that there was some kind of organization governing Baltic trade as early as the ninth century, and that Gotland was involved in this.[1]

---

[1] Åke Hyenstrand, *Socknar och stenstugor: Om det tidiga Gotland*, Stockholm Archaeological Reports 22 (Stockholm: Department of Archaeology, University of Stockholm, 1989),

Certainly the best-known source for the early history of Gotland is the so-called *Guta saga*, a narrative appended to the sole medieval manuscript containing the *Gutalagen*, or Gotlandic law code.[2] The precise age of the saga has not been determined, but it appears to be a compilation parts dating mainly to the thirteenth and fourteenth centuries.[3] The saga makes a strong argument for the independence and autonomy of the Gotlanders, stating that the Gotlanders themselves sought the alliance with the "king of the Svear" that resulted in their paying him a tax of sixty silver marks per annum. In exchange, the Gotlanders were to be granted free access to all parts of Sweden, as well as freedom from tolls and other fees. The Svear were to have corresponding rights in Gotland. Further, the Gotlanders could turn to the king for help and protection.[4] Like other medieval narratives, *Gutasagan* must be regarded as strongly tendentious. Historical sources from the medieval period tend to focus on the Svear as the most important sources of political influence for early Gotland. Hyenstrand notes, though, that the period from roughly 1000 to 1100 or 1150 is marked by a stream of coins from the south and west, including both Danish and Swedish coins. This suggests that, even in this early period, Gotland's trade contacts with other Nordic regions were not entirely dominated by the Svear. Both *Gutasagan* and a number of runic inscriptions bear witness to armed conflicts in the immediate area of Gotland, and these might be interpreted as an indication that several different northern European centers of power had an interest in the island. These would include not only groups emanating from the Swedish Mälar region, but also from Denmark, and perhaps even from Russia.[5]

The saga also has considerable information about the Gotlanders' conversion to Christianity. According to the third chapter of the saga, the first person to introduce Christianity to the island was the Norwegian king Olav Haraldsson (d. 1030), who after his death came to be venerated as one of the most popular saints in the entire Nordic region, and not least in Sweden. Although St. Olav made some converts, the greater movement toward Christianity is attributed to Gotlandic traders, who visited Christian lands and observed their customs. Some of them, according to the saga, underwent baptism, and brought Christian priests with them when they returned home. Several prominent Gotlanders built churches on their lands, and managed to convince their pagan neighbors

---

18–19; Kenneth Jonsson, "Hansatiden på Gotland i ett numismatiskt perspektiv," *Gotländskt arkiv* 69 (1997), 7–18, here 7.

[2] *Svenska landskapslagar: Skånelagen och Gutelagen*, ed. Åke Holmbäck and Elias Wessén (Stockholm: AWE/Gebers, 1979), LXIV.

[3] Hyenstrand, *Socknar*, 14; Sven-Erik Pernler suggests that *Guta saga* was probably completed by around 1220 (see *Gotlands medeltida kyrkoliv*. [Visby: Barry Press Förlag, 1977], 60).

[4] *Svenska landskapslagar*, 292–93.

[5] Hyenstrand, *Socknar*, 133.

not to destroy them. "Once the Gotlanders had seen the customs of Christian men, they obeyed God's commandments and the teachings of learned men. As a body, they accepted Christianity freely, without compulsion, so that no one forced them to Christianity."[6]

Once this voluntary and peaceful conversion had taken place, the saga tells us, the Gotlanders found themselves in need of a bishop. In the beginning, they were able to turn to bishops who visited Gotland as pilgrims on their way to or from Russia, Greece or Jerusalem. These bishops consecrated churches and churchyards at the request of the early church builders. Soon, however, the Gotlanders recognized their need for a bishop of their own, and, pragmatic as ever, they turned to the bishop of Linköping, "because he was closest." The saga specifies the conditions that the Gotlanders presented to the bishop, as well as the services that they expected from him.[7] Whether or not *Guta saga's* version of events, in which the independent Gotlanders steered their relationship to the developing Swedish kingdom and the diocese of Linköping, can be deemed reliable, the connection to the bishop of Linköping was a fact during the entire medieval period. Interestingly, the voluntary nature of the Gotlanders' connection to Linköping is confirmed in a charter issued in the early 1220s by the archbishop of Lund and the bishop of Linköping.[8] According to this document, "when this land first voluntarily accepted the Faith, it subjected itself, without anyone's compulsion, to the church of Linköping."[9] Numerous attempts have been made to determine when Gotland was incorporated into the diocese. It has been suggested that this had already occurred by around 1120, the date traditionally attributed to the so-called Florence Document, which lists a number of Swedish metropolitan centers (which can in their turn be interpreted as the names of most of the known Swedish sees). This document lists Gotland among other known regions of Sweden, which might suggest that the island's incorporation into Linköping diocese had already taken place.[10] In any case, most scholars are in agreement that it had occurred, at the latest, by the time that Sweden acquired its own archdiocese in the year 1164.[11] Even though the connection between Gotland and the diocese of Linköping appears to have been of long standing, it does not appear to have been a typical one, since the bishop of Linköping was not entitled to a portion of the tithes paid by Gotlanders.[12]

---

[6] *Svenska landskapslagar*, 293–94.
[7] *Svenska landskapslagar* 294–95.
[8] *DS* no. 832.
[9] Pernler, *Gotlands medeltida kyrkoliv*, 60.
[10] Hyenstrand, *Socknar*, 17.
[11] Pernler, *Gotlands medeltida kyrkoliv*, 58–63; Nilsson, *Sveriges kyrkohistoria I*, 79–83; Hyenstrand, *Socknar*, 17; Majvor Östergren, "Det gotländska alltinget och Roma kloster," *Gotländskt arkiv* 76 (2004): 40–45, here 43–44.
[12] See Pernler, *Gotlands medeltida kyrkoliv*, 133 ff.

Matters of land ownership, particularly those having to do with the aristocracy and the various ecclesiastical institutions, are well documented for most of
the medieval Swedish mainland. However, circumstances are somewhat different for Gotland. The aristocratic families of mainland Sweden never owned land
here, and there does not seem to have been a corresponding local nobility with
connections to royal power and freedom from land dues. This fact may be one of
the contributing factors in the popular assumption that medieval Gotland was
an "egalitarian republic of free peasants."[13] Rönnby suggests that this widespread
notion is a local variant of the idealized Nordic peasant farmer so prominent
in nineteenth-century Scandinavian political thought, as well as an important
aspect of the more recent marketing of the island as a center for tourism.[14] Furthermore, the absence of representatives of the established Swedish nobility does
not mean the absence of powerful local chieftains.[15] In fact, Gotland appears
to have been governed by a central assembly roughly equivalent to the medieval
Icelandic system. This means that Gotland was divided into a group of twenty
local assembly districts, each of which had its own judge or chieftain.[16] These
chieftains and their followers would undoubtedly have functioned as a local or
regional elite.

According to the Gotlandic Law Code, *Gutalagen*, land could not be sold
to buyers outside of a lineage. Even lands not deemed to be ancestral holdings
were to be sold only to potential heirs. If the heirs were for any reason unable
to purchase the lands, they were to be purchased by leading men in the local
district (hundred). Further, all sale and purchase of land had to be confirmed by
the members of the local assembly. Failure to follow any of these requirements
would result in significant fines.[17] This passage certainly strengthens the notion
that Gotland was in many ways a separate entity from the rest of the Swedish
realm, and it may well explain why none of the noble families of Sweden became
established here. Even the church and the various monastic houses, which came
to control a major part of medieval Swedish land holdings, held far smaller and
more isolated properties in Gotland.[18] It is also notable that Gotland was never
part of the "Eriksgata," the route the king of Sweden took when he visited the

---

[13] Jonas Rönnby, *Bålverket: Om samhällsförändring och motstånd med utgångspunkt från
det tidigmedeltida Bulverket i Tingstäde träsk på Gotland*, Studier från UV Stockholm, Arkeologiska undersökningar, skrifter nr. 10 (Stockholm: Riksantikvarieämbetet, 1994), 122.

[14] Rönnby, *Bålverket*, 122–23.

[15] See Hyenstrand, *Socknar*, 133.

[16] Östergren, "Det gotländska alltinget," 40–41.

[17] *Svenska landskapslagar*, 229.

[18] See Roger Öhrman, *Vägen till Gotlands historia* (special issue of *Gotländskt arkiv* 66
[1994]), 95.

various parts of his kingdom, and that the Swedish crown did not have royal officers in Gotland.[19]

Whatever the nature of the political relationship between Gotland and the Swedish mainland, it is clear that the island could and did develop its own trade routes, contacts, and treaties, independent of Swedish influence. Numismatic evidence suggests that Gotland had begun to develop strong ties to the increasingly important Russia trade early in the ninth century.[20] By the early twelfth century, Gotlanders had established their own trading station, the Gutenhof, in Novgorod, and the trade with Russia came to be a major source of the island's considerable wealth.[21] For much of the century that followed, Gotlanders exerted considerable control over Russian trade with western Europe, since German traders had to associate themselves with the Gutenhof. When the German-based Hansa finally acquired its own trading station in Novgorod in 1259, it was a major blow to the Gotlandic economy, and the beginning of the island's economic decline.[22] During the same period that the Gotlandic trade with Russia was at its height, another major trading partner was on the rise. During the middle of the twelfth century, Henry the Lion of Saxony brought the coastal lands formerly controlled by the Slavic Obodrites under his own rule. An earlier German trading center was rebuilt here at Henry's command, and the city of Lubeck came into being around 1159. Henry offered free trade agreements to the rulers of the Swedes, Danes, and Norwegians, and in 1161 he entered into a trade agreement with a leading group of Gotlanders.[23] In addition to their trading agreements with Russia and Lubeck, the Gotlanders also had early trading ties with the Danes. The Danish king Valdemar I is known to have given Danish traders permission to establish a guild in honor of St. Knut in Gotland, probably in Visby, around 1170, and runic inscriptions indicate that Gotlandic trade in Russian pelts was directed toward the Danes, perhaps as early as the eleventh century.[24] Because of agreements with the developing Hanseatic League, Gotlandic traders enjoyed free trading rights across a wide area of western Europe, and not least in England and Flanders, until the last decades of the thirteenth century.[25]

---

[19] Östergren, "Det gotländska alltinget," 40.

[20] Jonsson, "Hansatiden," 7.

[21] Gun Westholm, *Hanseatic Sites, Routes and Monuments* (Visby: Länsstyrelsen på Gotland, 1996), 12.

[22] Westholm, *Hanseatic Sites*, 19–20.

[23] Jonsson, "Hansatiden," 11.

[24] Curt Wallin, *Knutsgillena i det medeltida Sverige* (Stockholm: KVHAA, 1975), 99; Gun Westholm, "Gotland, hansan och de bevarade spåren av en epok," *Gotländskt arkiv* 69 (1997), 71–94, here 76.

[25] Westholm, "Gotland, hansan," 77–78.

Gotland's location in between the major trading centers of eastern and western Europe, and the advantages that Gotlanders were able to derive from it led to a level of prosperity that most inhabitants of the Swedish mainland in this period could only dream of. While the wealth of the island's inhabitants during the later Viking Age can be seen in the large and relatively frequent silver hoards deposited in or near Viking Age dwellings, the surplus income of medieval Gotlanders financed building projects, both stone houses and churches.[26] To a degree hardly seen in the rest of Sweden, the churches of Gotland reflect a remarkable prosperity during the early part of the Middle Ages, followed by a strong economic decline beginning in the late thirteenth century.

Up to the middle of the thirteenth century, the Gotland trade seems to have been relatively evenly distributed between the farming/trading families of the countryside and the townsfolk of Visby. Although Visby began as one harbor among many, by the twelfth century it was on its way to becoming Gotland's most prominent trading center. As such, it attracted not only Gotlanders but also traders of other nationalities, who gradually made it a base for their activities. By the late 1180s there was a colony of German traders in Visby who, together with visiting German merchants had formed a guild. By 1190, this guild had built and had consecrated the chapel in honor of the Virgin Mary that would eventually become the parish church for all Germans in Visby.[27] While the Germans seem to have been the most populous and most powerful group in Visby, they were not the only foreigners to establish themselves there. Russian sources record that traders from Novgorod began to visit Gotland during the 1130s, and at least up to 1371 they are known to have had a trading station in Visby, as well as a Russian Orthodox church.[28] In addition, a Danish traders' guild is known to have existed in Visby during the last decades of the twelfth century, while early thirteenth-century law codes from Slesvig also record the presence of traders from Gotland at markets on the Jutland peninsula.[29]

One result of the international presence in Visby was that the city gradually became more and more a center of Hanseatic trade, and less and less a part of the larger Gotlandic trading community. City and countryside began to regard each other as increasingly bitter rivals, a circumstance that culminated in the fortification of the city. During the 1280s, the German and Gotlandic residents of Visby cooperated to build a huge city wall around the entire settlement. The wall was intended not to protect Visby from enemies approaching by sea, but rather to divide it from the surrounding countryside. The farmer/traders of rural Gotland appear to have regarded the wall as a demonstration of hostility, and as proof that

---

[26] See Westholm, "Gotland, hansan," 78–79.

[27] Hugo Yrwing, *Visby – hansestad på Gotland* (Lund: Gidlunds, 1986), 36–37, 20.

[28] Yrwing, *Visby*, 44–45.

[29] Hugo Yrwing, *Gotlands medeltid* (Visby: Gotlandskonst AB, 1978), 117.

the long-established community of Baltic traders on the island was threatened. In 1288 a troop of rural Gotlanders attacked Visby and fell before the city wall. King Magnus Ladulås of Sweden, who had tightened his grip on the island's rural populations three years earlier, now intervened on their behalf, forcing the townsfolk of Visby to accept conditions that afforded the rural Gotlanders some degree of protection. Even if some degree of peace had been restored, however, the division between city and countryside was now a fact, and Visby's status as a Hanseatic, rather than a Gotlandic, center was greatly strengthened. A further result of this circumstance appears to have been a weakened position for the Gotlandic merchants residing in Visby. Now that they no longer had the support of the rural trading community, they were increasingly dominated by the German families, whose Hanseatic connections were much stronger.[30]

It is clear, then, that in spite of its status as a part of the Swedish diocese of Linköping and, at least by the later thirteenth century, a possession of the Swedish crown, Gotland was not fully integrated into the medieval Swedish kingdom. Although it is quite clear that members of the local elite were actively engaged in building and adorning the island's parish churches, these people did not record their transactions in written form as did the mainland aristocracy, with the result that they are not known by name.[31] It is much more difficult (perhaps even impossible) to connect Gotlandic churches and their inventory to specific individuals than it is to make similar connections for many mainland churches. As a result, the discussion of the importance and meanings of the cult of St. Katherine here is in many ways much more general than the corresponding discussion for other parts of medieval Sweden. Since Gotlanders left few charters, there are few seals to discuss. It is clear that the Cistercian monastery at Gutnalia (Roma) played an important role in the island's religious and even secular culture, and equally, that the Dominican and Franciscan friars who established themselves in Visby influenced a large number of Gotlanders. However, the lack of written documents makes the exact nature of these differences elusive.

St. Katherine of Alexandria in Gotland

Gotland's unique economic and political circumstances during the Middle Ages are to a great degree reflected in the island's churches, both in the rural parishes and in Visby. Interestingly, the cult of St. Katherine appears to have been important in Gotland from a relatively early period, and there is good evidence that devotion to the saint occurred among all of the major groups of Gotlandic society, from the monastic and mendicant orders to the laity of the country parishes and

---

[30] Yrwing, *Visby*, 114–15.

[31] See Yrwing, *Gotlands medeltid*, 12.

among the German/Hanseatic population of Visby. Although most of Gotland's medieval churches are still standing, and although a greater proportion of their early medieval paintings and inventory have been preserved than in most other parts of Sweden, it should be remembered that what remains is only part of what once existed. Although this chapter deals only with preserved or documented artworks, this does not exclude the possibility that St. Katherine was represented in other churches, from which she has disappeared without a trace.

Although late Viking Age Sweden, like Gotland during the same period, had considerable contact with the Russian and Byzantine realms, it is generally thought that the Orthodox church had relatively little influence on the introduction and development of Christianity in Sweden, and medieval Swedish churches on the mainland show little or no evidence of contact with the east.[32] However, because of its location and its close trading contacts with Novgorod, Gotland shows a greater degree of contact with the artistic traditions of the Byzantine world. As Gunnar Svahnström points out, a surprisingly large number of parish churches from rural Gotland have at least traces of mural paintings in Russian-Byzantine style. Stone churches with paintings in Byzantine style include Källunge, Garde, Mästerby, and Havdhem. Additional paintings in Byzantine style have been found on wooden planks originating from wooden churches that preceded the stone churches in the parishes of Sundre, Dalhem, and Eke. Swahnström suggests, cautiously, that the paintings on wood can be dated to approximately the later twelfth century, while the murals in the stone churches can be dated, allowing for a wide margin of error, to around 1200.[33] He considers it likely that this style of painting, and probably the artisans who produced it, came to Gotland as a result of the Gotlandic farmer/traders' visits to Novgorod, a city with a considerable number of churches. As the trade with Novgorod came increasingly under German control, the necessary preconditions for Russian influence on the decoration of Gotlandic churches disappeared, a circumstance that helps to explain why all paintings of this type in Gotland date from a relatively brief and early period.[34]

Alskog

Is there any connection between the cult of St. Katherine of Alexandria in Gotland and the strong eastward connections of the Gotlandic traders? It must be stated from the beginning that there are no surviving or documented images of St. Katherine among the murals in Russian-Byzantine style from the Gotlandic

---

[32] Nilsson, *Sveriges kyrkohistoria* I, 63–64.

[33] Gunnar Svahnström, *Rysk konst från Vladimir den helige till Ivan den förskräcklige: 1000–1550* (Visby: Ödins förlag, 1993), 158–78.

[34] Swahnström, *Rysk konst,* 178.

churches. Whether the saint's popularity in the Byzantine world had any influence on her cult in Gotland can neither be demonstrated nor disproved. Only one account suggests that there is even such a possibility. The parish church of Alskog was apparently dedicated to St. Katherine, and at least one of its surviving medieval sculptures, which an eighteenth-century artisan attempted to transform into a portrayal of an Old Testament prophet, once depicted St. Katherine.[35] Although much of the church's medieval inventory has disappeared, Bishop Jöran Wallin, during his visitation in the year 1737, noted that the church had three wooden altarpieces. One of these, on the high altar, depicted the passion of Christ, and also contained an image of St. Katherine. The second altarpiece, on the altar of the Virgin Mary, was in poor condition at Wallin's visit, but he notes that it included a depiction of the Wise and Foolish Virgins. The third altarpiece merits his particular attention:

> ... the other has been most lovely, with precious (*kostelig*) painting and well gilded. It contains the story of the life of St. Katherine. In the center we see St. Katherine whole and complete, in full dress, with 12 smaller sections, 6 on each side of her, and on each section its content is inscribed with Greek or Russian characters. This has been a precious object, and came from a far-off land.[36]

How are we to interpret Bishop Wallin's description? No trace of this altarpiece has been preserved to the present day, and Wallin's description is the only documentation of its existence. No other altarpieces or sculptures of Russian/Byzantine origin have been found in Gotland. Was Wallin's description accurate? Was this altarpiece an anomaly? Wallin's description does not allow a close estimate of the altarpiece's age, though the developments in the Gotlanders' trade with Russia suggest that impulses coming from that part of the world would tend to belong to the earlier rather than the later Middle Ages. Another interesting question is what relationship the altarpiece, assuming that Wallin's description is accurate, had to the cult of St. Katherine in Alskog's church. Certainly the cult of St. Katherine was well established in the Byzantine church before it spread to the west. It is not implausible that Gotlanders engaged in trade in Novgorod might have come into contact with the saint's cult there. However, there is no specific evidence linking this parish to the Gutahof. One farm in the parish is known to have had a stone building dating from the Middle Ages, which suggests that at

---

[35] Erland Lagerlöf, *Alskogs kyrka*, Sveriges kyrkor 118 (Stockholm: Almqvist & Wiksell, 1968), 208. Swahnström (see Erland Lagerlöf and Gunnar Svahnström, *Gotlands kyrkor* [Stockholm: Rabén & Sjögren, 1966], 79) suggests a date of around 1300 for this sculpture and the others assumed to have come from the same altarpiece. Jacobsson (*Höggotisk träskulptur*, 214) discusses this piece among a group of sculptures that she dates to around 1350–1375.

[36] Lagerlöf, *Alskogs kyrka*, 208–9.

least one household enjoyed significant profits from trade, but this in itself does not indicate where these traders had their contacts.[37] Like many other Gotlandic parish churches, Alskog's church was built and remodeled in stages, beginning around 1200 and continuing into the early fourteenth century. However, this church has no traces of Russian/Byzantine painting, and its well-known rood is classed among a group of high-quality, late twelfth-century sculptures thought to have been executed in Gotland, under the influence of both German and French style.[38] The architecture of the church does not seem to point to close ties with the Cistercian monastery of Gutnalia (Roma) or with the Dominican priory in Visby. In the absence of specific documentary evidence linking the parish to Novgorod, the altarpiece described by Wallin must be regarded as (at best) a mysterious anomaly. Still, the dedication of the church remains, and it raises an interesting question. Is it possible that, in this case, the choice of St. Katherine as church patron arises out of Gotland's close ties to Novgorod? This would, of course, suggest a devotion to the saint arising out of her popularity in the Byzantine church rather than the Western, which the altarpiece described by Wallin might well confirm. As uncertain as it is, Wallin's description at least opens the possibility that the cult of St. Katherine in Gotland might have arisen out of a greater variety of influences than in other parts of the Nordic region.

St. Katherine and the Cistercians

While the parish church of Alskog may be an exception, it is remarkable that the majority of churches in Gotland with one or more images of St. Katherine appear to have some connection to the Cistercian monastery of Gutnalia, frequently called "Roma kloster." In addition, the parish church in Björke, which has no known or surviving image of St. Katherine, was known to be dedicated to her, and is also known to have had a guild for which she was patron. Björke parish was a close neighbor to Roma, and is known to have been closely connected to the monastery.[39]

According to Kersti Markus, the parish church of Buttle belongs to Gotland's oldest group of Cistercian-influenced churches. At the end of the thirteenth century, or perhaps as late as the middle of the fourteenth century, Buttle's chancel was rebuilt with a straight east wall, a trait typical of Cistercian architecture, and a modification that also occurred in Björke.[40] A sculpture of St. Katherine

---

[37] Westholm, "Gotland, hansan," 79–84.

[38] See Jacobsson, *Höggotisk träskulptur*, 35.

[39] See Sven-Erik Pernler, "S:ta Katarina-gillet i Björke," *Gotländskt arkiv* 58 (1986): 67–92; Kersti Markus, *Från Gotland till Estland: Kyrkokonst och politik under 1200-talet* (Kristianstad: Mercur Consulting OY, 1999), 43; also below 000–00

[40] Markus, *Från Gotland*, 43.

in an altarpiece from this church has been dated to about 1400.[41] The corpus of the retable depicts the Crucifixion, while the doors contain four sculpted figures. In one door, St. Katherine, wearing a crown and holding a fragment of a wheel, stands beside a bishop whose only remaining attribute is a book. In the other door, St. Olav is shown together with a female saint wearing a wimple and holding a book, perhaps St. Birgitta.[42] Fide church, in the southernmost part of Gotland (Sudret), has a retable dating from the early sixteenth century, depicting the Madonna and Child surrounded by a group of saints, including St. Katherine and St. George. Although Markus considers Dominican influence to be stronger than Cistercian in this part of Gotland, she notes that the architecture of Fide church more closely resembles that of the group of churches in northern Gotland that are associated to a greater or lesser degree with the building workshop at Roma monastery. She also suggests that the parish church of Hall may be connected to the building workshop at Roma.[43] This church has a mural depicting St. Katherine, dated to the fourteenth century, in its chancel arch.[44]

The parish church of Kräklingbo is of particular interest in the present discussion. This church has four surviving images of St. Katherine, including a mural dated by inscription to the year 1211, a painted image on a choir bench dating from the early fourteenth century, and two images in a retable dating to the early sixteenth century.[45] Kräklingbo church, and indeed all of the churches in the law district (*ting*) of Kräklinge, show evidence of exceptionally close contact with the Cistercian monks of Roma. Roosval and Lagerlöf suggest that the extant stone church in Kräklingbo was built at the suggestion or initiative of a lay brother from Roma around the year 1180.[46] Markus detects strong Cistercian influence in the architecture of all the district's churches.[47] Among the architectural evidence for this statement is the structure of the chancel in Kräklingbo church. Citing Hilding Johansson, Markus notes that the high altar in Cistercian churches always had a free-standing position in the interior of the church, rather than being placed against a wall. This was because the space behind the altar had specific liturgical functions. Since the high altar at Kräklingbo is placed in the center of the widest part of the chancel, Markus concludes that

---

[41] According to the Catalog of Iconography at ATA.

[42] Sigurd Curman and Johnny Roosval, "Buttle kyrka," in *Kyrkor i Halla ting: södra delen*, ed. Johnny Roosval. Sveriges kyrkor 68, Gotland 4:3 (Stockholm: Generalstabens litografiska anstalt, 1952), 380–408, here 399.

[43] Markus, *Från Gotland*, 48, 57.

[44] Catalog of Iconography, ATA.

[45] Catalog of Iconography, ATA.

[46] Johnny Roosval and Erland Lagerlöf, "Kräklingbo kyrka," in *Kyrkor i Kräklinge ting: nordvästra delen*, ed. eidem, Sveriges kyrkor 84, Gotland 4:4 (Stockholm: Generalstabens litografiska anstalt, 1959), 466.

[47] Markus, *Från Gotland*, 52, 88.

the arrangement of this space may also have specific liturgical meaning here.[48] Another sign of Cistercian influence in the district of Kräklinge may be the degree of simplicity and restraint that these churches display, "almost as if there were strict rules for church buildings and the acquisition of inventory." Indeed, six of the seven churches in the district did not even acquire their baptismal fonts until the middle of the thirteenth century, even thought the churches themselves are much older.[49] All of the churches in this district are extremely basic in their architecture, especially up to the beginning of the fourteenth century. Only then does Kräklingbo, the leading church in the district, acquire a nave in Gothic style. All of these circumstances suggest a Cistercian connection.[50] One possible explanation for the apparent Cistercian influence in Kräklinge district might be that the monastery of Gutnalia held the right of patronage to the churches in the district. Although this was not entirely in accordance with Cistercian principles, it is known that Cistercian monasteries in Denmark had the right of patronage over several parish churches there.[51] Indeed, it could happen a good deal closer to home. In the year 1279, Bishop Henrik of Linköping conferred the right of patronage for the parish church of Ås, on the island of Öland, upon the Cistercian monastery of Nydala "to be used in any way allowed by the rules of the order."[52] It may be of interest that Nydala was the mother house of Gutnalia. As church patron, a monastery was responsible for the building and maintenance of the church, and for its decoration. It would also have to employ a parish priest to make sure that the needs of the parish were met. Church patrons had the right, in some circumstances, to a portion of the church's income, which was undoubtedly the main motivation for a spiritual institution to seek such a position.[53] The lack of early baptismal fonts in Kräklinge district may indicate that the Cistercian monks in Roma administered this sacrament for parishioners. Another possibility is that residents of this district were instead encouraged to baptize their children in the churches of the neighboring districts, since the monastery's main motivation in holding the right of patronage was to gain maximum economic benefit.[54]

---

[48] Markus, *Från Gotland*, 40.

[49] Markus, *Från Gotland*, 138.

[50] Markus, *Från Gotland*, 139.

[51] Markus, *Från Gotland*, 140.

[52] See *DS* no. 661; Axelsson, Janzon and Rahmqvist, *Det medeltida Sverige 4:3: Öland*, 320; see above, 29.

[53] See Markus, *Från Gotland*, 140–41.

[54] Markus, *Från Gotland*, 141. While no known documents confirm that the monks of Gutnalia held the right of patronage for the churches of Kräklinge district, or for the parish of Kräklingbo, the evidence is quite convincing, especially given that similar circumstances are known to have existed elsewhere in the diocese of Linköping.

Does St. Katherine's prominence in Kräklingbo church have any connection to Cistercian influence? It is worth noting that the saint is featured among the suite of very early paintings on the north wall of the chancel. According to a painted inscription, they date from 1211, which is also believed to be the year that the original "core church" was consecrated. The present-day nave is an addition dated to 1260–1285.[55] It should be noted that the chancel in the church as it now stands was originally the nave. The earliest chancel, which appears to have had an apse, was torn down, perhaps around 1300, and the original nave now became the chancel.[56] In this early mural, St. Katherine is portrayed as a woman standing inside a stylized, tower-like construction. Although the painting is in less than perfect condition, having been whitewashed in 1767 and uncovered in 1908,[57] it appears that the saint is wearing a crown. Her other attributes are much clearer, and confirm her identification. In her right hand she holds a wheel, while she carries a martyr's palm branch in her left. Outside of the tower, a larger figure is portrayed on St. Katherine's right. This figure, at least twenty-five percent larger, is a female saint with an ornate halo, wearing a wimple. She has no other visible attributes, and is thus difficult to identify. Given the difference in size between these two figures, and the fact that St. Katherine is portrayed within a castle- or tower-like construction, it does not appear that they are to be understood as connected to one another. The fact that St. Katherine is depicted standing in a tower (or the like) may be a reference to her legend, in which she was beaten, starved, and imprisoned in a tower for her refusal to sacrifice to the pagan gods of Rome. On the other hand, this is not a depiction of a scene from the legend, since the saint is depicted with her clothes intact, wearing a crown, and holding the wheel that is her most frequent attribute. The suite of paintings immediately below the image of St. Katherine depicts scenes from the life of the Virgin Mary, including the Annunciation, the meeting of Mary and Elizabeth, and the birth of Christ.

The choir bench from Kräklingbo is now housed at the Gotland Museum. Although it is damaged, it depicts a line of saints standing under a gothic canopy. The group of saints includes St. Olav, St. Katherine of Alexandria, and a male saint wearing a crown and holding what may be a spire.[58]

The most spectacular images of St. Katherine in this church are certainly the ones in the late medieval altarpiece, which has been attributed to the so-called "Ekeby Master," apparently a Gotlandic artisan who produced a number of well-known wooden sculptures from his workshop in Visby at the beginning of the sixteenth century.[59] The corpus is a depiction of the Virgin Mary's visit to

---

[55] Lagerlöf and Roosval, "Kräklingbo," 466.
[56] Lagerlöf and Roosval, "Kräklingbo," 474.
[57] Lagerlöf and Roosval, "Kräklingbo," 484.
[58] Lagerlöf and Roosval, "Kräklingbo," 506.
[59] Lagerlöf and Roosval, "Kräklingbo," 496.

her cousin, Elizabeth, mother of John the Baptist. Flanking this central motif are the figures of St. Nicholas of Myra and the apostle St. Bartholomew, who is thought to have been the patron saint of Kräklingbo.[60] Each of the doors contains two figures. On the right, the outer figure is St. George, dressed in armor and standing on a dragon. The inner figure is St. Katherine, wearing a crown and holding a sword. On the other door, the outer figure is St. Barbara, wearing a crown, holding a chalice, and standing beside a tower. Beside her is the figure of St. Olav, also crowned and dressed in armor, holding his axe and standing on a small dragon with a man's crowned head. Interestingly, the outer doors of this altarpiece also depict St. Barbara and St. Katherine. This means that these two saints were visible to the congregation whether the altarpiece was closed, as it undoubtedly was most of the time, or open as it would have been on the more important feast days. The image of St. Barbara on the exterior door is a very typical depiction of this saint. She is shown full length, wearing a crown and reading in an open book. Beside her is a tower, within which can be seen a chalice and the host.

The image of St. Katherine is more unusual. Certainly, the saint has her typical attributes, including a very large sword, and a wheel at her feet. Like St. Barbara, she is wearing a crown, but her dress is much more richly patterned, and is inscribed with her name at the bodice and at the hem. The difference in the quality of the painting may result in part from the restoration of the altarpiece in 1908, as a part of the general restoration of the church. Certainly the execution of the image of St. Katherine gives an impression of greater age and complexity than that of the details in the image of St. Barbara. In the background painting behind St. Katherine's head are several signatures, one of them including the date 1688. These appear to be graffiti rather than reference to an earlier restoration, and they may indicate that much of this painting is original. Some of the details, including the saint's hair and her shoes, the brick wall behind her, the wheel, and part of the sword, may show signs of a more recent hand. The most important aspect of this image, however, is the large gold ring, ornamented with a stone, that St. Katherine holds up in her left hand. Photographs taken prior to the restoration show that the depiction of the ring is unchanged. Although this motif is relatively unusual, it does occur in depictions of St. Katherine in the Nordic region and elsewhere, and it refers to the mystic marriage, in which St. Katherine is married to the Christ Child, and has a ring placed on her finger. The composition of this altarpiece may well point to Cistercian influence, even at the end of the Middle Ages. The central motif of the retable, the meeting of the Virgin Mary with her cousin Elizabeth, is consistent with the Cistercians' particular devotion to the Virgin, who was the patroness of the entire order and of all its monasteries and churches. It is interesting that three of the four preserved

---

[60] Lagerlöf and Swahnström, *Gotlands kyrkor*, 173.

images of St. Katherine in Kräklingbo place her in the immediate vicinity of an image of the Virgin Mary (with the focus on Mary herself, not on the Christ Child). It might be noted that the sculpted figures in the altarpiece fall into three categories: two spiritual leaders (the bishop St. Nicholas and the apostle St. Bartholomew), two armored defenders of the faith (St. Olav and St. George), and two brides of Christ, the virgin martyrs Barbara and Katherine. The image of St. Katherine on the exterior door of the retable underscores her role as the foremost bride among brides, since it emphasizes not only the instruments of her martyrdom (which is what constitutes the "marriage" for most virgin martyrs), but also the specific narrative in which Katherine becomes the bride of Christ before her death, and indeed, as a prologue to the events of her passion. It is tempting to suppose that the person or persons who commissioned this altarpiece wanted to encourage devotion to brides of Christ, perhaps by emphasizing their effectiveness as intercessors. I have suggested above that St. Katherine's status as the most prominent of the brides of Christ (after the Virgin Mary herself) might explain much of her appeal to the Cistercian order. It may be, then, that the composition of this altarpiece points to continued Cistercian influence in Kräklingbo at the end of the Middle Ages.

Although a small number of late medieval altarpieces such as the one in Kräklingbo can be found in its churches, it is widely recognized that Gotland's economic boom was over by the middle of the fourteenth century. This was the result of a number of different factors, including the German-based Hanseatic League's increasing control of the trade with the east. During this period, trading harbors also began to develop on the eastern shore of the Baltic. Reval (Tallinn) began to export grain from its own hinterland, but it also came to have increasing importance as a port for Russian goods. Together with Riga, Reval began to assume to leading role within the Hanseatic trade in the Baltic that Visby had once held.[61] The civil war between the residents of Visby and the rural Gotlanders in the 1280s had had severe consequences for the traders outside of the city, but now the residents of Visby also found themselves in difficult straits. After the arrival of the plague in 1350, the island and the city of Visby were invaded by the Danish king, Valdemar Atterdag, in 1361. Nonetheless, in this battle as in earlier ones, the greatest loss of life occurred among the rural population. According to contemporary sources, as many as 1800 men died in the final battle outside of the city wall of Visby in conjunction with Valdemar's invasion. Westholm notes that if this number is compared to the number of farms on the island during the fourteenth century, it can be concluded that, on average, each farm on Gotland lost more than one man of fighting age in this battle alone.[62] The Danish conquest of Gotland put Denmark in a position to compete with the Hanseatic League to a

---

[61] Westholm, "Gotland, hansan," 90.

[62] Westholm, "Gotland, hansan," 90.

degree that the Hanseatic leaders found intolerable. During the 1360s the kings of Sweden and Norway, together with the Hanseatic League and other enemies of Denmark, mounted a campaign the goal of which was to force the Danish crown to give up not only Gotland but also Öland and Skåne. Although the Danish king managed to maintain his hold on Gotland, the Hanseatic League attempted to levy a tax of 2000 marks on Visby, as a contribution to the cost of the war.[63] As if the loss of control over trade routes, the conquest of the island by a foreign power, and the human losses to disease and battle were not enough, the Gotlanders found themselves confronted with an even worse problem during the 1390s. From 1396 to 1398, the island was occupied by a league of pirates known as the Vitalians. This group was headed at least in part by Duke Erik of Mecklenburg, a son of the deposed Swedish king, Albrecht. The Vitalians attacked Hanseatic ships, but they also plundered Visby and the countryside. The reign of the Vitalians was finally ended by the arrival of the Teutonic Order of Knights in 1398. This group maintained control of the island for ten years, in part to keep it out of the hands of the Danish monarchs, whose policies continued to be hostile to Hanseatic interests.[64] In 1408, Erik of Pomerania, Queen Margaret's heir and co-regent over the Kalmar Union, gained control of Gotland in exchange for a large payment to the Teutonic Knights. When Erik found himself deposed and forced from his holdings in Sweden, Norway, and Denmark in 1436, he withdrew to Visby, which became a base for his own plundering and piracy until his death in 1449. After Erik's death the piracy continued, and it was not until 1525 that a fleet from Lubeck managed to uproot the last of the Danish pirates from the island.[65]

It is widely recognized that the churches of Gotland reflect the economic circumstances of the island to a high degree. During the twelfth and thirteenth centuries, residents of rural Gotland built and repeatedly remodeled their parish churches, decorating them with murals and sculptures of often exceptional quality. By 1350 or 1360, however, nearly all building activity connected to the Gotlandic churches ceased.[66] Although an occasional later altarpiece found its way to a church in rural Gotland, such as the ones in Buttle and Kräklingbo, for the most part, congregations and patrons had to be satisfied with inventory acquired before the economic crash.

---

[63] Westholm, "Gotland, hansan," 91.

[64] Westholm, "Gotland, hansan," 91–92; Jonsson, "Hansatiden," 14–15.

[65] Westholm, "Gotland, hansan," 92.

[66] Westholm, "Gotland, hansan," 78–79; Lagerlöf and Swahnström, *Gotlands kyrkor*, 22–23; Torsten Svensson, "Imponerande export och expanderande import - influenser i den gotländska kyrkokonsten under hansan," *Gotländskt arkiv* 69 (1997): 115–42, here 133.

Gotland under the Kalmar Union

Although the importation, and also the local production, of high-quality sculpture dwindled during the fourteenth and fifteenth centuries, a considerable number of parish churches acquired new suites of murals during the fifteenth century. These murals were of a very different kind from the works of the "Master of St. Michael" and other artists of the thirteenth century. While the earlier murals in Gotlandic parish churches are often notable for their high quality, the paintings of the fifteenth-century "Passionsmästaren" ("The Master of the Passion"), which should probably be called a school, rather than the work of a single individual, are sometimes noted for their esthetic poverty.[67] These paintings appear to be the work of native Gotlanders as opposed to professional artists trained in major cultural centers, and it has been claimed that they are based on German woodcuts.[68] The name of this workshop derives from the fact that churches painted by this school frequently have a detailed suite of the Passion of Christ on the north wall of the nave or chancel. It is now generally accepted that these murals date from the middle of the fifteenth century, since at least one mural attributed to the school, in Anga church, depicts St. Bernardin of Siena, who was not canonized until 1450.[69] The works of the Master of the Passion often display scenes from the martyrdom of a saint in close proximity to a suite depicting the Passion of the Christ. Often the torments of the martyrs are depicted as a close parallel to those endured by Christ, which must surely be intended to underscore the role of the saints as followers, or imitators, of Christ. Although murals produced by this school occur in a wide range of Gotlandic churches, some of which lack any known connection to the Cistercian monastery at Roma, several churches that have been shown to have ties to the Cistercians have murals depicting the passion of a female martyr. For example, the parish church of Anga, in Kräklinge district, has an extensive suite depicting the martyrdom of St. Margaret painted directly above a suite of the Passion of Christ. The architecture of this church shows evidence of strong Cistercian influence, and Markus has suggested that some or all of the churches in this district may have been controlled by the Cistercian monastery.[70]

The parish church of Norrlanda is located a short distance away from Anga and Kräklingbo churches, though it does not belong to Kräklinge district. Unlike the churches in Kräklinge, Norrlanda has a twelfth-century baptismal font, which suggests that sacraments such as baptism were administered by a parish priest. However, the church does have a large number of architectural

---

[67] See Svensson, "Imponerande export," 135.

[68] Svensson, "Imponerande export," 135; Mereth Lindgren, "Kalkmålningarna," in *Den gotiska konsten*, Signums svenska konsthistoria 4 (Lund: Bokförlaget Signum, 1996), 373–74.

[69] Lindgren, "Kalkmålningarna," 373.

[70] Markus, *Från Gotland*, 140–41.

details that suggest Cistercian involvement in its design. Among other things, Markus notes that the early round window in the lower level of the tower at Norrlanda (early thirteenth century) is typical of the style seen in Cistercian churches. Further, when the chancel was rebuilt in the later thirteenth century, it was given not only a typically Cistercian straight east wall, but also an unusually large area east of the altar. The area occupied by the high altar is also several steps higher than the rest of the chancel. According to Markus, this may indicate that the liturgy of this church had specifically Cistercian traits, as may also have been the case in Kräklingbo. Finally, the angle between the ceiling vault of the sacristy and that of the chancel in Norrlanda is identified as a direct descendent of the monastery church at Alvastra, the first Cistercian monastery in Sweden.[71] During the middle of the fifteenth century, Norrlanda church was decorated by a painter from the school of the Master of the Passion. The north wall of the nave displays an extensive suite of the Passion of Christ (with comic images of sinners and their punishment underneath), while the south wall shows St. Martin sharing a piece of his cloak with a beggar, and St. George fighting the dragon. In the chancel, the north wall has ten scenes from the martyrdom of St. Katherine of Alexandria. These paintings are interesting in many ways. For example, in every scene in which St. Katherine is shown speaking or preaching the hand of God is shown reaching down in a gesture of blessing over her head. Perhaps this motif is intended to remind the viewer that St. Katherine's wisdom, and her ability to preach were miraculous in themselves, and were a direct manifestation of the power of God. No amateur ought to follow her example and argue with those who know better! The scenes depicted in the chancel at Norrlanda are as follows:

> 1. St. Katherine appears before the king. She wears a crown, holds a book in one hand, and gestures with the other. The people are shown worshipping an idol, which is depicted as a small horned devil holding a banner and heraldic shield, and placed on a pedestal.

> 2. In the second scene, two men bring St. Katherine back before the king. One holds each of her arms, and they are clearly compelling her.

> 3. In the third scene, St. Katherine is shown in debate with the philosophers. She is turned toward the king and gestures toward him, while the seven philosophers are shown behind her.

> 4. In this scene the philosophers are burned to death as the king watches, punishment for allowing themselves to be converted by the preaching and arguments of St. Katherine.

---

[71] Markus, *Från Gotland*, 42–43.

5. Katherine is once again brought before the king by two men. The idol on its pedestal is seen to the right.

6. Katherine, who is lying on the ground and praying, is beaten by two men, in the presence of the king. A devil, which closely resembles the pagan idol, is seen floating by the king's throne.

7. Still in the king's presence, and with her crown still firmly in place, Katherine is shown with her wrists bound to a beam over her head, stripped to the waist. Her bloodied torso is beaten by two men holding what appear to be leafy branches (closely resembling the palm branches that are an attribute of martyrdom).

8. Katherine is once again shown preaching before the king. A small devil or idol whispers into the king's ear, while a small angel whispers into Katherine's. Behind her is a tower, which may be the tower in which Katherine was imprisoned after having been beaten for her refusal to sacrifice to the pagan gods. As in all the scenes in this suite in which Katherine preaches, the hand of God is seen over her head. The angel whispering in her ear both emphasizes the origin of her extraordinary wisdom and reinforces the fact that this is a confrontation between good and evil.

9. This scene is in relatively fragmentary condition. In the center of the scene, St. Katherine is seen in prayer. In the lower right-hand corner, pagans are seen lying, probably dead, with fragments of wheels over them. A series of dark streaks (clearly a part of the composition, not marks of damage) in the upper right corner may be flames, or perhaps dark birds flying. The male figure standing behind St. Katherine may be the king.

10. This scene is also fragmentary. An executioner is seen replacing his sword in its sheath. In the lower right corner, a figure, probably St. Katherine, is shown lying, apparently dead. Above her chest, a pair of hands is shown in prayer. The body to which they belong has been obliterated – they do not belong to the figure lying dead. In the upper right corner, a trio of small figures may represent St. Katherine's soul being carried to Heaven by two angels. The king is seen on the right side of the scene, apparently gesturing at the executioner. He is accompanied by several other figures.

Like many of the suites painted by the school of the Master of the Passion, this suite is somewhat repetitive. Several of the scenes in which Katherine preaches are identical except for relatively minor details. This emphasis suggests that

FIGURE 4.1
Norrlanda parish church, scenes 1-2.
Tracey R. Sands.

FIGURE 4.2
Norrlanda parish church, scene 3.
Tracey R. Sands.

FIGURE 4.3
Norrlanda parish church, scene 4.
Tracey R. Sands.

FIGURE 4.4
Norrlanda parish church, scene 5.
Tracey R. Sands.

FIGURE 4.5
Norrlanda parish church, scene 6.
Tracey R. Sands.

FIGURE 4.6
Norrlanda parish church, scene 7.
Tracey R. Sands.

FIGURE 4.7
Norrlanda parish church, scene 8.
Tracey R. Sands.

FIGURE 4.8
Norrlanda parish church, scene 9.
Tracey R. Sands.

FIGURE 4.9
Norrlanda parish church, scene 10.
Tracey R. Sands.

Katherine's wisdom and/or preaching are of major importance in this depiction. At the same time, the presence of the hand of God in all of these scenes reminds the viewer that the ability or right to preach does not belong to everyone.[72] Katherine's ability is a sign of God's special favor, and also a miracle in itself. Another interesting point about this mural is that Katherine is shown wearing a crown throughout. Beatings and death do not dislodge it from her head. This must indicate that the crown is an outward symbol of an innate, inner quality. A crown is a very common attribute for virgin martyrs as well as for the Virgin Mary herself, and it is possible that St. Katherine's crown in these paintings should be understood as a symbol of her virginity. However, it is interesting to note that in the suite of paintings of the legend of St. Margaret in nearby Anga church, also by a painter from the school of the Master of the Passion, that saint is shown without a crown for most of the series. Only in the third-to-last frame does Margaret receive a crown. This picture depicts the passage from her legend in which her tormentor attempts to drown her. As in all legends of virgin martyrs, this attempt to kill the martyr by other means than with a sword is unsuccessful, and here it results in the arrival of an angel, who places a crown on Margaret's head. In this legend, the crown is clearly a mark of martyrdom, and of the special favor God shows the saint because of her steadfastness. This is clearly distinct from the portrayal of St. Katherine, whose crown is in place from the beginning. Perhaps, then, St. Katherine's crown is a reminder that she alone among the virgin martyrs was a reigning monarch. Another possibility is that the crown is a reminder of Katherine's exalted status as the foremost of the brides of Christ. It is not known whether this attribute derives from the specific instructions of the commissioner of the murals, from an official of the church, or from a model used by the painter.

The parish church of Rute, in the northeastern corner of Gotland, also has a suite of murals depicting St. Katherine's martyrdom, this time in five scenes. These paintings are also attributed to the Master of the Passion, but they appear to have been painted by a representative of the school different from the one who painted the suite in Norrlanda. Markus notes that the churches in the district of Rute, like those in Kräklinge, acquired their baptismal fonts a long time after the churches themselves were built, a possible indication that the Cistercians in Roma held the right of patronage over the churches of this district as well. Some aspects of the architecture of Rute church may also point to Cistercian influence.[73]

---

[72] Interestingly, the hand of God appears over the head of Christ in one scene from the suite depicting the Passion in Norrlanda. In this scene, which directly follows the Last Supper, Christ is shown kneeling in prayer before a chalice and host. This is clearly a reference to transubstantiation, but perhaps an unusual means of depicting Christ's words regarding the meaning of bread and wine.

[73] Markus, Från Gotland, 42–43, 141.

In Rute, the suite of scenes from the martyrdom of St. Katherine is located on the south wall of the nave, grouped together with a suite of scenes from the life of the Virgin Mary, some of which have been obliterated. The scenes depicting the martyrdom of St. Katherine are as follows:

1. St Katherine is shown in confrontation with the king. Unlike the king in Norrlanda, this king is shown standing, not enthroned. He is accompanied by a male follower. St. Katherine is shown gesturing, though with greater restraint than the king, who is waving his arms. As in Norrlanda, St. Katherine wears a crown.

2. St. Katherine is shown in debate with nine wise men.

3. The wise men (now there are eleven of them) are burned in a bonfire, and a young man is shown raking the coals as Katherine looks on and prays.

4. This scene contains a good deal of implied action. At the far left, the king is shown arriving on horseback, gesturing wildly. In the center of the scene, St. Katherine is shown kneeling in prayer before a terrible wheelworks, the wheels of which are studded with sharp blades. The machine appears to be bursting apart, and at least two bodies are depicted lying under it, one gesturing in apparent pain or surprise, the other lying still.

5. In this scene, the king stands on the left. In the center, an executioner raises his sword to strike off the head of St. Katherine, who is kneeling in prayer. In this scene, though in no other from this suite, the hand of God is seen over St. Katherine's head in a gesture of benediction.

Like the murals in Norrlanda, those in Rute church also show her wearing a crown in all scenes. Although the suite in Rute has only half the number of scenes in Norrlanda, it is still interesting to note the difference in emphasis. Rute has no scenes that depict the beating of St. Katherine (Norrlanda has two). The initial meeting with the king (or more properly the emperor Maxentius) is the opening scene of both suites, but in Rute the discussion takes place in front of one male witness, while in Norrlanda, it appears that Katherine is confronting the emperor at the public sacrifice, as she does in the legend. Another difference is that in Norrlanda St. Katherine holds a book in each of the scenes in which she is shown preaching, including in her debate with the wise men. In Rute, neither St. Katherine nor any of the philosophers is shown holding a book.

In Norrlanda, when the philosophers are burned to death, the king is shown, enthroned, on the left side of the scene. Two men are shown with rakes in hand, apparently feeding the flames with considerable enthusiasm. On the other hand,

St. Katherine is not depicted in this scene. In Rute, however, St. Katherine is the only witness (other than the one man with the rake), and the king is absent. The fourth scene in Rute compresses a significant amount of narrative into one picture. Although this suite does not depict the tower that reminds the viewer of St. Katherine's imprisonment in the Norrlanda murals, the image of the king on horseback may serve a similar function. In the legend of St. Katherine, Maxentius has the saint beaten and imprisoned, and then he leaves on a long journey, expecting to find her dead – or at least very repentant – when he returns. The image of the king gesturing from horseback in the Rute murals suggests both the king's return from a journey and his surprise and indignation at the state of affairs he finds. In the same scene, Katherine's prayer in front of the wheelworks, which belongs to a slightly later chapter in the legend, reminds the viewer that she is as unbending in her refusal to meet the king's demands now as she was before his journey. In contrast to the fourth frame, the final scene of St. Katherine's execution is much more concentrated. Unlike Norrlanda, this scene does not depict the saint's actual moment of death, nor does it show her soul departing her body. It is likely, however, that the hand of God over her head in this scene serves to reassure the viewer that Katherine's salvation is immanent, and her death is anything but final.

Given that the suites of the martyrdom of St. Katherine in Rute and Norrlanda are attributed to the same painter (or school) and depict the same saint, the differences between them are remarkable. No scene from the one church is identical to any scene from the other. If the painters are working from woodcuts, as some scholars have claimed, they are clearly different woodcuts. Perhaps the placement of the Katherine suite in Rute, directly adjacent to scenes from the life of the Virgin Mary, is intended to connect St. Katherine closely to the Virgin. Possibly the implication is that both have suffered the ultimate punishment as a result of their obedience to the word of God. Because some of the scenes from the life of the Virgin Mary have been obliterated, it is difficult to assess whether any of these images might have emphasized the suffering of Mary, perhaps in the form of a pietà. In Norrlanda, it would appear that the suite of St. Katherine is intended to be paired with the Passion of Christ on the north wall of the nave. Although there is no documentation to support this claim, it is tempting to suppose that the differences in these murals have something to do with the interests of the commissioners. In spite of the strong Cistercian influence on the architecture of Norrlanda church, the content of the murals (in particular their apparent emphasis on preaching) seems more suggestive of the interests of the Dominican order. Perhaps the original commissioners of Norrlanda church, whether they were members of a powerful local elite, or a coalition of local farmers, employed members of the building workshop at Roma. The presence of an early baptismal font in this church would seem to exclude the likelihood that the monastery of Gutnalia held the right of patronage over the church, and thus the right to make decisions about the decoration of the church. Perhaps, then, the

Dominican friars of Visby, whose activities included preaching to the general populace, came to have some influence in the parish of Norrlanda by the middle of the fifteenth century. On the other hand, the murals in Rute seem to play down the role of preaching in the legend of St. Katherine. Perhaps this somewhat more generalized depiction of a well-loved and widely venerated saint was more compatible with a Cistercian view, in a parish where the Cistercian influence may have been stronger and more lasting than it was in Norrlanda.

Although many images of St. Katherine and many of other saints occur in churches that appear to have been strongly influenced by the Cistercian monastery at Roma, the Cistercian order in general is known for its aversion toward excessive decoration of its churches. This would suggest that Cistercian influence would tend to reduce the number of images in a given church to a minimum. How, then, do we account for the fact that so many of the images of St. Katherine in Gotland appear in churches that seem to be connected in some way to the Cistercian monastery at Roma? Markus argues that there is strong evidence that the Cistercians' view of images was not as negative as has often been supposed. Not only does she consider it possible that the famous twelfth-century Madonna from Viklau church may have come from the altar of the Virgin Mary in the monastery church at Roma, she suggests that it may even have been made there by Cistercian artisans. In this case, there would have been a workshop for the production of sculpture to correspond with the building workshop associated with the monastery. Presumably, both would have been staffed by lay brothers. [74] Whether or not Markus is correct in her assessment of the origins of the Viklau Madonna, it is intriguing to consider the possibility that Cistercian practice in Gotland, and perhaps elsewhere in Sweden, might have diverged somewhat from the stated ideals of the order. Certainly the order and its members seem to have been forced to accommodate themselves to a degree of contact with the world outside of their cloister walls. If members of the order were also flexible in other areas, it might open the possibility that certain images might have been created under the influence of Cistercian thought and ideals, if not by craftsmen and artists who were connected to Cistercian monasteries.

Parish churches without Cistercian connections

Although the Cistercian order seems to have been the single most influential force on Gotlandic churches, at least with regard to their architecture, there are Gotlandic parish churches with no apparent connection to the Cistercian monks of Roma or their building workshop. Several of these churches have one or more early images of St. Katherine, and these early images are of extremely high

---

[74] Markus, *Från Gotland*, 54–56.

quality. Although there are few or no written records to explain the prosperity of these congregations, as demonstrated by the decoration of their churches, it would appear that successful trading would account for the high quality of the artwork, and might perhaps provide an explanation for the importance of St. Katherine in these churches. One such church is Hejdeby, a relatively small church located just east of Visby. During the later thirteenth century, Hejdeby church was decorated with a suite of paintings of very high quality, executed by a painter known to present-day observers as "The Master of St. Michael" ("Mikaelsmästaren"). The suite of paintings in Hejdeby includes a series of apostles in large format, spaced evenly throughout the nave and chancel. The west wall of the chancel arch, facing the nave, has a depiction of the Coronation of the Virgin, surrounded by three pairs of saints. The pair closest to the central motif consists of the Virgin Mary herself and John the Baptist. The next pair of saints is St. Nicholas on the south side of the arch and St. Katherine on the north, flanked in turn by St. Lawrence on the south side and St. Martin, portrayed as a bishop, on the north. As Lindgren notes, the saints in this grouping are all of central importance in western Christendom.[75] While it is interesting to see St. Katherine paired with St. Nicholas, too little is known about the history of this parish church to make conclusions possible. The inclusion of St. Lawrence, the patron of the archdiocese of Lund, is interesting and could signal a connection to Denmark. Indeed, the Danish king Sven Estridsen is said to have chosen St. Lawrence as the patron of Lund Cathedral because of his relationship to the German emperor.[76] Perhaps the inclusion of St. Lawrence in the murals at Hejdeby could thus reflect a German connection. On the other hand, St. Lawrence was also the patron saint of the archdiocese of Uppsala, and also a prominent saint in the diocese of Linköping. His image occurs frequently in later medieval murals, both in Gotland and in other parts of Sweden. Hejdeby parish does seem to have had some international connections during the thirteenth century. Gotlanders were actively engaged in trade in England during this period, and one Gotlander named in English sources in 1226 was "Paul from Hedeby."[77] Perhaps success in trade explains how the parishioners of Hejdeby were able to afford the murals, and also the high-quality sculptures that were acquired for the church during the thirteenth and following centuries.

Another parish with a range of different images of St. Katherine is Väskinde, in the assembly district of Bro, northeast of Visby. Based in part on an analysis of the iconography of their baptismal fonts, Markus sees evidence that the churches in this district were closely connected to the Danish ecclesiastical province. Bro district had an exceptionally large number of secular buildings in

---

[75] Lindgren, "Kalkmålningarna," 335.
[76] See Beskow, "Kyrkodedikationer i Lund," 51.
[77] Westholm, "Gotland, hansan," 78.

stone, which is undoubtedly a sign of wealth. Another indicator of high status over a period of several centuries may be the presence of picture stones, of which there are many in this district. In fact, Gotland's largest known picture stone is built into the stairs leading to the high altar of Väskinde church. The churches in Bro assembly district seem to have been built largely through the initiative of private persons (which is to say local elites), but possibly under strong influence from the assembly.[78] If Väskinde indeed had local landowners as its patrons, they seem to have shown a strong interest in the decoration of the church. Two images of St. Katherine can still be seen there, and according to the Catalog of Iconography at ATA, a suite of murals from the early sixteenth century included a group of four scenes in the chancel depicting the mystic marriage of St. Katherine. The oldest apparent depiction of St. Katherine is in the limestone outer frame of a tabernacle in the north wall of the chancel. This construction has been dated to just after the middle of the thirteenth century.[79] The vertical components of this frame are comprised of a male (east side) and a female figure (west side). The male figure is bare-headed, and has bare feet and a beard. He carries a staff, and the scallop shell ornamenting his purse identifies him as the apostle St. James the elder. The female figure wears a crown, and holds a martyr's palm in one hand and a book in the other. She is depicted standing on a small male figure who brandishes a knife and wears some sort of helmet, or possibly a crown. Such male figures are usually understood as representations of the emperor Maxentius, St. Katherine's primary tormentor and adversary. Around the year 1300 a suite of murals was painted in the church. These include a depiction of Christ in majesty above the tabernacle. In this image, St. Mary Magdalene is shown wiping Christ's feet with her hair, while St. Lawrence is depicted opposite her, holding his characteristic grill and a martyr's palm. According to Mereth Lindgren, tabernacles in this period were primarily regarded as a means of protecting the holiest of holies, the sacramental wafers that through transubstantiation became the body of Christ. The carved stone figures of St. James the elder and St. Katherine of Alexandria can thus be regarded as sentries or guards against all unauthorized attempts to reach the holy contents of the tabernacle. The slightly later painted image expands on the meanings associated with the tabernacle: the figure of St. Mary Magdalene can be interpreted as a representative for the congregation's deep reverence for the body of Christ, as manifest in the sacrament.[80] The choice of the two saints to guard the tabernacle is fascinating. What makes these two figures so well suited to their task? Again, the lack of records in the parish makes it impossible to draw any final conclusions. It is known that Gotlandic traders

---

[78] Markus, *Från Gotland*, 136–37.

[79] Lagerlöf and Swahnström, *Gotlands kyrkor*, 250.

[80] Mereth Lindgren, "Sakramentsskåpens ikonografi," in *Ting och tanke. Ikonografi på liturgiska föremål*, ed. Ingalill Pegelow, KVHAA handlingar, Antikvariaka serien nr. 42 (Stockholm: KVHAA, 1998), 167–83, here 181, 171–72.

had connections not only with Novgorod and northern Germany, but also with other areas of Europe and perhaps beyond. It is also known that a number of Swedes and other Scandinavians went on pilgrimage during the twelfth and thirteenth centuries. Although it cannot be proven, perhaps the pair of saints guarding the tabernacle indicates that some member of the local elite made a pilgrimage during the early thirteenth century. Certainly Compostela was a well-established shrine by this period, and it was visited by many Swedes. Only one Gotlandic image of St. James the elder is older than the depictions of this saint on the tabernacle in Väskinde,[81] which might suggest that the interest in this saint derives from an individual's journey to the shrine. Of course, St. Katherine's monastery at Mount Sinai was also a known center of pilgrimage, though far more difficult to reach for most pilgrims. Is it possible that St. Katherine's placement on the tabernacle also arises from a pilgrimage? Even if Gotlandic pilgrims did not reach Sinai, it might be that they visited relics of St. Katherine in other centers, perhaps in Normandy. It must be admitted that such an argument is highly speculative. However, the continued depiction of St. Katherine in Väskinde church suggests that members of the congregation, or the members of the local elite with the power, authority, or wealth to commission the decoration of the church, regarded the saint as a figure of particular importance. Although other factors could certainly contribute to the specific choice of St. Katherine as one of the most prominent saints in this church, pilgrimage could be one means of establishing a bond of mutual regard with this particular saint.

The early fourteenth-century murals on the north wall of the nave in Väskinde are grouped in two major motifs: St. Michael weighing the soul of the emperor Henry, and the Coronation of the Virgin. The latter motif is flanked by the two beloved virgin saints. To the west St. Margaret is seen, brandishing her cross-ornamented staff and trampling a dragon. To the east St. Katherine is depicted, holding a palm frond and a wheel that closely resembles a consecration cross. This depiction suggests that the two virgin martyrs are understood as having a strong connection to the Virgin Mary, and the fact that both are depicted wearing crowns underscores this point. Other saints depicted in the nave include a bishop without specific attributes (perhaps St. Nicholas), St. Olav with his axe, the apostle St. Andrew, and, interestingly, St. Francis. Does this suggest a connection to the Franciscan friars in Visby?

Sadly, the four scenes from the mystic marriage of St. Katherine that ATA places in the chancel of Väskinde are no longer visible. If the information of their existence is reliable, it suggests that there was a certain degree of awareness of this particular aspect of the legend of St. Katherine in late medieval Gotland. It is interesting to note that the early sixteenth-century altarpiece from Kräklingbo

---

[81] See excerpt from ATA's Catalog of Iconography, printed in Pegelow, *Helgonlegender*, 293.

depicts St. Katherine holding a ring, which is a clear reference to her mystic marriage. Together, the depictions from Väskinde and Kräklingbo suggest that the legend of St. Katherine's conversion and mystic marriage was well established in Gotland by the beginning of the sixteenth century. At the same time, the depiction of this particular motif in Väskinde suggests an awareness of and interest in one of the aspects of the legend of St. Katherine that sets her apart from other virgin saints, and establishes her as Christ's foremost bride. It may well be that this suite should be regarded as a later complement to the earlier mural of the Coronation of the Virgin, where St. Katherine appears as a witness.

One other image of St. Katherine from medieval Gotland is of particular interest. The parish church of Vallstena has an especially rich inventory of wooden sculptures dating from the fourteenth century. These include an enthroned St. Olav, a retable depicting the Crucifixion surrounded by the figures of the apostles, and a pair of sculptures depicting St. Margaret and St. Katherine. Both saints are portrayed with their adversaries under their feet: St. Margaret is shown trampling the dragon, while St. Katherine stands on a crowned male figure. [82] After a thorough examination of thirteenth- and fourteenth- century wooden sculptures from the diocese of Linköping, Jacobsson concludes that the similarities between works from Gotland and those from the mainland areas of the diocese are too great to be coincidental. She suggests that this may mean that the workshops connected to Linköping Cathedral may have had a greater influence on Gotland than has been previously supposed. [83] Whether this means that Vallstena itself had close ties with the cathedral chapter at Linköping is not certain. [84] Extant records do not connect Vallstena church to any canonry, nor is any such connection documented for any parish church with an image of St. Katherine. Still, it is interesting to speculate whether there is a causal link between St. Katherine's demonstrated popularity in the mainland portions of Linköping diocese and her equally strong presence in Gotland.

---

[82] Jacobsson, *Höggotisk träskulptur*, 209–14, 300.

[83] Jacobsson, *Höggotisk träskulptur*, 252.

[84] In general, it is difficult to determine the degree to which individual parishes or their priests had ties to Linköping Cathedral and its chapter. It is known that a few parish priests from Gotland – some of them also rural deans – were also canons connected to the cathedral chapter at Linköping. Interestingly, this connection seems to have been on a strictly individual level. There is no indication that any parish church in Gotland was at any time a benefice associated with the cathedral chapter at Linköping, or, indeed, with any other chapter. Pernler notes that some ten canons are attested from Gotland. Most of these were connected to Linköping, but others held canonries in Åbo, Lund, or even Dorpat. The majority of these canons were associated with the Church of St. Mary in Visby, but others were parish priests in the country parishes of Stenkyrka, Gothem, Hablingbo, and Burs (Pernler, *Gotlands medeltida kyrkoliv*, 172–73, 176, 183; Schück, *Ecclesia Lincopense*, 427–28).

Although their origins are not documented, the images of St. Katherine in the churches of Hedeby, Väskinde, and Vallstena demonstrate the strength of the cult of St. Katherine in Gotland from an early date. In addition, they underscore the idea that this cult did not arise from a single source in Gotland, but had multiple origins. Not only could trade provide a source of wealth to fund the building and adornment of churches, it could provide the opportunity to travel, exposing Gotlanders to the influence of many different regions with their local religious practices and interests. The specific connection with Linköping indicated by the sculpture in Vallstena may suggest that the strong interest in St. Katherine in the mainland portion of the diocese contributed to her prominence in Gotland. At the same time, other sources were clearly of equal importance.

In addition to the churches discussed above, a handful of other churches from Gotland have images of St. Katherine dating from the Middle Ages. In addition to the more extensive suites attributed to the Master of the Passion, single images of the saint attributed to this school are found in the churches of Boge, Hemse, and Stenkumla. The image in Hemse was radically "restored" by C. W. Pettersson in 1896. It is located on the north wall of the bell-ringing chamber, and depicts St. Katherine wearing a crown and holding a wheel, as well as some other unidentified object, possibly acquired though the restoration. Beside her is St. Barbara.[85] The painting of St. Katherine in Boge escaped the brush of Mr. Pettersson. In this church, St. Katherine appears as one of a group of saints depicted in pairs on the south wall of the nave. From the east, these saints are: St. Francis and St. Lawrence; St. John the Evangelist and St. John the Baptist; St. Judas Thaddeus and St. Thomas; two unidentified saints; St. Peter and St. Paul; St. Andrew and St. Bartholomew; St. Katherine and a previously unidentified female saint.[86] The unidentified saint is holding a staff that, although fragmentary, appears to be topped with a cross. The green mass at her feet appears to have a large, curled tail, and possibly an equally curved neck. It strongly resembles a dragon. In my opinion, this is a representation of St. Katherine's frequent companion, St. Margaret of Antioch. St. Katherine is portrayed holding a fragment of a wheel. Neither saint wears a crown, though Margaret appears to have some sort of a band across her forehead. Because of the fragmentary condition of the mural, it is impossible to see whether St. Katherine is depicted with Maxentius under her feet.

St. Margaret and St. Katherine are also depicted together in Stenkumla church, along with St. Barbara. The paintings in this church are on the west wall of the nave. Beginning from the north, they depict St. Margaret with her dragon, sword and cross, St. Katherine with sword and wheel, and St. Barbara

---

[85] Catalog of Iconography, ATA.
[86] See Lagerlöf and Swahnström, *Gotlands kyrkor*, 91.

with a book and tower. All three saints are crowned.[87] Here, then, we find three of the Four Capital Virgins, or perhaps equally significantly, the three female members of the Fourteen Holy Helpers. The location of the image on the west wall of the nave means that the laity of the parish had ready access to it, which might suggest that it stresses the saints' intercessory function. Markus notes that Stenkumla parish had a very powerful local elite. She also notes that the patron saint of the church was St. Lawrence, whose cult in the Nordic region, she notes, had its center in Lund. Can this be an indication of a connection between the local elites of Gotland and Denmark?[88] The idea is interesting, not least in conjunction with her similar thoughts regarding Väskinde. With regard to the choice of St. Lawrence as church patron, however, care is required. Although it is clear that the cult of St. Lawrence in the Nordic region spread from Lund, he was also the patron saint of the archdiocese of Uppsala, and of a number of early churches in Linköping.

One of the best-known Gotlandic images of St. Katherine is an exquisite stained glass window in the south wall of the chancel in Lye church. This image has been dated to 1325–1350.[89] It is the only preserved window depicting St. Katherine, who is the only saint depicted in this particular window. There are three more stained glass windows in the east wall of the chancel, each of them depicting multiple scenes from the life of Christ and the Virgin Mary, and images of saints including St. Olav, the apostles Peter and Paul, and a "holy bishop" (or perhaps archbishop), whose only attributes are a crozier and pallium.[90] Although the churches of Gotland have preserved their medieval windows to a far greater extent than the churches in other parts of Sweden, it is known that several churches lost their medieval windows during the end of the eighteenth and beginning of the nineteenth century. Norrlanda church, for example, is known to have had a suite of medieval stained glass windows. Accounting records from the church include a payment to a glazier in 1787–1788 for "3 new windows," while another payment in 1801 covers the replacement of "the old painted windows in the chancel." According to the dean who visited the church in 1801, the parishioners of Norrlanda were eager to retain the old windows. After applying pressure, however, Dean Neogardt managed to convince them to

---

[87] Johnny Roosval and Bengt Söderberg, "Stenkumla kyrka," in *Gotland III: Hejde setting*, ed. Johnny Roosval, Sveriges kyrkor 54 (Stockholm: Generalstabens litografiska anstalts förlag,1942), 5–26, here 19.

[88] Markus, *Från Gotland*, 71.

[89] Catalog of Iconography, ATA.

[90] Erland Lagerlöf, *Kyrkor på Gotland: Lye och Etelhem*, Sveriges kyrkor, Gotland 5:1 (Stockholm: Generalstabens litografiska antalts förlag, 1965), 54–55.

sacrifice both the windows from the nave and those from the chancel.[91] There is no record of the images depicted in the windows from Norrlanda, though one wonders if they, like the extensive suite of murals in the chancel, might have depicted St. Katherine.

Two churches in Gotland have also preserved medieval altar cloths with embroidered images of St. Katherine. Both of these, from Endre and Vall parishes, date from the fifteenth century.[92] Both depict the saint with her typical attributes, including the wheel.

Other indications of St. Katherine's cult in medieval Gotland can be traced. The parish church of Björke, adjacent to the Cistercian monastery at Roma, was dedicated to St. Katherine. In 1443, the parish priest, named Botulf, founded a guild there in honor of St. Katherine. The charter for this guild survives through a number of post-medieval copies, though the original has been lost. Interestingly, this is the only documented example from medieval Gotland of a rural guild, whose membership consisted of men and women from the parish (see below). There is good evidence that Björke had close contact with the monastery, and made use of its services.[93] Markus points out that the shape of the chancel of Björke church suggests the influence of Cistercian liturgy, with a separate, apseless space for the altar. Non-figurative ornamental painting from Björke church, dated to the thirteenth century, may also have been executed under Cistercian influence.[94]

Visby: Hanseatic Influences

Although there are no preserved medieval images of St. Katherine from Visby, there is evidence that the saint was as important and popular among the urban population as she was in the parish churches of the countryside. As noted above, St. Katherine was a favorite of the Franciscan order, and the patron saint of their priory in Skara. Likewise, the Franciscans in Visby, who arrived in the city in the year 1233, made St. Katherine the patron saint of their house and its church.[95] Early on, there seems to have been a significant Gotlandic component in the friary's membership, though Wase points out that the majority of the Gotlandic friars always came from Visby, not from the rural parishes. However, the number of Germans from Visby was also significant from the beginning, and the

---

[91] Johnny Roosval and Henrik Alm, "Norrlanda kyrka," in *Kyrkorna i Lina Ting*, ed. Johnny Roosval, Sveriges kyrkor Gotland 4:1 (Stockholm: Generalstabens litografiska anstalts förlag, 1947), 110–48, here 130.

[92] Catalog of Iconography, ATA.

[93] See Pernler, "S:ta Katarina-gillet.

[94] Markus, *Från Gotland*, 43, 57.

[95] Dick Wase, "Kyrkorna i Visby," *Gotländskt arkiv* 62 (1990), 29–52, here 39.

relationship between the friars and the German community of Visby seems to have grown stronger as time went on. Wase suggests that, especially during the fifteenth century, Gotlanders from the countryside had very little interest in the Franciscan friary, based on its membership, and on burials there.[96] Nonetheless, images of St. Francis among the paintings of the Master of the Passion suggest that lack of contact with the convent itself did not necessarily imply lack of interest in or rejection of its patron saints.

St. Katherine's position among the German trading families in Visby is of particular interest. In 1349, Simon and Gregor Swerting, "two laymen from the diocese of Linköping," received permission from Pope Clement VI to build a chapel "in honor of and under the authority of St. Katherine, virgin and martyr, for the sake of your souls and those of your children...."[97] In addition to its benefits for the brothers and their families, the chapel was a memorial to a third Swerting brother. This brother, Herman, had been one of Visby's two mayors during the early 1340s. During this period, relations between the German Hanseatic cities and the Swedish king, Magnus Eriksson, were less than friendly, especially since Magnus had captured a number of German merchants and confiscated their goods. As king of Sweden, Magnus demanded that Visby contribute to the monetary cost of maintaining the conflict with the German cities. Herman Swerting, a Visby German himself, and his co-mayor, Johannes Moop, complied with the king's demand. This decision seems to have been taken without the assent of the leading burghers of Visby, who considered the king's demand without merit, and the payment treasonous. As a result, Herman Swerting and Johannes Moop were condemned to death and beheaded.[98] The church of St. Mary, and the chapel that preceded it, had been the foremost church for the German population of Visby since the end of the twelfth century.[99] It seems only natural that this prominent family should memorialize itself (and even its disgraced and executed member) in this church. Among the rights accruing to the Swerting brothers, like typical church patrons, was the right to choose the priest who would serve in their chapel. Interestingly, the choice of patron saint for this chapel is not the only indication that the Swerting family had an interest in St. Katherine. According to an unpublished testament from 1371, Simon Swerting had a daughter named Katarina.[100] The Swertings were a powerful family, not only in Visby but throughout the Hanseatic League. Both of the surviving brothers became mayors of Hanseatic cities, Simon in Lubeck and Gregor

---

[96] Wase, "Kyrkorna," 40.

[97] *DS* no. 4429, "...in honorem et sub vocabulo beate Katherine virginis et martyris pro vestra et progenitorum animarum salute unam capellam in parrochiale ecclesia beate Marie Visby, Lincopensis diocesis . . ."

[98] Yrwing, *Visby*, 136; Westholm, "Gotland, hansan," 91.

[99] Yrwing, *Visby*, 20–21, 36–37.

[100] *De svenska medeltidsbreven* nr. 10021.

in Stralsund, and both of them continued to support their chapel even when they no longer lived in Visby. This is evident in a charter issued by the bishop of Linköping in 1413, in which he notes that Gregor and Simon, mayors of Stralsund and Lubeck, had purchased land in Holstein for the benefit of their chapel in Visby.[101] St. Katherine seems to have enjoyed considerable popularity among Hanseatic traders as a group. It is known, for example, that the guild of Hanseatic traders in the Norwegian city of Bergen was dedicated to St. Katherine and St. Dorothy. St. Katherine was also the patron saint of the Franciscan friary in Lübeck.[102] Much like members of the Swedish aristocracy, individual members of the Hanseatic community seem to have maintained contact with churches and monasteries in several different locations throughout the Hanseatic sphere of influence. It may be telling, for example, that Elizabeth, widow of the Visby alderman Henrik Gildehus, chose her burial place in St. Katherine's Franciscan church in Lübeck.[103] Perhaps the Franciscan friary in Visby, or even the saint herself could be a symbolic link with Lübeck, the city that many Hanseatic traders, including Visby's German population, seem to have regarded as "home."

It appears clear that the cult of St. Katherine in Gotland has both strong similarities to and some differences from the cult of St. Katherine on the Swedish mainland. The possibility of a Russian or Byzantine aspect to the cult of St. Katherine in Gotland that Bishop Wallin's description of Alskog parish church brings up is unique. Indeed, Gotland is the only part of medieval Sweden from which artworks of clearly Russian/Byzantine origin can be found in the churches. Although there was certainly cultural contact between the developing Russian state and mainland Sweden during the Viking Age and the earlier Middle Ages, Russian contacts with Gotland appear to have been more frequent, and to have led to the establishment of a Russian community and at least one Russian church in Visby. None of these facts proves that Bishop Wallin was accurate in his description of an altarpiece with scenes from the life of St. Katherine, ornamented with Greek or Russian lettering. Still, the possibility that St. Katherine's popularity in the Orthodox Church may have played a role in her popularity among Gotlanders is intriguing, and suggests that the saint's cult in Gotland may have differed from its mainland counterpart in its origins and early composition.

Although Gotland's location in the Baltic Sea made it a crossroads for traders of many different nationalities, the multicultural nature of Gotland and Visby differ only in degree from other urban centers in Sweden and the rest of the Nordic region. The Hanseatic League was also well established in mainland Sweden, and a number of urban centers, including Stockholm, had a significant

---

[101] *De svenska medeltidsbreven* nr. 18062.

[102] Max Hasse,"Die Lübecker und ihre Heiligen und die Stellung des Heiligen Olav in dieser Schar: Die Heiligenverehrung in Lübeck während des Mittelalters," in *St. Olav, seine Zeit und sein Kult*, ed. Gunnar Svahnström (Visby: Museum *Gotlands* fornsal, 1981), 175–84.

[103] *DS* X no. 301.

German component to their populations and city governments. The presence of the various monastic and mendicant orders, and their influence, are comparable on Gotland and on the mainland. It is interesting to note the trend that churches with strong evidence of devotion to St. Katherine, whether that evidence is in the form of images or of dedication, often have some connection to the Cistercian order or to one of its monasteries. This trend is evident both in Gotland and on the Swedish mainland. Likewise, guilds dedicated to St. Katherine are known both from rural Gotland and from rural and urban areas of the Swedish mainland.

The apparent connections between Denmark and Gotland during the early Middle Ages may also reflect realities in other parts of Sweden. The various regions that made up medieval Sweden were often quite loosely associated, especially during the early part of the period. Even after the creation of the archdiocese of Uppsala in 1164, several of the other dioceses, including Linköping, continued to be strongly influenced by the archdiocese of Lund. The archbishop of Lund retained the title of "primas" over Sweden well into the fourteenth century, and some holders of the office were loath to give up the title even after that, but the degree to which Swedish bishops acknowledged this primacy varied widely. Danish influence on politics, architecture, art, and cult can be seen in many areas of medieval Sweden. Even the fact that Gotland was invaded by the Danish king in 1361 does not really imply its division from the rest of Sweden as much as might be supposed, since during the later fourteenth century and much of the fifteenth century, Sweden was ruled by the same Union monarchs who also ruled over Denmark.

Although in many ways it was clearly a semi-autonomous region within the Swedish realm, many aspects of religious life in Gotland seem to have been closely connected to those of the Swedish mainland. One possible explanation for this might be that priests were generally educated at the cathedral chapters of their respective dioceses. Although Gotlanders were zealous in protecting their right to appoint parish priests, at times even turning directly to the pope to support their cause against the bishops of Linköping,[104] there is no evidence to suggest that priests from Gotland were not educated at the cathedral chapter. Even though clerics from Gotland did not often attain positions as canons, and even though Gotlandic parish churches were not annexed to the Linköping cathedral chapter, the basic instruction that every parish priest received would have a normative influence on the religious life of medieval Gotland. Thus it is not surprising that a saint such as St. Katherine, who clearly had a variety of devotional and symbolic meanings and functions for other parts of medieval Sweden, would also find a wide following here.

---

[104] See Yrwing, *Gotlands medeltid*, 166.

Although many aspects of the medieval history of Gotland, and indeed several of the documented images of St. Katherine from the island, suggest that it really was in some ways "a law unto itself," the circumstances of both island and cult may be more complex. Both for the island and for the cult, it appears that the connection to mainland Sweden may have been relatively tenuous early in the period. By the late thirteenth century, when rural Gotland's trade connections to the east had largely been severed and the Swedish kings had begun to assert their authority there, manifestations of the Katherine cult began to show similarities to those of mainland Sweden, not least in terms of Cistercian influences. In spite of the invasion of Gotland by the Danish king in 1361, the island remained a part of the Swedish diocese of Linköping. At the same time, the cult of St. Katherine in mainland Sweden is known largely because of devotees to the saint among the clergy and the aristocracy. The latter group was not found at all in Gotland, and the former group is far less documented there than on the mainland. The evidence of the veneration of St. Katherine in Gotland thus emanates from different portions of the population, and this may account for some distinctions. The final echo of the cult of St. Katherine in Gotland, as on the mainland, is in the form of an oral ballad. This tradition, which is clearly linked to the non-noble lay population, will be discussed in the following chapter of this work.

V

Non-noble laity
(commoners, peasants, burghers)

In medieval Sweden, as in the rest of medieval Europe, the most extensively documented lives are those of the nobility, the clergy, and, to some extent, members
of the various religious orders. In contrast, the sources are often silent, or nearly
so, about the lives of peasants and tenant farmers, not to mention the slaves who
continued to be a part of Swedish society at least into the thirteenth century. In
the later Middle Ages, the lives of city dwellers, male and to some extent female,
begin to be documented in the city records known as "tänkeböcker."[1] Although
these sources do record city business such as the names of those holding political
office, matters of city finances, and judicial decisions, they do not tend to offer a
great deal of insight into individual devotions.

It may be argued, then, that a different methodology is required in order
to explore the religiosity of these groups than that of other classes of medieval
Swedish society. Although commoners occasionally produced testaments that
have been preserved to the present day, especially in the towns that gradually
developed in the Nordic region during the later Middle Ages, their ancestry
and familial relationships are generally not known to the same extent as those of
noble families. Thus it is much more difficult to trace naming traditions for these
families than for the nobility. Although a few late medieval seals did belong to
burghers, occasionally even to women from this class, their lives are not generally documented to an extent that allows comparison of sigillographic images,
naming, donations, and foundations of various kinds as a basis for determining a
family's (or individual's) veneration of a saint or saints.

It may not be possible, in all cases, to separate genuine manifestations of lay
piety from the norms prescribed for laity by clergy, However, in this chapter I
will attempt to argue that there are social institutions, oral traditions, and even
occasional church dedications that may reflect the interests of commoners, rural
populations, and other persons who belong neither to the clergy, to a religious
order, or to the economic and social elite of medieval Sweden. In some cases, it is

---

[1] Lars Svensson, "Tänkebok," *KHLM* 19: 195–99.

apparent that the interests of the laity overlap with those of other groups. In this chapter, the main focus will be on guilds dedicated to St. Katherine, on the cult of the Fourteen (occasionally Fifteen) Holy Helpers, and, especially, on the post-Reformation ballad tradition known as "Liten Karin." I will argue that similar trends or concerns may be discernable in both guild and ballad traditions, and also that there may be a connection between these phenomena.

Guilds

Guilds of many different kinds were an important part of the social landscape in medieval Europe as a whole, and certainly in medieval Sweden. Among the various guild types represented are clerical guilds, tradesmen's guilds with merchants as members, guilds for various kinds of craftsmen, and general guilds. Of these, the general guilds appear to have been the most widespread.[2] General guilds could be located in urban areas or in rural parishes. Their membership could include both men and women, and their primary function, in addition to the sense of community and opportunity for social contact they provided, was to provide for commemorative masses for their members. As Samantha Riches has remarked, "joining a guild was rather like taking out an insurance policy that promised treasures in Heaven in return for the payment of an annual premium."[3] Documentation has survived of some one hundred and twenty medieval Swedish guilds the names of which are known, along with some sixty the names are not known. Those whose names are known are dedicated to twenty-four different saints and seven important feast days.[4] No fewer than six of these guilds are known to have been dedicated to St. Katherine. Based on the surviving evidence for medieval Sweden, only the Virgin Mary, the ever-popular St. Olav, and perhaps St. Nicholas, who was a particular patron of sailors, were more frequent guild patrons. For most of the medieval guilds dedicated to St. Katherine there is very little surviving information other than the guild's name and location. Exceptions are the St. Katherine guild in Stockholm, which is mentioned several times in medieval sources in relation to real estate transactions, and the St. Katherine guild in Björke parish, Gotland, a copy of whose charter has survived. Three of the known St. Katherine guilds were located in urban centers, while the three others were located in more or less rural parishes.

The guild of St. Katherine in Skara is attested in two medieval charters, of which one is thought to be a counterfeit. The suspect document is dated 25 May 1301, and attributed to the mayor and aldermen of Skara. It acknowledges that

---

[2] Sven Ljung, "Gilde," *KHLM* 5: 302–3.

[3] Samantha Riches, *St. George: Hero, Martyr and Myth* (Stroud: Sutton, 2000), 127.

[4] Ljung, "Tänkeböcker," 304.

the lot on which the guild house for the Katherine guild stands belongs to the priests of the church of St. Nicholas, and that the guild rents the lot from them with the consent of the cathedral chapter and the bishop of Skara. Further, the priests of St. Nicholas agree to perform masses for the souls of the guild brothers and sisters for a fee of 1 *öre* per mass. The measurements of the lot are also provided, and it is noted that it shares a boundary with the residence of the priest of St. Nicholas.[5] Some scholars have argued that the charter is entirely counterfeit, while others consider that it is authentic except for its date, which is a century too early.[6] According to the disputed document, the Katherine guild had both male and female members, which would suggest that it was a general parish guild, rather than a clerical or trade guild. The guild is also mentioned in a document from 1361, the authenticity of which does not seem to be in question. This charter is a list of properties belonging to the prebend of St. Nicholas, also known as Hindsbo prebend, at Skara Cathedral. Among the properties listed is the "chapel of St. Nicholas in Skara," along with the lot and cabbage patch to its south, upon which the guild house of St. Katherine is built.[7] The document is sealed by two canons from Skara, Martin and Lars. According to Wallin, the guild of St. Katherine in Skara can be traced back to the late twelfth century, through entries in the Bishop's Chronicle appended to a manuscript of the Law of Västergötland. Bishop Bengt of Skara (d. before 1196) is said to have participated in the building of the church of St. Nicholas, which is said to have belonged to a guild of which the bishop was a member.[8] This conclusion does not seem consistent with later information about the guild of St. Katherine. Certainly it is not impossible that a guild dedicated to St. Katherine would be established in a church dedicated to St. Nicholas. Especially if such a guild involved a bishop, the combination of St. Katherine and St. Nicholas might well reflect the learned character of the guild membership, and perhaps even their studies at continental universities (see above). However, this might suggest that the guild was clerical in character, which seems inconsistent with the reference to female guild members in the disputed document.[9] The apparently authentic document from 1361 suggests that the relationship between the guild and the church (or chapel) is primarily an economic one, in which the guild rents its locale from the church. Whatever the guild's ultimate origins, however, the evidence seems clear that guild of St. Katherine, perhaps of general parish character, was well established in the metropolitan center of Skara by the middle of the fourteenth century.

A guild dedicated to St. Katherine in the metropolitan center of Linköping is attested only through the testament of Bishop Lars, written on St. Katherine's

---

[5] Printed as *DS* no. 1748.

[6] See Wallin, *Knutsgillena*, 179.

[7] *DS* no. 6520.

[8] Wallin, *Knutsgillena*, 179.

[9] *DS* no. 1748.

day (25 November) 1301. In this document, the bishop leaves to the brothers of the guild of St. Katherine a baldachin to be used at the burials of guild brothers.[10] No other guild is mentioned in this testament, though the bishop makes many bequests to cathedrals, churches, monastic foundations, and private persons in many parts of Sweden. Although it is not specifically stated that the bishop is a member of the guild, perhaps his obvious interest in it should lead us to conclude that this guild of St. Katherine was clerical in nature.

The guild of St. Katherine in Stockholm, which was combined in 1444 or 1445 with the guild of St. Knut, appears to have been a relatively well-endowed organization.[11] The consolidation of guilds appears to have been a fairly widespread phenomenon in Stockholm during the middle of the fifteenth century, a period which also saw the consolidation of the guild of St. Michael with the guild of Our Lady, and that of St. Olav with the guild of the Holy Cross, among others.[12] Judging by the list of patrons (saints and other holy objects) whose guilds were consolidated, it appears that these consolidations had little to do with the status or popularity of the guild patrons. There does not appear to be any written record of the existence of the guild of St. Katherine before its consolidation with the guild of St. Knut, but records from the later fifteenth century give the impression that the Katherine guild was wealthy and enjoyed a well-established reputation.[13] This impression is reinforced by several medieval documents detailing the foundation of a prebend connected to the guild of St. Katherine, as well as the construction of several buildings on the property belonging to the guild.[14] Clearly this guild and its guild house were well known and prominent in medieval Stockholm, for the guild house is occasionally mentioned as a landmark when referring to properties not belonging to the guild, as in a document from 1474 discussing the sale of a property "across from St. Katherine's guild house."[15] Interestingly, this document and others post-dating the consolidation of the Katherine guild with the guild of St. Knut continue to refer to to the guild under St. Katherine's name. This is hardly surprising, considering that there was a prominent altar dedicated to the saint in the town church (St. Nicholai) a short walk from the guild house (now the site of the post-medieval "Tyska kyrkan"), and another Katherine altar in the Franciscan friary church on the adjacent islet

---

[10] *DS* no. 1352; see also Wallin, *Knutsgillena*, 179.

[11] Wallin, *Knutsgillena*, 109, 180.

[12] See Wallin, *Knutsgillena*, 109.

[13] See Frans de Brun, "Anteckningar rörande medeltida gillen i Stockholm," *Samfundet Sankt Eriks årsbok*, 1917, 43–79, 42.

[14] *Stockholms stads tänkeböcker (1474–1488)*, ed. Emil Hildebrand (Stockholm: Samfundet för utgifvande af hansdskrifter rörande Skandinaviens historia, 1917), 195, 253; *Stockholms stads tänkeböcker (1492–1500)*, ed. J. A. Almquist (Stockholm: Norstedt och Söner, 1930), 252.

[15] See, for example, *Tänkeböcker (1474–1488)*, ed. Hildebrand, 3.

of Riddarholm. The Dominican order, which also venerated St. Katherine, also had a friary within a short walk of the house belonging to the Katherine guild. Stockholm's status as an important center for Hanseatic trade may also have helped to reinforce the status of St. Katherine there. According to Wallin, the aldermen of the guild of St. Katherine were generally craftsmen. Nonetheless, the character of the guild appears to have been entirely social and religious, and Wallin states that it does not appear to have been a trade guild.[16]

At least two of the guilds dedicated two St. Katherine were clearly rural parish guilds. The guild of the Holy Cross and St. Katherine in Skepptuna parish, Uppland, is attested in Archbishop Jöns Bengtsson's charter of sanction from 29 December 1452. This charter notes that the guild had received similar sanction from the previous archbishop. Both the parish itself and the guild connected to it were relatively rich and populous. For example, Skepptuna's contribution to monies collected in support of the Crusades ("sexårsgärden") in 1314 and 1315 was among the highest in the district, as was its contribution to the fee for Archbishop Hemming's pallium in 1343.[17] It is known that some sixteen pewter drinking vessels were confiscated from the guild in conjunction with King Gustav I (Vasa)'s efforts to raise capital. Documents from the late seventeenth century note that the foundations of the guild house could still be seen near the parish church at that time, and that certain items belonging to the guild were still known to be in the area.[18] It is not known how St. Katherine came to be one of the patrons of this guild. According to Pernler, rural parish guilds were generally named after the patron of the parish church.[19] The identity of the patron saint of the parish church in Skepptuna is not known. However, it has been assumed that it must have been St. Thomas Becket, since Skepptuna church had a remarkable sculpture depicting this saint (now at the Statens historiska museum in Stockholm). This late fifteenth-century work was clearly intended to be placed on an altar. It depicts St. Thomas as a richly clothed, life-sized, enthroned bishop. It seems unusual for a parish church to own such an extravagant image if the saint represented were not the patron of the parish. On the other hand, no written record from the Middle Ages names St. Thomas in conjunction with Skepptuna. The church also owned a large and richly decorated altarpiece of Flemish origin. Like many other Flemish works, this one depicts scenes from the life of the Virgin Mary and the life of Christ, including the Crucifixion. It has been assumed that the altarpiece was donated by the members of the guild, and and Wilcke-Lundqvist expresses surprise that there is no image of St. Katherine among its

---

[16] Wallin, *Knutsgillena*, 180.

[17] Ingrid Wilcke-Lindqvist, "Skepptuna kyrka," in *Upplands kyrkor*, vol. 4, Upplands kyrkor 45 (Uppsala: Stiftsrådet i ärkestiftet, 1953), 101–23, here 111.

[18] Wallin, *Knutsgillena*, 180.

[19] Pernler, *Sveriges kyrkohistoria II*, 85.

paintings or sculptures.[20] However, Lennart Karlsson has raised an interesting point regarding Flemish altarpieces. By the end of the fourteenth century, the Flemish workshops had apparently developed so stable an economic base that they were able to begin producing altarpieces for a speculative market, not just for specific orders. This, according to Karlsson, is the reason that Flemish altarpieces focus on scenes from the life of the Virgin Mary and Christ, which would fit into all local liturgical traditions, and tend to exclude figures of saints, since preferences for these vary greatly from one parish to another.[21] Unlike northern German altarpieces, then, Flemish ones may not contribute to specific knowledge about the cult of saints in a given church. While it is notable that no images of St. Katherine have been preserved from Skepptuna church, there are many instances in which no images of a known church patron survive. This is the case, for example, for Björke church (Gotland), as well as for Ununge (Uppland). The absence of a surviving image of St. Katherine in Skepptuna neither supports nor undermines assumptions about her status as dedication saint. If the church was not dedicated to the Holy Cross and St. Katherine, it is worth asking how the guild acquired its name and dedication. Although the archbishop's benefice ("ärkebiskopsbordet") owned several farms in the parish during the fifteenth century, Skepptuna was not an annex to the cathedral chapter.[22] The shared dedication to the Holy Cross and St. Katherine does not seem to reflect any obvious connection to Uppsala Cathedral and its special liturgy. Perhaps it might be said that both the Holy Cross and St. Katherine are exceptional for their closeness to Christ, the Cross as the instrument of the Passion, and St. Katherine as the foremost of the brides of Christ. If this interpretation is plausible, then perhaps the choice of guild patrons reflects a perception of their particular effectiveness as intercessors. This would seem an appropriate basis for the selection of guild patrons, given that one of the guild's major functions was to secure the salvation of members' souls through proper burial and votive masses.[23]

The best documented of all the medieval Swedish guilds dedicated to St. Katherine was certainly the one in Björke parish, Gotland. It has been discussed at length by Sven-Erik Pernler in an article in *Gotländskt arkiv* in 1986. The guild was founded in 1443 by Botulf, parish priest in Björke, and here it is clear

[20] See Wilcke-Lindqvist, "Skepptuna kyrka," 112–13, 118.

[21] Lennart Karlsson, *Kretsen kring Haaken Gullesen* (Stockholm: Carlsson Bokförlag, 2005), 18–22.

[22] Dahlbäck, *Uppsala domkyrkas godsinnehav*, 49.

[23] In spite of Pernler's observation that parish guilds tend to share the patron saint of the parish church, examples from other parts of medieval Christendom suggest that this pattern was hardly universal. For example, there was a guild dedicated to St. Katherine in the parish of Sts. Simon and Jude in Norwich, England. See Eamon Duffy *The Stripping of the Altars: Traditional Religion in England 1400–1580* (New Haven and London: Yale University Press, 1992), 220.

that the dedication of the guild derives from the dedication of the parish. Interestingly, this is the only guild documented from rural Gotland, as opposed to the city of Visby, during the Middle Ages. Of particular interest is the fact that the guild's charter has been preserved through copies made during the sixteenth and seventeenth centuries, even though the medieval original has been lost.[24] In addition to the other evidence of the guild's existence and activities, there is some indication that local oral tradition during the nineteenth century retained some awareness of the guild and its locale. As Pernler notes in his article, the original charter of the Katherine guild in Björke came to be housed in Church of St. Mary in Visby. This may explain how certain post-medieval writers came to link the guild to the Franciscan friary in Visby, which was also dedicated to St. Katherine. Pernler suggests that it is likely that this document came to St. Mary's (which would become Visby Cathedral when Gotland became an independent diocese after the Reformation) together with a collection of other documents from the Cistercian monastery of Roma. Björke was an immediate neighbor of the monastery, and the last abbot of Roma actually became the (Protestant) pastor of Björke after the monastery's confiscation by the crown.[25] The guild charter from Björke is particularly significant for the information it provides about the membership and activities of the guild, and the role played by its patron.

As the guild charter makes clear, this was not a craftmen's or traders' guild, but, like the guild in Skepptuna, a social guild with both male and female members. The charter refers to the membership throughout as "Brydir ock Systir" (Brothers and Sisters), and it is clear that the female members were full participants in guild activities. Most of the charter is concerned with rules governing the behavior of those attending guild meetings, addressing issues such as drunkenness, profane language, and fights between guild members. However, there is also an entry concerning the drinking of toasts. Three toasts were to be drunk at each meeting of the guild, the first to "Vår Herre" (Our Lord), the second to "Vår Fru" (Our Lady), and the third to "Sankta Katarina." Of these, Pernler suggests that the first toast was to be drunk by the guild brothers, the second by the sisters, and the third toast, to the guild patron, by the entire membership. The toast to St. Katherine was considered to be the most important of the three.[26] This suggests that the identity of a guild patron was of some importance for the membership, and that they experienced a sense of connection with her. Some possible consequences of a perceived bond between guild members and their patron saint will be discussed later in this chapter, in conjunction with the ballad tradition, as will aspects of guild meetings.

---

[24] Pernler, "S:ta Katarina-gillet i Björke," *Gotländskt arkiv* 58 (1986), 67–92, here 67.

[25] Pernler, "S:ta Katarina-gillet," 69–70.

[26] Pernler, "S:ta Katarina-gillet," 75.

The last of the known guilds dedicated to St. Katherine was located in Bredsätra parish, on the island of Öland off the southeast coast of Sweden. In spite
of its location in a more or less rural parish, this guild does not appear entirely
to resemble the general parish guilds in Skepptuna and Björke. According to an
entry for the year 1413 in the *Diarium Minoritarum Wisbyenum*, the annals of
the Franciscan friary in Visby, the brothers agreed to perform votive masses for
the souls of the members of the guild of St. Katherine in exchange for a yearly
payment of four marks of silver.[27] As Wallin notes, four silver marks is a considerable sum, and it seems unlikely that a general parish guild would have had
the means or the desire to pay such a high fee for services that could be secured
locally at a much lower cost.[28] As a point of comparison, it is worth remembering
that the tax paid by all of Gotland to the Swedish king for most of the medieval
period was only sixty silver marks per annum. Wallin suggests that the guild in
Bredsätra was in fact a traders' guild, connected to the small but active harbor
and trading center of Sikehamn, which was located within the parish. Traders
from Sikehamn would have regarded Visby, one of the most important Hanseatic
centers for much of the Middle Ages, as their natural destination. The Franciscan friary of St. Katherine enjoyed high prestige in Visby, not least among the
German-speaking Hanseatic traders in the city. Perhaps, then, the connection
to the friary could help with socio-economic concerns, as well as spiritual ones.[29]
For this guild, it appears likely that the choice of St. Katherine as guild patron is
a direct result of the members' connection to Visby, and especially to the Franciscan friary.[30] The high prestige of the Hanseatic community in Visby certainly
plays an important role here. It could be concluded that St. Katherine's position
as patron saint for the guild in Bredsätra is a direct result of her status among
the Hanseatic traders of Visby and elsewhere. Interestingly, explicit relationships
between guilds and mendicant or monastic foundations also occur elsewhere in
medieval Sweden and in other parts of the Nordic region. Pernler suggests that
the guild of St. Katherine in Björke might have had such a relationship to the
Cistercian monastery in Roma.[31]

---

[27] *Scriptores Rerum Suecicarum*, vol. 1, ed. Ericus Michael Fant (Uppsala: 1818), 37; Wallin, *Knutsgillena*, 180.

[28] Wallin, *Knutsgillena*, 180.

[29] See Wallin, *Knutsgillena*, 180–81.

[30] St. Katherine is known to have been the patron saint of at least one church in Öland,
the twelfth-century parish church in Ås (see chapter 2). However, Ås is the southernmost parish on the island, and it is located over 70 km from Bredsätra. The choice of St. Katherine as
patron saint of the Bredsätra guild is therefore unlikely to have been influenced by her status
as patron of Ås parish.

[31] Pernler "S:ta Katarina-gillet," 88.

The Cult of the Holy Helpers

Certainly guilds and their patrons played a role in the daily lives of their members. In at least some cases, it may be argued that the choice of a particular saint as guild patron actively reflected the specific interests and activities of the guild. The identity of the patron saint for a parish church would seem to be a related issue, though a much more complicated one. In some cases it seems possible to connect the patron saints of certain churches to the interests of their royal builders (see Chapter 1). In other cases, it appears that other interests may have taken priority. It has been noted, for example, that St. Olav was the patron saint for "practically every church in Roslagen (the coastal region of Uppland)."[32] Although St. Olav occasionally appears in obviously royal contexts (see Chapter 1), or as one of the patrons, official or not, of Uppsala Cathedral (see Chapter 2), it appears that his status in Roslagen reflects a sense that he is a particularly reliable intercessor, perhaps especially so for people who make their living at least in part at sea. If this is so, perhaps other dedications, especially in this part of Uppland, may also reflect local interests and concerns. In this context, the parish church of Ununge, located in the district of Närdinghundra in eastern Uppland, is of particular interest. According to an inscription on its great bell, dated 1521, the patron saints of the church were St. Christopher and St. Katherine.[33] Ununge is not among the churches identified by Ferm and Rahmqvist as possible magnates' churches. The date of its construction has not been determined with certainty. According to Norberg, the oldest parts of the present church must have been built around 1270, based on the age of a painted plank from an earlier church ceiling, and on the age of the church's rood. Later, around the year 1500, the church was enlarged in its western part, which doubled the capacity of the nave.[34] Others are inclined to date the church to the late fourteenth or early fifteenth century, which would suggest that the mid-thirteenth-century font, the ceiling plank, and the rood belonged to an earlier church on the site.[35] Although the thirteenth-century ceiling plank is decorated with a painted vine, there is no evidence that the late medieval interior had any painted decorations beyond the obligatory confirmation crosses, which have since disappeared. The church certainly had a collection of medieval sculptures, including a reredos and

---

[32] Rune Norberg, "Ununge kyrka," *Upplands kyrkor*, vol. 11 (Uppsala: Stiftsrådet i ärkestiftet, 1972), 185–99, here 192.

[33] Mats Åmark, *Kyrkopatroner i ärkestiftet: Julhälsning till församlingen i ärkestiftet 1951*, (Uppsala, 1951), 13.

[34] Norberg, "Ununge kyrka," 191–92.

[35] See Bonnier, *Kyrkorna berättar*, 288; M. Erichs and I. Wilcke-Lindqvist, *Närdinghundra härad, östra delen. Uppland III: 4*, Sveriges kyrkor vol. 70 (Stockholm: Generalstabens litografiska anstalt, 1953); Janson, Rahmqvist and Skoglund, *Det medeltida Sverige: Uppland: 4. Tiundaland*, 310.

a number of statues for its secondary altars. None of these has been preserved, however.[36] In any case, Norberg asserts that St. Christopher and St. Katherine are not the original patron saints. Rather, two reliefs on the great bell depict the original patron saints, St. John the Baptist, and the ubiquitous St. Olav. Norberg suggests that the choice of John the Baptist can be connected with the fact that the church received the right to perform baptisms in the later thirteenth century. He does not suggest a rationale for the replacement of these earlier patrons with St. Christopher and St. Katherine. Indeed, he is uncertain whether the St. Katherine in question is Katherine of Alexandria or Katherine of Vadstena, daughter of St. Birgitta, beatified in 1489.[37] I would assert, however, that the fact that St. Katherine is co-patron with St. Christopher makes it virtually certain that this is St. Katherine of Alexandria. Although this appears to be an unusual pairing among Swedish church patrons, it provides a clue to the aspect of the saints that interested those responsible for this church. These two saints were clearly chosen because of their shared status as Holy Helpers. The collective cult of the Fourteen Holy Helpers is certainly known in the late medieval Nordic region. For example, the city church of Jönköping and Strängnäs Cathedral are both known to have had altars dedicated to the Fourteen Holy Helpers. However, the Holy Helpers do not figure prominently in the missals and breviaries published by the Nordic dioceses in the late fifteenth and early sixteenth centuries. Both in Germany, the original homeland of the collective cult, and in the Nordic region, where it appears around 1500, this appears to have been a cult that originated among the laity. When it begins to appear in liturgical books, it is more as a confirmation of existing popular piety than as an innovation from on high.

As Kilström notes, the individual members of the Holy Helpers were not necessarily of equal standing or popularity. Several of them do not appear to have had an individual cult at all. The trait that unites all of these saints was that they are all considered to have been granted the particular privilege of helping those in need or danger.[38] Some of the saints venerated as Holy Helpers in Sweden and elsewhere in Scandinavia, however, did have well-established individual cults. These include St. Aegidius or Giles (known in Sweden as Illian), St. Blaise, St. Dionysius, St. Erasmus or Elmo, St. George, St. Margaret, St. Vitus, St. Christopher, and St. Katherine. St. Eustachius, St. Cyriacus, and St. Pantaleon are attested in early calendars and occasional images or church dedications, but were not venerated in Sweden on a wide scale.[39] Although both St. Christopher and St. Katherine were well established in Swedish devotional life before the introduction of the cult of the Holy Helpers, the dedication of Ununge church suggests

---

[36] Norberg, "Ununge kyrka," 192.

[37] Norberg, "Ununge kyrka," 188.

[38] B. I. Kilström, "Nödhjälparna," *KHLM* 12: 458–66.

[39] Kilström, "Nödhjälparna."

that the new grouping made it possible for these old friends to appear in new contexts. It appears clear that the dedication to St. Christopher and Katherine as co-patrons does not reflect the liturgical practices of Uppsala Cathedral. Nor does the pairing of these two saints suggest any particular political standpoint or affiliation. Instead, the dedication seems to reflect the concerns of ordinary people. The saints appear here as powerful intercessors with a particular interest in helping their devotees. It was, of course, standard practice to rededicate a church after a major change such as an expansion. Given what is known about the origins and spread of the cult of the Fourteen Holy Helpers, it is clear that Norberg must be correct in asserting that St. Christopher and St. Katherine are not the original patron saints of Ununge. The presumed arrival of the cult in Sweden corresponds exactly to the apparent date of the expansion of the church. We do not know who chose the patron saints for this church. However, whether the choice reflects the decision of the local parish priest, the archbishop of Uppsala, or the parish residents who made up the congregation, it certainly shows a concern for the spiritual needs of the laity. The Old Swedish life of St. Katherine (see Appendix 6) includes the line in which the saint requests, and is granted, salvation for those who call on her. This, together with her status as the foremost of the brides of Christ among the other virgin saints, suggests that St. Katherine could be regarded as a favored intercessor by members of the non-noble laity who had no reason to view her as a symbol of royal origins or political affiliation.

The Katherine Ballad

It is difficult to find certain examples of the devotional needs, practices, and interests of commoners and laity from medieval Sweden. Whether or not the majority of them had possessions enough to justify a written testament, there were few whose land holdings were sufficient to motivate the preservation of such a document. It is to be expected that the laity were exposed to the legends of the saints through the sermons of parish priests and mendicant friars, and indeed, through visual images. However, although the murals and sculptures that decorated the parish churches may give a good indication of what parishioners saw when they attended church, and how they were influenced, it is difficult to prove that any of these arise out of the active devotional choices of this group. There is, nonetheless, one other source of potential information about the interests and concerns of the laity, and that is oral tradition. It is admittedly impossible to prove that a particular oral narrative or tradition has its origins in the Middle Ages, or in any other specific time. Traditions of this nature must always be treated with extreme care, and all conclusions based upon them must be recognized as speculative and provisional. However, there appears to be a sound basis for looking to oral tradition as a source of information about the extent, if not always about the details, of lay devotion to St. Katherine of Alexandria in medieval Sweden.

Even when there is good reason to conclude that an oral tradition really does stem from the Middle Ages, it must be remembered that all living traditions must have some justification for existing in their own time. Narratives, ideas, points of view, or beliefs that lack meaning for their traditors are not preserved or passed on: they are forgotten. For reasons that will be discussed below, the ballad tradition that will be the main topic for the rest of this chapter did not come to the attention of ballad collectors until the early nineteenth century. Yet if the ballad really has a connection to the cult of St. Katherine of Alexandria, and not just to her legend, it must have existed in oral tradition in some form well before the National Romantic movement of the early nineteenth century inspired members of Sweden's educated classes to go out into the field. For this reason, the discussion of the ballad "Liten Karin" will address not only how the medieval cult of the saint might have included some form of secular, vernacular, sung narrative, but also the ways in which a continued ballad tradition might indicate a degree of post-Reformation continuity of certain aspects of Roman Catholic belief and practice, at least among certain populations.

The traditional ballad known as "Liten Karin" is published as number 42 in the Swedish ballad edition, *Sveriges medeltida ballader* (abbreviated as *SMB*). It is assigned the number B 14 in *The Types of the Scandinavian Medieval Ballad*, (abbreviated as *TSB*) which is an index over all "traditional" ballad types from Nordic oral tradition. The terms "medieval ballad," "traditional ballad," and "ballad type" are not transparent, and require definition. Like the Anglo-American term "traditional ballad," the Nordic term "medieval ballad" ("medeltida ballad") refers to a genre of stanzaic narrative song, known or assumed to have been transmitted orally. The structural components typical of this genre reflect its oral transmission. These include the use of formulaic phrases or sequences, such as "commonplaces" (stereotyped descriptions of characters or actions), incremental repetition, and a particular kind of pacing known as "leaping and lingering." This last term refers to the way traditional ballads devote several stanzas to one single motif, and then jump over large segments of action without comment. A further trait typical of the traditional ballad genre is concentration of action, which means that these ballads tend to focus on one or a few pivotal episodes in the lives of their characters. The term "medieval" as used (primarily) by Nordic ballad scholars does not necessarily refer to the known or assumed age of any particular ballad "type" (which might be defined as a ballad "story," though it is conceded that verbal and stanzaic patterns are also crucial to delineating types).[40] Rather, it refers to the fact that this ballad *genre* is thought to have its roots in

---

[40] See *TSB*, 15.

the Middle Ages.[41] Other ballad genres, such as the so-called "broadside ballad," characterized by even pacing, journalistic attention to detail, and a style more suggestive of written origin and transmission, are assumed to have originated at a later date. It should be noted that the terms "broadside ballad" and "traditional ballad" do not exclude the possibility that both of these ballad genres can be sung and transmitted orally, as well as printed and distributed in broadside form (i. e., printed as single, inexpensive sheets, often sold at markets or in similar contexts). Further, as I have argued elsewhere, there are ballads the style of which meets the definition of a broadside ballad, that nonetheless are among the earliest documented of Swedish ballads.[42] The term "medieval" ballad can thus be misleading, both because it might imply that certain ballad types are medieval in their origin when they are not, and because it could be taken to suggest that all ballads belonging to other ballad genres are younger by definition. Any discussion of a given medieval ballad type that hinges upon the individual ballad's supposed medieval origins must therefore include some evidence that the ballad really can be traced back that far.

The style of "Liten Karin" clearly places it in the category of traditional or medieval ballads, though the earliest known variants of the ballad were collected during the second decade of the nineteenth century.[43] In spite of its relatively late appearance in the written corpus of Scandinavian or Swedish balladry, it has been collected from oral performance well over a hundred times (twenty-six variants published in *SMB*), and was, in addition, frequently published as a broadside during the nineteenth century.[44]

"Liten Karin" is known in roughly the same form in Swedish, Danish, and Norwegian oral tradition, and is clearly based on the legend of Saint Katherine of Alexandria. It is not certain that those who sang this ballad in the nineteenth and twentieth centuries regarded the protagonist of the ballad as a saint at the same time that they portrayed her as a threatened young woman. However, the elements in the ballad that connect it with the legend are sufficiently many and sufficiently obvious that the ballad must be regarded as, at the very least, an outgrowth of the cult of St. Katherine of Alexandria. It is my contention that the Swedish version of this ballad either originated among, or was popularized at an early point by, people who had a personal interest in the saint's cult.

---

[41] See *TSB*, 14.

[42] See T. Sands, "'Riddar sanct orrian': the Cult of St. George in Late Medieval Sweden," *The Nordic Storyteller: Festschrift for Niels Ingwersen*, ed. Susan Brantly and Thomas DuBois (Newcastle-upon-Tyne: Cambridge Scholars' Press, 2009), 6–19.

[43] See *SMB* 42, A-G.

[44] See *SMB* 42, 2:93–115.

The "Liten Karin" Story

Before attempting to draw any conclusions about the origin, spread, or function of "Liten Karin," it is necessary to examine the textual tradition in detail. Although there is considerable variation among the many recorded texts of the ballad, there are a number of elements common to most or all of them. With very few exceptions, the protagonist of the ballad is referred to as "Liten Karin" ("little, or young Karin") and is said to be a "tärna" at the king's court. Most of the scholars who have addressed the ballad have interpreted this word to mean a kind of servant girl, perhaps a synonym for "piga," which definitely has that connotation. However, "tärna" can also mean "a young girl or maiden," or a girl who waits on a woman of very high rank — a lady-in-waiting.[45] Karin is thus a young woman who serves at the royal court in some capacity, but her social rank is not clearly determined. It should not be forgotten that it was common in medieval Sweden, as later, for members of the high aristocracy to serve as personal attendents at the royal court. Birgitta Birgersdotter (St. Birgitta), for example, served at the court of King Magnus Eriksson as *magistra* (advisor) for the newly crowned Queen Blanche.[46] The only thing that is absolutely clear about Karin's social status is that it is lower than that of the king and queen. In all variants of the ballad, it becomes apparent that the king is attracted to Karin, and the greater part of the narrative is comprised of the king's attempts to woo her, with gifts and threats, into becoming his mistress. Nearly all variants of the ballad include a line that seems to make it clear that the king is already married, and thus is not wooing Karin as a potential bride: "Giv den/det/dem åt unga drottingen, låt mig med äran gå" (give it/them to your young queen, let me go with my honor). The most extensive segment of nearly all variants of "Liten Karin" is this sequence, in which the king offers Karin rich gifts in exchange for her consent. These gifts are often monetary in nature, such as "guld och gröna skogar" ("gold and green woods"), "ett gångande skepp i floden" ("a ship sailing in the river"), "ett stenhus uti staden" ("a stone house in the city" — or in Stockholm), or "mitt halva kungarike" ("half of my kingdom"). However, intangible items may also occur, most notably "mitt halva kungahjärta" or even "mitt helade hjärta" ("half of my kingly heart"/"my whole heart"). Once the king in the ballad understands that it is impossible to woo Karin with gifts and pleas, he threatens her. In many variants, he has her imprisoned in a tower or dungeon, which exactly corresponds with the Katherine legend and, again, is a consistent aspect of the virgin martyr tradition as a whole. In a few variants the king dreams of Karin as she sits in

---

[45] See Elof Hellquist, *Svensk etymologisk ordbok*, 3rd ed. (Lund: C. W. K. Gleerups förlag, 1966), 2:1266–67.

[46] Per Beskow, "Birgitta: en kronologi," *Birgitta av Vadstena, pilgrim och profet 1303–1373*, ed. idem and Annette Landen (Stockholm: Natur och Kultur, 2003), 13–17, here 14.

the tower, and wonders how she can survive without food. She replies that there is a lord in Heaven who takes care of her.[47] In nearly all variants, however, the king threatens that he will have Karin placed into a spiked barrel if she does not yield to him, and he makes good his threat. When Karin is confronted with this threat, she generally comments that God (or His angels) knows that she is innocent of all accusations, or that God's angels are with her. She is then rolled to her death. From this point, the ballad tradition allows a degree of variation. In many variants of the "Liten Karin" ballad type, Karin's body is removed from the barrel, placed on a golden bier, and attended by women who "krusa hennes hår" ("crimp her hair"). In one of the earliest known variants, collected in 1811,[48] the king goes and writes a letter, turns over his hourglass, and then stabs himself with his sword. A frequent motif is that the dead Karin speaks when she is removed from the barrel, saying "Gif unga konungen till" ("Forgive the young king"). In a somewhat unusual variant form, Karin prays to God to forgive the king before she dies.[49] In the final verse, she is placed "i mörka graven in" (into the dark grave) and "alla Guds små änglar de stodo omkring" (all God's little angels stood around it). Another memorable ending is well represented in the "Liten Karin" tradition. Two doves fly down from Heaven, and when they fly back up, Karin has been transformed to a third dove and rises with them to Heaven. In many variants, a corresponding pair of ravens then flies up from hell to fetch the king to his well-earned punishment. This ending may also be combined with the "forgive the young king" motif, as in *SMB* 42 I.

Earlier Scholarship on "Liten Karin"

Ballad scholars who have studied the "Liten Karin" tradition are generally in agreement that the ballad ultimately derives from the legend of St. Katherine of Alexandria. While this derivation is thought to be strong evidence that the ballad was already in existence during the Middle Ages, it is widely assumed that its form was very different from the ballad that came to be collected beginning in the early nineteenth century. This assumption is perhaps most attractively formulated by Svend Grundtvig, who remarked "this well-known little folksong has managed, in a remarkable way, to follow the times: since the Reformation it has so to speak doffed its convent-habit and donned worldly clothes."[50] Grundtvig and his followers compare the Danish and other Nordic traditions

---

[47] *SMB* 42 M.

[48] *SMB* 42A.

[49] *SMB* 42 C, originally printed in E. G. Geijer and A. A. Afzelius, *Svenska folk-visor från forntiden* (Stockholm: 1814–1818).

[50] Grundtvig, *DgF*, 2, 543.

of this ballad with songs about St. Katherine in other European languages.[51] Grundtvig is particularly interested in songs from German tradition, an interest that seems justified given the considerable influence of the largely German Hanseatic League in medieval Scandinavia. He notes that the German songs he examines more closely resemble the vita of St. Katherine than the Liten Karin ballad does, even though some German Katherine ballads contain motifs not found in written versions of the saint's legend. He suggests that the German ballads could be regarded as a "transitional form" between a hypothetical medieval Katherine ballad, the content of which must have been close to that the of vita, and the secularized Liten Karin tradition.[52] Grundtvig does not make the specific claim that the German Katherine ballads (or the tradition from which they derive) gave rise to the Nordic tradition, though he also does not dismiss it. It is equally possible to interpret his statements as suggesting a parallel development for the German and Nordic ballad types.

Like Grundtvig, Greni considers the question of possible German origin for the Nordic Liten Karin ballad, and concludes that it is impossible to determine the ballad tradition's ultimate origin. The core of his discussion of the ballad is a further development of Grundtvig's comment on the Liten Karin ballad's ability to "follow with the times:"

> We must thus believe that the ballad lived in Catholic times as a *Saint's ballad*: it must have had more or less the same content as most of the German songs. But during the period after the Reformation people lost interest in legendary material and—as we know—the clergy also warned strenuously against all forms of "popery" and thus also against Catholic folk songs. The Katherine ballad in its "old form" was thus no longer sung. But for all that it was not forgotten, but instead it turned itself into the song about the young, chaste maiden who would rather suffer death than live in shame. Nor is this recasting of the ballad difficult to understand and explain, for if we strip one of the many saint's ballads concerning Saint Katherine which we know from German folk tradition of all legendary material, we arrive at a song that in every way corresponds to the content of the Nordic variants. The Catholic ballad about Saint Katherine had a twofold content; for on the one hand the heroine appeared as a martyr and courageous confessor of Christ's teaching, and on the other hand we see her as the woman who defends her honor. This is probably also the reason that the ballad was able to continue to exist in Scandinavia after the Reformation; but from the ballad about Saint Katherine, there arose the ballad of "Liten Karin."[53]

[51] Most notably Toralf Greni, "Folkevisen om den hellige Katharina." *Edda* 13 (1920), 18–27.

[52] Grundtvig, DgF, 2, 545–46.

[53] Greni, "Folkevisen," 27–28.

Grundtvig's basic thesis of the ballad's ability to adapt to changing times, like Greni's refinement of it, is in many ways a logical and intuitively satisfying way of understanding the ballad's content, especially in view of the way that the Reformation was typically regarded by Nordic researchers in the nineteenth and twentieth centuries. As Magnus Nyman has pointed out, earlier Swedish historians are practically unanimous in regarding the late medieval Roman Catholic faith as primitive, degenerate, corrupt, and fundamentally unsuited to the Swedish people. These works almost invariably portray late medieval clergy, from parish priests to archbishops, as lazy, ill-educated, and uninterested in the people they are charged with serving, and suggest that the gospel of the Protestant reformers filled a great spiritual void for the Swedish laity.[54] Nyman's findings with regard to Swedish scholarship may also be valid for other parts of the Nordic region, and for certain other areas of northern Europe as well. Not least, Greni's comment that people lost interest in legendary material after the Reformation seems to arise out of an assumption that late medieval Catholicism had little to offer the general populace, that the Protestant Reformation in the Nordic region was quickly and throughly implemented, and that the reforms were readily accepted at all levels of society.

Beginning in the later twentieth century, a number of scholars have begun to reevaluate the motivations for and the effects of the Protestant Reformation in various northern European countries, not least in terms of the beliefs and practices of the laity.[55] In his study of Roman Catholicism in Sweden during the sixteenth and seventeenth centuries, Nyman has argued that the Protestant Reformation in Sweden arose out of King Gustav Eriksson (Vasa)'s interest in economic and political power rather than from his religious conviction. Lutheran doctrine developed only gradually, and Lutheran reformers could not provide parishioners with customs, beliefs, or institutions to take the place of those they sought to suppress. Not surprisingly, then, reformers often met with considerable resistence from clergy and laity alike. In some cases, this resistance could take the form of violent peasant revolt, such as the so-called "Dacke Uprising" in Småland during the 1540s. While the people of Småland had many reasons for complaint, the one they voiced most emphatically was the throne's rapacious plundering of churches and monasteries. Although the rebels were largely crushed after the execution of their leader, Nils Dacke, in 1543, much of Småland remained inhospitable to Protestant clergy. As late as the 1580s, some local parish priests continued to provide their parishioners with the Catholic rites they considered essential to their spiritual well-being.[56] Not only in Småland,

---

[54] Magnus Nyman, *Förlorarnas historia: katolskt liv i Sverige från Gustav Vasa till drottning Kristina*, 2nd ed. (Stockholm: Veritas förlag, 2002), 12–19.

[55] See especially Duffy, *Stripping of the Altars*.

[56] Nyman, *Förlorarnas historia*, 84–91.

but also in other parts of Sweden, Lutheran clergymen thoughout the sixteenth, seventeenth, and eighteenth centuries complained about the "superstitions" of their stubborn and ignorant parishioners, including their insistence on "praying to dead saints, saints' images, or remains."[57] Mass was still being celebrated in the churches of Gotland on a general basis throughout the seventeenth century, and in some parishes even into the eighteenth century. As Pernler remarks, this circumstance came to be a problem for the island's ecclesiastical leadership, since it contributed to the continued survival of the cult of the saints and the Catholic faith in general.[58] A good deal of material that Greni would certainly deem "Catholic" continued to exist and prosper in Swedish culture for many years after the Roman Catholic faith was outlawed.

It could be argued that the Liten Karin ballad tradition in its present form is entirely consistent with the vita of St. Katherine of Alexandria as it was known in medieval Sweden and throughout medieval Christendom. In contrast to Grundtvig and Greni, I would contend that the relatively concise narrative of the ballad tradition is a distillation of the legend of St. Katherine as it is known in medieval Swedish textual tradition, and to some extent from visual representations. The tendency to concentrate on a single episode is a well-known trait of the "traditional" or "medieval" ballad genre. The two surviving Old Swedish versions of the vita, like the vita in the widespread *Legenda aurea*, focus on St. Katherine's martyrdom and the events immediately preceding it. The Liten Karin ballad tradition does precisely the same thing, though in a distilled and concise form. Certainly, the ballad narratives omit certain episodes that are of great importance in the vita, such as St. Katherine's debate with and conversion of the fifty pagan philosophers, and her conversion of the empress and Porphyrius, the captain of the royal guard. As important as these episodes are in ecclesiastical/clerical settings, however, they can be regarded as supporting details to the central core of the narrative, which is the confrontation between the pagan emperor, Maxentius and the Christian queen, St. Katherine. Although the central issue in this confrontation is the clash between two religions, various versions of the legend of St. Katherine also depict the emperor's attraction to the saint, such that her rejection of his pagan worship also involves a rejection of his advances, including, eventually, a proposal of marriage.[59] Some versions of the

---

[57] See Nyman, *Förlorarnas historia*, 112, 196, 285; see also Roger Andersson, "Den fattiges värn: Marias roll i det medeltida predikoexemplet," in *Maria i tusen år: föredrag vid symposiet i Vadstena 6–10 oktober 1994*, ed. Sven-Erik Brodd and Alf Härdelin (Skellefteå: Artos, 1996), 517–38, here 529–31.

[58] Pernler, "S:ta Katarina-gillet," 90.

[59] Although the emperor's attraction to the saint is apparent in most versions of the vita of St. Katherine, the motif is consistently less prominent in the Katherine legend than it is in the legends of most other virgin martyrs, who are generally portrayed as making a specific defense of their virginity.

legend, including the versified Old French vita composed by the twelfth-century Anglo-Norman nun Clemence of Barking, place a much stronger emphasis on the emperor's personal attraction to the saint, so that the conflict between the two characters becomes to some degree, if only from the emperor's side, a kind of courtship.[60] By means of its use of what I have termed the "offer and rejection sequence," found in so many Swedish ballads, the Liten Karin ballad tradition manages to convey the essence of the conflict between the pagan emperor and the Christian woman he not only woos, but also threatens, torments, and kills. Although the individual motifs of the offer and rejection sequence vary quite a bit from one ballad variant to another, the impact of the narrative, and its general contours, remain consistent.

As noted above, the ballad generally opens with the information that "Little Karin served at the young king's hall/court." Although St. Katherine of Alexandria is a reigning monarch in her own right, and does not serve at the court of the emperor Maxentius in any capacity, her status as a queen of a smaller kingdom confronting an emperor may be comparable to the difference in status between Karin and the king in the ballad. In some variants of the ballad, most notably *SMB* variants D and E, collected during the second decade of the nineteenth century in Västergötland and Uppland respectively, and also alluded to by Olof Dalin (see below), the text comments that "she shone like a star among the little maids." Most versions of the legend of St. Katherine, including the fourteenth-century Old Swedish translation/adaptation of the one from the *Legenda aurea*, emphasize the saint's remarkable beauty, as this ballad line also does. Other variants of the ballad accomplish much the same purpose by stating that the king "till henne fann behag" ("took a liking to her"). One of the most consistent elements of the ballad tradition is Karin's nearly invariable reply to every offer the king makes her: "give it (or them) to your young queen, and let me go with my honor." Although this ballad line arouses our sympathies for a vulnerable young girl in a way that the saint's legend perhaps does not, it nonetheless reflects an important element of the confrontation between St. Katherine and the emperor Maxentius. Both of the Old Swedish versions of the legend follow the broader Latin tradition, in which, following the martyrdom of the fifty philosophers, Maxentius tells Katherine that if she will sacrifice to his gods, she will be the greatest lady in his empire, second only to the empress. Later, when the empress has converted to Christianity, confessed her faith, and been martyred because of it, Maxentius offers to make Katherine his wife if she will participate in the sacrifices. The wording of Karin's rejection of the king's offers in the ballads manages to encapsulate several different ideas from the legend at once, including the fact that the emperor is already married, that the status he is offering Katherine in some

---

[60] See *Virgin Lives and Holy Deaths*, ed. and trans. J. Wogan-Browne and G. S. Burgess (London: Everyman, 1996), 6–40.

way resembles that of a wife, and even the considerable solidarity that develops between the saint and the empress. Although the ballad does not explicitly state that Karin is rejecting the king because she has already pledged herself to Christ, the fact that she is as unmoved by the king's threats as by his offers may suggest that she is more focused on Heaven than she is on earthly life and values. Much as in the saint's life, Karin's continued refusal to bow to the king's wishes in the ballad narrative has severe consequences. In a significant number of ballad performances, the king tries to force Karin to accept him by imprisoning her in a tower, or by threatening to do so.[61] The prison tower is, of course, a central scene for the vita of St. Katherine. Not only is it the place in which the saint is fed and healed of her wounds by angels and saints, and where she speaks with her heavenly bridegroom, but it is also the location of the first, pivotal, meeting between St. Katherine and the empress who will precede her in martyrdom. In most of the ballad variants, it remains primarily a threat, though at the same time it is certainly an explicit reference to the biography of the saint. However, in two ballad variants, the king dreams of Karin as she sits in the tower.[62] The M variant is especially reminiscent of the saint's vita:

> Unga Konungen han drömde, han drömde om en natt/ Han drömde att liten Karin hon satt i tornet fast –
>
> Hur mår du liten Karin når du ej föda får?/
> Det sitter en härre i himmelen, han försörjer mig nog ändå. [63]
> (The young king he dreamed, he dreamed one night/He dreamed that little Karin she sat fast in the tower--. How do you feel, little Karin, when you get no food?/ There sits a lord in Heaven, he'll surely take care of me anyway.)

Like the legend, the ballad tradition has further torments in store for Karin after the episode in the tower. No variant of the Liten Karin tradition in any Nordic language depicts a contraption of bladed, interlocking wheels such as the device on which St. Katherine is to be torn apart in the vita. Instead, the ballad tradition substitutes a means of torture that can be described in a single word: *spiketunna* – a spiked barrel. The spiked barrel as an instrument of painful death is fairly well represented in oral tradition, perhaps especially in prose genres such as the fairy tale, both within and outside of the Nordic region. Although this torture device appears in only a small number of other ballad types, it is clearly a useful means

---

[61] Among them the texts printed in *SMB* as variants A, B, E, H, J, K, L and M.

[62] J, sung by a soldier's wife from Östergötland in 1843, and M, sung by another soldier's wife in Södermanland between 1860 and 1883.

[63] *SMB* 42 M: verses 13, 14.

of conveying a cruel reality in a single word.[64] Although the idea has never, to my knowledge, appeared in print, there is a fairly well-established assumption among people who know the Liten Karin ballad that the spiked barrel derives from a misunderstanding of the wheel that is St. Katherine's most frequent attribute in visual images. Examination of a wide range of such images shows that there is no good basis for this assumption. Many depictions of the wheel show it in pieces, but even when the wheel is whole, it is always recognizable as a spoked wheel. In the ballad, in contrast to the vita, Karin's torment and her death are condensed to a single episode.

The angel who destroys the wheelworks in the vita is absent from the balladic tradition. However, the vita does mention that angels carry the headless body of the saint to her final resting place at Mount Sinai. This motif is occasionally depicted in the murals and other artworks that decorated the parish churches of medieval Sweden. While the doves that carry Karin's soul off to heaven in the ballad do not have a precise counterpart in the saint's vita, they may very well derive from the angels that carry the saint to her grave, and may especially reflect the images depicted in churches. In such suites, at the moment of the martyr's death, a small, naked human figure is often seen being carried upward by a pair of angels. Among the paintings discussed in this study, the motif can be seen in Vendel church, Uppland, and in Norrlanda, Gotland. A related motif can also be seen in the final scene of twelve from St. Katherine's martyrdom in Gökhem church, Västergötland. Here we see Katherine just before her head is struck off. Although no angels have yet arrived on the scene, the hand of God is seen over Katherine's head, and the small haloed figure that seems to be emerging from her side is undoubtedly a depiction of her soul, about to free itself from her body.[65] The doves that carry Karin and other murdered innocents to heaven in Nordic ballad tradition function as an unequivocal sign of salvation, apparent both to those who witness the event in the narrative, and to the audiences of the ballads.[66] The painted motifs function in a similar way. Not only do they proclaim the will of God to the saint's tormentor and his followers, they also proclaim it to those who see the painted image. In many parish churches, medieval murals and sculptures were left in place, more or less unaltered, at least into the late eighteenth or early nineteenth century. It is very likely indeed that they form at least part of the background for the ballad motif. Are the ravens that carry off the soul of the king in "Liten Karin" and his equivalent in a handful of other ballads

---

[64] *SMB* 44, "Fru Gunnel och Eluf Väktare," which exists in only a single variant collected in 1667; described, but not called by name in *DgF* 178, "Folke Lovmandsøn og dronning Helvig."

[65] Viola Hernfjäll, *Medeltida kyrkmålningar i gamla Skara stift* (Stockholm: Institutionen för konstvetenskap, 1993), 177–78.

[66] Tracey R. Sands, "'Det kommo tvenne dufvor. . .': Doves, Ravens, and the Dead in Scandinavian Folk Tradition." *Scandinavian Studies* 73 (2001): 349–74

also derived from images in churches? This is far less certain. It is quite possible that ballad motif of the ravens arises out of a sense of aesthetic and emotional symmetry. Just as the innocence of the protagonist is made apparent through the doves and their flight, the tormentor is carried off to his well-earned reward. Just as the evil king's behavior is the opposite of the holy Karin's, the ravens are a negative image of the doves.[67] However, in at least one church, it is at least possible that ravens have also been associated with St. Katherine and her martyrdom. In the extensive suite of murals depicting St. Katherine's martyrdom in Gökhem, the individual scenes are depicted in separate roundels, each encircled in a decorative border. The eleventh of the twelve scenes depicts the wheelworks that was intended to tear Katherine apart, and the angel who destroyed it. Above this roundel, outside of the decorative frame, a pair of black, raven-like birds are depicted in flight. Certainly these have no part in the legend, which may explain why they are seen outside of the frame. However, Hernfjäll suggests that, at least in this context, the birds can be interpreted as an ominous sign of Katherine's impending death.[68] The association is interesting, not least because it suggests the possibility that some later observers of such images in churches might draw their own conclusions about their meaning. In any case, even if the images of dark birds in Gökhem were understood by their painter or donors as signs of the saint's impending martyrdom, they do not correspond to the use or meanings of the ravens in the ballad tradition.

While the general plot of the Liten Karin ballad narrative follows the central core of the saint's legend quite closely, the extensive use of a formulaic offer and rejection sequence in all variants of the ballad means that the tradition also contains highly stereotypical elements that are common to a large number of different ballads. In this sequence, the gifts offered to Karin are often quite distinct from those Maxentius offers to Katherine in the saint's vita. No variant of the ballad, for example, mentions a golden statue. However, in certain cases it might be possible to speculate about a relationship between the gifts offered in the ballad and aspects of the cult of St. Katherine, and some of the offers might be understood as a translation of some elements of the legend into a ballad idiom. Saints' altars, including some documented Katherine altars, often owned considerable property. Thus offers of real estate ("gold and green woods," "a stone house in the city") appearing in the ballad are consistent with gifts sometimes offered to the saints via their altars in medieval Sweden.[69] The "stone house in the city" (or in Stockholm, as in at least one variant) might also conceivably suggest a link to a saint's guild, which often owned such houses. Guild houses were

---

[67] See Sands, "Doves, Ravens, and the Dead," 371–72.

[68] Hernfjäll, *Medeltida kyrkmålningar*, 110.

[69] See, for example, the listing of properties belonging to the altar of St. Katherine at Åbo Cathedral in *Registrum Ecclesiæ Aboensis eller Åbo domkyrkas svartbok*, ed. Reinhard Hausen (Helsingfors: Finlands statsarkiv, 1890), 579–82.

often known by the name of the guild patron, even long after the Reformation, if they continued to stand. For example, a song collected by P. A. Säve from a singer born in Björke parish, Gotland, included the lines "De lyste där med ljus / uti Karins hus" (approx. "They illuminated (the room) with candles / there in Karin's house").[70] According to Pernler, these lines may refer to a preserved medieval building in the parish, which may have been used by the guild of St. Katherine, and which has sometimes been associated with it in later oral tradition.[71] The word "hus," though cognate with English "house," does not typically refer to ordinary dwellings in rural areas, which adds weight to the argument that the song collected by Säve refers to a (perceived) guild locale, and not to a home. The ballad stanza in which the king offers Karin a crown might be understood as a reference to the fact that Katherine of Alexandria, like other virgin saints, is often portrayed wearing a crown in ecclesiastical art, or it might refer to the emperor's offer in the vita that Katherine will share the status of the empress. Likewise, the offer of "mitt halva kungarike" (half of my kingdom),[72] which occurs in a large number of variants, or "halva mitt kungahjärta" (half of my royal heart), which is found in the O variant, may also reflect that offer of shared imperial status.

Offer and Rejection Sequences

While it is quite possible that ballad singers did make a connection between the legend, image, and cult of St. Katherine and the well-established ballad formulas they were singing, the stereotypical nature of these commonplaces means that such connections cannot be taken for granted. The formulaic stanzas and sequences found in "Liten Karin" are employed in a wide range of different ballad types. Many of the ballads that employ formulaic sequences resembling those of "Liten Karin" are courting songs. Unlike "Liten Karin," most of the courtship ballads in this group end in marriages, to the ultimate satisfaction of all involved parties. In other ballads that contain the sequence, the offers are made by a young woman who bargains unsuccessfully to save her own life. A number of other scholars have noted the relationship between "Liten Karin" and another ballad which clearly belongs to this group, "Liten vallpiga."[73] Bengt Jonsson has

---

[70] *Svenska visor I: gotländska visor samlade av P. A. Säve*, ed. Erik Noreen and Herbert Gustavson (Uppsala and Stockholm: Kungl. Gustav Adolfs Akademien/Almqvist & Wiksells boktryckeri AB, 1941), 232.

[71] Pernler, "S:ta Katarina-gillet," 81–85.

[72] Perhaps a reference to Herod's offer to Salome in Mark 6:23.

[73] *TSB* D 405, *SMB* 182. See Bengt R. Jonsson, *Svensk balladtradition. Balladkällor och balladtyper*, Svenskt visarkivs handlingar 1 (Stockholm: Svenskt visarkiv, 1967), 733; Bengt R. Jonsson, "Något om Katarinavisan," unpublished essay, Svenskt visarkivs bibliotek nr. 2729,

also noted that these formulas appear in *SMB* 181/*TSB* D 399 ("Tærningspillet," or as he calls it in his 1952 paper, "Gångarpilten"). Sequences identical or closely related to those in "Liten Karin" or "Liten vallpiga" occur also in *SMB* 183/*TSB* D 409 ("Allebrand harpolekaren"), *SMB* 6/*TSB* A 20 ("Varulven" – The Werewolf), *SMB* 13/*TSB* A 38 ("De två systrarna" – The two sisters), *SMB* 20/*TSB* A 48 ("Näcken bortför jungfrun" – The neck/nixie kidnaps the maiden), *SMB* 86/*TSB* D 90 ("Broder prövar syster" – Brother tests sister), and *SMB* 127/*TSB* D 255 ("Herr Apelbrand och lilla Lena" – Sir Apelbrand and little Lena). It is quite clear that these sequences should be regarded as "commonplaces," formulas with more or less fixed form, which may contain specific semantic content, but may also be employed in quite diverse narrative situations. What is most striking about the formulaic sequence, however, is the the variety of contexts in which it may appear, and outcomes to which it may lead. In situations related to courting, the "offer-and-rejection" sequence is generally set in motion by the character who has the highest apparent social or economic status in the ballad. The intent in these ballads is to entice or convince a character whose power and economic position appear to be weaker, to consent to a situation ardently desired by the more powerful figure. However, the nature of this situation may vary considerably. While the sequence often occurs in ballads which also have a courtship theme, or which result in a marriage, it is not always directly linked to the actual courtship. In the "Liten Karin" tradition, as discussed above, the object of the king's efforts and desire is the protagonist herself. The king offers a series of rich gifts, some of which may imply a degree of political influence, in exchange for which he expects Karin to become his mistress. Each "offer" verse from the king is followed by a "rejection" verse from Karin, in which she repeats the offer he has just made, rejects it ("jag passar inte på"), and tells him to give it to the queen and let her go. As noted above, this ballad never results in a successful courtship, and always results in the death of the protagonist. At the same time, from the point of view of the protagonist, this outcome is clearly preferable to capitulation. In the "Liten Karin" ballad, the offer and rejection sequence tends to be extended over a large number of verses. Although in many ballad variants the verses offering rich gifts form a distinct section preceding the verses in which the protagonist is threatened with punishment if she refuses to comply with the king's demands, the "threat" verses, which are also answered by rejecting verses, may also be mixed in with the "offer" verses. In spite of the relatively widespread occurrence of the offer and rejection sequence, the verses in which the protagonist is threatened appear to be unique to "Liten Karin."

"Liten vallpiga" is another ballad that makes extensive use of the offer/rejection sequence also seen in "Liten Karin," as several scholars have noted.

1952, 21–22; Sixten Belfrage, *Våra vanligaste folkvisor*, Verdandis småskrifter 187 (Stockholm: Albert Bonniers förlag, 1912), 12.

Although this ballad type allows considerable variation, the narrative focuses on a young woman of apparently low social status, who has a remarkable singing ability. The king hears her singing from a distance, and has her brought before him. Many variants of this ballad include a long sequence in which the protagonist dresses herself in fine clothes for her audience with the king, and the clothing is described in detail. Once the protagonist and the king are face to face, the offer and rejection sequence generally commences. In this ballad type, the gifts are offered in exchange for a song, not for the girl's person. The rejection verses occasionally employ the phrase "jag passar inte på" found in most variants of "Liten Karin," but in many cases the protagonist either replies "det kan jag väl få" (That I can certainly get) and then refuses to sing, or states that it will take a much better gift to win a song from her. In these variants, the gift she wants is the king himself, and she consents to sing once she has secured the king's promise. In a number of variants the offer and rejection sequence is omitted. However, the ballad always ends with the marriage of the king and the protagonist.

The instigator of the offer and rejection sequence in courting ballads is always the character whose apparent social and economic status is highest. However, the role is not necessarily restricted by gender. In *SMB* 181, "Liten båtsman," a maiden challenges a young man who happens by to a game of dice. Although the game goes back and forth, he eventually wins, and the implication is that the maiden herself is his prize. This situation generates an offer/rejection sequence:

"Hörer tu goda gångepilt, tu skynda tigh bort från migh, een silkesticka skiorta, then will iagh gifwa tigh." (Listen, good travelling boy, hurry away from me, and I'll give you a silk-embroidered shirt.")

The young man replies that a fine silken shirt is all very well, but he wants the maiden he won at dice. The sequence generally continues for several verses, often including the same gifts offered in "Liten Karin" and "Liten vallpiga," such as a fine horse and saddle, a ship, a house of stone in the city, a castle and fortress, or even half a kingdom. After several verses, the maiden realizes that she has no choice, and consents, unwillingly, to marry the young man. At this point he reveals that he is the son of a king, and a much better match than she has the right to expect. When she hears this news the maiden experiences a change of heart, pledges her troth, and gives us every reason to expect that a wedding will take place.

SMB 183 (*TSB* D 409), "Allebrand harpolekaren (Allebrand the harper)," collected several times in Småland during the eighteenth century, also employs a variant of the offer and rejection sequence. The situation that triggers it is perhaps slightly more complex than in the other ballads incorporating the sequence, and the relationship between the figure who offers and the one who rejects is also quite interesting. In this ballad, a man who has seduced the king's daughter persuades his sister to let her son be executed in his stead, noting that she can have another son, but never another brother. The son, however, has a golden harp, and he plays it as he goes to meet his fate. As in "Liten vallpiga," the king hears his playing, and is enchanted. When Allebrand is brought before the king, the offer and rejection sequence is set in motion, and the king offers the young man a series of gifts, if he will play for him "så länge du lefver" ("as long as you live"). In one of the *SMB* variants (A), the first gift offered is "en silkesstucken klädning" ("a silk-embroidered dress"—though the word could also refer more generally to a set of clothes, or "costume"), which suggests that the exact content of the individual verses of the sequence is not necessarily of primary importance for all singers. The rejection verses could as easily be placed in "Liten vallpiga," which has a closely related plot:

"En silkesstucken klädning den passar jag ej på, men jag spelar intet för eder ändå."

When the king offers the young musician his oldest daughter, the rejection verse becomes explanatory: she has slept with my uncle this year. The king then offers his youngest daughter, and the offer is accepted. In one of the variants he also asks that the uncle's life be spared, and in another the king takes this initiative himself. In all cases, the ballad ends happily for Allebrand, who marries the youngest princess.

In addition to these courting ballads, several Swedish ballads employ nearly identical offer and rejection sequences in situations that force the protagonist to bargain, always unsuccessfully, for her life. The objects offered in these ballads are familiar from "Liten Karin" and the other ballads discussed above: a golden crown, a golden circlet, silken dresses,and so on. Many singers are also careful to include elements that are particularly appropriate to the narrative at hand. For example, in *SMB* 13 ("De två systrarna"), the ugly, dark, older sister tires of being taunted by her beautiful, blond, younger sister, and pushes her into the water. The younger sister offers a series of gifts, including golden circlets and golden crowns, often concluding with "min fästerman" (my betrothed). The older sister replies:

"Ditt röda gullband / gullkrona grann / fästerman får jag väl ändå
Men aldrig skall du mer på Guds gröna jord gå." (Your red golden circlet / crown of gold / betrothed I'll certainly get anyhow / But nevermore will you walk on God's green earth.)

In *SMB* 6, "Varulven" (The Werewolf), a young woman is attacked in the woods by a wolf. In most variants, she tries to pacify him by offering her shift of silk, her golden circlet or golden crown, her silver-buckled shoes or her little gold rings. In some variants, her offers include items more likely to appeal to a wolf, such as "my cow and my calf," or "my grey charger." The wolf's reply is typically "Jag passar inte på," familiar from "Liten Karin." In most variants of "The Werewolf," however, the second line of the stanza explains why the item offered is of no use to the wolf, or asserts that he wants the maiden nonetheless. On the other hand, in *SMB* 20 ("Näcken bortför jungfru" --The Nixie kidnaps a maiden), the offer and rejection verses are nearly interchangeable (though generally fewer in number) with those of *SMB* 13. The supernatural male rejects the maiden's pleas that he let her go in exchange for her golden circlet and golden crown. He generally replies:

> "Ditt röda gullband / gullkrona röd det passar jag ej på / Men aldrig mer skall du ur wagnen min gå / på guds gröna jord gå." (Your red golden circlet doesn't interest me at all / But nevermore shall you go out of my wagon / walk on God's green earth, etc.)

It is well known and widely accepted that formulas consisting of individual half-lines or full lines, or even full verses, may be used interchangeably in a variety of individual ballads.[74] However, the existence of interchangeable sequences consisting of several or many verses raises interesting questions about the nature of ballad narratives. How integral is the relationship between the content of the offer and rejection sequence and the ballad narrative as a whole? Is it defensible to attempt an interpretation of the individual verses of the offer and rejection sequences in the "Liten Karin" variants on the basis of the legend, or should these elements be regarded as independent narrative units the meaning of which resides mainly or solely in their function as the means through which the personal confrontation between the two main characters is expressed? In this context it may be of interest to note that at least three Swedish ballad singers had repertoires from which both "Liten Karin" and "Liten vallpiga" were collected, and the repertoire of one of these singers also included "Liten båtsman." None of these singers provided ballad collectors with a variant of "Varulven," "De två systrarna," or "Näcken bortför jungfru," which means that this comparison of formulaic sequences looks only at ballads with a courting theme, and not with those that depict a murder or abduction. Nonetheless, by comparing the variants of each of these ballads as sung by these three singers, it may be possible to determine, at least to some extent, whether the singers themselves considered the ballads to be related or wholly separate.

One singer, "Stina i Stensö," from Östra Husby parish in Östergötland, provided the ballad collector L. Christian Wiede with variants of "Liten vallpiga," "Liten båtsman," and "Liten Karin" during the 1840s. Happily, Wiede recorded not only the ballad texts, but also the melodies. Stina's version of "Liten Karin" is printed as *SMB* 42 K. As is typical of the "Liten Karin" tradition as a whole, Stina's ballad does not have a refrain, but instead the melody is repeated, so that

---

[74] Flemming G. Andersen, *Commonplace and Creativity*, Odense University Studies from the Medieval Centre 1 (Odense: Odense University Press, 1985), 37.

each line of the ballad is sung twice. The first two verses of her version introduce the characters and the situation. Karin serves at the king's home, the king is fascinated with her and wants to spend the whole day and night talking with her (v. 1–2). The offer and rejection sequence begins with the third verse, in which the king offers Karin material for a dress:

> "Och hör du lilla Karin hvad jag nu säga vill
> Och Linelång till klädning det vill jag gifva dig."

Karin's reply to this offer is less closely bound to the usual formulaic pattern than those that follow, possibly because the reason for the offer has not yet been made explicit:

> "Och linelång till klädning det passar jag ej på
> Men Herren Gud i himmelen gif unga kungen nåd." (v. 4)
> (And linen cloth for a dress won't interest me at all / But Lord God in Heaven have mercy on the young king)

The king's next offer, "Gullkrona och gullspira," ("a golden crown and scepter") leads to the more typical rejection verse, "Gif dem åt unga Drottningen, låt mig med äran gå." Having failed in his attempt to woo her with material objects, the king now changes tactic and threatens Karin, while also clearly stating what he expects of her:

> "Och hör du lilla Karin, vill du ej blifva min
> Så sätter jag dig i fångatorn och fängslar hårdt ditt sinn." (v. 7)
> (And listen, Little Karin, if you will not be mine/I'll put you in the prison-tower and sorely try your mind)

The following four strophes describe how Karin is threatened with the spiked barrel, how the punishment is carried out, and how she dies. Her body is carefully tended (v. 13), and buried (v. 14). The ballad ends with the familiar sequence in which angels carry Karin to Heaven, and ravens carry the king off to hell.

Stina's version of "Liten vallpiga" (*SMB* 182 Q) does not call the main character by name, but instead makes her "bondens getpiga" (the farmer's goat-girl). The ballad has a refrain, "Herren min" (my lord), following the first line, and "Om sommaren, när alla små foglar de sjunga väl" (in the summer when all the little birds sing well), following the second line of regular text. The text has no offer and rejection sequence at all. Instead, the girl complies immediately with the king's request that she sing for him, and he responds by making her queen.

Stina's version of "Liten båtsman" (*SMB* 181 L) contains the refrain "Och de spela, de spelade gulltärning" ("and they play, they played golden dice") following the second of the verse's two lines. The offer and rejection sequence begins in verse ten, with the following offer:

"Gack borrt, gack borrt, du gångarpilt, Gack långt borrt ifrån mig, sju gårdar uti Skåne dem vill jag gifva dig." ("Go away, go away, thou wandering boy, go far away from me / seven farms in Skåne, these will I give to thee.")

The young man replies:

"Sju gårdar uti Skåne, dem tar jag när jag kan / men nog tar jag min jungfru, som jag med tärning vann." ("Seven farms in Skåne, I'll take them when I can / but sure I'll take my maiden, the one at dice I won.") (v. 11)

The maiden's second offer as she tries to rid herself of her apparently low-born suitor is "halfva utaf mitt rike" — ("half of my kingdom") (v. 12), and after the lad's formulaically consistent reply, she gives up, and he reveals that he is the emperor's son.

In Stina's repertoire, the three ballads seem to be fully independent of one another. Although two of the three employ offer and rejection sequences, the gifts offered in the two ballads are not the same, and there does not seem to be any other correspondence between the three ballad texts or their melodies.

Maja Hansdotter, the widow of a crofter in Slaka parish, Östergötland, was the most respected ballad singer in her area, according to J. H. Wallman, who collected a large number of ballads from her in the early nineteenth century.[75] Her version of "Liten Karin," printed as *SMB* 42 A, was collected by J. H. or D. S. Wallman in 1811, unfortunately without the melody. The offer and rejection sequence begins in the second verse with the offer of a golden dress:

"Och hör du lilla Karin vill du nu blifva min
den rödaste Gullklädning den vill jag gifva dig."

Karin's reply is the typical one for this ballad type, ". . .den passar jag ej på, Gif den åt er unga Drottning, låt mej med äran gå." The king then threatens to imprison Karin in "mörka tornet," followed by a verse offering her "den rödaste gullkrona" in exchange for her consent, and Karin's formulaic reply. In verse eight the king threatens to condemn Karin to the spiked barrel, and the narrative omits her reply, moving directly to the action. Karin's lifeless body is laid on a golden bier (v. 10). The king then goes in to write a letter, turns over his hourglass, and when it has run out, stabs himself (v. 11,12).

Maja's version of "Liten vallpiga," with the refrain "månde jag få sofva hos dig, Inga, liten och väna!" ("may I sleep beside you, Inga, little and fair!") was also collected by the Wallmans in the early 1800s. It is not printed in *SMB*, but occurs under two different numbers in the first and second editions of *Svenska*

---

[75] Jonsson, *Svensk balladtradition*, 385–86.

folkvisor. The ballad is assigned number 75 in the first edition, but printed as number 60 in the second edition, in which Maja's text appears as 60:4. Inga works in the mill, where she sings as she works. The king hears her, and sends his page to fetch her. The offer and rejection sequence is introduced in verse eight, with the offer of "the best stone house in my city":

> "Och Inga lilla, Inga lill', du sjunger för mej!
> Det bästa stenhus i min stad det vill jag gifva dig."

She refuses to sing:

> "Och intet har jag sjungit eller väjet deruppå,
> Det bästa stenhus i er stad det kan jag väl få."

The king then offers "the best ship in the river," "the best horse in my stables," "a golden saddle," and "one of my servants," all of which elicit the same formulaic refusal from Inga. In verse 18 he offers himself, and she begins to sing. Everyone dances, after which the king makes Inga queen and the ballad ends.

Like Stina i Stensö, Maja Hansdotter uses different offer and rejection sequences for "Liten Karin" and "Liten vallpiga." There is nothing in either text to suggest that the singer considers the two ballads to be related. Rather, it appears that the offer and rejection sequence is a tool used consciously and intentionally to advance the narrative.

A third singer, Anna Stina Hallman in Landeryds parish in Östergötland, also provided J. H. Wallman with variants of "Liten Karin" and "Liten vallpiga." Her origin and background are unknown, and Bengt Jonsson suggests that she was only a temporary visitor in Landeryd. Wallman collected a total of three ballads from Hallman, but she also provided A. M. Weselius with a number of singing games.[76] Hallman's version of "Liten Karin" (*SMB* 42 B) lacks a refrain, but includes a repeat of the second line of several, but apparently not all of the verses.[77] Hallman's version of "Liten Karin" is unique, to the best of my knowledge, in that the protagonist is named Inga. While this name commonly occurs in variants of "Liten vallpiga," the "Liten Karin" tradition is otherwise extremely consistent in retaining the name Karin. The male antagonist is called "unga Hertingen" (the young duke) in the first verse, and he actually catches Inga in his arms, a situation that does not occur in other variants of the ballad. The offer and rejection sequence begins in the second verse with the offer of a golden crown, and the reply is the standard one:

---

[76] Jonsson, *Svensk balladtradition,* 393–94.
[77] See notes to text, *SMB* 2:94.

"Den rödaste Gullkronan den passar jag ej på
Gif den åt Er unga Drottning, låt mig med äran gå." (v. 3)

Interestingly, it appears that the formulaic tradition is strong enough that no adjustment is made in the status of the duke's consort. She remains "drottningen," the queen, in spite of the title accorded her (presumed) husband in the ballad. The offer and rejection sequence continues with "den rödaste gullklänning," and "ett gångande skepp i floden." In verse eight the sequence shifts to threats, beginning with "mörka tornet." This theme is actually accorded four verses (8–11), and the king makes his threat more specific by stating that Inga will be left in the tower for two months. The next threat is the spiked barrel, and as usual the king makes good his threat. Hallman's version of the ballad ends with two stanzas in which two doves fly down from Heaven and three fly back up (v. 16), and two ravens fly up from hell to carry off the young duke, body and soul (v. 17).

Hallman's version of "Liten vallpiga" (*SMB* 182 E) has the refrain "I minunnen Ekelund så gröna" (approx. "Remember an oak-grove so green"). The protagonist in the ballad is "Kari lille," which is interesting in comparision with Hallman's "Liten Karin." However, the name of the main character in the many variants of "Liten vallpiga" is highly variable, and Karin or some variation thereof is among the names which occur. It is typical of this ballad that there are several narrative episodes before the offer and rejection sequence begins, and Hallman's variant follows tradition, introducing the sequence first in verse 12, with the offer of a golden crown. Although the crown also occurs in the offer and rejection sequence of Hallman's version of "Liten Karin," the reply, or rejection stanza, does not resemble that of "Liten Karin":

"Nej inte jag quäda ej heller quäda må förr än jag bättre gåfva får." ("No, I will not sing, nor can I sing until I get a better gift") (v. 13)

Unlike the sequence in "Liten Karin," the reply stanza in this variant of "Liten vallpiga" does not include a repetition of the king's offer. Although some variants of this ballad also employ the phrase "jag passar inte på," which occurs regularly in "Liten Karin," in the rejection stanza, this variant does not. The sequence continues with the offer of "gull och gröna skogar" ("gold and green woods"), "Den likesta Riddaren" ("the finest knight"), half a kingdom, the whole kingdom, and "halva mitt unga liv" ("half of my young life"). The rejection stanza remains the same for each of these offers, and only when the king offers his whole life does the girl yield to his request and begin to sing. The ballad ends with the observation that it is not a bad thing to be queen:

"Drottningenamn det är ej så tungt till att bära
Men väljes den jungfru som får det med ära." (v. 31)

(approx. "Being named queen is not hard to bear, when the girl who is chosen gets it with honor.")

Generally speaking, it does not appear that the singers whose repertoires include
more than one of the ballads employing an offer and rejection sequence consider
these ballads to be closely related. None of the variants discussed above appears
to make any intertextual reference to any other ballad (something which does
occasionally occur in ballad tradition), unless a case can be made for the stanza
cited just above as a reference to "Liten Karin"'s "låt mig med äran gå," which
seems unlikely. Of the three singers discussed here, only Hallman uses the same
offer in the offer and rejection sequence in two different ballads, and even she
repeats only a single stanza. This argument is nonetheless limited by the fact that
only one recording of each ballad and singer has been available for examination.
Thus it is not possible to determine whether the singers always used exactly the
same offer and rejection sequence each time they sang a given ballad, or whether
the stanzas could vary with each performance. To judge from the material available here, however, the singers seem to regard the various ballads as separate,
discrete narratives, and the lack of overlap between the offer/rejection sequences
in the ballads sung by each individual seems to reflect this circumstance. It may,
however, be possible to suggest that the "Liten Karin" tradition contains elements, even in the offer and rejection sequence, that separate it further from the
other ballads that also employ such sequences. Although the offer verses may be
more or less identical—at least in the second line—in all of these ballads, the
reply in "Liten Karin" is always distinct from the other ballads in this group.
Although this comparison involves only three singers, and only three ballad
types, it suggests that ballad singers were well in control of their material, and
were able to deploy established, stereotypical formulas and formulaic sequences
in very intentional and conscious ways, so that they could make use of a broad
range of meanings implicit (or potentially so) in any given commonplace. In spite
of the formulaic nature of the offer and rejection sequences in "Liten Karin,"
there is no evidence that excludes the possibility that the gifts might have been
understood as having some connection to the saint's legend or cult.

The connection between the legend and the ballad is widely accepted by
ballad scholars, and no one has advanced a dissenting opinion. Given this background, and given the wide geographic distribution of the ballad in early nineteenth-century Sweden, it seems very unlikely that the ballad was first composed
or borrowed into Scandinavian tradition shortly before the nineteenth-century
ballad enthusiasts began writing it down. If the ballad had existed in tradition
for a longer time, however, why does it not occur in any of the ballad collections
of the sixteenth, seventeenth or eighteenth centuries?

One of the most important points that must be recognized in any study of
ballad tradition is that there is no such thing as an unbiased source. Every ballad collector, whether he or she records the ballads with a pen and paper or with

advanced video and sound equipment, makes decisions about the nature of the material, and what is to be included. These decisions include definitions of the ballad genre, as well as opinions as to what kinds of ballads are of interest. In some cases this process of selection is intentional and conscious, while in other cases it may result from the way the collector unconsciously guides the informant. Although the tastes and values of the individual collector, or indeed, the informant, may be important in this process, it is also crucial to realize that there have been very strong trends in Scandinavian ballad collecting through time, and that these trends have been extremely influential in determining which ballads were recorded. Bengt Jonsson has discussed these trends in his dissertation, *Svensk balladtradition* :

> The occurrence of the various ballad categories in the sources from different periods is closely related to the varying nature of the source materials and the attitudes of the collectors. The heroic ballads ("kämpavisorna") were clearly appreciated during the 1500 and 1600s, and were therefore included in the ballad books and discussed by historians during these centuries. It is also clear that these ballads were attractive to the promoters of the antiquarian movement; it is thus telling that of Ingierd Gunnarsdotter's repertoire, it is the heroic ballads which were most often written down. Otherwise, a man like Johan Hadorph had clear intentions about which ballads he most wanted from her: one about Brakelund and one about the Battle of Lena in 1208. This kind of selective approach is something we must assume for the seventeenth-century antiquarians. Similarly, with regard to the spontaneously written ballad books of the sixteenth and seventeenth centuries, we must of course assume that their owners included only the ballads they themselves had enjoyed or come into close contact with. It is far from certain that a member of the high nobility knew or enjoyed the same ballads as, for example, the peasants under his leadership. Anything which could be considered an expression of peasant superstition (the magical ballads) or "popery" (the legendary ballads) would be unlikely to appeal, either to the ballad-interested circles of aristocrats and students, on the one hand, or the antiquarian collectors on the other. The eighteenth century is the century when the broadside assumes a relatively more dominant position among ballad sources than either before or after. There is reason to assume that the content of the broadsides corresponded to the tastes of their principal consumers, who were mainly found among the lower classes during this period. It should thus be possible, with regard to selection, to consider the broadsides as a separate source. It is thus notable that the legendary ballads are relatively better represented among the broadsides than in other sources before the collections of the National Romantic generation. From the eighteenth century there are also relatively many examples of historical, or locally connected ballads in the dissertations and other works of historical or topographic content. With regard to the collectors of the nineteenth and twentieth centuries, it should be possible to assume that they did not have any particular preferences—although it may be that the men of the

early nineteenth century had a particular weakness for the "nixie ballads," and other magical ballads, whose motifs inspired the poets of the time to compose their own poems on these themes—but that they wrote down all the ballad types they encountered.[78]

Jonsson's description of Scandinavian ballad collectors' preferences offers a very strong explanation of the absence of "Liten Karin" in the early ballad manuscripts. While the ballad's legendary origins are not necessarily evident to the singers of the nineteenth and twentieth centuries, they might have been much more obvious to collectors in an earlier period. Further, it is difficult to connect this ballad to anything resembling an historic event or heroic tradition, whether classical or Germanic. There is very little in the ballad that might have been attractive to the early antiquarians, and, as Jonsson suggests, the material might have seemed inappropriate to the owners of the private ballad books. It is also important to note that early ballad collectors, including Johan Hadorph, whom Jonsson mentions above, were often closely connected to circles around the royal court, and thus representatives of the very authorities who were most interested in promoting the reformation of the church in Sweden. If ballad singers in the seventeenth century did have ballads with specifically Roman Catholic content in their repertoires, and if these ballads in any way reflected their own devotional practices or beliefs, such songs are the last thing they would have been likely to perform for a collector. The very great popularity of "Liten Karin," and for that matter "Maria Magdalena," another legendary ballad absent from ballad sources until the very end of the eighteenth century, once they began to be collected in the nineteenth century, seems also to argue for a long and well-established tradition with roots deep in the past. The fact that "Liten Karin" is a legendary ballad, based on Roman Catholic material, not only accounts for its omission from the early written sources, but may also be one of the most important arguments for a medieval origin. As Vésteinn Ólason notes:

> For some strange reason, ballad scholars have tended to think that these (legendary) ballads are a relatively late phenomenon in the history of Scandinavian balladry. Such an idea probably began with Grundtvig and his contemporaries, who thought the ballad genre had its roots as far back as pagan times. Few Scandinavian ballads, however, have a stronger claim to being really medieval than these ballads that are based on literature and ideas of the time before the Reformation when all of Scandinavia was Roman Catholic. Ballads of this kind are generally not found in the ballad books of the sixteenth-century aristocracy in Denmark and Sweden because such poetry could not be regarded as proper for well-educated people to read or hear while the Protestant agitation against everything that had to do with Catholicism was at its height. The common people, on the

---

[78] Jonsson, *Svensk balladtradition*, 797–98.

other hand, continued to cherish these old songs, regardless of the attitude of the church.[79]

The Danish ballad scholar Iørn Piø has similar thoughts:

> Even though these Catholic songs are known to have been popular among "the folk" also after the Reformation of 1536, they were only rarely written down in the circles that were interested in folksongs during the seventeenth and eighteenth centuries. The hatred for everything "Papist" was still too strong for that.[80]

Like many other legendary ballads, "Liten Karin" is featured on a number of nineteenth-century broadsides, and these undoubtedly served to enhance its popularity and spread. Jonsson's comments about the target market for broadsides suggest that the legendary ballads as a genre, at least after the Reformation, were sung mainly by members of the lower classes, an idea with which Ólason clearly concurs. These general circumstances regarding the collection of legendary ballads give a degree of credibility to the idea that many legendary ballads, including "Liten Karin" may be much older than the date of their earliest collection would indicate. On the other hand, the fact that ballad collectors avoided certain kinds of ballads cannot be used as proof that all ballads of that kind are medieval in origin. In the absence of an early text of "Liten Karin," it is worth turning to circumstantial evidence in order to trace the history of this individual ballad back in time.

A Reconstructed History of "Liten Karin"

"Liten Karin" depicts a virtuous young woman's efforts to fend off the amorous advances of a powerful male, who tries to woo her first with gifts, and then with threats. The girl's refusal to yield leads to her painful death, but the ballad does not generally end here. Instead, a pair of angels in the shape of doves descend from Heaven and rise again with Karin as a third dove, while a pair of ravens appears to carry the king off to hell. While the "Liten Karin" ballad is clearly to be regarded as a distinct narrative tradition, the general plot outline of the unfairly persecuted girl unjustly executed for defending her virtue, along with its accompanying dove and raven motif, is also found elsewhere in Scandinavian ballad tradition. In fact, a written record of such a ballad, a variant of "Herr

---

[79] Vésteinn Ólason, "Literary Backgrounds of the Scandinavian Ballad," in *The Ballad and Oral Literature*, ed. Joseph Harris, Harvard English Studies 17 (Cambridge, MA and London: Harvard University Press, 1991), 116–38, here 131.

[80] Iørn Piø, *Nye veje til folkevisen* (Copenhagen: Gyldendal, 1985), 315, n. 14.

Peder och hans syster" ("Sir Peder and his sister"),[81] may provide the first opportunity of tracing "Liten Karin" back in time. This variant, *SMB* 46 C, was collected in Östergötland during the 1790s. It incorporates a two-line refrain, the second line of which is "stolts Karin och jag." The protagonists of these two ballads are placed in very similar situations, which might justify the assumption that the "Karin" mentioned in the refrain is a reference to "Liten Karin." This would in turn suggest that the "Liten Karin" ballad was sufficiently well established in oral tradition by the 1790s that it could influence variants of other ballads. Unfortunately, the collector did not write down the melody, which makes it difficult to test the common assumption that refrains may be more closely related to the melody than to the body of the ballad text. If this refrain actually does refer to the ballad in which it occurs, however, it seems quite possible that this line is a comment on the similarity of the two protagonists' situations. If this is the case, it may help to establish that "Liten Karin" existed in tradition at least some thirty years earlier than the earliest known written text.

Olof Dalin, one of eighteenth-century Sweden's most important cultural figures, provides the next opportunity of tracing "Liten Karin" backward in time. Dalin composed a number of poems in which he parodied or made use of folk ballads, and one of these ballads appears to have been "Liten Karin." In a poem dated 25 November 1738, Dalin commemorates the name-day of a daughter of his patron:

På Karins-mässo dagen den 25 November 1738, En
gammal Wisa Til Fröken Catharina Charlotta Ribbing

Nu wele we qwäda om fordom tid,
För aderton år sen i werlden,
Då Karins-mässo kom på jorden här nid
Ibland den werdsliga flärden:
In dulci gaudio, på Karins-mäss frögdar sig Fogden.

Herr Lennart han axlade kappan blå,
Han månde för Fru Elsa framträda.
Han sade: hwad namn skal wår Dotter få,
Som skal oss i ålderdomen gläda?
In dulci gaudio, på &c.

Fru Elsa hon hade sig wäl betänkt,
Din Moder uppkallar jag så gärna;
Och alt sen den dagen har Karin blänkt
I Allmanackan liksom en Stjerna:
In dulci gaudio, på &c.

---

[81] *TSB* B 20/*SMB* 46.

Sankt Brita hon skaffade en Dotter fram
Sanct Karin med ära och lydna.
Hon spådde, att en Karin skull' födas af dess stam,
Sitt Kön til heder och prydna.
In dulci gaudio, på &c.

Hon sade, du stolts Karin, som bära skal mitt namn,
Wist hafver dig Himmelen i minne
En ypperlig Ungerswän får du i famn
Och tusend' slags frögd i ditt sinne.
In dulci, på &c.

Stolts Karins Fogde, den trogna träl,
Har denna uppenbarelse funnit:
Han önskar nu stolts Karin til kropp och til själ
Mer godt, än nånsin Karin har wunnit:
In dulci gaudio, på Karin-mäss frögdar sig Fogden.[82]

(Now we sing of times long past
18 years ago in the world
when Karin's mass came down to earth
among worldly vanity.
--In dulci gaudio, on Karin's mass the bailiff rejoices.

Herr Lennart threw back his blue cape
He went before Fru Elsa.
He said: what shall we name our daughter,
the joy of our old age?
-- (refrain)

Fru Elsa, she was well prepared:
we'll name her after your mother;
and since that day Karin has shone
in the almanac like a star.
-- (refrain)

Saint Brita bore a daughter,
Saint Karin, with honor and glory.
She said that a Karin would be born of their lineage,
to the honor and adornment of her sex.
-- (refrain)

She said, you, proud Karin, who will bear my name,
Heaven remembers you well:

---

[82] Olof von Dalin, *Witterhets-Arbeten*, vol. 4 (Stockholm: Carl Stolpe, 1767), 95.

You shall embrace a fine young man
and a thousand kinds of joy.
-- (refrain)

Proud Karin's bailiff, that faithfull thrall,
has found this revelation:
He wishes proud Karin in body and soul
more good than ever Karin has won.
--(refrain)

Dalin's poem is by no means a copy of any known version of "Liten Karin," but certain elements link it with the ballad and, much more loosely, with the cult of St. Katherine of Alexandria. November 25 is the feast day of St. Katherine of Alexandria, and is to this day celebrated as "Katarinadagen" in Sweden. It has never been associated with St. Katherine of Vadstena, whose feast days (in those few calendars that included them) are 25 June and 2 August. It does not necessarily follow that Dalin was aware of this distinction. The strong emphasis on Katherine of Vadstena and her mother Saint Birgitta (including the reference to Birgitta's Revelations in the last stanza) may result from a misunderstanding of which saint lay behind "Katarinadagen," but it may also be an expression of Swedish patriotism to associate a young Swedish noblewoman with an earlier, much admired, aristocratic Swedish "virgin,"[83] and indeed, the poem suggests that the family it depicts claimed descent from St. Birgitta. The reference to Katherine of Vadstena and St. Birgitta may also be intended as a compliment, not only to the recipient of the poem, but also to her mother, who is thus made a parallel to Birgitta. The content of Dalin's poem diverges considerably from "Liten Karin," which should surprise no one. However heroic and sympathetic the protagonist of "Liten Karin" appears in the ballad, her story is at least partly tragic, and as such is not really appropriate material for a poem dedicated to the young daughter of a wealthy patron. Perhaps the most important detail in Dalin's poem which may link it to the "Liten Karin" tradition is the line "Och alt sen den dagen har Karin blänkt / i Allmanackan liksom en Stjerna" ("And ever since that day Karin has shone in the almanac just like a star"). This seems very close indeed to "Hon lyste som en stjärna/bland andra tärnor små" ("She shone just like a star / among the other little maids"), a line found in Afzelius's famous recording of "Liten Karin" "efter en vallpigas sång" ("from a herding-girl's song"). It seems very unlikely that Dalin's occasional poem, composed for the commemoration of a single individual on a specific occasion, would exert influence on oral folk tradition. On the other hand, Dalin's "Karins-mässo" poem, like a number of

---

[83] Although Katherine of Vadstena was married, her legend stresses that she and her husband lived in chastity. See Tryggve Lundén, *Sveriges missionärer, helgon och kyrkogrundare: en bok om Sveriges kristnande* (Storuman: Bokförlaget Artos, 1983), 386.

his other ballad parodies, shows that the poet had considerable familiarity with the formulaic language of ballad tradition (e.g., ". . .han axlade kappan blå / Han månde för Fru Elsa framträda. . ."). Dalin's references to Katherine of Vadstena and Saint Birgitta, and his explicit references to 25 November not only as a name day but also as a saint's feast day (albeit the wrong saint), reflect a surprising interest in and tolerance of certain aspects of Roman Catholicism among secular aristocratic circles, and even among some clerics, during the eighteenth century. The celebration of name days directly based on the Roman Catholic liturgical calendar was very much in vogue among the educated classes during this period, to such an extent that, by 1768, a book was actually published in Sweden explaining the legends behind the names in the calendar.[84] Still later in the century, King Gustav III attempted to repeal the law banning the practice of non-Lutheran religion (primarily Catholicism and Judaism) in Sweden. It is significant, however, that the king was thwarted in this attempt by the powerful clergy, so that the increasing curiosity about and tolerance toward Roman Catholicism among certain circles did not lead to greater religious freedom under the law. For a Swedish Lutheran (a category which by definition included all Swedes), to convert to Roman Catholicism remained a crime punishable by law - and the penalties included exile and loss of inheritance - until 1870.[85] Thus it seems unlikely that a newly composed ballad about a saint would have the opportunity to achieve widespread popularity across class boundaries during this period. This suggests that Dalin's poem may be regarded as a marker in the history of the "Liten Karin" ballad, but not as the earliest boundary of the ballad's existence.

The next record that may help to trace "Liten Karin" backwards in time is not an example of intertextuality, but rather a comment in a dissertation from 1860 that "under Sigismund's vistelse i Upsala sjöngs vid ett tillfälle visan om 'Liten Karin'" ("on one occasion during Sigismund's stay in Uppsala, the ballad 'Liten Karin' was sung").[86] Sigismund, son of Johan III, and grandson of Gustav Vasa, was king of Sweden from 1592 until 1599, when he was deposed by his uncle, later King Karl IX. Bengt Jonsson notes that a number of historical works from the seventeenth century mention that a ballad containing the phrase "Jagh passar intet på" was sung at Sigismund's coronation.[87] It appears, then, that Piscator based his statement on the fact that this phrase occurs repeatedly in the offer and rejection sequence that forms the core of the "Liten Karin" ballad. As Jonsson points out, this does not absolutely constitute certain identification of the

---

[84] *En kort berättelse utaf hwad tillfälle de Personers Namn Blifwit införde uti Almanachen/ som der, för hwarje dag, hela året igenom, står antecknade* (Västerås: Printed by Johan Laurentius Hornn at his own expense, 1768).

[85] Sten Carlsson, "Katolicism i svenskt kulturliv," *Kyrkohistorisk årsskrift* (1989), 25–31.

[86] Johan Anders Conrad Piscator, *Historisk översigt af Musiken i Sverige under Gustaf III* (Uppsala: Edquist, 1860), 1.

[87] Jonsson, *Svensk balladtradition*, 733.

ballad. As I have discussed at length above, this phrase may occur in many other ballads. However, examination of a large number of variants of each of these ballads shows that the line occurs in "Liten Karin" almost without exception, while it is only one of several possible variants for this part of the sequence in other ballads. In "Liten Karin," the line "jag passar inte på" and its close variants "det/den/de passar jag ej på" and "jag passar intet på" (all of which mean roughly "I'm not interested" or "It doesn't/they don't mean a thing to me") is an expression of deep conviction. It is clear from the beginning that no offer or threat will induce Karin to consider a closer relationship with the king. In the offer sequences, the second part of the rejection stanza is always "Gif den/det/dem åt unga drottningen låt mig med äran gå" (Give it/them to your young queen, let me with honor go). In these phrases, variation occurs only in minor, "filler" words, not in meaning-bearing components of the phrase. In other ballads, the phrase "jag passar inte på" is often found alongside "det kan jag väl få" (approximately "I can certainly get / take that"- more loosely, perhaps, "nothing wrong with that") or "det får jag väl ändå" ("I'll be getting that anyway"), all of which fulfill the same rhyme function as "det passar jag ej på." It may be that the consistency with which the phrase occurs in "Liten Karin" is an argument in favor of Piscator's assumption that it really was "Liten Karin" that was sung in Uppsala in the 1590s. Sigismund's religious background may also suggest that "Liten Karin" would have been considered an appropriate song for the festivities surrounding his coronation. His mother was the Polish princess Katarina Jagellonica, a fervent Catholic, and his father, Johan III, is known for his (ultimately unsuccessful) attempts to reconcile the Catholic and Lutheran faiths. One of Sigismund's major concerns during his short reign was to try to promote tolerance between Lutherans and Catholics, and this also contributed to his strongly Pietist uncle's successful move to depose him.[88] It might also be noted that the content of the ballad does not portray Karin as an intercessor, though it does emphasize her status as a holy martyr. Thus, while the ballad's appeal is obvious for those who still clung to their Roman Catholic faith, it would not be offensive to those who had accepted Lutheran doctrine. According to the reforms adopted in Sweden in

---

[88] In another somewhat uncertain note roughly a century later (published in 1695), the Danish ballad editor Peder Syv mentions a ballad about "S. Karen" among other songs with religious subject matter in the foreword to his ballad edition (Peder Syv, *Et hundrede udvalde danske viser forøgede med det andet Hundrede Viser om Danske Konger, Kæmper og Andre*, 2nd ed. (Copenhagen: printed and published by P. M. Høpffner, 1787),"Fortale," section 21 –unpaginated). Unfortunately he does not describe the song in detail, and it does not appear in his ballad edition. Still, Katherine of Alexandria appears to have been as popular in Denmark as she was in Sweden, and "Liten Karin" is represented in later Danish tradition. While not reliable in isolation, Syv's mention might form a small building block in a reconstruction of the ballad's earlier history, as well as suggesting the possibility that the ballad might date back further in Denmark, as well as in Sweden, than the manuscript record would indicate.

1544, it was forbidden to pray to the saints, or call on them for intercession. On the other hand, it was still permissible to regard them as examples of holy behavior, and to commemorate them. During this period, some few saints' days were allowed to remain in the liturgical calendars.[89] In this way, the performance of "Liten Karin" might well have reflected Sigismund's own interests or concerns.

If there is reason to believe that "Liten Karin" existed in Swedish oral tradition by 1592, the year of Sigismund's coronation, we find ourselves only a generation or two after the inception of the Protestant Reformation. From this position it may be possible to argue that this ballad, the content of which is based on a solidly Roman Catholic legend, actually dates from the period during which Catholicism was the official religion of Sweden. If this is so, is it possible to speculate about its origin and early spread? The question of the ballad's possible earlier form has already been discussed in this chapter, and will not be repeated here. But what information do we have that might have bearing on the ballad's possible medieval history?

In her study of the "Maria Magdalena" ballad, Ann-Mari Häggman asserts that this ballad[90] is clearly of medieval, religious character, and that it has many traits pointing to strong Dominican influence.[91] Although the "Liten Karin" ballad and that of Mary Magdalene differ considerably in content, they also have important aspects in common, and Häggman's conclusions regarding "Maria Magdalena" may also to a certain extent be applicable to "Liten Karin." Like Katherine of Alexandria, Mary Magdalene was a favored patron saint of the mendicant orders. It is well known that the Dominican and Franciscan friars had a great deal of contact with ordinary laymen and women, often outside the context of the parish church. In conjunction with preaching, hearing confession and administering absolution, and other aspects of ministering to the souls of the laity, these friars undoubtedly retold the legends of their patron saints. Contact with the mendicant friars could occur in various ways. While their influence on an official, institutional level can be seen in the liturgical history of the various Swedish dioceses, it is also possible that their influence on the laity can be seen in Scandinavian ballad tradition. At the same time, it might be noted that the cult of St. Mary Magdalene, like that of St. Katherine of Alexandria, can be documented in Sweden not only before the arrival of the mendicant orders there, but even before the foundation of those orders. Like the feast of St. Katherine, the feast day of St. Mary Magdalene, 22 July, is found in the earliest Swedish liturgical calendar, the Vallentuna calendar dated to 1198. Just as for St. Katherine,

---

[89] Åke Andrén, *Sveriges kyrkohistoria 3: Reformationstid* (Stockholm: Verbum, 1999), 111.

[90] *SMB* 43, *TSB* B 16.

[91] Ann-Mari Häggman, *Magdalena på källebro: en studie i finlandssvensk vistradition med utgångspunkt i visan om Maria Magdalena*, Skrifter utgivna av Svenska litteratursällskapet i Finland 576, Humanistiska avhandlingar 6 (Helsingfors: Svenska litteratursällskapet i Finland, 1992), 67–72.

the notation for the Magdalene's feast is in the original hand, with a cross beside the name added in a later hand.[92] Although this saint, like St. Katherine, is frequently named in letters of indulgence issued for Dominican churches, she was clearly venerated also by other groups in medieval Swedish society. For example, Mary Magdalene's feast day is named as one of those on which visitors to the church of the Cistercian convent at Vreta could receive forty days' indulgence in a charter issued by Brynolf, Bishop of Skara, dated 1289 (*DS* no. 1004). Although the mendicant orders clearly played an important role in the popularization of the cult of St. Mary Magdalene, as they did for the cult of St. Katherine of Alexandria, it may be misleading to assume that they alone were responsible for the widespread devotion these saints enjoyed.

As I have already suggested in this chapter, I find little reason to believe that the "Liten Karin" ballad has undergone a radical change of form or content since the Middle Ages. While it is clear that mendicant orders played a role in the ultimate popularity of the cult of Saint Katherine, the aspects of the legend emphasized in the ballad are not the ones most closely associated with the ideals of the Dominican and Franciscan orders. Rather, it seems most likely that the ballad was composed by non-clerics, laypersons, who extracted from the legends told orally by the mendicant friars or parish priests, and perhaps also learned from other sources, the motifs and episodes which had most meaning for their own lives. It should not be surprising, for example, that Katherine's extraordinary learning and her conversion of fifty pagan philosophers by means of their own pagan Greek texts fail to appear in the ballad. An intimate knowledge of Plato or Aristotle might be important to a Dominican friar, but it would have little meaning to a farmer in rural Uppland. However, the legend of Saint Katherine is not only about the conversion of pagan Greek philosophy to Christian theology, it is also about rebellion against authority. In the legend, as well as in the ballad, a young woman is subjected to extreme and unjust torture by an authority figure who tries to force her from the position she knows to be correct. Although the antagonist, both in the legend and in the ballad, appears to win the battle, subjecting the young female protagonist to a painful death, his victory is only apparent and quite temporary. Both the miracles that precede and accompany her death and the voice from Heaven that welcomes Katherine as the beloved bride of Christ make it abundantly clear to the audience of the legend that the real triumph is Katherine's. The ballad also depicts the triumph of Right over Might, of truth and justice over earthly authority, in the dove-and-raven stanzas that often comprise the conclusion of "Liten Karin." Although the ballad could certainly be seen as a depiction of the vulnerable position of women in medieval, and later, society — and as a pious man's affirmation that the king's treatment of Karin is wrong and sinful — it is just as likely that much of its appeal lay in

---

[92] See Schmid, *Liber ecclesiae Vallentunensis*, 89.

the triumph of the oppressed. "Liten Karin" has been recorded from both male and female traditors. This fact makes it clear that the conflict in the ballad was not regarded as being strictly a problem of women. Clearly men were also able to find significance in the narrative, whether that significance lay in the perceived class conflict or in the clear theme of salvation. If the ballad really is an expression of lay spirituality, where might we look to discover its origins, or at least an environment in which it might have been sung?

Although it may be impossible to prove conclusively, it may well be that the guilds dedicated to St. Katherine played a role in the popularization of "Liten Karin," perhaps providing, at the least, a venue for its performance. As noted above, guilds, perhaps especially the rural parish guilds, were strongly rooted in the local communities of medieval Sweden. At least some guilds had both male and female members, and one of the primary functions of these guilds seems to have been to provide for the members' spiritual health through the funding of masses for the souls of the deceased and participation in their funeral processions. Solidarity among guild members was certainly encouraged and reinforced through the regular guild meetings, which appear to have had a festive aspect. Among the most important activities at any guild meeting was the drinking of a toast ("minne"). In the case of the guild of Katherine of Alexandria in Björke parish, Gotland, the three toasts drunk were to "Our Lord," "Our Lady," and most importantly, "S:ta Katarinas minne."[93] The custom of toasting, or drinking in honor of the saints, especially the guild patron, was apparently well established in medieval Europe and not least in Scandinavia, and it is possible that the custom reflects similar practice from pre-Christian times.[94] At least in the medieval Swedish guilds, the "minnen" were sung, not spoken, and the word "minne" thus refers not only to the act of drinking to the saint's honor, but also to the song sung during the ceremony, in which all guild members were expected to participate.[95] It appears, however, that the official toasts were not the only songs sung at guild meetings. Guild charters typically place heavy emphasis on rules for proper behavior at guild meetings. In particular, members are warned against excessively noisy and disturbing behavior, and in many charters (though not specifically in the Björke charter), specific fines are levied against those who talk or sing during the toast, or those who loudly sing impolite or blasphemous songs.[96] It is important to note that singing is not forbidden in all contexts, and further, that only a specific category of song is forbidden at guild meetings. This suggests that song was a normal element of these meetings, not only the com-

---

[93] Pernler, "S:ta Katarina-gillet," 71, 75.

[94] Pernler, "S:ta Katarina-gillet," 76.

[95] Christina Mattson, *Helan går: 150 visor till skålen samlade och kommenterade* (Hedemora: Gidlunds förlag, 1989), 15.

[96] Pernler, "S:ta Katarina-gillet," 77.

munal toast, but also other songs unrelated to this ceremony. Songs that met a certain standard of decency were presumably tolerated and performed.

One possible explanation of the popularity of "Liten Karin" might be that some version of the ballad was sung at guild meetings of the various guilds of Saint Katherine. Several factors may contribute to such a suggestion. The ballad's point of view and choice of motifs from the legend suggest that it was composed and sung by laypersons. The ballad portrays the guild patron in a flattering light, and retells a recognizable episode — though somewhat condensed, as is typical of the ballad genre — from her legend. Further, the ballad contains no vulgarities or scandalous elements, and should not in itself have constituted a violation of typical guild rules regarding seemly behavior. Thus it could have functioned both as entertainment and as a reminder of the guild's relationship to its patron. If, as seems likely, the ballad is medieval in origin, it is quite possible that it either has its origin among the members of the guilds of Saint Katherine, or that these guilds may have contributed to the popularization of the ballad at an early point. Once the ballad became established in oral tradition, it would not have been dependent on the guilds for its continued survival, and thus the fact that the guilds in their medieval form ceased to exist as a result of the Reformation would not necessarily hinder the spread of the ballad.

Echoes of the Saint's Cult

Although the "Liten Karin" ballad derives from the legend of Katherine of Alexandria, and although the ballad's later popularity is undoubtedly related to the influence of the Katherine cult in medieval Scandinavia, the relationship between the cult and the ballad does not demonstrate unbroken continuity through time. While certain aspects of the cult of St. Katherine have remained part of Swedish culture up to the twentieth century, these are mainly linked to calendar traditions, and do not reflect continuity of devotion, or even any specific awareness of the saint as such. The same may be said of the "Liten Karin" ballad in nineteenth- and twentieth-century oral tradition. Although ballad scholars have unanimously identified the source of the ballad as the legend of Katherine of Alexandria, there is no indication that either the ballad singers themselves or their audiences were aware of the legend or the saint by the middle of the nineteenth century. Certainly many of the specific stanzas in the offer and rejection sequences used in "Liten Karin" could be interpreted as specific references to the saint's cult and legend, but the ballad also functions effectively as a narrative in its own right and for its own sake, and does not require a connection to the saint to have meaning. The nineteenth century was a time of significant changes on the religious front of Swedish society. As Nyman has noted, there is no continuity between any Roman Catholic family now living in Sweden and those who practiced the faith in Sweden before the Reformation. Although many identifiably Roman Catholic beliefs and prayers were documented from oral tradition through the early part of the nineteenth century, Nyman sees evidence that these last links to the pre-Reformation faith ceased to exist by the 1860s, when, paradoxically, the laws forbidding practice of Catholicism by native-born Swedes began to be relaxed.[97]

The immense popularity of the ballads "Liten Karin" and "Maria Magdalena" when they begin to appear in the written record in the nineteenth century is strong evidence that these ballads existed in oral tradition long before they began to be collected by ballad enthusiasts. Whether or not the ballad singers would have identified themselves as Roman Catholics, the popularity of these two ballads shows clearly that the narratives continued to have significance for performers and their audiences long after the public devotion to the saints was suppressed. While there is no doubt that St. Katherine and St. Mary Magdalene were among the favorite patrons and intercessors of medieval Sweden, there is no exact correspondence between the popularity of a saint's cult in Sweden before the Reformation (as based on the number of known dedications, images, altars, and the like) and the existence or popularity of a ballad about that saint in Sweden after the Reformation. An important example is St. Olav, the royal saint of Norway who seems to have dominated the devotional life not only of Norway, but also of Sweden, Denmark, and other parts of the medieval Nordic region.[98] In spite of this saint's enormous popularity, apparently on all levels of society, the Swedish ballad based on St. Olav's life[99] has been collected only four times, in all cases in clearly fragmentary form. Of these four variants, three (*SMB* 41 A, B, and C) were collected in areas that lay outside of Sweden during the Middle Ages. The D variant, recorded in Småland in 1925, consists only of a single verse.[100] Since no saint was more frequently chosen as dedication saint or more

---

[97] Nyman, *Förlorarnas historia*, 285–86.

[98] See Anne Lidén, *Olav den helige i medeltida bildkonst: legendmotiv och attribut* (Stockholm: KVHAA, 1999); Lilli Gjerløw, Aarno Maliniemi, Bernt. C. Lange, C. A. Nordman, Olav Bø, Kustaa Vilkuna, "Olav den hellige," *KHLM* 12: 561–83; *Helgonet i Nidaros: Olavskult och kristnande i Norden*, ed. Lars Rumar, Skrifter utgivna av Riksarkivet 3 (Stockholm: Riksarkivet, 1997).

[99] *SMB* 41/*TSB* B 12.

[100] Interestingly, the circumstances of the St. Olav ballad are similar in Denmark, and even in Norway. The Olav ballad (*NMB* 44) was collected only four times from Norwegian oral tradition. With the exception of one text of 16 verses, all were highly fragmentary. Further, all of the collected variants appear to be based on a late printed text (See *NMB* 1: 45–47). Two different poems about St. Olav (*DgF* 50, 51) are published by the Danish ballad editor Vedel, and these also appear in a handful of seventeenth-century Danish ballad manuscripts. However, only one later oral version of a ballad of St. Olav was ever recorded in Denmark, and Grundtvig considers it to be derived from Vedel's printed text. It would appear that the only significant nineteenth-century oral ballad tradition concerning St. Olav was found in the Færoes (see *DgF* 2, 134–39; *DgF* 4, 877–89).

often depicted in Swedish churches, the rarity of the ballad in Swedish tradition does not reflect medieval attitudes toward the saint himself. Nor is it likely to reflect the preferences of ballad collectors, since, by the time that "Liten Karin" and "Maria Magdalena" begin to appear in the written record, ballad collectors were happy to write down more or less all the texts available to them.[101] Because Norway was joined in a union with Sweden in the early nineteenth century, only a few years after Sweden lost Finland to Russia, it seems unlikely that ballad collectors en masse would choose to ignore narratives about Norway's patron saint for nationalistic reasons. Further, the content of this ballad, which centers on St. Olav's famous sailing race and his conflict with trolls, seems if anything more likely to appeal to collectors inspired by the ideals of National Romanticism than the narratives of the murdered innocent of "Liten Karin" and the penitent sinner of "Maria Magdalena." Thus it seems reasonable to conclude that these two ballads fulfilled a need or satisfied an interest for singers and audiences that the ballad of St. Olav did not. The key may be that, in contrast to the ballad of St. Olav, both "Liten Karin" and "Maria Magdalena" focus on the issue of individual salvation.

Kathleen Stokker has argued convincingly that Norwegian prose legends depicting Lutheran clergy ("Black Book ministers") actually suggest that the doctrinal changes resulting from the Reformation created for the laity a sense of powerlessness over their own salvation, in spite of Martin Luther's insistence that the individual would achieve salvation through his own purity of heart.[102] A considerable corpus of material from Sweden and Denmark expresses similar concern over the fate of individual souls, and seems to suggest a belief that Protestant ministers possessed both knowledge of and control over the salvation of souls to a degree that caused their parishioners considerable anxiety. At the same time, however, ballads such as "Liten Karin" and others that depict the souls of the blessed carried up to Heaven, or those of the damned to hell, present an essentially Roman Catholic worldview, in which salvation and damnation are dependent on individual behavior. In these ballad narratives, the signs of salvation or damnation are apparent to everyone, not just to the Lutheran clergy.[103] In the Swedish legendary ballad corpus, the only ballad whose popularity, based on the number of times it has been collected from oral tradition, surpasses that of "Liten Karin" and "Maria Magdalena" is "Staffan Stalledräng," or "Sankte Staffan."[104] This ballad was associated with a processional tradition connected to

---

[101] See Jonsson, *Svensk balladtradition*, 797–98.

[102] Kathleen Stokker, "Between Sin and Salvation: the Human Condition in Legends of the Black Book Minister," *Scandinavian Studies* 67 (1995): 91–108.

[103] Sands, "Doves, Ravens, and the Dead."

[104] *SMB* 38/*TSB* B 8.

the celebration of Christmas,[105] and it remains an important part of Christmas celebrations in Sweden to this day. "Liten Karin" and "Maria Magdalena" do not seem to have been associated with a specific time of year, or any other restricted performance context. Their immense popularity in later tradition may very well reflect the fact that each depicts a protagonist who achieves salvation as a direct result of her own choices, including her ability to resist or obey authority figures as appropriate. As I have argued above, the legend of St. Katherine of Alexandria, like those of other virgin martyrs, can be read as a narrative of resistance to Muslim expansion, and even as a symbolic reconquest of formerly Christian territories now in Muslim hands. Olof Dalin's ballad parody shows clearly that the ballad singers he knew (or knew of) were aware that they were singing of a holy person, and not just about a girl in trouble. In the case of "Liten Karin," it may be that Karin's resistance to the king might, in some situations, have been seen as a symbol of resistance to Protestant doctrine or ideology, not least to the notion that salvation arises out of grace alone, and that good deeds play no role.

The wide-scale publication of edited narratives from oral tradition during and after the early nineteenth century brought a major change to the mode of transmission of many oral genres, including the ballad. The Romantic Era's interest in traditional oral narratives as a source of collective national identity also meant that the audience for such narratives expanded far beyond those groups of people who were in a position to experience them through traditional, oral performance. It has often been remarked that, beginning in the nineteenth century, "Liten Karin" became particularly popular as a more or less literary ballad among the educated middle class, as a result of the influence of Geijer and Afzelius's *Svenska folkvisor*. The song is thus familiar to a large number of Swedes who are not otherwise interested in folk tradition. Although the general public's familiarity with the ballad now derives from published works, and not from oral tradition, the conclusions of Grundtvig and the other scholars who have discussed "Liten Karin" seem to have had little or no influence on the way the ballad is understood by a general audience, and present-day Swedes do not tend to associate the ballad with any saint. Instead, it has become quite common to link the ballad with a well-known historical figure from the Swedish Renaissance. It appears to be a relatively widespread popular belief that the "Karin" of the ballad can be identified as Karin Månsdotter, a footsoldier's daughter who became the mistress and then the consort of King Erik XIV, the oldest son of Gustav Vasa. This association must ultimately depend on the fact that the ballad protagonist and the soldier's daughter have the same name, and that the ballad depicts a girl of apparently low social status who is pursued by the king. Whatever their personal qualities might or might not have been, both Erik XIV and

---

[105] Dag Strömbäck,"Kring Staffansvisan," in *Folklore och filologi*, Acta Academiæ Regiæ Gustavi Adolphi 48 (Uppsala: Almqvist & Wiksell, 1970), 34–53.

Karin Månsdotter seem to have been much in vogue at the turn of the twentieth century, and they were frequently depicted in music, painting, and drama
from this period. One such work was Ivar Hallström's opera "Liten Karin," written—but not performed—in 1897, with a libretto by Frans Hedberg. Hallström
was apparently fascinated by folk ballads, and composed several operas based
on ballad narratives. The "Liten Karin" ballad appears to have been one of his
main sources of inspiration for the opera, and is worked into the score. Although
this opera was not performed until 1997, and thus is not likely to be the ultimate
source of the tendency to regard the ballad as a depiction of Karin Månsdotter, it may be one of the earliest examples of the trend. Interestingly, Hallström
wrote at least one other operatic work, "Herr Magnus och sjöjungfrun" (1865),
in which he uses a known traditional ballad in a narrative about members of
the Vasa dynasty. Hallströms's "Herr Magnus" is about Magnus Gustavsson, a
brother of Erik XIV.[106] Another interesting example of this clearly widespread
interpretation of the ballad occurred in the 1950s, when the cabaret performer
Karl Gerhard made use of the popular connection between the ballad character
and Karin Månsdotter in one of his satirical revue numbers:

> Att Konung Erik på lutan har lekt
> vet vi, och dessutom, att han har smekt
> ej bara strängarna, än ej något hult,
> ett kvinnligt väsen, så oskuldsfullt.
> Men nu har en historiker, en aldrig mera skarpa,
> avslöjat att liten Karin var en riktig harpa.
> Med Jöran Persson hon hade en son;
> mot höga räntor gav kärringen lån.
> Mån hon var ock om sig, därav namnet som vi känner.
> Erik flydde hemmet och gick in i Visans vänner
> för att slippa höra hennes snåla falsett
> — Så var det med det lilla helgonet![107]

(That King Erik on the lute has played, / we know, and moreover that he
has caressed / not only the strings, if not something hidden / — a womanly
being, so innocently. / But now a historian, and never a sharper one, / has
revealed that "liten Karin" was a real harpy / — to Jöran Persson she bore a
son / — for high interest she'd give you a loan. / She looked out for herself,
hence the name we know well / — Erik fled from home and joined "Visans

[106] See *Sohlmans musiklexikon*, 2nd revised and expanded edition (Stockholm: Sohlmans, 1976–1979), 3: 301.

[107] Karl Gerhard, "Så var det med det lilla helgonet," melody by Gideon Wahlberg. Recorded 3–4 December 1955, complete version not previously released. Reproduced on EMI Svenska AB record no. 4751142, 1994.

vänner" ("Friends of the Ballad"), / in order to escape hearing her stingy falsetto. / And that's how it was with that little saint!)

Unlike many other non-scholars who have considered, used, or referred to this ballad—but like Dalin—Karl Gerhard was apparently aware that the ballad had some connection to a saint. It is to this connection that the refrain of his revue number "Så var det med det lilla helgonet" alludes. Karin Månsdotter thus becomes one of a considerable group of Swedish cultural and historical icons skewered in Gerhard's satirical "couplet," beginning with Saint Birgitta, but also including Joan of Arc and a number of contemporary celebrities.

Although the tendency to associate the protagonist of "Liten Karin" with the historical figure Karin Månsdotter appears to be of relatively recent date, it highlights an important development in the history of the ballad and its relationship to the cult of Saint Katherine of Alexandria. While it may be assumed that medieval singers of the ballad, and quite possibly many of those who must have sung it at least into the nineteenth century were aware of the saintly status of the protagonist, it appears that at some point by the middle or end of the nineteenth century, the association between the ballad and the saint's legend and cult weakened and finally disappeared from tradition. There is much evidence to suggest that rural peasant populations were much slower to accept the changes in religious doctrine arising from the Reformation than their counterparts at other levels of society. The liturgical reforms did not only mean that people were expected to turn their backs on the intercessors and rituals they had trusted for generations. Changes to the liturgical year also meant that the number of mandatory working days each year increased radically during the seventeenth and eighteenth centuries. While peasant populations often made their objections known on religious grounds, representatives of the Estates, who held the power in society, invariably dismissed their concerns as evidence of laziness or even of a predilection for drunken behavior.[108] Under such circumstances, a continued private awareness of, or even devotion to, the saints could both provide solace and a means of symbolic resistance to unjust authority. If, as Nyman suggests, the middle of the nineteenth century marks the end of any remnants of pre-Reformation belief or practice in any part of Swedish society, it may be that the increasing integration of rural and urban populations played a role in their demise. The widespread publication of ballad texts also made them available and of interest to a middle- and upper-class audience, whose understanding of the meaning of the texts was quite distinct from that of the ballads' oral traditors. For these largely urban, financially comfortable, and politically connected groups, Swedish history must have seemed a much more obvious inspiration for a ballad narrative than the biography of a fourth-century Alexandrian queen.

---

[108] Gustaf Lindberg, *Kyrkans heliga år* (Stockholm: Svenska kyrkans diakonistyrelsens bokförlag, 1937), 439–47.

Although this study deals mainly with the relationship between the saint's cult and the later ballad tradition, and thus concentrates on the narrative aspects of the ballad to a much greater extent than the melodic tradition, all ballads by definition are both text and melody. For this reason it is necessary to make some comments on the musical aspects of the "Liten Karin" ballad. Previous scholarship on this ballad has almost exclusively concerned the textual tradition, and comments of any kind on the melody are few and far between. The comprehensive Swedish ballad edition, *Sveriges medeltida ballader,* does not include commentaries, and the commentaries in the older ballad editions, including *Danmarks gamle folkeviser* and *Svenska folkvisor,* make little or no reference to the melodic tradition. The most important discussion of the melodic tradition of "Liten Karin" up to the present time is that in Sture Bergel's *Musikkommentar till Geijer-Afzelius: Svenska folkvisor.*[109] Perhaps the earliest published comment on the melodic tradition of "Liten Karin" is Afzelius's remark that the ballad "is sung in nearly all parts of the country, and it is seldom sung the same way from one place to another. The melody is also different from one place to another."[110] Bergel, who analyzes a considerable number of tune variants, concurs, and notes that the wide variation noted by Afzelius may be explained by the ballad's strophic form. He notes that "a traditional four-line stanza without refrain is such a well-trodden path, that melodies easily move back and forth." He goes on to note that the strongest influence on the choice of ballad tune seems to have been the ease with which "Liten Karin" ballad's strophic form can be adapted to broadside form. A number of tune variants thus seem to have been influenced by organ grinders' tunes.[111] Another example of the relatively "modern" impression made by a tune variant of "Liten Karin" is a remark by the collector Carlheim-Gyllenskiöld in 1879. Commenting on his informant, he notes, "She knew some ballads, which she sang for me, quite badly. Most of the melodies were modernized, and I include them here only as an example of how the old romances have degenerated in our time."[112] Such a comment may, of course, remind the reader that one of the most cherished assumptions of collectors of folklore schooled in the Romantic tradition is that they were preserving the last, degenerate fragments of a great, dying tradition. If it is difficult to trace a text backward through time, however, it is even more difficult to trace an undocumented melody. A specific connection between the melodic tradition and the cult of Saint Katherine seems unlikely, and there is certainly no reason to suppose any link with medieval church music.

---

[109] Sture Bergel, *Musikkommentar till Geijer-Afzelius: Svenska folkvisor* (Uppsala: offprint from Kungl. Gustav Adolfs Akademiens ed. of Geijer and Afzelius' *Svenska folkvisor,* 1957–1960).

[110] *Svenska folkvisor,* 3:12.

[111] Bergel, "Musikkommentar," 133.

[112] Cited in Bergel, "Musikkommentar," 136.

On the other hand, a newer melodic sequence is no proof that "Liten Karin" was not sung earlier.

While it is not possible to prove conclusively that the "Liten Karin" ballad was composed and sung in Scandinavia during the Middle Ages, it appears quite reasonable to assume that the ballad's history in Sweden goes further back in time than its written record would indicate. There appears to be no cause to doubt that the ultimate origin of the plot of this ballad lies in some form, written or oral, of the legend of St. Katherine of Alexandria, and that the ballad's popularity in the centuries after the Reformation is in some way linked to the popularity of the saint's cult in medieval Sweden. Although there is no evidence of continuity of veneration of Katherine of Alexandria by the early nineteenth century, it is certainly appropriate to regard this ballad as an important outgrowth of the saint's cult, and thus an essential object of inquiry in an investigation of this cult and its influence on the culture of medieval and post-Reformation Sweden. It can be shown that Swedish ballad tradition was an important narrative genre among rural populations at least as far back as the seventeenth century, when the nationalistically inspired Antiquarian movement first sent collectors into the field to gather oral traditions. It is not known whether legendary ballads such as "Liten Karin" were ever sung by the nobility, but if they were, the practice was not documented. On the other hand, it appears that the ballad tradition does provide some insight into a segment of medieval Swedish society whose devotions are otherwise little documented. Along with a handful of references to church dedications and parish guilds, the "Liten Karin" ballad may be our best evidence of the veneration of St. Katherine of Alexandria among the non-noble laity of medieval Sweden.

VI
CONCLUSION

The cult of St. Katherine in medieval Sweden both resembles and differs from her cult in other parts of medieval Christendom. Some of the differences may lie in the fact that the means by which the Swedish cult is documented differ significantly from those of other regions. While many areas, perhaps most notably England, have large numbers of manuscripts of the life of St. Katherine and many other saints, many of them produced by known authors for specific individuals, such texts are few and far between in Sweden. Although some medieval Swedish testaments do survive to the present day, these are far fewer in number, and represent a far narrower segment of the population than in many other areas. On the other hand, Sweden's medieval parish churches, in spite of the advent of the Protestant Reformation in the sixteenth century, are preserved to a degree encountered almost nowhere else in Europe, and their images, in the form of murals and other paintings, sculptures, embroideries, and even engravings on liturgical vessels, are still found in remarkable numbers. In spite of the great losses known to have occurred, not least at the hands of eighteenth- and nineteenth-century clergymen, some three hundred images of St. Katherine alone survive or are documented in the present day. Other important sources for an understanding of the cult include sigillographic images, family naming traditions, and the occasional records of donations to altars dedicated to the saint.

By the time the cult of St. Katherine arrived in Sweden, it had become more or less well-established throughout the Christian world. We know that the cult was established there by 1198, based on the saint's inclusion in the earliest known Swedish liturgical calendar. It is possible, however, that the saint and her cult were known considerably earlier, given that the name "Katarina" occurs in Swedish royal families as early as the late eleventh century.

Throughout the medieval period, both for groups and for individuals, it is clear that a central aspect of St. Katherine's importance was her status as an especially powerful intercessor, arising out of her unique position as the foremost of the brides of Christ. To a great extent, medieval Swedish devotion to the saint parallels international trends. At the same time, however, it is clear that the legend and image of the Greek-speaking, Alexandrian-born queen and scholar came to embody a range of specific meanings for individuals and groups across the range of social classes in medieval Sweden. While St. Katherine's conflict with a heathen emperor may have alluded to the international conflict between Christianity and Islam for clergy across Europe, for many Swedish clerics, the saint's image also became a symbol of their studies at the prestigious European universities, especially the University of Paris. Although St. Katherine was never among the official patron saints of any Swedish cathedral, her image became closely associated with the activities of cathedral chapters. At least in the case of Uppsala, the image of St. Katherine, especially in the company of one or more of the patron saints of the archdiocese, appears in several churches closely linked to the cathedral chapter as a symbol of that connection. Thus, both on an individual and on an institutional level, St. Katherine came to symbolize the important intellectual aspects of the work of the cathedral chapters.

Among the medieval Swedish nobility, circumstances may be similar. Throughout Europe in the high and late Middle Ages, St. Katherine was a favorite patron saint of noble or wealthy women. This is clearly also the case in Sweden, but here we can also observe specific personal motivations for individual devotion to the saint. In many cases, it appears that these devotions, established on the basis of donations in the saint's name, family naming traditions, and, especially, sigillographic images, arise at least in part out of women's relationships to devotees of St. Katherine's among the clergy or religious orders. In other cases, devotion and imagery appear to arise out of an identification with specific aspects of the saint's legend. Thus, for several generations of one important Swedish family, the name and image of St. Katherine come to symbolize their royal ancestry. Although only women, among the laity, depict St. Katherine in their seals, the saint's image could also be used in other ways by aristocratic males. During the later fifteenth century, St. Katherine was enlisted as symbol and intercessor for a political movement. In several murals and altarpieces St. Katherine appears in the company of St. George in contexts that suggest that the two saints are associated with the movement to establish Sweden as an independent kingdom, in opposition to the Kalmar Union that united Sweden with Norway and Denmark under the rule of a single monarch.

Although medieval Sweden comprised a single ecclesiastical province under the authority of the Archbishop of Uppsala, and was for the most part more-or-less politically united under a single king, some regions could nonetheless function with considerable autonomy. This is especially true of the Baltic island of Gotland, which was for several centuries only loosely tied to the Diocese of Linköping and the Swedish crown. Gotland's exceptionally strong trade connections with Russia and the Byzantine world during the early Middle Ages may have contributed to a different development of the cult of St. Katherine here than in other parts of medieval Sweden, though the cult gradually came to manifest itself in ways recognizable from other areas.

The lives of medieval Swedes who were neither clergy nor nobility are more difficult to document than those of other groups, and their concerns are only seldom recorded. It is especially difficult to draw any conclusions about the devotions of individual members of this large and varied group, which may include both urban traders of German nationality or origin in Hanseatic centers, and rural peasants living in country parishes. Still, I argue that there is evidence of devotion to St. Katherine among the urban and rural laity. In the case of urban populations, forms of documentation may resemble those seen among nobility, such as naming traditions and donations in the name of the saint. Guilds dedicated to St. Katherine are known from several of Sweden's urban centers, and suggest that at least some urban dwellers were active participants in her cult.

The devotions of rural populations may also be connected to guilds of St. Katherine, which are well-documented in several country parishes. However, the most compelling piece of evidence of the importance of St. Katherine to rural Swedes may be the one that comes from oral tradition. Oral narratives are notoriously slippery things to use as historical sources. Their origins are seldom discoverable, and their meanings tend to shift over time and according to the concerns of individual narrators and their audiences. Nevertheless, I argue that the widespread Swedish traditional ballad "Liten Karin," which was first collected in the early nineteenth century, can be connected to medieval guilds and to other aspects of the medieval cult of St. Katherine. Further, I argue that the ballad shows the same traits of flexibility and multifunctionality that characterize the image and cult of St. Katherine both in specifically Swedish contexts and in other parts of medieval Christendom. I assert that, in the generations following the advent of the Protestant Reformation, the narrative of St. Katherine's martyrdom continued to have meaning for its traditors, in spite of the official suppression of the cult of the saints. Indeed, the fact that this ballad was so widely sung by the time that collectors finally began to write it down suggests that this narrative, still recognizable as a highly condensed version of the legend of St. Katherine, may have helped to fulfill spiritual needs that went unmet under the new Protestant doctrine. Only by the middle of the nineteenth century, when all continuity with Sweden's Roman Catholic past finally disappeared, did the connection between the ballad and the saint's cult finally break down.

Thus, the cult of St. Katherine of Alexandria provides a window on the cultural and spiritual life of medieval Sweden. The highly flexible and multifunctional nature of the cult accommodates both universal and highly individual meanings, and suggests that medieval Swedish religious life was at the same time integrated with the rest of the medieval West, and also concerned with specific, local, and individual issues.

APPENDIX 1
VISUAL IMAGES

Sculptures depicting St. Katherine are known from or found in the following churches:

(Names in boldface denote provinces or regions; names in parentheses denote national affiliation during the Middle Ages, if different from present boundaries).

Ångermanland: Multrå (early 1500s), Nordmaling (end of 1400s), Skog (early 1500s)

Bohuslän (Norway): Skee (late 1400s)

Dalarna: By (late 1400s), Sollerö (1480s), Stora Skedvi (late 1400s), Vika (late 1400s)

Finland (Sweden): Hammarland (1400s), Houtskär (1508), Karis (late 1300s), Korpo (c. 1500), Lemland, Pargas, Raumo, Rusko (after 1350), St. Karins (before 1350), Sund, Tyrvis (1400s?), Virmo (apparently had an entire reredos devoted to St. Katherine, from the early 1300s, also two panels of reliefs from an antemensale, early 1400s)

Gotland: Alskogs (c. 1300; crown and other attributes removed and mustache added 1759, turning St. Katherine into an Old Testament prophet, placed into a new altarpiece), Buttle (c. 1400), Fide (early 1400s), Kräklingbo (early 1500s), Vallstena (1300s), Väskinde (stone surround for an aumbry, early 1200s, depicting St. Katherine and St. James)

Gästrikland: Hedesunda (after 1450), Hille (mid. 1400s)

Hälsingland: Bollnäs (early 1500s), Enånger (c. 1500), Hög (early 1500s), Njutånger (early 1500s), Segersta (late 1400s)

Medelpad: Alnö (end of 1400s), Sättna (early 1500s)

Närke: Edsberg (early 1500s), Glanshammar (two sculptures: one of alabaster, early 1400s, one of wood, early 1500s), Hidinge (after 1450), Täby (late 1400s)

Östergötland: Björkeberg: (early 1300s), Hägerstad (end of 1400s), Kaga (1450–1500), Kullerstad (early 1500s), Normlösa (early 1400s), Stora Åby (c. 1500), Söderköping St. Lawrence (end of 1400s), Tidesrum (end of 1200s), Vadstena Abbey Church (early 1400s), Vånga (end of 1400s), Östra Eneby (end of 1400s)

Skåne (Denmark): Håstad (early 1500s), Lund Cathedral (1398), St. Olof (1400s), Trelleborg (c. 1500), Östra Tomarp (early 1500s)

Småland: Hakarp (after 1450), Hjorted (after 1450), Näshult (late 1400s), Rumokulla (late 1400s), St. Sigfrid (early 1500s), Västra Ed (early 1500s), Åseda (after 1450)

Stockholm: Storkyrkan (reredos from 1468 sold to Österåker church, Uppland, by 1640s)

Södermanland: Hammarby (1470s-1480s), Sorunda (c. 1495), Strängnäs Cathedral (1430–1440), Toresund (early 1400s), Torshälla (late 1400s), Vansö (c. 1480)

Uppland: Bälinge (two altarpieces, both featuring St. Katherine, late 1400s. One of these may have come from the chapel of St. Katherine and St. Nicholas at Uppsala Cathedral), Börje (late 1400s), Edebo (1475–1500; reredos sold to Gräsö church, Uppland, during 1700s), Ekerö (early 1470s), Färinge (c. 1470–1480), Frötuna (c. 1440), Funbo (c. 1500), Harg (late 1400s; reredos sold to Singö church, Uppland, c. 1760), Husby-Sjuhundra (1400–1450), Kalmar (mid. 1400s), Knivsta (c. 1500), Kårsta (late 1400s), Lagga (late 1400s), Litslena (c. 1480), Munsö (c. 1470), Odensala (1514), Sigtuna St. Mary (figures in two different reredos from the late 1400s), Skuttinge (1475–1500), Sollentuna (1475), Tegelsmora (c. 1500), Vaksala (early 1500s), Vidbo (later 1400s), Värmdö (1470–1480, altarpiece sold to Möja church, Uppland, c. 1729), Älvkarlaby (c. 1490), Össeby-Garn (1475–1500), Östra Ryd (c. 1300)

Värmland: Gräsmark (c. 1500; reredos older than church)

Västerbotten: Skellefteå (late 1440s)

Västergötland: Edsvära (late 1400s), Husaby (1300s), Ljungsarp (1475–1500), Näs (early 1500s)

Västmanland: Irsta (Early 1400s), Järnboås (early 1400s), Munktorp (end of 1300s), Västerås Cathedral (1450–1500), Västra Skedvi (c. 1500), Ängsö (c. 1490; reredos sold to Tillinge church, Uppland in 1753)

Murals in chancel:

Finland (Sweden): Ingå (1500–1510), Kumlinge (c. 1500), Sjundeå (1500–1510)

Gotland: Kräklingbo (1211, according to inscription), Norrlanda (later 1400s, scenes from martyrdom), Väskinde (early 1500s, scenes from legend including mystic marriage)

Östergötland: Asby (early 1200s, prison scene from Katherine legend), Fivelstad (end of 1400s), Mogata (later 1400s), Risinge (mid. 1400s, four scenes from martyrdom)

Skåne (Denmark): Bunkeflo (later 1400s), Gässle (1475–1525), Ivö (later 1400s), Söfvestad (early 1500s), Tosterup (later 1400s), Trollenäs (1400–1500), Västra Sallerup (1303)
Småland: Askeryd (two different murals from the early 1500s), Lofta (later 1400s), Säby (end of 1400s)
Södermanland: Vänsö (before 1470)
Uppland: Härnevi (1480s), Litslena (c. 1470), Nora (large painting on east wall from the end of 1400s; possibly also scenes from her martyrdom on the south wall), Rasbokil (1520–30), Rimbo (c. 1500), Söderby-Karl (c. 1500), Tensta (1437), Tolfta (1490s), Vallby (1510–1520), Västeråker (c. 1470), Östervåla (c. 1525)
Västerbotten: Umeå (1520s)
Västergötland: Husaby (1400s)
Västmanland: Sala (1465–70), Tortuna (early 1500s)

Murals in nave:
Finland (Sweden): Hattula (two murals from the 1510s), Lojo (1510s; ten scenes from Katherine's legend, along with two other depictions in the nave), Nykyrko (1470–71, together with a female donor), Rimito (late 1400s), Sund (early 1300s), Tövsala (c. 1470–1490)
Gotland: Boge (1400s), Rute (later 1400s, 5 scenes from martyrdom), Stenkumla (later 1400s), Väskinde (c. 1300)
Östergötland: Kaga (two murals: one from the middle 1200s, the other from the later 1400s), Östra Eneby (1400s, scenes from legend)
Skåne (Denmark): Bjällerup (later 1300s), Borrby (early 1300s), Brunnby (later 1400s), Bunkeflo (later 1400s; nine scenes from the legend of St. Katherine), Fjälie (later 1300s), Frenninge (?), Hörup (later 1300s), Knislinge (later 1400s), Kyrkoköpinge (later 1400s), Östra Vemmerlöv (later 1400s)
Småland: Säby (end of 1400s)
Uppland: Almunge (end of 1400s), Alunda (end of 1400s), Björklinge (c. 1469, scenes from martyrdom), Färentuna (1440s), Husby-Sjutolft (1480s), Håtuna (1450–1470s), Häverö (c. 1500; scene from martyrdom), Knivsta (before 1467), Norrsunda (scenes from the martyrdom of Sts. Katherine and Stephen, ca. 1450), Rasbo (1456, according to inscription), Roslags-Bro (1471), Tierp (shortly after 1469), Vallby (1510–20; Katherine's martyrdom), Valö (c. 1527), Vendel (1451–52; Katherine's martyrdom), Ärentuna (c. 1435)
Västmanland: Arboga town church (c. 1440), Kumla (1482), Ängsö (c. 1340)

Murals in chancel arch:
Småland: Dädesjö (late 1200s; identification uncertain — may be a donor)
Uppland: Gamla Uppsala (1455–1469), Löt (end of 1400s), Spånga (later 1400s), Vendel (1451-52)

Murals in transept:
Östergötland: Örberga (mid. 1400s)

Murals in tower arch:
Skåne (Denmark): Farstorp (1475–1525)
Uppland: Frötuna (1503)

Murals in church porch:
Uppland: Markim (mid. 1400s), Tensta (early 1500s), Viksta (1503; 3 scenes from martyrdom. Nilsén identifies this saint as St. Barbara)
Västergötland: Gökhem (1487)

Murals in chapels:
Västmanland: Odensvi (ca. 1450)

Murals in "ring chamber" (= sacristy?):
Gotland: Hemse (late 1400s)

Paintings on wood (on altarpieces, unless noted):
Ångermanland: Fjällsjö (early 1500s), Ytterlännäs (early 1500s)
Dalarna: Ore (c. 1520)
Finland (Sweden): Ackas (c. 1480), Jämsä (later than Ackas), Tövsala, Vörå
Gotland: Kräklingbo (early 1500s; also plank from choir bench, early 1300s), Lau (early 1400s)
Härjedalen (Norway): Älvros (before 1550)
Hälsingland: Bollnäs (two reredoses, one from late 1400s, the other from early 1500s)
Medelpad: Njurunda (after 1450)
Östergötland: Järstad (predella; early 1400s), Kumla (early 1400s), Risinge (1475–1500), Tjällmo (?)
Skåne (Denmark): Helsingborg St. Mary (c. 1450)
Småland: Djursdala (after 1450; depiction of mystic marriage), Högsby (end of 1400s), Kråksmåla (1450–75), Svarttorp (1450–75)
Södermanland: Råby-Rekarne (end of 1400s), Sorunda (end of 1400s), Torpa (two pieces: one early 1400s, the other after 1450), Tumbo (after 1450)
Uppland: Frösunda (1425–1450), Haga (1514), Harg (end of 1400s), Knutby (early 1400s), Värmdö (1514)
Värmland: Ekshärad (c. 1520), Hammarö (wooden plank from chancel ceiling, 1450–60)
Västmanland: Arboga country church (predella, 1510–20), Köping (1510–20), Västerås Cathedral (two reredoses, after 1450), Ängsö (after 1450).

Windows:
Gotland: Lye, south window of chancel (1325–1350)

Embroideries: (from altar cloths or vestments — chasubles or copes — unless noted)
Ångermanland: Sollefteå (after 1450)
Dalarna: Mora (1400s), Rättvik (end of 1400s)
Gotland: Endre (c. 1500), Vall (1400s)
Gästrikland: Hedesunda (after 1450), Hille (c. 1500)
Hälsingland: (Hedesunda (end of 1400s), Hassela (end of 1400s)
Medelpad: Alnö (c. 1500)
Närke: Kumla (1522), Skollersta (c. 1500), Viby (end of 1400s)
Östergötland: Borg (c. 1500), Börrum (end of 1400s), Söderköping St. Lawrence
    (late medieval), Vadstena Abbey (mid. 1400s), Vånga (end of 1400s), Västra
    Skrukeby (after 1450), Östra Ny (c. 1500)
Skåne (Denmark): Lund Cathedral (end of 1400s), Malmö St. Peter (end of
    1400s)
Småland: Blackstad (c. 1500), Eksjö (c. 1500), Hässleby (1475–1525), Höreda
    (1475–1525), Jälluntofta (1475–1525), Karlstorp (c. 1500), Lidhult (1350–
    1400), Norra Sandsjö (end of 1400s), Västra Ed (after 1450)
Södermanland: Fogdö (tapestry, c. 1475), Huddinge (later 1400s), Jäder (end of
    1400s), Nyköping St. Nicholas (c. 1500), Sorunda (after 1450), Svärta (later
    1400s), Taxinge (late 1400s to c. 1500)
Uppland: Fasterna (c. 1500), Jumkil (1475–1500), Söderby-Karl (c. 1500), Upp-
    sala Cathedral (end of 1400s), Åkerby (2 pieces from the late 1400s, both
    previously belonging to Bälinge in Uppland)
Västergötland: Ullene (late 1400s to beginning of 1500s)
Västmanland: Västerås Cathedral (after 1450), another late medieval embroidery
    from an unknown church in Västmanland

APPENDIX 2
SEALS DEPICTING ST. KATHERINE
OF ALEXANDRIA

Seals belonging to clerics:

Andreas Andreasson And, Dean of Uppsala Cathedral
Bearer depicted kneeling before St. K, who has crown and sword
Pointed oval. Appears as main seal on documents beginning 1280 (publ. in Hildebrand) Also on *DS* no. 2029 (23 August 1315) as counterseal (RA)

Nils Alleson, deacon at Uppsala Cathedral (later archbishop)
Small round seal depicting saint with sword, palm frond and wheel
Used as counterseal on two documents from 1291; may have been his seal as canon (Hildebrand) (Also in RA)

Nils, a "monk" (actually friar) in the Dominican priory in Skänninge
Pointed oval seal shows bearer venerating crowned St. K with wheel, palm frond together with St. Nicholas. *DS* no. 1098 (1293) (Hildebrand) (Also in RA)

Ödhin, parish priest in Husby in Linköping Diocese
Pointed oval depicting bearer venerating St. K, who is crowned, carries a wheel and palm frond, and has short hair. *DS* no. 1451 (1304) (Hildebrand) (Also in RA)

Odinkhar, another parish priest in the diocese of Linköping
Pointed oval depicting crowned female saint holding palm frond and book.
DS no. 1451 (1304) (Hildebrand) Hildebrand notes that he is not among the sealers named in the document.

Jakob, parish priest of St. Katherine's church in Nummis, Finland
Pointed oval, bearer venerates crowned St. K, who holds a book. *DS* no. 1626 (1309) Hildebrand) (Also in RA).

Lars Agmundsson, Dominican friar and confessor to Archbishop Nils Kettilsson
Pointed oval shows bearer venerating St. Laurentius (patron of Uppsala Cathedral), crowned St. K with wheel, palm frond, Virgin Mary and Child at top of
seal. *DS* no. 1968 (1314) (Hildebrand)

Johannes of Söderby, presumably a parish priest (Strängnäs)
Round seal depicts bearer kneeling in veneration of crowned St. K with wheel,
sword. *DS* no. 2041 (1315) (RA)

Algot, parish priest in Åby church, Möre, Småland
Small round seal shows bearer venerating crowned St. K, who holds wheel and
palm frond. *DS* no. 2174 (1318) (Hildebrand) (also in RA)

Styrbjörn, priest in Götlunda, (probably Närke)
Pointed oval seal depicts St. K with crown, wheel, bearer venerating from below
DS no. 2319 (1321) (RA)

Johannes Dansson, priest or monk, also nobleman
Pointed oval depicts St. K with crown, wheel, inscription "time devin", coat of
arms below. *DS* no. 2485 (1324) (RA)

Vemund, canon in Linköping and Växjö
Pointed oval depicts St. K with wheel, crown and sword, together St. Andrew (?)
DS no. 2839 (1331) (RA)

Nils, parish priest in Estuna, Uppland (NB: Acc. to a parchment strip dated 14
Dec. 1298, found when high altar was rebuilt 1733, the church was ded. to Sts.
Lars, Olof and Erik—as was altar)—by Nils Alleson, archbishop of Upps.—relics of St. Mauritius and 11000 virgins).[1] Interestingly, this church has no known
depictions of St. K. Nils Alleson did have K's image in his counterseal)
Pointed oval seal depicts St. K with sword, crown, wheel. *DS* no. 2862 (1331) (RA)

Björn, parish priest in Vassunda, Uppland (no known K images—church radically rebuilt in 1800s)
Pointed oval seal depicts bearer kneeling in veneration of St. K with crown, wheel
and sword. *DS* no. 3306 (1337, 1339) (RA)

Gödkin, parish priest in Skärkind, Östergötland
Round seal depicts crowned St. K with wheel. *DS* no. 3914 (1345) (RA). (Letter
of mortgage)

---

[1] Ingrid Wilcke-Lindqvist, "Estuna kyrka," in *Upplands kyrkor*, vol. 7 (Uppsala: Wretmans Boktryckeri AB, 1960), 105–6.

Lekr Salmonsson, parish priest priest in Vist (immediate vicinity of Linköping) and the Bishop of Linköping's "officialis."
Pointed oval depicts crowned St. K holding wheel and sword, bearing venerating from below. *DS* no. 4211 (1347) (Hildebrand)

Hook Ofradsson, canon in Linköping
Pointed oval depicts St. K with crown and wheel. *DS* no. 6764 (1353) (RA).

Johan, parish priest in Floda, Södermanland (no known K images in this church) Fragmentary round seal depicts St. K, wheel clearly visible. (*DS* no. 6129) RPB no. 422 (1359) (RA)

Johan Petersson, parish priest in Vadsbro (near Katrineholm), canon at cathedral chapter, Strängnäs.
Partially fragmented pointed oval seal depicts St. K with crown, wheel, sword. (*DS* no. 7944 / RPB no. 858 (1369) (RA). Letter dated from Strängnäs: Johan's brother mortgages property to abbot of Eskilstuna (Order of St. John)

Hemming, monk at Vadstena, former parish priest of Östra Eneby church in Östergötland.
Pointed oval seal with standing St. Katherine. RPB no. 3105 (1400)
Ö Eneby had a mural in nave with scenes from K's legend, also a candlestick with a sculpture depicting her. Hemming = treasurer ("syssloman") of Vadstena Abbey.

Povel Thordsson, holder of prebend in Stockholm, later also Uppsala.
Round seal depicts K with crown, sword, small wheel, and shield with personal mark". RPB (RA) (1444)

Arvid, parish priest in Värnamo (Östergötland), apparently also rural dean in Östbo. Round seal depicts crowned K with wheel, sword. RPB no. 1456 (RA). Seal on 5 documents from 1450s.

Martin Frome, holder of a prebend in Stockholm. Round seal: K with crown, sword, wheel, small shield with bird. (1475) (RA)

Aristocratic women

Katarina Sigridsdotter of Steninge, widow of Anund

Round seal shows bearer, kneeling with chalice in veneration of St. K, crowned with wheel and palm frond. *DS* no. 1281 (1299) (Hildebrand)

Rangfrid (aka Ramfrid) Göstafsdotter (Gustavsdotter), daughter of Hafrid Sigtryggsdotter and widow of Tiundalands magistrate Israel Andreasson And. Large, elaborate round seal depicts bearer kneeling before crowned St. K, who has wheel, sword and palm frond and halo (sharp detail). Known from *DS* no. 1156 (1296), *DS* nos. 1372–3 (1302) (Hildebrand) (Also in RA)

Katarina Sigridsdotter of Steninge (same as above, but a new seal) Elaborate round seal depicts bearer kneeling in veneration of enthroned, crowned St. K with halo, detailed wheel, sword, lily. *DS* no. 1818 (and several other preserved documents) (1311) (Hildebrand) (Also in RA).

Ingeborg Birgersdotter (maternal aunt of Birger Petersson) Detailed round seal shows bearer kneeling in veneration below two crowned female saints, on left St. K with wheel and sword, on right unidentifiable saint with palm frond. *DS* no. 1984 (1314) (Hildebrand)

Cecelia Glysingsdotter, widow of Knight Karl Nilsson Pointed oval depicts bearer kneeling in veneration of St. K with crown, halo, palm frond and wheel, while an angel reaches a hand toward the wheel. Husband's coat of arms below. *DS* no. 2941 (1322) (Hildebrand) (also in RA)

Ingegierd Svantepolksdotter Round seal depicts bearer kneeling before St. K with crown, wheel, palm or lily. *DS* no. 2333 (1322) (RA). Her daughter, Birgitta Bryniolfsdotter (see below) also depicted St. Katherine in her seal.

Christina Röriksdotter Pointed oval (upper portion missing) shows St. K with wheel and sword, coat of arms below. *DS* no. 2493 (1325) (RA). Daughter of Rörik Birgersson and Helena Anundsdotter (a niece of Birger Jarl).

Benedikta Algotsdotter (later entered Dominican convent in Skänninge). Through her mother Botild (daughter of Lars Boberg, son of Bengt Sigtryggsson), apparently a great-niece of Hafrid Sigtryggsdotter. Damaged pointed oval seal depicts St. K with wheel, sword (head missing). *DS* no. 3266 (1336) (RA).

Birgitta Bryniufsdotter Round seal depicts St. K with crown, wheel, palm, bearer kneeling below. Two shields. *DS* no. 4711 (1351) NB: daughter of Ingegierd Svantepolksdotter. (RA)

Also: One of her children with Gregers Magnusson was Katarina Gregersdotter (*ÄSF*, 44)

(Other known bearers of seals depicting St. Katherine: Ingeborg Eriksdotter (probably Bielke -- mother of Katarina Glysingsdotter) (1374 RPB no. 1077); Birgitta Aronsdotter (probably daughter of Arendt Pinnow and widow of Karl Magnusson) (1475)

Non-noble women:

Katarina Ragvaldsdotter
Round seal depicts St. K with crown, wheel, upright sword. Very clear. *SD* no. 1570, 7 May 1412. Katarina was apparently not of aristocratic origin, but was married to Hemming Olofsson, burgher in Västerås.

Appendix 3
Saint Katherine and other selected saints in various medieval Scandinavian Calendars

Note: **Boldface** indicates red ink in original entry, generally indicating a *festum fori* – a general feast day – rather than a *festum chori*, celebrated only by the clergy, without the attendance of the laity.

Vallentuna Parish, Uppland, 1198 (degree not indicated)
25 November Katerine virginis

Breviarium Aarhusiense 1519
18 May Erici regis m.
20 July **Margarete v.**
22 July **Marie Magdalene**
29 July **Olavi regis m.**
10 August **Laurentii m.**
25 November **Katherine v.**
4 December Barbare v. IX.
6 December **Nicolai ep. cf.**

Missale ecclesie Aboensis (1448)
18 May **Erici regis m.** Totum duplex
13 July **Margarete v.** Duplex
22 July **Marie Magdalene** Duplex
29 July **Olavi regis m.** Duplex
10 August **Laurentii m.** Totum duplex
25 November **Catherine v.** Totum duplex
4 December Barbare v. Simplex
6 December **Nicolai ep.** Totum duplex

Missale Hafnienese (1510)
18 May Erici regis
20 July Margarete v.
22 July **Marie Magdalene**
29 July **Olavi regis m.**
10 August **Laurentii archidiac. m.**
25 November **Katherine v.**
4 December Barbare v. m.
6 December **Nicolai ep. cf.**

Breviarium sec. chorum Lincopense (1493)
18 May **Erici regis m.** Totum duplex
20 July Margarethe v. m. Simplex
22 July **Marie Magdalene** Duplex
29 July **Olavi m.** Totum duplex
10 August **Laurentii m.** Duplex
25 November **Katherine v.** Duplex (According to edition of *Breviarium Lincopense* publ. 1950-1558 St. K. has Totum duplex)
4 December Barbare v. Simplex
6 December **Nicolai ep. cf.** Duplex

Breviarium ecclesiae Lundensis (1517)
18 May **Erici regis m.** Totum duplex
20 July **Margarite v. m.** simplex Festum terre
22 July **Marie Magdalene v.** <sic!> Festum vicariorum
29 July **Olavi regis m.** Duplex
10 Augusti **Laurentii m.** Festum prelatorum (= highest degree)
25 November **Katherine v. m.** Duplex
4 December Barbare v. m. Duplex
6 December **Nicolai ep. cf.** Duplex

Breviarium Othoniense (1497)
18 May Erici regis m. IX
20 July Margarete v. IX
22 July **Marie Magdalene**
29 July **Olavi regis m.** Historia
10 August **Laurentii m.**
25 November **Katherine v.** Historia
4 December Barbare v. IX
6 December **Nicolai ep. cf.** Hist.

Breviarium Roeskildense (1517)
18 May **Erici regis m.** IX
20 July Margarete v. m. IX
22 July **Marie Magdalene** Festum canonicorum historia
29 July **Olavi regis**
10 August **Laurencii m.** Festum canonicorum historia
25 November **Katherine v. m.** Historia
4 December Barbare v. IX
6 December **Nicolai ep. cf.** Festum canonicorum historia

Breviarium Scarense (1498)
18 May **Erici regis Suecie m.** Duplex
20 July Margarethe v. m. Simplex
22 July **Marie Magdalene** Duplex
29 July **Olavi regis Norwegie m.** Duplex
10 August **Laurentii m.** Duplex
25 November **Katherine v. m.** Duplex
4 December Barbare v. Simplex
6 December **Nicolai ep.** Duplex

Kalendarium Scarense (1470s)
18 May Erici regis et martyris. Duplex
20 July Margarete virginis et martyris. Simplex
22 July Marie Magdalene. Est festum terre. Duplex
29 July Olauj regis et martyris. Semiduplex
11 August Laurencij martyris. Duplex
25 November Katherine virginis et martyris. Duplex
4 December Barbare virginis et martyris. Memoria
6 December Nicolai episcopi et confessoris. Semiduplex

Breviarium Strengnense (1495)
18 May **Erici regis m.** Totum duplex
20 July Margarete v. Simplex
22 July **Marie Magdalene** Duplex
29 July **Olavi regis** Duplex
10 August **Laurentii m.** Totum Duplex
25 November **Katherine v.** Duplex
4 December Barbare v. Simplex
6 December **Nicolai ep. cf.** Duplex

Breviarium ad usum Nidrosiensis ecclesiae (1519)
18 May Erici regis m. Semiduplex
20 July **Margarethe v.** Simplex

22 July Marie Magdalene Semiduplex
29 July **Olavi regis m.** Summa
10 August **Laurentii m.** Duplex
25 November Katherine v. m. IX
4 December Barbare v. m. Simplex
6 December **Nicolai ep. cf.** Duplex

Breviarium Uppsalense (1496)
18 May **Erici regis m.** Totum duplex
20 July Margarete v. m. IX
22 July **Marie Magdalene** Semiduplex IX
29 July **Olavi regis m.** Semiduplex IX
10 Augusti **Laurentii m.** IX Totum duplex
25 November **Katherine v. m.** IX Duplex
4 December Barbare v. m. IX
6 December **Nicolai ep. cf.** IX Semiduplex

Breviarium ecclesiae Arosiensis (1513)
18 May **Erici regis m.** Totum duplex
20 July Margarete v. Duplex
22 July **Marie Magdalene** Duplex
29 July **Olavi regis** Duplex
10 August **Laurentii m.** Duplex
25 November **Katherine v. m.** Totum duplex
4 December Barbare v. Simplex
6 December **Nicolai ep. cf.** Duplex

Appendix 4
Saint Anne and Saint Katherine

(Stephens 3:11–13, Cod. UUB 9 Benz.)

A merchant had two daughters in the same city. When they went to be shriven for the first time, the confessor gave one of them St. Anne as her patroness, because her name was Anna, and he thought that it would be easy for her to remember her patroness's name. The other girl was named Katarina, and her patroness was St. Katherine, for the same reason. After some years, the girl named Anna grew very unhappy, because she saw how the eve of St. Anne received so much less honor than the eve of St. Katherine. She began to envy her sister, who had a greater patroness than she did, though she did not tell anyone of it, but kept her thoughts to herself. On St. Anne's day she again despaired that her feast was celebrated with so little dignity. She began to ponder, and decided that it must be because St. Anne was less honored in Heaven than St. Katherine and the other virgins. That was why she received so much less honor here on earth. That night as she slept, it seemed to her that she was in a great palace, where innumerable knights and squires were sitting at a table, with innumerable ladies and maidens. In the highest seat sat a lady in the richest of raiment, and the greatest of kings served the meal to all those who sat there, and the loveliest of maidens poured for them. When those who were eating had praised and honored the king and the maiden for all the joy and honor they had brought them, they began to praise the great lady who sat in the high seat. This was St. Anne, and they bowed to her, saying "Eternal honor and praise be thine, oh great Mother Saint Anne, and the thanks of all God's creatures for the blessed fruit of thy womb. We hold thee next to our lord and king Jesus Christ and thy daughter Mary over all the creatures of Heaven and Earth." When the maiden who was pouring was given gifts, she went to St. Anne and said, "My dearest mother, these gifts were given me by my friends and servants on Earth. As is my custom, I wish to give them to thee, for all those who honor me honor thee, and it is especially well for all those who have thee as their patroness, for they shall be my brothers and sisters in eternal honor." This was where the girl awoke. She understood her dream well, and thanked St. Anne with all her heart. After that she was most satisfied to have her as her patroness. She became a nun, the better to serve her and give thanks. This occurred in the year 1317 after the birth of our lord. Amen.

Appendix 5
Old Swedish Translation of the
Life of St. Katherine of Alexandria

About Saint Katherine (from Codex T 153 a, Linköping library. Paper manuscript from beginning of sixteenth century, 32 pp., 4:0. Beginning missing). Published by George Stephens in vol. 3 of *Ett fornsvenskt legendarium*.[1]

St. Katherine's answer to the fifty wise men.

. . . he shall only be of the two either god or man, then he must be other than god or man, which is impossible for him. The virgin answered him and said "It seems so to me that since you do not wish to believe what is said, you by your sophistry cause others to follow you and believe that it is true, and that which is whole and complete in itself, you knock over, and men say that because he is God, he cannot be a man, as if anything could be impossible for almighty God, that he who from the power of his divinity created everything should not be able to be a man, or to take upon himself a man's nature. Though he had been invisible before, he became visible, and though he had been invulnerable, he became vulnerable and mortal. It is so that if you want know the truth of this, you must cast aside your false wisdom, which fools and sickens you, and you shall become a new disciple, and as you now know and understand God's strength and power by created things, then you shall begin to believe in God, and what will you not know then of God's power and strength, for he is the one who binds together body and soul, he gives the dead life and the blind man eyes, makes the lame man able to walk, and he cures leprosy and heals the sick, and he does this not with spells or with bookish art, but of his divine power. And if you cannot believe that God is thus powerful, then ask among Christians who believe in him, and you shall find it to be wholly true that such miracles and wondrous deeds are done in his holy name. If he were not God, he could not give life to dead men, and if he

---

[1] Svenska fornsällskapets skrifter 42 (Stockholm: P. A. Norstedt & söner, 1865–1874), 108–53.

were not also a man, he could not have endured death like other mortal men, and thus it can be proved that Christ, God though he is, with his holy body endured death and torment. If he is a man, and not God, how could he overcome death, and rise from the dead? He is truly a man, and in his holy divinity he overcame all death and torment because he is Christ, the son of God. He who could not be subject to death and torment in his divinity, let himself be tortured and slain in his body and the mortal coil that he took upon himself. Though he was immortal in his divinity, and that same Jesus Christ, the son of God, when he was killed in his body and his mortality, he arose from the dead, though he completely lost the immortality that he had because of his divinity and let himself be tortured and killed as a man. Thus one must declare that death did not kill Christ, but that Christ killed death by choosing to suffer pain and death himself. And if you still doubt and refuse to believe what I say, then pay attention and listen to the unclean spirits that live in your idols. They are devils that you worship in the place of God. They fear and tremble before God's name, and they do not deny that Jesus Christ is God and the son of God, and although they do not want to, they recognize that he is their god. If you will not believe our words, then you must believe your own gods. If that does not make you believe, then your shame is all the greater, that you deny that he is our creator and god whom even the devils in hell recognize as their god and lord."

St. Katherine continues her answer.

"Now you may say, and think to yourself that I have no better evidence than to support my faith with the devils as witnesses. I do not do it because Jesus Christ had to rely on the witness of devils. Rather I do it to make you understand and know that even the devil is compelled to bear witness of his god and say the truth to honor his god, whether he wishes to or not. It astonishes me greatly that so great a master as yourself doubts, then, that Jesus Christ is the true God, when you know well that your own books bear witness that he is God, and your books tell of his cross, though you mock and hate it. Therefore I will prove with the evidence that is in your own books, starting with the great master Plato, whom you think the wisest of masters. With these words he speaks of Jesus Christ and his strength and power. Then he speaks of Jesus Christ's sign of the cross. Another is the wise woman Sibilla. She speaks in her book of his holy name and his powerful nature. Of his divinity and his cross she writes in a verse, and says 'so hale is that god who shall be hanged up on the high tree.' Thus you must see that and hear that both Plato and the Sibyl recognize his divinity, and Plato says that he is of man's nature, while the Sibyl says that he is hale and healthy, for she tested and understood in her prophecy that in his human nature he had the power and virtue of divinity, and that he would be victorious over the devil through the death and torment that he would endure on the cross. I say this not so that you in any way follow their knowledge, because it was granted to them by God, that they spoke this wisdom as if they were sleeping and dreaming, for pagans are not worthy to taste and to know from God the things that will come. For I shall prove that, though they are false and misled in their knowledge, still your masters bear witness in their books, and Jesus Christ is God and the true son of God. I have told you a little of what is great. If you will not believe that which you hear with your ears, and see in miracles revealed to your eyes, then believe the devils who recognize that he is God against their will. And if you do not want to believe them, believe your own masters, and do not judge me for supporting my wisdom and faith with the devils that you worship as your gods. I could as well support my faith with the holy scripture that was compiled by the holy spirits, I can also support it with hundreds of miracles and wondrous deeds, but it seems most honest and most fair to me that I convert you with your own learning. Look and see, I have no other weapon than the holy faith. If it is so that your gods have ears with which to hear, then listen carefully to what I say, and have something to deny my speaking, then let me see it. If they cannot speak themselves, speak on their behalf, and I will answer on God's behalf."

The masters' reply to St. Katherine.

When the masters had heard this they answered it and said, "If it is so that God made such miracles as you tell me, while he was on earth in his manhood, why should he then suffer torment and death on the cross, and why should he let himself be killed if he had the power to give others life? Indeed, how could he be good to others when he was evil to himself? How could he save others if he did not have the power to save himself?"

St. Katherine's answer to the masters.

The virgin replied to the master's words and said: "If you think in your heart that he endured death on the cross in his divine nature, you are greatly mistaken, for God is invulnerable. You must know that he let himself be tormented in his manhood, which he took upon himself, and not in his divinity, for God is manifest and he is immune to all suffering, so that he cannot be tortured or imprisoned or held. And thus Jesus Christ was victorious over the devil in the manhood that he assumed, and not in his divinity. For as it was a man who sinned and broke the commandments by the tree, so was also the one who atoned for the sins and let himself be crucified on the tree, so that the sins that humankind had committed would be forgiven. Thus God himself wished to become a man. God had the power to strike down the devil through one of his angels, and could have taken humanity in his hands if he wished to, for his wisdom is great. But he wished to overcome the devil in the same way that the devil had overcome mankind. And he who overcame mankind and bent him down under his control must in turn be overcome by a man."

The fifty wise men accept the Christian faith.

When the virgin had spoken these and other great words, then the master and all his men were greatly astonished and did not know how to answer her. They were perplexed and shamed by God's virtue, and they were as silent as if they had been mute, and they looked at each other, one after another. The emperor was enraged, and with great and bitter anger he spoke to them and said, "Oh, you poor fools and false men, how is it that you are so dull in your senses? You stand and hold your tongues like mutes, and you should be ashamed that a woman can overcome you, as if you had lost both might and main. It would be shame enough that fifty women and one more could seduce you with their words. That is shameful, and it is even more shameful that fifty masters who are chosen and called from foreign lands let themselves be overcome by a mere girl, and cannot answer her with the merest word." Then one of the bravest and wisest of the masters, who was their leader, spoke for them all and answered the emperor. He said, "Lord Emperor, you should know that all the masters in your kingdom will bear witness that until this day there was no master who was our equal in words or in the bookish arts, for anyone who debated us was immediately overcome, and departed in shame. But this virgin is something quite different, for if I tell the truth, it is no human spirit which speaks in her, however that has come to pass. A holy spirit is speaking through her, and by his virtue we wonder greatly at her words, so that we neither dare nor can say anything about this same Jesus Christ, whom she calls her lord. As soon as she began to preach for us in the name of Jesus Christ, about his divine power and his great cross, all of our organs and our hearts began to shake and tremble, and all our senses wondered at her words. Know this, O Emperor, that we no longer desire frivolous or foolish things. We say to you that unless you can give us more certain proof of the gods we have worshipped until now, we wish to be converted to Christ, for we believe steadfastly in our hearts that he is God and the true son of God, of who we have heard so much good from this maiden."

The masters are burned — St. Katherine resists both Emperor Maxentius' temptations and his threats.

When the emperor heard that he was crazed with anger, and in his rage he had a bonfire lit in the middle of the city, and ordered that all the masters should be bound hand and foot and thrown into the fire. And as they were led to the fire where they were to be burned, one of them spoke to another and said, "O Emperor, brothers, and honorable companions, what are we doing? God, in his great mercy, has pitied us and the state of error in which we long found ourselves, and has called us to his mercy, so that we arrive at the Christian faith in our last moments, and are able to know his holy name before we leave this earth. Why do we not hurry before we die to embrace the holy cross and holy baptism?" When he had said this, they all begged the holy virgin Katherine with one voice that they might receive baptism. God's chosen bride replied thus: "Ye strongest knights of God, be steadfast in your faith and be not afraid, and have no fear for your baptism, for you shall be baptized in your own blood and the fire that burns and torments you will also light the fire of the Holy Spirit in your hearts. When the maiden had said this, the emperor's servants came, and in accord with the emperor's orders they bound the masters' hands and feet and threw them into the midst of the bonfire, and there they were tortured for the holy faith, and traveled to their blessed lord Jesus Christ. Their honor is great, for they were crowned as martyrs on the thirteenth day of November, and God wrought a great miracle on their behalf, for their clothes were not singed nor burned, not a hair was burnt from their heads, and their faces were as red and fair as the loveliest rose, so that their faces looked as though they were asleep rather than dead. Many people who saw it were converted to Jesus Christ by that miracle, and took the holy faith. Christian men quickly took their holy bodies and buried them. When this had been done, the emperor saw that he could not overcome the holy virgin with threats or force, for she was steadfast in her faith. Instead he tried to tempt her, to see whether he could persuade with sweet words her to worship the gods. And so he spoke to her and said, "O honorable maiden, your face is so lovely and fair that you are well worthy to be an empress. I wish that you could find it in your heart not to insult our gods, for you still say that they are devils and all those who worship them are sick and fools who will descend to the torments of the depths of hell. I would rejoice to see you renounce such words and not shame our gods, for I am afraid that they will not have much more patience with you, and that their revenge will be all the harder when it comes, if you do not change your ways. I advise you to sacrifice to our gods, and then I will gladly do you the honor of making you the greatest lady in my palace, second only to the empress. All the business of the kingdom shall be conducted according to your will, those you approve of shall be honored and made bodyguards to the emperor, and those you find unworthy will be shown little honor. You shall be powerful, and bring into the kingdom those you wish, and exile those you do not like. You shall be influential with the king's royal guard, dispensing justice and appointing and dismissing men as you wish. You and the empress with be equals in all matters, and she will have no advantage over you other than the right to lie with me in my bed, for she is my wedded wife. Otherwise, in bodily glory and in the matters of the kingdom, you shall be a mediator and a princess. Not only will I do you all the honors I have just named, I will also make a platform in the middle of the city.

On it I will place your image, and all those who are in the city will fall upon their knees in front of your image. And anyone who does not fall on his knees will be as guilty as if he had committed a crime against the emperor. Nor shall any crime be so great that the man who falls humbly to his knees before your statue and begs for mercy shall not be shown forgiveness. I can do you no greater honor than to construct for you a temple of precious marble, adjacent to those of the gods." When the emperor was finished, the maiden smiled, and said: "O, what great honor and advantage I should then receive, that everyone should greet me and fall upon their knees before my image. What great ceremony I should have! Up to now, I have been flesh and blood, and now I shall be made of gold. Surely it would be more than enough to make me out of silver. It is too much to make me of pure gold! I am greatly afraid that the goldsmiths and the coinmakers will begin to fight over me, the one saying that I am heavy and worth a great deal, another saying that I am light and worth but little. Thus it seems to me a better idea to make my image of some other, less precious metal, or of marble. Surely it would be honor enough that everyone must bow to me and fall on their knees before me. If it were also the case that you could make an image that resembled me as much as you say, I have but one thing to ask you. Where will you get life and breath to place into the body? How will you quicken the limbs, and give it the power to see with its eyes, and to move its limbs, to have soul and sense, so that it can see and hear and distinguish whether people greet it or not? If you cannot do that, you might just as well make my statue with an ape's head as with a maiden's face. You may say that it is not in vain, that all who go up to the statue remember my name and to honor me say, 'There is the honorable maiden Katherine, who abandoned her god and received this payment.' And you must also see what an honor it would be for me to provoke every child to words and lies. What kind of an honor would it be if the people, for fear of you, fell on their knees in front of my statue, when the birds in the sky sit upon my head and pollute my face? Indeed, what honor would small children and little boys show me, they who do not fear you nor understand what you have ordered. Imagine what the dogs would do! They are not so shy as to avoid doing indecencies before my eyes. O Emperor, what do you intend? Do you think that for the sake of such trifles and flattery I would abandon my faith and deny my God and Lord Jesus Christ, to worship your devils and idols? I ask you, Emperor, does erecting the statue during my lifetime mean that you promise me that things will go better for me, that I shall live longer, or be any richer than if it is put up after I am dead? Does the statue have the power to hide my body so that the maggots cannot devour it when I am dead, or does it have the power to keep my body uncorrupt in the earth until it is time to rise for the Last Judgement? What grace can this statue offer my soul? Will the statue stay in Heaven and receive everlasting life with the saints? Reconsider this frivolity, for it is a great sin to think thus, all the more to speak, and I think you are a great fool for doing this when you know nothing of Jesus Christ. He has taken me as his bride, and I have given him all my troth, so steadfastly that none can part us. He is my honor, he is my love, my glory and sweetness, he is my dearest lover. I was given to him for all time, and you should know with certainty that neither temptation nor force, neither sweet nor sour, will ever cause me to deny him." Emperor Maxentius replied: "For the sake of your youth, I had thought to advise you for your own benefit, if only you had obeyed me. But I see that you not only despise all the honor I have offered you in your stubborn heart, but even despise your own life and health. I shall now try something better, and see if I can make you more humble and right the error of your ways. You will sacrifice to our gods or suffer the hardest of deaths." Katherine answered: "When the king of Heaven, Jesus Christ, my Lord, once sacrificed himself on the cross to God the Father in Heaven for my sake, it is a great joy to me that I can be sacrificed for him in return. O poor Emperor, you think that it is a great honor to you that you have power over me and other servants of God. But the time is coming all the sooner that the devil in hell will regain his power over you. The torments that you inflict for a short time upon the servants of Jesus Christ will be repaid you without end. My Lord Jesus Christ finds me so much lovelier and dearer and better because for a short time I suffer torment for his sake. Do you think that your unjust judgment can judge and kill me? No, it will not happen, for I shall come to my Lord Jesus Christ, and a great crowd from your palace will follow him, and they will live with him in joy and happiness for eternity."

St. Katherine is tortured and thrown into prison.

When the maiden had replied to the emperor as is written, he grew crazed with rage, and in his furor he ordered his servants to take the maiden, tear her clothes from her and flog her with lead-tipped flails, and then to throw her into the dungeon. As she was led away, she said to the cruel emperor, "I submit gladly to being flogged and beaten, and thrown into the dungeon, for the sake of him who let his whole body be flogged, and his skin struck for my sake. You will know for certain I shall be saved from the darkness into which you would cast me by an eternal light, while you shall receive darkness without end." When the maiden had said this, the emperor's servants came and did as they were ordered; they took away her clothes and flogged her fragile body with iron points. And when they tired and could not continue, others took their places. The harder they flogged her, the more she praised and thanked God. The emperor asked if she would be willing to do as he bid her, if he stopped torturing her. But she took more comfort in this herself than did the emperor and all his executioners who flogged her. She answered: "O, you most pitiful and shameful dogs, torment me as much as your evil hearts can imagine. I am happy to endure and suffer every kind of torture for the sake of the love of the one who was willing to ransom me with his suffering. When this torment is over, the time will come that you see me in the glory of Heaven among the saints, and you shall be cast into everlasting torment, in woe and pain, because of what you are doing now to me and to all other servants of Jesus Christ." Next the maiden was thrown into the dungeon, and the emperor ordered that she should be starved there for twelve days, and it was forbidden for anyone to bring her food or drink, on pain of grievous revenge, nor should any light reach her. She was to see nothing but heavy darkness. But God did not forget his handmaiden while she was in that dark place. He sent to her his holy angels, who comforted and healed her, and the dungeon shone with unspeakable clarity, so that the guards who were outside the dungeon were astonished and afraid in their hearts. They would have liked to tell of the miracle they had witnessed, but did not dare to because of the emperor's great cruelty and rage.

The Queen's conversation with Porphyrius.

Before St. Katherine was put into the dungeon, it happened that the emperor had to travel away on business to the furthest parts of his realm. While he was away, the empress found out about the heavy judgement he had placed on the holy virgin St. Katherine, and how the wise masters had debated the mildest of virgins with strong words, and how they were converted to the holy faith, and how they let themselves be tortured and slain for the holy faith, and how her husband the emperor was cruelly enraged by the wise men's conversion, and how the maiden was flogged with leaden flails for refusing to sacrifice to the gods, and how she was cast unjustly, innocent as she was, into the dungeon, to starve there for twelve days without food or drink. When the empress heard how cruelly the emperor had behaved, she sorrowed greatly in her heart, for her nature was kind and good, and though she was a pagan she began to mourn and worry for the delicate maiden. In her heart, she wondered how she might manage to see her face and speak with her without the emperor's knowledge. By herself in her palace, she paced back and forth thinking about this. Unexpectedly, she met the captain of the king's guard, a very honorable and noble man, wise in all the things of this world and schooled in all secret knowledge. He was called Porphyrius, and the queen called to him secretly, asked his advice and told him of her wish, and asked whether there was any way that he, with temptation and sweet words, could gain the good will of the watchmen who guarded the dungeon, so that she could speak with the maiden. Among other words she said to Porphyrius she said, "Know, good Porphyrius, that I have had strange dreams, and I have pondered these in my heart, for I do not know if they portend good or evil until I see what will come. I dreamed last night about the same maiden of whom we are speaking. I saw her sitting in a house, and around her there was a clear and unspeakably lovely light, and there sat many men, all dressed in white clothes, and their faces were so shining and fair that I could hardly look upon them. And when she caught sight of me, she asked me to come toward her. She took a golden crown from the hand of one of those sitting near her, and placed it on my head, saying, 'Good Empress, do you know that this crown has been sent to you from Heaven, by my Lord Jesus Christ?' My heart is filled with the light of this dream. I cannot sleep at night, nor can I rest for a moment, so much does my heart long to see the maiden. I beg you, dear Porphyrius, find a way for me to meet and speak with her."

Porphyrius replied: "Good lady Empress, it is clear that you have the right to give me orders as you will, and it is for me to obey and do as you say. I tell you the truth that I am ready to do all that you ask in this errand, even though I know well that the emperor will be enraged and will show me no mercy if he comes to know of it. It is certainly true that the emperor has treated the maiden of whom we speak very cruelly, for I was there when he sent for all of the wisest masters of his realm to debate with her. He promised them great gifts if they overcame her. Yet when they arrived, they could not gain any ground from her, and immediately let themselves be converted and confessed that the God of whom she preached was theirs as well. And at this the emperor was furious, and ordered all the masters to be thrown into a roaring bonfire. In the bonfire, a great miracle occurred. I saw with my own eyes that they were dead, but not a hair was burned on their heads, nor a thread from their clothes, and this I confess to you, O Empress, that from the day I saw that miracle, her words have been fastened in my heart, those with which she punished our gods so piously. If she says that all of our gods are devils, then I count them as devils and vanity. If our laws were not so cruel to the Christians as they are, I would quickly turn to her and worship and honor Jesus Christ. Since you and I have the same desire, I see no better advice than that we bribe and tempt the jailers who are guarding the dungeon to let us visit the maiden, so that they will promise us faithfully that no one will come to know." And with that Porphyrius went to the jailers of the dungeon, and with gifts and sweet words he tempted them, and they declared themselves willing to do all that he asked.

The queen and Porphyrius visit the prison.

At midnight the empress and Porphyrius went to the dungeon. When they entered it, it was filled with the most wondrously clear light shining in all directions. When they saw it, they were greatly astonished, and fell down to the ground. As soon as they had fallen, they smelled a good and precious scent in their nostrils and they soon quickened again because of these precious odors. The honorable maiden Katherine spoke to them and said, "Arise and be not afraid, for my Lord Jesus Christ has called you and chosen you for a crown of honor." When they stood up they could see that the maiden was seated on a glorious seat, and God's angel was healing her wounds and anointing her with the most precious salve, so that her wounds closed and were covered with skin in that moment, and her body was fair and white. Around her they saw a number of honorable old men, with unspeakably clear and shining faces, and from one of these men the maiden took a crown that shone like the brightest gold, and placed this crown on the head of the empress. She spoke to the glorious old men who sat around her, saying, "This is the queen of my Lord Jesus Christ, whom I have long awaited. I have prayed that she will get a noble crown with you and with me, to her eternal honor. And this knight whom you see standing here will be among us, and he shall be counted in our number." One of the honorable old men replied, "O finest and most precious pearl of Jesus Christ, because you were not afraid of the dungeon and endured its evil stench for the sake of your Lord Jesus Christ, he has heard your prayers on behalf of those present here. It is granted to you by your Lord Jesus Christ that your prayers will be answered on behalf of those you ask for. These people who have sought you out and visited you in your wretchedness will also be included in your reward. You shall see them allow themselves to be tortured and killed and they shall gain martyrs' crowns and the honor of Heaven. As soon as their torment is over, your immortal bridegroom Jesus Christ will lead them through the gate of life. There they will hear the sweet music of organs and see the fair flock of maidens who amuse themselves and rejoice among roses and lilies, and who follow after the innocent lamb Jesus Christ wherever he goes . . ."[2]

St. Katherine's speech to the queen.

When that was spoken, the maiden St. Katherine turned to the empress, comforted her and said, "O Empress, be steadfast in your heart, for in three days you will travel hence from this world to your God and to your Lord. Be not afraid of any torment before you, for in a short moment all of the torments that you can endure and suffer in this little time are nothing to the great honor that you will gain as your reward. Do not be afraid of abandoning your bridegroom who is a devilish man, for he will be emperor but a short time, and his rule will soon be over. Today he is an emperor and a lord in his power. Tomorrow or the next day toads and serpents will rend his body. Do not be afraid to part from the worldly king, for in exchange you will gain as your bridegroom the immortal king Jesus Christ, who will give you the reward that never perishes, and honor that will never end."

---

[2] Allusion to Revelation 14:4.

St. Katherine's speech to Porphyrius.

When virgin St. Katherine had spoken the words written here, because Porphyrius was a great lord and captain of all the emperor's men, and had great riches, he asked St. Katherine what reward he would gain for his injuries, if he became the knight of Jesus Christ and fought for his sake. The maiden answered him and said, "You know well, my good Porphyrius, that no mortal man is so powerful and so rich and so healthy, nor can he look after himself so well that he is not sometimes shifted from his own proper place. See for yourself how short a human life is. The land and money that people amass over many years and with great effort vanish in an hour, and in a blink of an eye, everything dear to you has vanished. See for yourself how that lands and cities are much worse off now than they were a few years ago when they were newly built. Because you ask me what reward Jesus Christ will give his servants, who for his sake abandon these fleeting things, see for yourself that while these things seem to be important down here on earth and yet shall so soon perish, how great and important must be those things in Heaven that never perish, but exist for eternity. This world is like the ugliest of dungeons. All those who enter it will die and be killed. Those who abandon the world for the sake of God will gain the kingdom of Heaven. It is a noble place, which needs no light from sun or moon. There is no wretchedness, no failure, no anxiety. There is eternal joy and happiness without end. If you want to know, finally, about the joy of Heaven, let me tell you in a few words, that Heaven is the place where there is everything good and nothing evil. If you ask me what is there that is good, I will tell you that human eyes have never seen it, nor human ears heard it, and the heart cannot imagine the great honors God has given to his friends who love him.[3] The rich man that scripture tells of[4] desired these honors and joys, and he spoke to himself in his heart and said, 'O my dearest God, how long will my soul, which thirsts and longs to come to you, stay in these dark rooms that are my sinful body? How long will the time last that I must stay in my mortal body?' This is the glorious ancestral land that every person must desire and wish for, for there is no sighing and weeping there, no cries or striving, no sorrow or wretchedness. When a person gains these honors, she rejoices in her soul. Everything I have told you about Heaven is but little before what it is in truth. This you will come to know if you remain steadfast in your Christian faith to the end."

---

[3] 1 Corinthians 2:9.
[4] Luke 18:28.

Porphyrius' speech to the knights. — St. Katherine's judgement.

When St. Katherine had spoken the above-mentioned words about the glory of Heaven, the queen and Porphyrius rejoiced greatly in their hearts, and they left the dungeon and knew in their hearts that they would gladly obey and endure all the torments the cruel emperor would visit upon them, for the sake of the name of Jesus Christ. When they came out of the dungeon, all of the emperor's bodyguards asked each other where Porphyrius or the queen had been the whole night. Then Porphyrius answered and said, "Where I have been you may not ask. I will tell you one thing that will be of great help to you, if you will heed and place my words in that time, for I have had a holy watch this night. The path of life was revealed to me tonight, and my God and my creator was shown to me. If you want to remain with me and rejoice with me, you must abandon the idols we have worshipped and loved up to now, and instead worship and honor a true God who created you and everything. You must also believe in his son Jesus Christ, honoring and worshipping him, for he is the true God and true Lord over everything that is in the world. All those who believe in him shall receive everlasting blessedness, and those who do not will receive everlasting condemnation. This same omnipotent God who has so long tolerated our error has now revealed himself through this holy maiden St. Katherine whom the Emperor Maxentius threw into the dungeon. Porphyrius spoke these words to two hundred knights who were the foremost in the emperor's bodyguard, and they immediately renounced the worship of idols and were converted to Jesus Christ. Before this was spoken, the holy maiden St. Katherine was again hidden in the dungeon according to the orders of the emperor. And because the emperor had given the strictest of orders that she should be given neither food nor drink during the twelve days she lay there, the same God who fed the prophet Daniel in the lions' den also fed the innocent virgin where she lay, sending her food and drink with a white dove from Heaven above, and when the twelve days had passed Jesus Christ himself came to her with a great flock of angels and a great flock of virgins, and he spoke to her and said: "O my dearest daughter, now you may see and look upon your God and your Lord, for whose name you have endured these trials. Remain steadfast in your heart and be not afraid, for I am with you, and I will never leave or abandon you. It is so that many men will believe in me for your sake." And when he had spoken those words he went once again back up to Heaven, and the maiden stood looking up after him as long as she could.

When the emperor had finished his business away in the kingdoms, he came back to the city of Alexandria, and the next day after that he sat in his court and called together all his masters and his highest advisors. When they were all present, the emperor spoke to those who stood around him, and said: "Bring the stubborn girl before us, and we will see and hear if we can compel her with hunger and thirst to worship our gods." At once the maiden was led in from the dungeon before the emperor's court. As she stood before him and he saw that her face was fair and shining, while he had expected her face to be pinched and strained from her long fast, he grew suspicious in his heart. He began to think that someone must have given her food in secret, against his orders. In his anger and rage, he ordered that the guards who had watched the dungeon be seized and tortured and beaten, until they were willing to reveal who had fed her. They were tortured for her sake without cause, for they were innocent. The maiden felt herself compelled to reveal what she would have preferred to keep hidden from the men, and she said: "O Emperor, you who have such great honor and worth before other men, it would be better if you punished those who are guilty and criminal, and leave those who have committed no crime free from torture. Otherwise it is clear for all to see that you are unworthy to rule in the city where you reign. Know that no living person gave me food or drink since I was placed in the dungeon. Rather, a God who does not abandon his knights when they obey and endure hunger and thirst for his sake, of his greatness he sent me food and sustenance from Heaven above with his heavenly angel. He is my God and my lover, he is my sanctuary and my bridegroom."

St. Katherine's steadfastness.

The emperor turned his back on those who stood nearby, so that his cruelty and grimness toward those who had committed crimes would not be seen. He pretended to be concerned for the maiden, and spoke sweet words to her with a false heart, and said: "I pity this girl, who is born of royal family and honorable people, but she is spellbound in her heart with magic and sorcery, so that she is no longer able to worship our immortal gods, but instead blasphemes and insults them with her words. She calls them devils and unclean spirits, and says that they deceive and fool all those who believe in them." Then he turned to the maiden herself and said, "I would much rather help and save you than slay and destroy you. We advise you that you tell us your will, as you have thought about your interests during the long days you were in prison. Now you must choose whether you would rather sacrifice to our gods and keep your life, or I shall torture your body with the hardest of deaths."

St. Katherine replied: "I would gladly give my life for Jesus Christ, I am not afraid to die for his sake, indeed, I desire of my free will to suffer death and torment for his sake, for then I will gain everlasting life. As you wound and torture my body, my Lord Jesus Christ will exchange this mortal body for an immortal body. You have power over me now, and I know that it is according to nature that I die, but you have no power over my soul. You are lying to yourself, for as soon as you have killed my body, my soul shall fly, free and saved, as quickly as the quickest bird, up to Heaven, to see God with the greatest of joy and gladness. I say to you, cruel Emperor, think of all the torments you can find in your evil heart and let them come, for my Lord Jesus Christ is calling me, and I have no wish to offer him cattle or sheep, but rather my own flesh and my own blood, for he sacrificed himself to God the Father in Heaven for my sake. You shall know the truth of this, for in a short time the vengeance of God will come upon you, for Jesus Christ will awake a great warrior[5] against you, who shall do battle against you for the sake of the holy faith, and he will avenge your wrongs against God. With his sword he will cut off your head, and your sinful blood will be sacrificed to your gods, a cursed sacrifice to the devils in hell. If you listen to my advice, and renounce your idols, and with a godly heart accept the holy faith, you may yet escape this severe judgement which stands over you, because the mercy of God is upon you."

St. Katherine and the people.

When the maiden had spoken the emperor was as furious and grim as a lion, and began to snort and gnash his teeth, and in his raging he spoke boastful words, saying: "How long must we endure that this cat so greatly insults our gods? Surely it is better to tear her whole body to pieces, one limb from another. Then other Christians will not be comforted and emboldened by her to insult and mock our gods. All those who wish to avenge the wronging of our gods, step forward and take hold of this witch-cat, beating her and torturing her so that she ends her life most cruelly, and then she will see what help she gets from this god of hers, whom she praises so much." As she was led away to be tortured, there gathered people who pitied her beauty, and grieved that such a fair maiden should be so shamefully executed. They advised her to obey the emperor rather than lose her young life, saying: "O fairest maiden, lovely and shining as the sun, what is the hardness in your heart, that you who are born of royal family and are offered honor, riches, and fame, that you willingly reject, preferring to die rather than live? Maiden, you are worthy of being an empress. Remember that you are now in your youth, like the fairest flower. Do not cast away such a fair body with such a shameful and evil death." The honorable maiden replied, saying: "Cease your foolish weeping and ungodly encouragement, and do not pity my youth or my beauty, for the body that to you seems blooming and fair is like a withered tree, for as soon as the soul or spirit leaves it, the body is at once withered and dead, and all its beauty gone. Serpents and toads will tear at it, and it will be earth and ashes, from whence it came. Have no sorrow, nor do not weep for the death that I now confront, for that shall not be my final end, it shall be my departure for an eternal life. He will slay me and torment me wretchedly, and for the sake of that death I shall arise to everlasting honor. Weep and mourn rather over yourselves,

---

[5] Constantine

for after your deaths you will not have a hope of honor or life. For you nothing awaits but eternal damnation." When the maiden had spoken thus, some people repented in their hearts because of her words, and they withdrew in secret from the worship of idols and from the society of the emperor, though they did not dare confess the publicly, for fear of the emperor. And so they remained silent long enough to see what kind of ending the maiden might find to her torment.

The wheel of torment — salvation.

When the maiden was to be tortured, a man came forth by the name of Chrusates, the emperor's bailiff in the city. He was a devilish man, who with his words aroused the emperor to new fury against the maiden, and made the emperor even grimmer and crueler than he had been before. He ordered them to inflict torture upon torture, and he spoke smarmily to the emperor, saying, "O great and powerful Emperor, do you not think it shameful that a woman should hold you with many words? Mark my words, this girl Katherine has not yet seen torments sufficiently frightening and fearsome. It is no wonder that she refuses to sacrifice to our gods. I advise you, Emperor, to make a stronger command and a greater revenge. Before three days have passed, have built four wheels according to the plans that I will tell you. These wheels are to be studded all around, on all sides, with sharp spikes. The hubs and spokes must be shod with sharp nails and iron saws. When the wheels have been constructed to my orders, put her before them so that she can see how they run together up and down, and so that she can hear how the spikes spark together when they meet. Then her heart will be gripped with fear, and by this she will be forced to worship our gods. If she should still refuse to be persuaded, throw her immediately into the wheelworks so that her body will be torn into a thousand pieces by the iron spikes. Then all the worshippers of Christ will see and understand that they have never seen such torment."
As soon as that foul advisor had spoken, the cruel emperor ordered the machine constructed without delay. The pagans were ready and willing to follow all of the emperor's orders to harm the maiden. When the third day had arrived the emperor gave orders that word should be spread of the machine's completion. The maiden was to be thrown into the center of it if she resisted the emperor's will. He ordered the wheels to be set in motion at great speed, to show her how her slender body would be torn to pieces, and to inspire fear in other Christians of such a cruel death. The cruel emperor's servants fulfilled all his orders. The wheels were set up before the judicial building, and they stood there so sharp and so cruel that all those who saw them trembled in their hearts at the horror of it. Only St. Katherine was unafraid of any torment, for her heart was so steadfastly devoted to our Lord Jesus Christ that she could not be persuaded with fair words or foul ones. The wheels were constructed so that they turned against each other, so that two went up and two went down. The holy maiden was to be thrown into

the midst of those wheels. Her body would be torn to pieces by the sharp iron spikes, and her life would be brought to an end in a wretched death. When she was led forth, and was about to be thrown into the machine, she raised her eyes to Heaven, and secretly in her heart she prayed to her God, saying, "O almighty God, you who always help those who call upon you in need, hear my prayer as I call on you in my peril. Grant that this wheelworks, which has been constructed to torture me, be struck down by lightening. Thus may those gathered around see the power of your divinity, so that they will have to honor your eternally blessed name. You know well, my dear lord, that I do not ask this out of fear of torment, for my heart longs to suffer any pain and death that is meant for me, so that I may come swiftly to you and see your holy visage. I pray this prayer so that those who believe in your holy name for my sake should be strengthened in their faith, and more steadfastly proclaim your holy name." Before the maiden had finished her thought, God's angel came from Heaven and struck the wheelworks with a fierce storm. It was struck so hard that the fragments killed four thousand pagans who were nearby. The pagans wailed and mourned and were ashamed, but the servants of Jesus Christ, who believed in him, rejoiced in their hearts. The emperor was so enraged that he gnashed his teeth in fury, and did not know what to do.

The queen proclaims Christ.

The honorable empress, standing among the others, witnessed God's great miracle and justice, and the vengeance he visited upon his enemies. She had long hidden her heart and her faith for fear of her husband. But now she stepped forth toward the evil emperor, chastising him. "O, you poorest of men," she said, "how long must you strive against God? You wretched man, what madness is too great for your cruel heart? Are you so cruel and mad toward your own creator that you use the time you have left to strive against God and all his servants? Look and see what great deeds God has just done before your eyes! This should make you see how mighty and powerful the God of the Christians is, and how he will condemn you. He is so mighty that with a wind he slew thousands of people, and by this miracle many pagans who saw it were turned to Jesus Christ. They shouted aloud, saying, 'Truly, truly, the God of the Christians is a great god. From this day forward who confess that we are his servants.' Your gods are no more than useless idols, of no good to anyone."

The queen's martyrdom. — Porphyrius buries her.

When the emperor heard this his rage grew even more bitter, and his fury was greatest toward the queen. In his anger he spoke to her, saying, "O Queen, what are you saying, why do you speak such words as you have just uttered? Are you ill or mad, or have you been deceived by Christians into believing their faith, and abandoning our almighty gods, who, as you know, are the source of all our might and honor? This causes me great sorrow and pain, that I, who have always compelled all others to worship our gods, should now find within my own house such a poisonous betrayal. My own wife and only bedmate is now infected with error just like the others. Am I so mad and so foolish that I should let myself be deceived and made a fool of out of love for a woman? That I should not avenge the outrage which has been done to our gods? What can come of this? All the women in our Roman Empire will follow these women, and turn their husbands away from the worship of our gods. That way they will convert the entire kingdom to the wretched creed called the Christian faith. Therefore I swear, O Empress, by my mighty gods, that if you do not swiftly turn from your madness and sacrifice to our gods, that I will cut off your head and throw your corpse into the open to be torn by birds and beasts. Nor shall you have the favor of a quick death. I shall plague you for a long time, and I shall have the nipples torn from your breasts." The cruel emperor ordered his executioner and his foul servants to seize the queen, and to tear the nipples from her breasts with sharp iron links. As they were taking her to the place where she would be tortured, she saw St. Katherine, and said to her: "O most honored maiden of Jesus Christ, pray for me to my lord Jesus Christ, for the sake of whose love I have entered this great battle. Ask him to comfort me and strengthen me in my heart as I am tortured. My body is sick and frail, and no loss, but do not let my soul despair or be lost as I suffer. Let me not lose the crown that God has promised to the knights who fight for his sake, and of which you told me."

Great St. Katherine replied, "Honorable queen, be steadfast in your heart and deeds, and do not fear. Today God will make you a glorious exchange. For this transitory kingdom he will give you a kingdom that will never perish. For your bridegroom, who is a mortal man, he will give you an immortal bridegroom. For the torments that await you, you will receive everlasting rest and peace. For the death which you endure but a little while you will gain a new life without end." These words so comforted and strengthened the honorable empress that she called to the executioners that they should hurry to do as the emperor had ordered. The emperor's servants seized her and, when they had arrived at the place of torture, they threw sharp iron hooks at her breast, tearing off both of her nipples and doing her grievous pain. Then they cut off her head and she became a holy martyr, and left this world to a martyr's crown, and to her bridegroom Jesus Christ. This occurred on a Wednesday, the twenty-third of November. The night after she was slain, Porphyrius and some of his trusted servants laid her body secretly in a grave and buried her with precious herbs and fragrant spices.

Porphyrius' speech to the emperor.

Early in the morning, just after the queen was buried, people began to ask what had become of her body, or who might have taken it. Porphyrius saw how the emperor seized one man after another, blaming them all. And so he went before the emperor, saying, "Emperor, why do you torture innocent men, who have committed no crime against you? If only you understood the ways of nature, when your own nature tells you that you must not throw dead bodies to the birds and beasts. You are clearly mad in all your senses, for you do not allow a dead body to be buried. Do you know of anyone in the world who has been as cruel as you have, not to bury a body in the earth from which it came? Before I allow you to kill an innocent man for burying her, I will proclaim that I did it myself. Do with me what you will, I put her in a grave against your will. I ask that you release all the others, for I did this by myself. She is a martyr of Jesus Christ, and I proclaim that I too worship Jesus Christ."

Maxentius' fury

When the cruel emperor heard this he was wounded to his heart with great distress. He did not weep, but he began to shout with rage like a madman, and his howls were heard throughout the kingdom. He spoke to himself, saying, "Oh, I may well call myself more wretched than anyone in the world. Why was I ever born to such wretchedness? Why is all my glory taken away? Porphyrius was all my peace, my only help, he bore all my burdens. I cannot understand the devilishness with which he is betraying me, for he refuses now to worship and honor my gods. Instead he has turned to this Jesus Christ, whom Christians worship in their foolishness. And he is a madman to proclaim it openly. I can test whether it is true beyond a doubt that he infected and turned the queen from worshipping our gods. If the honorable women have betrayed none other than him, though it is an unequaled injury that he betrayed my wife, yet it would still seem to me only half as great a sorrow if I could retrieve him from his madness so that he worships our gods as he used to do. If he did this, I would forgive him and remain his friend."

The steadfastness of Porphyrius's knights.

When the emperor had spoken, he called in all the knights and well-born men whom Porphyrius commanded on his behalf. When they arrived, he called them all over to one side, telling them how Porphyrius had been converted. At this, the knights shouted with one voice that they too believed in Jesus Christ, and that neither death nor torture would cause them to renounce that faith or their dear lord Porphyrius. At that, the cruel emperor decided to torture some of them so long that they would be happy to renounce the holy faith. He had them led off to one side, and ordered them to be severely tortured and tormented. When Porphyrius saw them being led away, his heart was gripped by fear. . .(ending missing).

Appendix 6
Saint Katherine's Saga

This version of the vita of St. Katherine of Alexandria is found complete in two manuscripts, Cod. C 528 ("Codex Bildstenianus") and Cod. Holm A 3. The former, dated to 1440–1450, has certainly belonged to Vadstena Abbey, and may or may not have been produced there. It is considered to be derived from an older source, either Cod. Holm A 34 ("Codex Bureanus", dated 1340–1385, connected by some scholars to the Dominican friary or convent at Skänninge, Östergötland), or an older, lost source common to both C 528 and Holm A 34.[1] Codex Bureanus contains a fragment of the life of St. Katherine below, but it, along with the rest of the manuscript, extends only to the third line of the second chapter of the life below. The text produced here is a translation of the life of St. Katherine published by George Stephens in the first volume of *Ett fornsvenskt legendarium*.[2] Stephens' text is taken from Codex Bureanus up to its end, in the middle of section two, line three. The remainder of the text is taken from Codex Bildstenianus.

How Maxentius became Emperor

The judges removed Diocletian and Maximian from power and reduced them to the status of regular free men. They appointed three emperors: Varian, Constantinus and Licinias, and their reign lasted two years. With his sword, Constantius brought Britain under Roman rule, and as his wife he took Helen, the daughter of the king of Britain. Maxentius killed all three of them. He wanted to become emperor, but was never crowned so. But still he called himself Emperor, and confiscated the lands of many Romans against their will, until young Constantine grew up.

---

[1] See Jansson, *Fornsvenska legendariet*, 25; Carlquist, *Fornsvenska helgonlegenderna*, 25–32.

[2] Stockholm: Svenska fornsällskapets skrifter/P. A. Norstedt & söner, 1847–1858), 533–39.

Katherine and Maxentius. — The 50 Wise Men. — The Queen. — The Conversions.

About St. Katherine.

Maxentius came to Alexandria, the capital city of the land of Egypt, and commanded that everyone in the kingdom come together to sacrifice to the gods and to kill Christians. Costus, the king of Egypt, had died recently. His only child, Katherine, was his heir. She was the fairest of maidens, and the wisest in book-learning. She was eighteen years old. As she sat in her palace, she heard the bellowing of oxen and the baaing of sheep, and the chanting of the heathen priests who called upon their gods and sacrificed every kind of animal to them. Katherine could no longer tolerate this insult to God and worship of devils. She went bravely forth from her palace to the emperor, and spoke to him, and said: "It would be well for you if you recognized your creator and did not worship devils. Why do you call people together to insult God and sacrifice to devils that which God created as food? Do you think that these monsters are so fair? For these images of gold were made by the hands of men, and it is wrong to sacrifice to the works of man. Lift your eyes up to the heavens, and examine the path of the sun and the stars, day and night, from the beginning of the world, from east to west, from west to east, and ask, if you know it not, who steers them to the benefit of mankind. Who sends rain for the growth of the earth? Who lets gold and treasure and every kind of ore grow in the earth? He is worthy of your worship. He and no other gave you your soul in your mother's womb, and your natural reason, if you will only follow them. Therefore offer Him your praise. His alone is the honor which is turned from Him and offered to devils."

Maxentius was full of wonder at her beauty and her eloquent words. He had her brought to his palace with honor, where the sacrifices were being held. "We heard your words and your quick tongue, and we cannot understand your hatred for the gods and their worship, nor have we found an answer for it.. But we say to you now that you will either suffer torture or you will sacrifice to the gods."

Katherine replied: "A wise philosopher wrote that a king shall always rule over his anger, anger shall not rule over the king. He who rules over many must first rule over himself. Speak to me with reason, not with anger." Maxentius understood that she was very wise in the bookish arts, and he sent out a letter throughout the kingdom of Egypt, in search of the best masters, and all of the best masters in the land in all the bookish arts, fifty in all, came to him. When they heard why they had been called, they spoke mockingly to the emperor, and said: "What is wrong with the emperor, who calls together so many wise masters from foreign lands, to debate with a single girl-child?" Maxentius said that he thought it a greater honor to convert her with reason than with torment, especially since she herself relied more on books. Jesus Christ himself supported his maiden, and comforted her before her battle with the fifty wise masters, and promised her that they would become Christians. The next day their battle began. Katherine said: "If I should be victorious over these masters, I know what my reward will be, for I expect a better reward from Jesus Christ. And thus I will do his errands and his work. He is my God and my Lord, he is true wisdom and eternal blessedness. To all those who believe in him, he is what the roads of life have proven with his holy commandments. And all those who fulfill his commandments shall be rewarded with eternal life. He is the same one who had mercy on mankind, when we were deceived and damned by the cleverness of the devil. He took on humanity and was born of the purest of virgins, without sin, in a true body of man. He showed himself to be both God and man, God in that he performed great miracles and wondrous deeds, restoring the dead to life, and the blind to sight. He purified lepers and performed innumerable other wonders, as it pleased him. He showed that he was a man, for he went visibly as a man among others here in the world, and he let himself be tormented and killed in his manhood, for the sake of mankind. He arose from the dead and went up to Heaven. He is my victory and my crown, he is my wisdom, and with his virtue and power, I know that I can overcome every obstacle."

The masters replied that it was impossible for a god to take human form or to suffer death. Katherine told them what was true, that they must have read very little in the books of Christian men, and that they did not know what the prophets had predicted. And then she spoke to them of heathen books, and surprised them, with Plato and the Sibyl. "Plato wrote, and proved with reason that the world rotates,[3] the smallest sphere inside the highest ones. It was in the age of the gods / about that time / put into a virgin's womb / and is now seen each day in the shape of bread. The Sibyl predicted that God would become flesh, and be tormented, and suffer death. If you do not believe what you hear with your ears, or with your eyes see the miracles manifest before you, then you must believe the devils who recognize him as God against their will. If you do not want to believe them, then believe your own masters, who bear witness in their books that Jesus Christ is the true son of God."

The masters were beaten with their own swords, and they gave in to her logic. Truly it is as Paul has said, that God overcomes the greatest power with the slightest of means, so that none may despair. Maxentius commanded that the masters should be burned to death. Katherine gave comforted them and gave them the strength to endure what was to come, and told them that they would be baptized in their own blood. Thus they burned in divine faith, and no mark was found on their bodies.

Maxentius spoke again to Katherine: "You are well born. Heed my advice, and you shall be as an empress. Your portrait will be made of gold and put into

---

[3] *Timaeus* 34a.

the middle of the street. All those who pass by will fall on their knees." Katherine replied that it would be little honor to have birds soil her head. "Jesus is my betrothed, he is my honor, he is my lover, and neither threats nor soft words will turn me from him."

Maxentius had her beaten and thrown into a dungeon. She was there for twelve days, and was given neither food nor drink. But God's angel in the form of a dove brought her food each day. During those days, Maxentius had an errand in the far reaches of his kingdom, and he traveled away. His queen came to hear how Katherine preached, though she had been beaten, and she went to visit her, and took with her Marshal Porphyrius. They saw a light shining in the dungeon, and saw how God's angel healed and cared for her wounds. And they fell to the ground in fear of God. Katherine preached the Christian faith to them until midnight, and they became Christian, and a hundred knights with them. Katherine placed a crown on the queen's head, and prophesied that she would become a martyr within a few days. Jesus himself visited her with a host of angels, and bade his daughter recognize her creator. He said that he was the one of whom she preached, and for whom she suffered torment. He bade her not to be afraid.

Maxentius returned, full of rage that she was neither starving or dead. He demanded that she make a choice. Either she could worship idols and enjoy earthly glory, or she could suffer torture. Katherine said that she would gladly sacrifice her blood for Jesus Christ, who had redeemed her with his own blood. Maxentius had four wheels made, and had all of them set with iron spikes. The mechanism was constructed so that two of the wheels went against the other two. He commanded that Katherine should be placed on top, between the wheels, so that when they were set in motion, her body would be torn asunder. Saint Katherine prayed for God's help, and help came. God's angel destroyed the wheel as Katherine had prayed, and slew four thousand heathen men. The queen, who before had been Christian in secret, rejoiced at God's miracle. She chastised the emperor for the way he treated innocent people, and revealed that she was a Christian. In his rage, Maxentius commanded that she should have the nipples cut from her breasts, and then she should be beheaded. Katherine comforted her with fair words, and told her that she should rejoice to exchange the honor of this world for eternal Heaven. Porphyrius buried her body, and was asked about this, and confessed. He was condemned to be beheaded, and with him the hundred knights who had converted to Christianity with him. Then Maxentius had Katherine called to him. He told her to sacrifice to the gods, and become his (first) wife after the death of the queen, or else lose her life. Katherine chose death, and was condemned to be beheaded. She prayed to God, saying, "For thy sake I am happy to face the sword, Jesus, son of God. Accept my soul, and have mercy on all those who call upon my name." A voice came from Heaven and said, so that everyone could hear it, "Betrothed of God, come to God's happiness. Those who honor thee will be saved." Then she stretched out her neck, unafraid, and instead of blood, milk ran from her body. Angels took her beheaded body, and in a short while they had traveled twenty days' distance, to Mount Sinai, where they buried her with honor.

Saint Katherine's Finger.

A good man who served St. Katherine traveled from Rome. He was a monk at Mount Sinai, and he served there for fifty years in her church. He wished to have something from her shrine before he traveled back home. St. Katherine came to him as he slept and gave him her finger. With this he went happily to that land, and wherever he came, many miracles occurred. Her feast comes six days before the feast of St. Andrew.

APPENDIX 7
CHURCH BELLS

Medieval Swedish church bells could convey important information about the patron saint(s) of their church. In some cases, bells had their own patrons, which could be separate from the patron saint of the church itself. During the Middle Ages, church bells were commonly consecrated by the bishop, in a ceremony that could include the naming of the bell. This ceremony has popularly been called "klockdopet" (bell baptism).[1] This appendix includes medieval Swedish church bells that name or depict St. Katherine of Alexandria. However, even bells that are not inscribed with the name of the saint could be called by her name. In several cases, local tradition has preserved bell names, and this information is also included in this appendix. As Åmark notes, "A witness to the loyalty with which the old church bells have been regarded in Västergötland is the way that the names of the bells have been preserved here. Even bells that lack inscriptions have had names in many places. One common name is Maria. Other names have been Magdalena, Susanna, and especially Katarina, or its Swedish form, Karin."[2] Except where otherwise noted, this appendix is derived entirely from Mats Åmark's *Sveriges medeltida kyrkklockor* (Stockholm: Almqvist & Wiksell, 1960).

Uppland: Ununge parish church. Cast 1521. Inscription: "Per me [Johannem] hoc opus factum est ad honorem sanctorum Christofferi et Katerine patronorum huius ecclesie, tempore domini mathie curati." Norberg notes that the surface of the bell also has several reliefs depicting St. John the Baptist, and one depicting St. Olof. He suggests that these two were the original patron saints of the church, and that St. Katherine and Christopher achieved this distinction when the church was reconsecrated after renovations in the late fifteenth century.[3]

Västergötland: Asklanda parish church. Age of bell unknown. No inscription, but the bell is known as "Karin."

---

[1] M. Åmark, *Sveriges medeltida kyrkklockor* (Stockholm: Almqvist & Wilsell, 1960), 91.

[2] Åmark, *Kyrkklockor*, 191.

[3] Norberg, "Ununge kyrka," 188.

Bollebygd parish church. Small bell (lillklocka) dated to thirteenth century. Latin inscription in runes: "hic sonus auditur hic mens turbata blanditur dat katerina sonum fideli populo bonum."

Böne parish church. Great bell. Age of bell unknown, and no inscription, but bell is known as "Karin" in local tradition.

Dalstorp parish church. Great bell. Age unknown, no inscription, bell is called "Karin."

Flakeberg parish church. Small bell, probably 14th century. Inscription: AVE: MARIA: GACIA [sic]: PLENA: DOMINVS: TECV [sic]: BENEDICTVS: TV: IN: MVLIERIBVS: ET: BENEDICTVS: FRVCTSVENRISTVI [sic]:. Above final letters in lower register, written right to left: SANCTA: CATERINA.

Fors parish church. Small bell. Cast 1300–1350. Bell called "Karin."

Hemsjö parish church. Great bell. Age unknown, "late medieval" in style. Bell called "Karin."

Hyssna parish church. Great bell. Age unknown, "late medieval" in style. Recast 1915. Called "Karin."

Knätte parish church. Great bell. Late medieval, recast 1915. Inscription (based on photos taken before recasting): Ave maria sancte Katrnsa."

Möre parish church. Small bell. Probably late 13th century (destroyed in fire 1947, examined by Åmark 1940. Called "Karin."

Rångedala parish church. Small bell. Age unknown, "late medieval" in style. Called "Karin."

Östergötland: St. Lars (town of Söderköping). Cast 1474. Inscription, partly in Latin, partly in Low German: "anno domini millesimo quadringentisimo septuagesimio quarto/ thakrai sradh mt ilforin help got unde Maria." Åmark suggests that the words "thakrai sradh mt ilforin" refer to St. Katherine and her wheel (Radh), as well as to her role as a Holy Helper ("ilforin").[4] It may be worth noting that this church has a large (76 cm) wooden sculpture of St. Katherine, dating from roughly the same period as the bell, as well as a 15th-century chalice with two images of the saint, and a late medieval embroidery from a cope. Thus Åmark's interpretation of the inscription has a context.

---

[4] Åmark, *Kyrkklockor*, 116.

APPENDIX 8
"ABOUT A FATHER- AND MOTHERLESS COUNT (A MIRACLE ABOUT SAINT KATHERINE OF EGYPT)"

(Codex Holm A3, dated 1502. According to Jonas Carlquist, this manuscript was produced and used at Vadstena Abbey, to be read aloud during nuns' meals.[1] Published in *Helige mäns lefverne jämte legender och järtecken efter gamla handskrifter*, ed. Robert Geete.[2])

A count who was both fatherless and motherless served St. Katherine joyfully and well. And by his castle he had a chapel that was dedicated to St. Katherine's honor, to which he went each day, and there recited his pious prayers. Once it occurred that as he was there praying, three maidens came to him. He was instantly shy, and dared not look up at them, but cast his gaze down to the ground. Then one of them spoke to him, saying, "Why do you behave like a peasant when you are born of a noble, powerful, and well born family? Look up at us, for we have come here for your sake." And the maiden who stood between the other two said to the count, "Which of us will you take as your bride?" And as he stood there, silent, not speaking, and could not reply, then the one of the maidens that stood on the right side of the maiden in the middle said to him, "Make your choice and take the maiden in the middle, for she is Saint Katherine, who is the patron of this chapel." He did as he was advised. And the maiden and he pledged each other their faith. And instantly Saint Katherine made for her betrothed a noble and sweet-scented wreath of roses and of noble and fair lilies. And afterward, as he stood and doubted what had happened, he touched his hand to his head and found the wreath sitting there. And he rejoiced greatly at this, and he took the wreath home, and hid it with great care for the rest of his lifetime. And he honored Saint Katherine even more after that than he had before. When some time had passed after

---

[1] Jonas Carlquist, *De fornsvenska helgonlegenderna: källor, stil och skriftmiljö*. Svenska fornskriftsällskapets skrifter 262, vol. 82 (Stockholm: Svenska fornskriftsällskapet, 1996), 25.
[2] Svenska fornskriftsällskapets skrifter 34 (Stockholm: P A Norstedt & Söner, 1902), 269–72.

that, his friends and relations came to him and asked and advised him to make a pious marriage with a good and noble, high-born maiden, which he did. When their wedding had been held, he served St. Katherine as steadfastly and piously as he had before. And he stood up quite early each day, and went immediately to Saint Katherine's chapel, and there prayed his pious prayers. Some time thereafter, his wife became pregnant, for which he thanked God, the Virgin Mary, and Saint Katherine, and he served the honorable virgin all the more piously, in that he arose very early each day, and went immediately to Saint Katherine's chapel. And his noble wife mourned at this, and thought that he must love some others more than herself, and so she had it investigated where her lord went so faithfully each day. And she asked her serving maids about this, and they said to her, "A good burgher lives here in the city by St. Katherine's churchyard, and he has a lovely and noble daughter, and we believe that your good and noble lord goes to her." And at that she mourned much more than before. It happened one evening that the lord and lady both went to bed, and the lord understood and saw that his wife was very unhappy in her heart. He spoke to her, and asked why she was so sorrowful. His wife answered, "I can certainly tell, dearest lord, that you love another much more than me, and you go to her faithfully each morning." Then the lord replied, "Dearest wife, who is it, tell me which one she is." His wife said that it was the burgher's daughter who lived by Saint Katherine's churchyard, and to that the count answered thus: "My dearest wife, it is true that the one I go to and serve each day is fairer than you. And that is why I go to her." The next day, the count arose quite early and put on his clothes and went to Saint Katherine's chapel. Once he had gone his wife took her knife into her chamber, and with it she killed both herself and the child. Later on the same day, the count came to the castle, and found both his wife and the child dead. He mourned greatly at this, and cried out, "Woe, woe, woe is me, wretched man, that I did not tell you the truth when you asked me about it." And filled with sorrow, he went straight away to Saint Katherine's chapel, with great and humble weeping, and he prayed fervently for help from the honorable virgin. As he stood thus in his pious prayers, the three maidens came to him who had been there before. And one of them said to him, "Why did you insult me and take another bride?" And she took a noble and very fair cloth, and dried the count's face and eyes and said to him, "Go home now. And know this to be true: for the pious service you have done me, I have saved your wife, so that she is alive now, and she has a lovely daughter, who was born while you were here, who will be named Katerina. And you and your wife shall build a convent in my honor, and your daughter Katerina will be the first abbess in that convent. And she will save the soul of your father from the torments of Purgatory." All this was done, and the wife confessed what she had done, and said that if Saint Katherine had not helped her soul, that she would have come to eternal damnation. And the convent was called the *monasterium ad crineum rosale*, which is the same as "The Convent of the Wreath of Roses." And the count and his wife entered the convent, and there they served God all the days of their lives, and now they are in eternal blessedness.

WORKS CITED

Adam of Bremen. *Adam av Bremen, Historien om Hamburgstiftet och dess biskopar.* Trans. Emanuel Svenberg. Comm. Carl Fredrik Hallencreutz, Kurt Johanneson, Tore Nyberg, and Anders Piltz. Stockholm: Proprius förlag, 1984.

Ahnlund, Nils. "Vreta klosters tidigaste donatorer," *Historisk tidskrift* 89 (1945), 301–51.

Äldre svenska frälsesläkter. Eds. Folke Wernstedt, Hans Gillingstam and Pontus Möller. Stockholm: Riddarhusdirektionen, 1957–2001.

Åmark, Mats. *Kyrkopatroner i Ärkestiftet: Julhälsning till församlingen i ärkestiftet 1951.* Uppsala, 1951.

———. *Sveriges medeltida kyrkklockor.* Stockholm: Almqvist & Wiksell, 1960.

Andersen, Flemming G. *Commonplace and Creativity.* Odense University Studies from the Medieval Centre 1. Odense: Odense University Press, 1985.

Andersson, Roger. "Den fattiges värn: Marias roll i det medeltida predikoexemplet." In *Maria i tusen år: föredrag vid symposiet i Vadstena 6–10 oktober 1994*, ed. Sven-Erik Brodd and Alf Härdelin, 517–38. Skellefteå: Artos, 1996.

Andrén, Åke. *Sveriges kyrkohistoria 3: reformationstid.* Stockholm: Verbum, 1999.

d'Ardenne, S. R. T. O., and E. J. Dobson. *Seinte Katerine, Re-Edited from MS Bodley 34 and the Other Manuscripts.* Early English Text Society s. s. 7. Oxford: Oxford University Press, 1981.

Axelsson, Roger, Kaj Janszon, and Sigurd Rahmqvist. *Det medeltida Sverige 4.3: Öland.* Stockholm: Riksantikvarieämbetet, 1996.

de Baumgarten, N. "Généalogies et mariages occidentaux des Riurikides russes du Xe aux XIIIe siècle." *Orientalia Christiana* 9 (1927), 1–94.

Beatie, Bruce A. "Saint Katharine of Alexandria: Traditional Themes and the Development of a Medieval German Hagiographic Narrative." *Speculum* 52 (1977): 785–800.

Belfrage, Sixten. *Våra vanligaste folkvisor.* Verdandis småskrifter 187. Stockholm: Albert Bonniers förlag, 1912.

Bergel, Sture. *Musikkommentar till Geijer-Afzelius: Svenska folkvisor* Uppsala: 1957–1960.

Berglund, Louise. *Guds stat och maktens villkor: politiska ideal i Vadstena kloster, ca. 1370–1470.* Acta Universitatis Upsaliensis, Studia Historica Upsaliensia 208. Uppsala: Historiska institutionen vid Uppsala universitet, 2003.

Bernau, Anke. "A Christian Corpus: Virginity, Violence, and Knowledge in the Life of St Katherine of Alexandria." In *St Katherine of Alexandria. Texts and Contexts in Medieval Western Europe*, 109–130, ed. Jacqueline Jenkins and Katherine Lewis. Medieval Women: texts and contexts 8. Turnhout: Brepols, 2003.

Berntson, Martin. *Klostren och reformationen: upplösningen av kloster och konvent i Sverige 1523–96.* Skellefteå: Artos och Norma bokförlag, 2003.

Beskow, Per. "Kyrkodedikationer i Lund." In *Nordens kristnande i ett europeiskt perspektiv. Tre uppsatser av Per Beskow och Reinhard Staats*, 37–62. Occasional papers on medieval topics 7. Skara: Viktoria bokförlag, 1994.

Beskow, Per. "Birgitta: en kronologi," *Birgitta av Vadstena. Pilgrim och profet 1303–1373*, ed. idem and Annette Landen, 13–17, Stockholm: Natur och kultur, 2003.

Blomkvist, Nils. "När hanseaterna kom: en stadshistorisk jämförelse mellan Visby och Kalmar." *Gotländskt arkiv* 69 (1997): 47–70.

Bonnier, Ann Catherine. "Hammarlands kyrka." In *Ålands medeltida kyrkor*, ed. Armin Tuulse, 84–102. Acta Universitatis Stockholmiensis. Stockholm Studies in Art 25. Stockholm: Almqvist & Wiksell, 1973.

――――. *Kyrkorna berättar. Upplands kyrkor 1250–1350.* Upplands fornminnesförenings tidskrift 51. Uppsala: Upplands fornminnesförening och hembygdsförbund/Almqvist & Wiksell, 1987.

Borelius, Aron. *Romanesque Mural Paintings in Östergötland.* Norrköping: Norrköpings museum, 1956.

Börjesson, Birger. *Om Vreta klosters kyrka.* Vreta kloster: Vreta klosters hembygsförening, 1986.

Brandel, Sven, O. Johanson, and Johnny Roosval. *Uppland I: Danderyds, Värmdö och Åkers skeppslag.* Sveriges kyrkor. Stockholm: Riksantikvarieämbetet och Statens historiska museer, 1931–1942.

Breviarium Lincopense. Ed. Knut Peters. 4 vols. Lund: Laurentius Petri sällskapet, 1950–1958.

Broomé, Catharina, and Kajsa Rootzén. *Katolska ordnar och kloster.* Stockholm: Petrus de Daciaföreningen, 1963.

de Brun, Frans. "Anteckningar rörande medeltida gillen i Stockholm." *Samfundet Sankt Eriks årsbok* (1917): 34–79.

Carlquist, Jonas. *De fornsvenska helgonlegenderna. Källor, stil och skriftmiljö.*
Stockholm: Svenska fornskriftsällskapet, 1996.

Carlsson, Sten. "Katolicism i svenskt kulturliv." *Kyrkohistorisk årsskrift* (1989): .

Chadwick, Henry. *The Early Church.* The Pelican History of the Church 1.
Middlesex: Penguin, 1967, repr. 1997.

Collijn, Isak, and Andreas Lindblom, eds. *Birgitta utställningen 1918.
Beskrivande förteckning över utställda föremål.* Statens historiska museum.
Uppsala: Almqvist & Wiksell, 1918.

Cotsonis, John. "The Contribution of Byzantine Lead Seals to the Study of the
Cult of The Saints." *Byzantion* 75 (2005): 383–497.

Crossley, Paul. "The Man From Inner Space:Architecture and Meditation in
the Choir of St. Laurence, Nuremburg." In *Medieval Art: Recent Perspectives: a memorial tribute to C. R. Dodwell,* ed. Gale R. Owen-Crocker
and Timothy Graham, 165–82. Manchester and New York: Manchester
University Press, 1998.

Curman, Sigurd and Johnny Roosval. *Riddarholmskyrkan.* Sveriges kyrkor 28.
Stockholm: KVHAA, 1937.

———. "Buttle kyrka." In *Kyrkorna i Halla ting: södra delen,* ed. J Roosval,
380–408. Sveriges kyrkor 68, Gotland 4:3. Stockholm: Generalstabens
litografiska anstalt, 1952.

Dahlbäck, Göran. *Uppsala domkyrkas godsinnehav med särskild hänsyn till
perioden 1344–1527.* Studier till det medeltida Sverige 2. Stockholm:
KVHAA/ Almqvist & Wiksell International, 1977.

———. "Uppsalakyrkans uppbyggnadsskede. Om kyrka och kungamakt under
äldre medeltid." *Kärnhuset i riksäpplet.* (Upplands fornminnesförening och
hembygdsförbunds årsbok) Uppland, 1993, 135–72.

Dalin, Olof von. *Witterhets-Arbeten.* Vol. 4. Stockholm: Carl Stolpe, 1767.

Danmarks gamle Folkeviser. 1853–1976. Eds. Svend Grundtvig, Axel Olrik, et
al. 12 Vols. Copenhagen: Den danske Litteraturs Fremme, J. B. Schultz.

*De svenska medltidsbreven i Svenskt Diplomatariums huvudkartotek.*Stockholm:
Riksarkivet, 2001. CD ROM, Version 2, Macintosh.

Duffy, Eamon. "Holy Maydens, Holy Wyfes': The Cult of Women Saints in
Fifteenth- and Sixteenth-Century England." In *Women in the Church,* ed.
W. J. Sheils and D. Wood, 172–96. Studies in Church History 27. Oxford:
Blackwell, 1990.

———. *The Stripping of the Altars: Traditional Religion in England 1400–1580.*
New Haven and London: Yale University Press, 1992.

En kort berättelse utaf hwad tillfälle de Personers Namn Blifwit införde uti Alma-nachen/som der, för hwarje dag, hela året igenom, står antecknade. Västerås: Printed by Johan Laurentius Hornn at his own expense, 1768.

Erichs, M., and I. Wilcke-Lindqvist. *Närdinghundra härad, östra delen.* Sveriges kyrkor 70, Uppland III: 4. Stockholm: Generalstabens litografiska anstalt, 1953.

Etzler, Allan. "S. Örjens gille." *Med hammare och fackla* 3 (1931): 1–55.

Fant, Ericus Michael. *Scriptores Rerum Suecicarum.* Vol. I. Uppsala: 1818.

Fawtier, R. "Les Reliques Rouennaises de Sainte Catherine d'Alexandrie." *Analecta Bollandiana* 41 (1923): 357–68.

Ferm, Olle, and Sigurd Rahmqvist. "Stormannakyrkor i Uppland." In *Studier i äldre historia tillägnade Herman Schück 5/4 1985*, ed. Robert Sandberg, 67–84 Stockholm: Minab/Gotab, 1985.

Ferm, Olle, Mats Johansson and Sigurd Rahmqvist. *Det medeltida sverige 1:7 Attundaland.* Stockholm: Riksantikvarieämbetet, 1992.

Fichtenau, Heinrich. *Living in the Tenth Century: Mentalities and Social Order.* Trans. Patrick J. Geary. Chicago and London: The University of Chicago Press, 1993.

Fischer, Ernst. "Sankta Katarinas kapell." In *Västergötland, Bd. I, Kållands härad*, 48–51. Sveriges kyrkor. Stockholm: Gunnar Tisells tekniska förlag, 1913–1922.

Franklin, Simon, and John Shepard. *The Emergence of Rus 750–1200.* London and New York: Longman, 1996.

Fritz, Birgitta. "Privata böcker och boksamlingar under folkungatiden." In *Helgerånet: från mässböcker till munkepärmar*, ed. Kerstin Abukhanfusa, Jan Brunius, and Solbritt Benneth, 37–45. Stockholm: Carlsson Bokförlag/ Riksarkivet/ Stockholms medeltidsmuseum, 1993.

Fröjmark, Anders. "Kyrkornas skyddshelgon i Östergötland 'västanstång' under tidig medeltid." *I heliga Birgittas trakter: nitton uppsatser om medeltida sam-hälle och kultur i Östergötland "västanstång,"* ed. Göran Dahlbäck, 133–49. Uppsala: Humanistisk-samhällsvetenskapliga forskningsrådet (HSFR), 1990.

———. *Mirakler och helgonkult. Linköpings biskopsdöme under senmedeltiden.* Acta Universitatis Upsaliensis Studia Historica Upsaliensia 171. Uppsala/Stock-holm: Almqvist & Wiksell, 1992.

Gad, Tue. "Legenda aurea." *KHLM* 10: 410–11.

———. "Margareta (af Antiochia)." *KHLM* 11: 346–47.

Gallén, Jarl. *La province de Dacie de l'ordre des frères prêcheurs. I. Histoire générale jusqu'au grande schisme*. Helsingfors: Söderström & C:o Förlagsaktiebolag, 1946.

———. "Dominikanerorden," *KHLM* 3: 174–85.

———. "Korståg." *KHLM* 9: 210–15.

———. "De engelska munkarna i Uppsala—ett katedralkoster på 1100 talet."*Historisk tidskrift för Finland* 61 (1976). Pp. 1–21.

———. "Knut den helige och Adela av Flandern. Europeiska kontakter och genealogiska konsekvenser." *Studier i äldre historia tillägnade Herman Schück 5/4 1985*, ed. Robert Sandberg, 49–66. Stockholm: Minab/Gotab, 1985.

Gerhard, Karl. "Så var det med det lilla helgonet." Melody by Gideon Wahlberg. Recorded 3–4 December 1955, complete version not previously released. Reproduced on EMI Svenska AB record no. 4751142, 1994.

Gillingstam, Hans. *Ätterna Oxenstierna och Vasa under medeltiden. Släkthistoriska studier*. Stockholm: Almqvist och Wiksell, 1952–1953.

Gíslason, Jónas. 1990. "Acceptance of Christianity in Iceland in the Year 1000 (999)." *Old Norse and Finnish Religions and Cultic Place Names*, ed. Tore Ahlbäck, 223–255. Åbo: The Donner Institute for Research in Religious and Cultural History, 1990.

Gjerløw, Lilli, and Aarno Maliniemi, Bernt. C. Lange, C. A. Nordman, Olav Bø, Kustaa Vilkuna. "Olav den hellige." *KHLM* 12: 561–83.

Grape, Anders. *Studier över de i fornsvenskan inlånade personnamnen*. Doctoral dissertation, Uppsala, 1911.

Grell, Ole Peter. *The Scandinavian Reformation: From Evangelical Movement to Institutionalization of Reform*. Cambridge: Cambridge University Press, 1995.

Greni, Toralf. "Folkevisen om den hellige Katharina." *Edda* 13 (1920): 18–27.

Grotefend, Hermann. *Zeitrechnung des deutschen Mittelalters und der Neuzeit*. Hannover, Leipzig: Hahn, 1891–1898.

Gurevich, Aron. *Medieval Popular Culture: Problems of Belief and Perception*, trans. János M. Bak and Paul A. Hollingsworth. Cambridge Studies in Oral and Literate Culture 14. Cambridge: Cambridge University Press, 1988.

Häggman, Ann-Mari. *Magdalena på källebro: en studie i Finlandssvensk vistradition med utgångspunkt i visan om Maria Magdalena*. Skrifter utgivna av Svenska litteratursällskapet i Finland 576. Humanistiska avhandlingar 6. Helsingfors: Svenska littertursällskapet i Finland, 1992.

Hasse, Max. "Die Lübecker und ihre Heiligen und die Stellung des Heiligen Olav in dieser Schar. Die Heiligenverehrung in Lübeck während des Mittelalters." In *St. Olav, seine Zeit und zein Kult*, ed. Gunnar Svahnström, 171–88. Visby: Museum Gotlands fornsal, 1981, 171–88.

Hedlund, Monica. "Medeltida kyrko- och klosterbibliotek i Sverige." In *Helgerånet. Från mässböcker till munkepärmar*. Eds. Kerstin Abukhanfusa, Jan Brunius, and Solbritt Benneth. Stockholm: Carlsson Bokförlag/Riksarkivet/Stockholms medeltidsmuseum, 1993, 25–36.

Heffernan, Thomas. *Sacred Biography: Saints and their Biographers in the Middle Ages*. Oxford and New York: Oxford University Press, 1988.

Helander, Henrik. *Hammarland Sta Catharina kyrka*. Mariehamn: Mariehamns tryckeri, 1991.

Helander, Sven. *Ordinarius Lincopensis c:a 1400 och dess liturgiska förebilder*. Bibliotheca theologiae practicae 4. Lund: Gleerup, 1957.

————. *Den medeltida Uppsalaliturgin: studier i helgonlängd, tidegärd och mässa*. Lund: Arcus förlag, 2001.

Hellquist, Elof. *Svensk etymologisk ordbok*. 2 vols. 3rd ed. Lund: C. W. K. Gleerups förlag, 1966.

Hernfjäll, Viola. *Medeltida kyrkmålningar i gamla Skara stift*. Stockholm: Institutionen för konstvetenskap, 1993.

"Hervarar saga ok Heidreks." *Fornaldar sögur Nordurlanda*. Vol. 2. Ed. Gudni Jónasson. Íslendingasagnaútgáfnan. Reykjavík(?): Prentverk Odds Björnarssonar H. F., 1959 1–71.

Hildebrand, Bror Emil. *Svenska sigiller från medeltiden*, 3 vols., Stockholm: KVHAA, 1862–1867.

Holmqvist, Wilhelm. "Mariakyrkan och klostret." In *Sigtuna Mariakyrkan 1247 1947*. Eds. Holger Arbman, Wilhelm Holmqvist & Rolf Hillman. Sigtuna: Sigtuna fornhems förlag, 1947, 7–44.

Hyenstrand, Åke. *Socknar och stenstugor: om det tidiga Gotland*. Stockholm Archaeological Reports nr. 22. Stockholm: Department of Archaeology, University of Stockholm, 1989.

Jacobsson, Carina. *Höggotisk träskulptur i gamla Linköpings stift*. Visby: Ödins förlag, 1995. (Doctoral dissertation, Art History, Stockholms Univ.)

Jacobsson, Carina. *Beställare och finansiärer: träskulptur från 1300-talet i gamla ärkestiftet*. Visby: Ödins förlag, 2002.

Jacobus de Voragine. *The Golden Legend: Readings on the Saints*, trans. William Grainger Ryan. 2 vols. Princeton: Princeton University Press, 1993.

Janson, Henrik. *Templum nobilissimum: Adam av Bremen, Uppsalatemplet och konfliktlinjerna i Europa kring år 1075.* Avhandlingar från Historiska institutionen i Göteborg 21. Göteborg: Historiska institutionen, 1998.

Janson, Rune, and Sigurd Rahmqvist, Lars-Olof Skoglund. *Det medeltida Sverige: Uppland: 4. Tiundaland.* Stockholm: Almqvist & Wiksell, 1974

Jansson, Sven. Bertil. "'Och jungfrun hon skulle sig till ottesången gå': om kyrkan i den medeltida balladen." In *Kyrka och socken i medeltidens Sverige,* ed. Olle Ferm, 521–43. Studier till Det medeltida Sverige 5. Stockholm: Riksantikvarieämbetet, 1991.

Jansson, Valter. *Fornsvenska legendariet. Handskrifter och språk.* (Doc. Diss., Uppsala University) Stockholm: Hugo Gebers förlag, 1934.

Jenkins, Jacqueline and Katherine Lewis. "Introduction." In *St Katherine of Alexandria. Texts and Contexts in Medieval Western Europe.* Eds. Jacqueline Jenkins and Katherine Lewis, . 1–18. Medieval Women: texts and contexts 8. Turnhout: Brepols, 2003

Jones, Charles W. "The Norman Cult of Sts. Catherine and Nicholas Saec. XI." In *Hommages à André Boutemy,* ed. Guy Cambier, 216–30. Brussels: Latomus, 1976.

Jonsson, Bengt. "Något om Katarinavisan." Unpublished essay. Svenskt visarkivs bibliotek nr. 2729, 1952.

Jonsson, Bengt. *Svensk balladtradition I: balladkällor och balladtyper.* Svenskt visarkivs handlingar 1. Stockholm: Svenskt visarkiv, 1967.

The Types of the Scandinavian Medieval Ballad: A Descriptive Catalog, ed. Bengt Jonsson, Svale Solheim, and Eva Danielson. Skrifter utgivna av Svenskt visarkiv 5. Stockholm: Svenskt visarkiv, 1978.

Jonsson, Kenneth. "Hansatiden på Gotland i ett numismatiskt perspektiv." *Gotländskt arkiv* 69 (1997): 7–18.

Jørgensen, Ellen. *Helgendyrkelse i Danmark.* Copenhagen: H. Hagerups Forlag, 1909.

Karlsson, Jan O. M and Ragnar Sigsjö. *Varnhems kloster: kyrkan, ruinerna, museet.* 2nd ed. Varnhem: Varnhems församling, 1987.

Karlsson, Lennart. *Kretsen kring Haaken Gullesen.* Stockholm: Carlsson Bokförlag, 2005.

Kilström, Bengt Ingmar. "Nödhjälparna." *KHLM* 12: 458–66.

———. "Patronus." *KHLM* 13: 144–48.

———. "Älvkarleby kyrka." In *Upplands kyrkor* 10: 17–32 Uppsala: Stiftsrådet i Uppsala ärkestift, 1969.

———. *Franciskanska perspektiv.* Stockholm: Verbum/studiebokförlaget, 1974.

———. *Dominikanska perspektiv.* Lund: Verbum/studiebokförlaget, 1976.

———. *Litslena kyrka,* Upplands kyrkor 14. Fifth edition. Strängnäs: Strängnäs tryckeri AB, 1981.

———. *Heliga trefaldighets kyrka i Arboga.* Västerås: Västerås Stifts kyrkobeskrivningskommitté, 1998.

Kjellberg, Carl M. "Erik den heliges ättlingar och tronpretendenterna bland dem." *Historisk tidskrift* 43 (1923): 351–74.

"Knytlinga saga." In *Danakonunga sögur,* ed. Bjarni Gudnason, 91–321. Íslensk fornrit 35. Reykjavík: Hid Íslenzka fornrítafélag, 1982.

Knytlinga saga. The History of the Kings of Denmark, trans. Hermann Pálsson and Paul Edwards. Odense: Odense University Press, 1986.

Kulturhistorisk leksikon for nordisk middelalder. 21 vols. Copenhagen: Rosenkilde og Bagger, 1956–1978.

Lagerlöf, Erland and Gunnar Svahnström. *Gotlands kyrkor.* Stockholm: Rabén & Sjögren, 1966.

Lagerlöf, Erland. *Alskogs kyrka,* Sveriges kyrkor 118. Stockholm: Almqvist & Wiksell, 1968.

Lagerlöf, Erland. *Gotland och Bysans: bysantinskst inflytande på den gotländska kyrkokonstern under medeltiden.* Visby: Ödins förlag AB, 1999.

Langberg, Harald. *Gunhildskorset.* Copenhagen: Selskabet til udgivelse av danske Mindesmærker, 1982.

Lawrence, C. H. *Medieval Monasticism: Forms of Religious Life in Western Europe in the Middle Ages.* London and New York: Longman, 1984.

Lewis, Katherine J. *The Cult of St Katherine of Alexandria in Late Medieval England.* Woodbridge, Suffolk: Boydell Press, 2000.

Liber ecclesiae Vallentunensis, ed. Toni Schmid. Stockholm: KVHAA, 1945.

Lidén, Anne. *Olav den helige i medeltida bildkonst: legendmotiv och attribut.* Stockholm: KVHAA, 1999.

Liepe, Lena. *Den medeltida träskulpturen i Skåne: produktion och förvärv.* Skånsk senmedeltid och renässans 14. Lund: Lund University Press, 1995.

Lindberg, Gustaf. *Kyrkans heliga år.* Stockholm: Svenska kyrkans diakonistyrelsens bokförlag, 1937.

Lindblom, Andreas. *Johan III och Vadstena nunnekloster.* Antikvarist arkiv 16. Stockholm: KVHAA, 1961.

———. *Kult och konst i Vadstena nunnekloster.* KVHAAs handlingar Antikvariska serien 14. Stockholm: Almqvist & Wiksell, 1965.

———. *Vadstena klosters öden.* Vadstena: Vadstena affärstryck, 1973.

Lindahl, Göran. *Uppsala domkyrka*. Excerpt from *Kyrkorna i Uppsala*. Upplands kyrkor, new series 1:1. Uppsala: Almqvist & Wiksell tryckeri, 1997.

Lindgren, Mereth. "Kalkmålningarna." In *Den romanska konsten*, Signums svenska konsthistoria 3, 299–335. Lund: Bokförlaget Signum, 1995.

———. "Kalkmålningarna." In *Den gotiska konsten* Signums svenska konsthistoria 4, 309–411. Lund: Bokförlaget Signum, 1996.

———. "Sakramentsskåpens ikonografi." In *Ting och tanke. Ikonografi på liturgiska föremål*, ed. Ingalill Pegelow, 167–84. KVHAA handlingar. Antikvariaka serien nr. 42. Stockholm: KVHAA, 1998.

Lindroth, Sten. *Svensk lärdomshistoria: medeltiden, reformationstiden*. 2nd ed. Stockholm: Norstedts, 1989.

Lindström, Fredrik. *Jordens smartaste ord: språkliga gåtor och mänskligt tänk*. 2nd ed. Stockholm: Albert Bonniers förlag, 2004.

Ljung, Sven. "Gilde." *KHLM* 5: 302–3.

———. "Hospital." *KHLM* 6: 677–93.

Lundén, Tryggve. *Sveriges missionärer, helgon och kyrkogrundare: en bok om Sveriges kristnande*. Storuman: Bokförlaget Artos, 1983.

Lundmark, Efraim, and Johnny Roosmark. *Gotland. I: Bro setting*. Sveriges kyrkor. Stockholm: Generalstabens litografiska anstalt, 1931.

Malin(iemi), Aarno. *Der Heiligenkalender Finnlands. Seine Zusammensetzung und Entwicklung*. Finska kyrkohistoriska samfundets handlingar 20. Helsingfors: Finska kyrkohistoriska samfundet, 1925.

Maliniemi, Aarno. "Grundandet av dominikankonventet i Åbo och dess förhållande till Sigtuna: några kritiska randanteckningar." In *Sigtuna Mariakyrka 1247–1947*. Eds. Holger Arbman, Wilhelm Holmqvist, and Rolf Hillman, 83–95. Sigtuna: Sigtuna fornhems förlag, 1947.

Markus, Kersti. *Från Gotland till Estland. Kyrkokonst och politik under 1200–talet*. Kristianstad: Mercur Consulting OY, 1999.

Mattson, Christina. *Helan går. 150 visor till skålen samlade och kommenterade*. Hedemora: Gidlunds förlag, 1989.

McCormick, Michael. *Origins of the European Economy*. Cambridge: Cambridge University Press, 2001.

Medeltida bilder. Medeltidens konst, kultur, och historia sedd genom västsvensk kyrkokonst. 1999. CD-ROM, SINOPIA digitalproduktioner.

Medeltidens ABC. Ed. Karin Orrling. Stockholm: Statens Historiska Museum/ Prisma, 2001.

Myrdal, Janken. *Jordbruket under feodalism 1000–1700*. Det svenska jordbrukets historia 2. Stockholm: Natur och kultur/LTs förlag, 1999.

Necrologium Lundense: Lunds domkyrkas nekrologium, ed. Lauritz Weibull (Monumenta scaniæ historica). Lund: Berlingaska boktrykeriet, 1923.

Nestorskrönikan. Trans. A. Norrback. Stockholm: P. A. Norstedt & söners förlag, 1919.

Nilsson, Bertil. *Sveriges kyrkohistoria I: missionstid och tidig medeltid.* Stockholm: Verbum, 1998.

Nilsén, Anna. *Program och funktion i senmedeltida kalkmåleri. Kyrkmålningarna i Mälarlandskapen och Finland 1400–1534.* Stockholm: KVHAA, 1986.

———. "Kult och rum i svensk bondbygd. Om gudtjänstens inverkan på kyrkorummet." In *Tidernas kyrka i Uppland*, ed. Karin Blent, 57–78. Upplands fornminnesförening och hembygdsförbunds årsbok. Uppland: 1997.

Nisbeth, Åke. *Ängsö kyrka och dess målningar.* Stockholm: KVVAA/Almqvist & Wiksell International, 1982.

———. *Bildernas predikan: medeltida kalkmålningar i Sverige.* Stockholm: KVHAA/RÄÄ, 1986.

———. *Ordet som bild: östgötsk kalkmåleri vid slutet av 1300-talet och början av 1400-talet.* Scripta maiora 1. Stockholm: Sällskapet runica et mediævalia, 1995.

Norberg, Rune, "Ununge kyrka." In *Upplands kyrkor*, vol. 11: 185–99. Uppsala: Stiftsrådet i ärkestiftet, 1972.

Norén, Hjorvard, Inga Norrby, Curt Sandin, and Carola Selbing. "Östra Ryds kyrka." In *Upplands kyrkor*, vol. 13: 233–55. Uppsala: Stiftsrådet i ärkestiftet, 1978.

Norske mellomalderballadar 1. Legendviser. Ed. Ådel Gjøstein Blom. Oslo, Bergen and Tromsø: Universitetsforlaget, 1982. NB: as of 2007, this is the only published volume of the collection.

Nyberg, Tore. *Monasticism in North-Western Europe, 800–1200.* Aldershot: Ashgate, 2000.

Nygren, Olga Alice. "Helgonen i Finlands medeltidskonst." *Finska fornminnesförenings tidskrift* 46 (1945): 1–94.

Nylander, Ivar. "Patronatsrätt." *KHLM* 13: 136–38.

Nyman, Magnus. *Förlorarnas historia: katolskt liv i Sverige från Gustav Vasa till Drottning Kristina.* 2nd ed. Stockholm: Veritas Förlag, 2002.

Odenius, Oloph. See Gad et al, "Katarina av Alexandria," *KHLM* 9.

Öhlin, Eric. "Nils Alleson (Nikolaus Allonis)." *Svenska män och kvinnor. Biografisk uppslagsbok.* Ed. Torsten Dahl. Vol. 5. Stockholm: Albert Bonniers förlag, 1949.

Öhrman, Roger. *Vägen till Gotlands historia*. Special issue of *Gotländskt arkiv* 66 (1994).

Ólason, Véstein. "Literary Backgrounds of the Scandinavian Ballad." In *The Ballad and Oral Literature*, ed. Joseph Harris, 116–38. Harvard English Studies 17. Cambridge, MA and London: Harvard University Press, 1991.

Östergren, Majvor. "Det gotländska alltinget och Roma kloster." *Gotländskt arkiv* 76 (2004): 40–45.

Otterbjörk, Roland. "Helgner (Sverige)," *KHLM* 6, 338.

———. "Namngjeving," *KHLM* 12: 210–11.

Parikh, Kristin. *Kvinnoklostren på Östgötaslätten under medeltiden: asketiskt ideal -- politisk realitet*. Lund: Lund University Press, 1991.

Pegelow, Ingalill. "En sky av vittnen: om ett märkligt altarskåp i Bälinge." In *Den ljusa medeltiden. Studier tillägnade Aron Andersson*, 219–38. The Museum of National Antiquities, Stockholm Studies, 4. Stockholm: Statens historiska museum, 1984.

Pegelow, Ingalill. *Helgonlegender i ord och bild*. Stockholm: Carlssons förlag, 2006.

Pernler, Sven-Erik. *Gotlands medeltida kyrkoliv*. Visby: Barry Press förlag, 1977.

Pernler, Sven-Erik. "S:ta Katarina-gillet i Björke." *Gotländskt arkiv* 58 (1986): 67–92.

Pernler, Sven-Erik. *Sveriges kyrkohistoria II. Hög- och senmedeltid*. Stockholm: Verbum, 1999.

Piø, Iørn. *Nye veje til folkevisen*. Copenhagen: Gyldendal, 1985.

Pira, Sigurd. *Om helgonkulten i Linköpings stift*. Lund: Svenska kyrkans diakonstyrelses bokförlag, 1952.

Piscator, Johan Anders Conrad. *Historisk översigt af Musiken i Sverige under Gustaf III*. Uppsala: Edquist, 1860.

Rahmqvist, Sigurd. *Sätesgård och gods*. Uppsala: Upplands Fornminnesförening och Hembygdsförbund, 1996.

Rahmqvist, Sigurd, and Lars-Olof Skoglund. *Det medeltida Sverige: Uppland: 5. Attundaland Lyhundra, Sjuhundra*. Stockholm: Riksantikvarieämbetet, 1986.

Reames, Sherry L. "St Katherine and the Late Medieval Clergy: Evidence from English Breviaries." In *St Katherine of Alexandria. Texts and Contexts in Medieval Western Europe*, ed. Jacqueline Jenkins and Katherine Lewis, 201–20. Medieval Women: texts and contexts 8. Turnhout: Brepols, 2003.

Redelius, Gunnar. *Kyrkobygge och kungamakt i Östergötland*. Stockholm: KVHAA/Almqvist & Wiksell, 1972.

Registrum Ecclesiæ Aboensis eller Åbo domkyrkas svartbok, ed. Reinhard Hausen Helsingfors: Finlands statsarkiv, 1890.

Rhodin, Leon, Leif Gren and Werner Lindblom. "Liljestenarna och Sveriges kristnande från Bysans." *Fornvännen* 95 (2000), 165–81.

Riches, Samantha. *St. George: Hero, Martyr, Myth.* Stroud: Sutton, 2000.

Rimbert. "Vita S. Anscharii." In *Scriptores Rerum Suecicarum,* vol. 2, ed. E. M. Fant, E. G. Geijer, and J. H. Schröder. Uppsala: Palmblad, 1828.

Roelvink, Henrik. *Franciscans in Sweden: Medieval Remnants of Franciscan Activities.* Assen: Van Gorcum, 1998.

Rönnby, Jonas. *Bålverket. Om samhällsförändring och motstånd med utgångspunkt från det tidigmedeltida Bulverket i Tingstäde träsk på Gotland.* Studier från UV Stockholm. Arkeologiska undersökningar, skrifter nr. 10. Stockholm: Riksantikvarieämbetet, 1994.

Roosval, Johnny, and Henrik Alm. "Norrlanda kyrka." In *Kyrkorna i Lina ting.* ed. J. Roosval, 110–48. Sveriges kyrkor, Gotland, 4:1. Stockholm: Generalstabens litografiska anstalts förlag, 1947.

———, and Erland Lagerlöf. "Kräklingbo kyrka." In *Kyrkor i Kräklinge ting: nordvästra delen,* ed. eidem, 463–529. Sveriges kyrkor 84, Gotland 4: 4. Stockholm: Generalstabens litgrafiska anstalt, 1959.

———, and Bengt Söderberg. "Stenkumla kyrka." In *Sveriges kyrkor. Gotland, band III. Hejde setting,* 5–26. Stockholm: Generalstabens litografiska anstalts förlag, 1942.

Rosenstock, Leif H. "Kalendarium." *KHLM* 2: 577–78.

Rumar, Lars, ed. *Helgonet i Nidaros: Olavskult och kristnande i Norden.* Skrifter utgivna av Riksarkivet 3. Stockholm: Riksarkivet, 1997.

Sands, Tracey R. "'Det kommo tvenne dufvor…': Doves, Ravens, and the Dead in Scandinavian Folk Tradition." *Scandinavian Studies* 73 (2001): 349–74.

———. "The Saint as Symbol: the Cult of St Katherine of Alexandria Among Medieval Sweden's High Aristocracy." In *St Katherine of Alexandria. Texts and Contexts in Medieval Western Europe,* ed. Jacqueline Jenkins and Katherine Lewis, 87–108. Medieval Women: texts and contexts 8. Turnhout: Brepols, 2003.

———. "'Riddar sanct orrian': The Cult of St. George in Late Medieval Sweden." In *The Nordic Storyteller: Festschrift for Niels Ingwersen,* ed. Susan Brantly and Thomas DuBois, 6–19. Newcastle-upon-Tyne: Cambridge Scholars' Press, 2009.

Säve, P. A. *Svenska visor I. Gotländska visor samlade av P. A. Säve.* Eds. Erik Noreen and Herbert Gustavsson. Uppsala: Almqvist & Wiksel, 1949.

Sawyer, Birgit, and Peter Sawyer. 1993. *Medieval Scandinavia*. Minneapolis: University of Minnesota Press, 1993.

Schmid, Toni. "Om Sigtunabrödernas böcker och böner." In *Sigtuna Mari-akyrka 1247–1947*, ed. Holger Arbman, Wilhelm Holmqvist, and Rolf Hillman), 45–82. (Sigtuna: Sigtuna fornhems förlag, 1947.

Schück, Herman. *Ecclesia Lincopensis. Studier om Linköpingskyrkan under medeltiden och Gustav Vasa*. Acta Universitatis Stockholmensis 4. Stockholm: Almqvist & Wiksell, 1959.

Scriptores Rerum Suecicarum Medii Ævi. Vol. I. Ed. Ericus Michael Fant. Uppsala: Zeipel & Palmblad, 1818.

Sinding-Larsen, Staale. *Iconography and Ritual. A Study of Analytical Perspectives*. Oslo: Universitetsforlaget AS, 1984.

Smedberg, Gunnar. *Nordens första kyrkor. En kyrkorättslig studie*. Lund: CWK Gleerups förlag, 1973.

Sohlmans musiklexikon, 2nd revised and expanded ed., 5 vols. Stockholm: Sohlmans, 1975–1979.

St Katherine of Alexandria: The Late Middle English Prose Legend in the Southwell Minster MS 7. Ed. Saara Nevanalinna and Irma Taavitsainen. Cambridge: Brewer, 1993.

Ett fornsvenskt legendarium. 3 vols. Ed. George Stephens. Svenska fornskriftsällskapets skrifter. Stockholm: P. A. Norstedt & Söner, 1844–1874.

Stockholms stads tänkeböcker (1474–1488). Ed. Emil Hildebrand. Stockholm: Samfundet för utgifvande af handskrifter rörande Skandinaviens historia, 1917.

Stockholms stads tänkeböcker (1492–1500). Ed. J. A. Almquist. Stockholm: Norstedt och Söner, 1930.

Stokker, Kathleen. "Between Sin and Salvation: the Human Condition in Legends of the Black Book Minister." *Scandinavian Studies* 67 (1995): 91–108.

Stolt, Bengt. "Bälinge kyrka." In *Upplands kyrkor* vol. 2: 137–52. Uppsala: Stiftsrådet i Uppsala ärkestift, 1949.

Strömbäck, Dag. "Kring Staffansvisan." *Folklore och filologi*, 34–53. Acta Academiæ Regiæ Gustavi Adolphi 48. Uppsala: Almqvist & Wiksells, 1970.

Sundquist, Nils. "Tegelsmora kyrka." *Upplands kyrkor* vol. 10: 33–68. Uppsala: Stiftsrådet i ärkestiftet, 1969.

Svahnström, Gunnar. *Rysk konst från Vladimir den helige till Ivan den förskräcklige. 1000–1550*. Visby: Ödins förlag, 1993. (Pp. 179–184 written by Sven-Erik Pernler).

Svanberg, Jan. "Ett helgonskåps historia: från altare i Ängsö till predikstol i Tillinge." In *Kyrka och socken i medeltidens Sverige*, 321–51. Studier till det medeltida Sverige 5. Stockholm: Riksantikvarieämbetet, 1991.

Svanberg, Jan and Anders Qwarnström. *Sankt Göran och draken.* Stockholm: Bokförlaget Rabén-Prisma, 1993, repr. 1998.

Svärdström, Elisabeth. *Kalenderstickan från Lödöse.* (Antikvariskt arkiv 21). Stockholm: Almqvist & Wiksell, 1963.

Svenska böner från medeltiden. Ed. R. Geete Samlingar utgifna af Svenska fornskriftsällskapet, nrs. 131, 133, 135. Stockholm: Svenska fornskriftsällskapet, 1907–1909.

Svenska landskapslagar: Skånelagen och Gutelagen. Eds. Åke Holmbäck and Elias Wessén. Stockholm: AWE/Gebers, 1979.

Svenska riks-archivets pergamentsbref från och med år 1351. 3 vols. Stockholm: P. A. Norstedt & Söner, 1866–1872. (Index and description of unpublished parchment charters in Swedish National Archive = RPB).

Sveriges medeltida ballader. Eds. Bengt R. Jonsson, Margareta Jersild and Sven-Bertil Jansson. 5 vols. Stockholm: Svenskt visarkiv/Almqvist & Wiksell International, 1983–2001.

Svensson, Lars."Tänkebok." *KHLM* 19: 195–99.

Svensson, Torsten. "Imponerande export och expanderande import— influenser i den gotländska kyrkokonsten under hansan." *Gotländskt arkiv* 69 (1997): 115–42.

Syv, Peder. *Et hundrede udvalde danske viser forøgede med det andet Hundrede Viser om Danske Konger, Kæmper og Andre.* 2nd ed. Copenhagen: printed and published by P. M. Høpffner, 1787.

Thordeman, Bengt. "Erik den helige i medeltidens bildkonst." In *Erik den helige. Historia. Kult. Reliker,* ed. Bengt Thordeman, 173–232. Stockholm: Nordisk rotogravyr, 1954.

Tuulse, Armin. "Munsö kyrka." In *Upplands kyrkor* vol. 6: 161–75. Uppsala: Stiftsrådet i ärkestiftet, 1957.

———. *Romansk konst i Norden.* Stockholm: Albert Bonniers förlag, 1968.

———. "Färentuna kyrka." In *Upplands kyrkor* vol. 5: 97–112. Uppsala: Stiftsrådet i ärkestiftet, 1955.

Tångenberg, Peter. *Mittelalterliche Holzskulptur und Altarschreine in Schweden.* Stockholm: KVHAA, 1986.

Ullén, Marian. "Kyrkobygnnaden." In Sven-Erik Pernler, *Sveriges kyrkohistoria II: hög- och senmedeltid,* 254–67. Stockholm: Verbum, 1999.

Unestam, Gustaf. "Börje kyrka." *Upplands kyrkor* vol 8: 153–76. Uppsala: Stiftsrådet i ärkestiftet, 1964.

Virgin Lives and Holy Deaths: Two Exemplary Biographies for Anglo-Norman Women, ed. and trans. Jocelyn Wogan-Browne and Glyn S. Burgess. London: Everyman, 1996.

Wallin, Curt. *Knutsgillena i det medeltida Sverige. Kring kulten av de nordiska helgonkungarna.* Historiskt arkiv 16. Stockholm: KVHAA, 1975.

Walsh, Christine. "The Role of the Normans in the Development of the Cult of St Katherine." In *St Katherine of Alexandria. Texts and Contexts in Medieval Western Europe*, 19–36. Eds. Jacqueline Jenkins and Katherine Lewis. Medieval Women: texts and contexts 8. Turnhout: Brepols, 2003.

Wase, Dick. "Kyrkorna i Visby." *Gotländskt arkiv* 62 (1990): 29–52.

———. "Kyrkorna i Visby — nya rön." *Gotländskt arkiv* 74 (2002): 53–68.

Westholm, Gun. *Hanseatic Sites, Routes and Monuments.* Visby: Länsstyrelsen på Gotland, 1996.

———. "Gotland, hansan och de bevarade spåren av en epok." *Gotländskt Arkiv* 69 (1997): 71–94.

Westman, Knut B. "Erik den helige och hans tid." In *Erik den helige. Historia. Kult. Reliker.* Ed. Bengt Thordeman, 1–108. Stockholm: Nordisk rotogravyr, 1954.

Wilcke-Lindqvist, Ingrid."Skepptuna kyrka." *Upplands kyrkor* vol. 4: 109–23. Uppsala: Stiftsrådet i ärkestiftet, 1953.

Wilcke-Lindqvist, Ingrid. "Estuna kyrka." *Upplands kyrkor* vol. 7. Uppsala: Stiftsrådet i ärkestiftet, 1960. 103–16.

Williamson, Beth. "Altarpieces, Liturgy and Devotion." *Speculum* 79 (2004): 341–406.

Winstead, Karen. *Virgin Martyrs: Legends of Sainthood in Late Medieval England.* Ithaca and London: Cornell University Press, 1997.

Winstead, Karen. 2003. "St. Katherine's Hair." In *St Katherine of Alexandria. Texts and Contexts in Medieval Western Europe.* Eds. Jacqueline Jenkins and Katherine Lewis, 171–200. Medieval Women: texts and contexts 8. Turnhout: Brepols, 2003.

Yrwing, Hugo. *Gotlands medeltid.* Visby: Gotlandskonst AB, 1978.

Yrwing, Hugo. *Visby—hansestad på Gotland.* Lund: Gidlunds, 1986.

INDEX

This index covers the main text and those footnotes containing discussion, as opposed to strictly bibliographical references. It does not index the appendices or bibliography. Because medieval Swedes generally used patronymics rather than inherited surnames, this index follows established Swedish practice and lists persons who lived during the Middle Ages by their first names. Later times have assigned surnames to some of these individuals, even though they did not use these during their lifetimes. In these cases, the surname is given in parenthesis following the patronymic. Post-medieval individuals are listed here by their surnames. It should further be noted that Scandinavian names are alphabetized according to English-language practice, so that the letters <å> and <ä> are treated as <a> while <ö> is treated as <o>.